CAROLINAS
GARDENER'S HANDBOOK

Brimming with creative inspiration, how-to projects, and useful information to enrich your everyday life, Quarto Knows is a favorite destination for those pursuing their interests and passions. Visit our site and dig deeper with our books into your area of interest: Quarto Creates, Quarto Cooks, Quarto Homes, Quarto Lives, Quarto Drives, Quarto Explores, Quarto Gifts, or Quarto Kids.

© 2012 Quarto Publishing Group USA Inc.
Text © 2004 Toby Bost and Jim Wilson, Revised and Additional Content © 2012
Text © 2000 Bob Polomski, Revised and Additional Content © 2005 and 2012
Text © 2007 Joe Lamp'l
Text © 2007 Steve Dobbs
Text © 2002 James A. Fizzell

First published in 2012 by Cool Springs Press, an imprint of The Quarto Group, 401 Second Avenue North, Suite 310, Minneapolis, MN 55401 USA. T (612) 344-8100 Fax: (612) 344-8692 www.QuartoKnows.com

All rights reserved. No part of this book may be reproduced in any form without written permission of the copyright owners. All images in this book have been reproduced with the knowledge and prior consent of the artists concerned, and no responsibility is accepted by producer, publisher, or printer for any infringement of copyright or otherwise, arising from the contents of this publication. Every effort has been made to ensure that credits accurately comply with information supplied. We apologize for any inaccuracies that may have occurred and will resolve inaccurate or missing information in a subsequent reprinting of the book.

Cool Springs Press titles are also available at discount for retail, wholesale, promotional, and bulk purchase. For details, contact the Special Sales Manager by email at specialsales@quarto.com or by mail at The Quarto Group, Attn: Special Sales Manager, 401 Second Avenue North, Suite 310, Minneapolis, MN 55401, USA.

Library of Congress Cataloging-in-Publication Data
Bost, Toby.
Carolinas gardener's handbook : all you need to know to plan, plant, & maintain a Carolinas garden / Toby Bost, Jim Wilson, Bob Polomski.
p. cm.
Includes bibliographical references and index.

ISBN: 978-1-59186-539-1

1. Landscape plants--North Carolina. 2. Landscape plants--South Carolina. 3. Landscape gardening-- North Carolina. 4. Landscape gardening--South Carolina. 5. Gardening--North Carolina. 6. Gardening-- South Carolina. I. Wilson, Jim, 1960- II. Polomski, Robert, 1960- III. Title. IV. Title: All you need to know to plan, plant, and maintain a Carolinas garden.

SB407.B58595 2012
715.09756--dc23

2011023102

Project Editor: Kathy Franz
Design Manager: Brad Springer
Design: S. E. Anderson
Layout: Kim Winscher

TOBY BOST AND BOB POLOMSKI

PHOTOGRAPHY CREDITS

Cool Springs Press would like to thank the following photography and illustration contributors to the Carolinas Gardener's Handbook:

André Viette: 48, 50a, 200a, b, 207
Bill Adams: 54a, 79b, 80b, 148a
Charles Mann: 14, 17, 37a, 79a, 185c
Dave MacKenzie: 182a
Fielder Rushing: 11, 22, 23, 73, 199b
Jerry Pavia: 10, 28b, 156, 30b, 31b, 33a, 34a, 36b, 49c, 52a, 55b, 56b, 58b, 59b, 62a, 63b, 78 both, 81a, 84b, 129b, 136b, 161a, 162a, 174a, 175a, 179a, 181b, 182b, 185a, 186a, 187b, 188a, 198, 199a, 203a, 205 both, 218b, 221 both, 222b
Katie Elzer-Peters: 25a, 26c
Laura Coit: 144
Liz Ball: 36a, 77a, 83b, 108b, 159, 114a, 135b, 186b, 187a, 201a, 203b, 215b, c, 223b, 224a, 225a, 226b, 228
Lorenzo Gunn: 173b
Michael Turner: 146
Peter Loewer: 134a, 136a, 232
Pamela Harper: 174b, 188b, 202 both, 204a, 216a, 217b
Ralph Snodsmith: 51a, 75, 178b, 218a
Rob Proctor: 107b
Thomas Eltzroth: 25b, c, 26a, 27 all, 28a, c, 29a, b, 30a, 31a, 32 both, 33b, 34 b, 35 both, 37b, 38 both, 39, 49a, b, 50b, 51b, 52b, 53 both, 54b, 55a, 56a, 57 both, 58a, 59a, 60 both, 61, 63a, 64 both, 65 both, 66 all, 80a, 81b, 82 both, 83a, 84a, c, 85b, 87, 95-106 all, 107a, 108a, c, 109-110 all, 111b, c, 112 all, 113a, b, 114b, c, 115c, 116 both, 124, 127a, c, 128b, 130a, 131-133 all, 134b, 135a, 136c, 142, 147a, 148b, 168, 160, 161b, c, 162b, c, 172, 173a, 175b, 176a, 177b, 178a, 179b, 180 both, 181a, 183-184 all, 185b, 186c, 187c, 201b, 204b, 210, 212, 216b, 217a, 219 both, 220a, 222a, 223a, 224b, 225b, 227a
Tom Koske: 147b
Toby Bost: 177a

EDITOR'S NOTE

When I was approached about working on this project, I wondered how we would improve on a series of books written by some of the gardening world's best-known authors, including the legendary Jim Wilson. What emerged was a blending of *The Carolinas Gardener's Guide, Month-by-Month Gardening in the Carolinas*, and bits and pieces of other volumes. The goal was not to re-write any of them in their entirety, but to pull together the *best* information from each volume, update it, add to it where we could, and compile it into a single volume that would allow gardeners throughout the Carolinas to have a complete garden reference at their fingertips. I believe we have accomplished what we set out to do.

While doing my editing work and compiling multiple volumes into one, it was my goal to leave the voices of the original authors—whom so many of you already know and trust—intact. At the same time, the final product had to have a common thread running through it, and I hope that thread is my own voice blending with those authors.

With more than twenty-five years of professional gardening experience behind me, and hopefully many more ahead, I am honored to be included among such an esteemed group of authors. I hope that I did their original works justice. It was my goal that this new volume of gardening information should inspire gardeners throughout the Carolinas to update their gardens, just as we have done with these books. Better yet, I hope we inspire a generation of new gardeners to pick up their gardening tools for the first time, get some dirt under their nails, and join us on a journey that has brought these authors and gardeners so much pleasure. Happy gardening!

—*Troy B. Marden*

DEDICATION

This is Jim Wilson's final book, his last contribution to a long legacy of books and articles that have enriched millions of readers over the years. On August 1, 2010, Jim Wilson passed away at his home in Columbia, Missouri. I had the good fortune of knowing Jim for more than twenty years as a mentor, friend, and colleague. In fact, Jim gave me my first break in the book writing business when he passed on an opportunity to write *Month-by-Month Gardening in the Carolinas*. He recommended me—a "non-celebrity"—to write this book for Cool Springs Press. Writing that book has changed my life.

I've followed Jim's career over the years as he was an award-winning garden writer and sought-after speaker on the lecture circuit that took him across the U.S. and abroad. He was not the stereotypical celebrity. As the host of the PBS program *The Victory Garden*, and later HGTV's *Great Gardeners*, Jim was the same on or off camera. What you saw was what you got—a knowledgable Southern gentlemen with a rich, distinctive voice and affable manner who engaged, inspired, and empowered viewers. Jim had the uncanny ability to connect with newbie gardeners and accomplished veterans alike.

I admired Jim for his mastery of the spoken and written word. In his unpublished memoir, *My Life and Times*, Jim wrote, "Words to me are like good tools in the hands of an artisan." Jim Wilson's handiwork as a wordsmith lives on in these pages as he fulfills his lifelong love of gardening and passion for learning.

Of all of the important lessons Jim taught me over the years, this one comes to mind:

"It costs you nothing to thank people who help you; give credit to everyone who helps you along the way."

So, I want to say thanks, Jim, for your friendship and your wisdom, and for the opportunity to co-author this book with you. This one's for you.

— *Bob Polomski*

CONTENTS

FEATURED PLANTS

WELCOME TO GARDENING

in the Carolinas

If you are new to gardening or new to gardening in the Carolinas, you will quickly discover that success depends on knowing how to perform certain tasks and when to perform them. Creating a flower bed that draws admiring looks from passersby; complementing the look and style of your home with well-placed trees, shrubs, and ground covers; and brightening your indoor living area with the colorful blooms and enchanting fragrances of indoor plants do not happen by chance. You can be assured that all of these are achieved with careful planning, know-how, and proper care.

Every season in the Carolinas presents a gardening opportunity. Start vegetables in the summer for a fall garden. Divide and replant fall-flowering perennials in the spring when their new growth emerges. Start or renovate a warm-season lawn in late spring and early summer. Just knowing how and when to perform certain tasks makes gardening easier and more fun, and greatly improves your chances of success.

With the help of a number of seasoned gardeners from both North Carolina and South Carolina, we have attempted to place each activity into the appropriate month for both states. However, some fine-tuning will be necessary in your own garden and landscape. The seasons do not always arrive when expected, and most landscapes have microclimates within them—nooks and pockets that have environmental conditions that are different from the other areas.

THE BENEFITS OF A GARDENING PLAN

Folks smitten by the beauty and excitement of gardening in the Carolinas quickly discover that they need two additional gardening tools: pen and paper. Although you can write in the margins of this book, you are strongly encouraged to start a gardening diary in a separate notebook. A 100-page, wide-ruled composition notebook works perfectly. You should record observations on weather, especially first and last freezes, as well as the names of vegetables, flowers, and shrubs that you've grown. It is also helpful to note the bloom dates of choice flowering plants. Notes about fertilizer applications and pest problems are also helpful. When talking with and learning from other gardeners, jot down interesting techniques or plants that interest you. All of these handwritten comments will become a "gardening memory." A journal is a tool, just like a shovel or a hoe, and will help you raise the best garden possible.

BUILDING HEALTHY SOIL

Gardeners often get caught up in the beauty of their plants without remembering that the foundation for any healthy garden, landscape, or lawn is the soil. Good soil allows air, water, and nutrients to be absorbed by plant roots and lets those roots roam freely.

How do you build healthy soil? Begin with a soil test through your County Extension Service. The test will tell you the pH of the soil and the levels of nutrients available for plant growth. Stated in numbers, pH is a measurement of the acidity or alkalinity of the soil. On a scale of 0 to 14, a pH of 7 is neutral. Numbers below 7 indicate acid conditions and readings above 7 are basic or alkaline. Soil pH affects not only plant health, but also the availability of nutrients. If the soil is too acidic or too alkaline, minerals such as nitrogen, phosphorus, potassium, calcium, and magnesium can be "tied up" and unavailable to your plants. Adding more fertilizer will not help. The soil pH will have to be corrected by either mixing in the recommended amount of limestone to raise the pH and "sweeten" the soil, or by adding sulfur if you need to lower the soil pH.

Maintaining the right soil pH is very important. It affects the uptake of nutrients by plants and creates an environment that supports helpful soil-dwelling organisms, including earthworms. The results of your soil test will indicate the amount of limestone or sulfur required to bring the soil pH into an ideal range, between 5.8 and 6.5 for most vegetable and flower gardens, shrubs, trees, and lawns. Mix pulverized or pelletized limestone into the top 6 inches of soil to raise the pH; mix in sulfur to lower it.

The soil test also measures the levels of phosphorus, potassium, calcium, and magnesium. Since calcium and phosphorous move slowly in the soil, these minerals should be incorporated into the top 6 inches of soil. Knowing the nutrient content of your soil will help you determine which nutrients need to be added and in what amounts.

Good gardeners also add organic matter. It improves soil tilth—its physical condition or structure. When added to clay soil, organic matter holds the clay particles apart, improving air and water movement in the soil. In sandy soil, organic matter helps to bind the soil particles together and improves water and nutrient retention in soils that are otherwise dry and infertile. This translates to deeper and more extensive root development from your plants.

IMPORTANT NOTE: Sand has often been touted as the perfect fix for improving drainage in clay soils. Unless you add it at the rate of at least 6 inches of sand per 8 inches of soil, your soil will be better suited for making bricks than growing

plants. Sand is *not* the perfect fix for clay soils! Organic matter is.

The kind of organic matter you mix into your soil is your choice. Well-rotted cow, horse, rabbit, or chicken manure is excellent for vegetable and flower beds. If you are squeamish about using these organic materials, then add compost or shredded leaves. Cover crops or "green manure," such as crimson clover or annual rye, are relatively inexpensive sources of organic matter. Sow these crops in the fall and then turn them under in the spring to enrich the soil.

To avoid damaging soil structure, never dig or cultivate when the soil is too wet. Follow this simple test: If the soil sticks to your shovel—the soil is too wet. Postpone digging until the soil dries out.

PLANTING

Plant properly. The health and long-term survival of plants that you set into their new home—indoors or out—is affected by how they're planted. Follow the step-by-step planting instructions in the introduction to each chapter to learn about proper planting. Your plants' survival depends on it.

LIGHT LESSONS

We all know that in order to thrive, plants need light. It can get confusing, though, when you're looking at plant labels or reading a gardening book like this one and you see references to terms that seem vague or that you may not be familiar with. What is full sun? How much shade is "deep" shade? Or perhaps the most confusing of all, is there really a difference between "part sun" and "part shade"? Let's see if we can clear up some of the uncertainty.

FULL SUN—Full sun is the easiest of the light levels to understand and is simply described as any area of your garden that receives six or more uninterrupted hours of sun each day. It is important to note the word "uninterrupted." You may have areas of the garden that receive six or more hours of sun each day, but at different times of the day. For instance, a place that gets three hours of morning sun and three hours of late afternoon sun, but is shaded by a tall tree at midday. These areas will fall into different light categories, described below.

PART SUN—Part sun refers to those areas of the garden that receive direct sun for four to six hours each day, but not more than six hours of uninterrupted sun at a time in a given location. These could include areas of bright morning sun, late day sun, or a burst of sun as it passes overhead at midday. Part sun areas of the garden receive more sun than shade, but not enough sun to qualify as "full sun." A "half-day" of sun might be another way to interpret this exposure.

PART SHADE—Part shade is the part of the garden where shade is prevalent, but some sun still gets through as it moves from east to west during the day. It is difficult to assign a specific number of hours, but you might use three to four hours of sun each day as a general guideline. Part shade would also include areas that receive very bright dappled shade from overhead trees throughout the day.

SHADE—The shady areas of the garden are those areas that receive little or no direct sun during the day. To put it in terms of hours, you might think of areas of your garden that receive less than three hours of sun each day. Shady areas can still be bright from ambient light and will allow a wide variety of plants to be grown.

DEEP SHADE—Deep shade is the part of the garden that receives no direct sun at any time of the day. It can be solid shade from a building, such as the north side of a house, or it can be very dense shade cast by the canopy of a tree like a Southern magnolia whose foliage is so thick that it never allows any sun to reach the ground.

Full Sun

Part Sun

Part Shade

Shade/Deep Shade

WATERING

Anyone can water; however, watering efficiently to meet the demands of the plant while conserving water requires some attention to detail. The upcoming chapters provide information on when and how often to water. The aim is to avoid the common mistakes of overwatering or underwatering—two practices that can injure or kill plants.

Water needs depend on the plant and the situation. Moisture-loving plants require more frequent watering than plants adapted to dry conditions. Newly set-out plants need to be watered after planting and during their establishment period. Once they become established, however, they may not require supplemental watering even during the hot, dry summer months. Some shrubs and trees are quite drought-tolerant and can withstand long periods without rain or irrigation. Soil also affects watering. Plants growing in clay soils need to be watered less often than plants growing in sandy soils, because sandy soils drain so rapidly.

FERTILIZING

Fertilizing could be the gardening practice that causes the greatest confusion. Besides knowing when, how often, and how much to fertilize, the choices seem endless. Should you choose a fast- or slow-release nitrogen fertilizer? Would your plants prefer a diet of organic or inorganic nutrients? What do those numbers on the bag mean? Should you choose the 10-10-10 or the 16-4-8? Dry or liquid fertilizer? Before making an application, realize that fertilizing should be guided by soil-test results, the appearance of the plants, and the purpose of fertilizing.

Fertilizers are minerals added when the soil does not supply enough of those nutrients. The three most important—nitrogen, phosphorus, and potassium—are represented by three numbers on a fertilizer bag. For example, 16-4-8 gives the percentage by weight of nitrogen (N), phosphate (P_2O_5), and potash (K_2O). In this example, nitrogen makes up 16 percent of the total weight, phosphate—which supplies phosphorus—accounts for 4 percent, and potash, a source of potassium, makes up 8 percent. The remaining weight (the total must add up to 100 percent) consists of a nutrient carrier.

A fertilizer containing all three nutrients, such as a 16-4-8, is referred to as a "complete" fertilizer. If soil tests indicate high levels of phosphorus and potassium, then apply an "incomplete" fertilizer, one that supplies only nitrogen, such as 21-0-0.

In addition to the primary elements (N-P-K), the fertilizer may contain secondary plant nutrients including calcium, magnesium, and sulfur, or minor nutrients such as manganese, zinc, copper, iron, and molybdenum. Apply these nutrients if dictated by soil-test results.

You can choose dry or liquid fertilizers. Dry fertilizers are applied to the ground around your plants. They are available in fast- or slow-release nitrogen forms. Fast- or quick-release liquid nitrogen fertilizers dissolve readily in water and are almost immediately available to plants. They can also be quickly leached out of the root zone in fast-draining, sandy soils.

Liquid fertilizers can be absorbed through the leaves as well as the roots of plants. These have to be applied more frequently than granular types, usually every two to four weeks.

Slow-release fertilizers make nutrients available to a plant for an extended period of up to several months. While more expensive than conventional fertilizers, they reduce the need for supplemental applications and the likelihood of fertilizer burn. Select a slow-release fertilizer that has at least one-half of the total amount of nitrogen listed as "water-insoluble nitrogen."

Alternatives to synthetic slow-release fertilizers are organic fertilizers derived from naturally occurring sources such as composted animal manure, cottonseed meal, and bloodmeal, among many others. Although they contain relatively low concentrations of actual nutrients compared to synthetic fertilizers, they increase the organic matter content in the soil and improve soil structure.

Organic fertilizers also tend to be "slow release," lasting longer in the soil and releasing their nutrients over a longer period of time, making them more available to plants.

A slow-release fertilizer is a good choice, especially for sandy soils—which tend to leach—or for heavy clay soils, where runoff can be a

problem. If the soil is properly prepared at the start, supplemental fertilization may not be necessary for several years after planting. When fertilizing your perennials, let their growth rate and leaf color be your guide. Rely on soil-test results to help you make the right decision. If the bed is already highly fertile, the soil test will save you from the other equally undesirable results of overfertilizing, such as encouraging a lot of leafy growth at the expense of flowers.

PRUNING

Pruning improves the health and appearance of plants. It can be as simple as nipping the spent flowers from your zinnias (deadheading) or removing a large limb from your maple tree. In the following chapters, read the step-by-step instructions for pruning roses, shrubs, and trees. You'll find that pruning will require you to have a purpose in mind. It can be to encourage more flowers on perennials, to reduce the height of plants, or to create a strong structure of trunk and limbs to support future growth in young trees.

PEST CONTROL

You are bound to confront the three most common pests in your Carolina garden: insects, diseases, and weeds. (Deer, voles, and rabbits can also be considered pests and are addressed in the following chapters.) Deal with them sensibly. When referring to pest control in this book, we use the term "Integrated Pest Management" or "IPM." IPM is a commonsense approach to managing pests that brings Mother Nature into the battle on the gardener's side. It combines smart plant selection with good planting and maintenance practices, and an understanding of pests and their habits. It starts with planning and proper planting to produce strong, healthy plants that, by themselves, can prosper with minimum help from you. As in nature, an acceptable level of pests can be accommodated. Suppression is the goal, rather than elimination. Several techniques can be used in a home garden or landscape IPM approach.

IPM CULTURAL PRACTICES

PROPER SOIL MANAGEMENT: Maintain the appropriate soil pH for your plants by testing your soil at least every three years. Add generous amounts of organic matter to build up soil fertility.

PLANT SELECTION: Match plants suited to the soil and climate of your area, and select species and cultivars resistant to pests. But remember, these plants are resistant—not immune—to damage. Expect them to exhibit less insect or disease injury than susceptible varieties growing in the same environment.

WATERING: Water late at night or early in the morning when dew has formed. Avoid watering in early evening when leaves may remain wet for an extended period of time, which favors fungal infections.

MULCHING: Apply a shallow layer of organic mulch such as compost, shredded leaves, or bark to conserve moisture, suppress weeds, and supply nutrients as they decompose.

SANITATION: Remove dead, damaged, diseased, or insect-infested leaves, shoots, or branches.

IPM MECHANICAL CONTROLS

HANDPICKING: Remove any insects by hand, or knock them off with a strong spray of water from the hose.

EXCLUSION: Physically block insects from attacking your plants. Aluminum foil collars can be placed around seedlings to prevent cutworms from attacking plant stems. Plants can be covered with muslin or spun-bonded polyester to keep out insects.

IPM BIOLOGICAL CONTROLS

PREDATORS AND PARASITES: Some bugs are on our side. Known as beneficial insects, they are the natural enemies of damaging insects. They fall into two main categories: predators and parasites. Predators hunt and feed on other insects. They include spiders, praying mantises, lady beetles, and green lacewings. Parasites, such as braconid wasps and trichogramma wasps, hatch from eggs inside or on another insect and they eat their host insect as they grow.

Releasing beneficial insects into your landscape or garden may offer some benefit, but it is better to conserve the beneficial insects already there. Learn to distinguish between pests and beneficial insects in your garden and landscape. Avoid applying broad-spectrum insecticides that will harm beneficial insects if it looks as if the harmful insects are already being kept to tolerable levels.

BOTANICAL PESTICIDES AND INSECTICIDAL SOAPS: Botanical pesticides, or "botanicals," are naturally occurring pesticides derived from plants. Two common botanicals include pyrethrins, insecticidal chemicals extracted from the pyrethrum flower (*Tanacetum cinerariifolium*), and Neem, a botanical insecticide and fungicide extracted from the tropical neem tree (*Azadirachta indica*) that contains the active ingredient azadirachtin. Insecticidal soaps have been formulated specifically to control insects. Soaps are effective only against those insects that come into direct contact with sprays before they dry.

These "natural" pesticides break down rapidly when exposed to sunlight, air, and moisture, and are less likely to kill beneficial insects than insecticides that have a longer residual activity.

MICROBIAL INSECTICIDES: These insecticides combat damaging insects with microscopic living organisms such as viruses, bacteria, fungi, protozoa, or nematodes. Although they may seem like out-of-the-ordinary insecticides, they can be applied in ordinary ways—as sprays, dusts, or granules. The bacterium *Bacillus thuringiensis* (*Bt*) is the most popular pathogen. Formulations from *Bacillus thuringiensis* var. *kurstaki* (*Btk*) are the most widely used to control caterpillars—the larvae of butterflies and moths.

HORTICULTURAL OILS: When applied to plants, these highly refined oils smother insects, mites, and their eggs. Typically, horticultural oils such as Sunspray, Scalecide, and Volck are derived from highly refined petroleum products that are specifically manufactured to control pests on plants. Studies have shown that horticultural oils derived from vegetable oils, such as cottonseed and soybean oil, also exhibit insecticidal properties.

Dormant applications generally control aphid eggs and the egg stages of mites, scale insects, and caterpillars like leaf rollers and tent caterpillars. Summer applications control adelgids, aphids, mealybugs, scale insects, spider mites, and whiteflies.

Oils have limited effects on beneficial insects, especially when applied during the dormant season. Additionally, insects and mites have not been reported to develop resistance to petroleum or vegetable oils.

TRADITIONAL SYNTHETIC PESTICIDES: Synthetic pesticides, developed by people, should be your last resort when confronted by damaging pest levels. Use them sparingly to control the targeted pest. Specific names of synthetic pesticides are avoided in this book because products and their labels change rapidly along with the pesticide registration and use process. When buying any pesticide, read the label and follow *all* directions and precautions before mixing and applying it, and before storing or disposing of it.

FURTHER HELP

Clemson University or North Carolina State University have Extension centers or offices in every county of the Carolinas. Many are staffed by Master Gardeners trained in horticulture. These volunteers are also available to answer your questions at many arboretums and botanical gardens. Help is available from the Garden Clubs of North Carolina and South Carolina, an array of societies devoted to specific plants, and from seminars and informative newsletters as well.

USDA HARDINESS ZONES

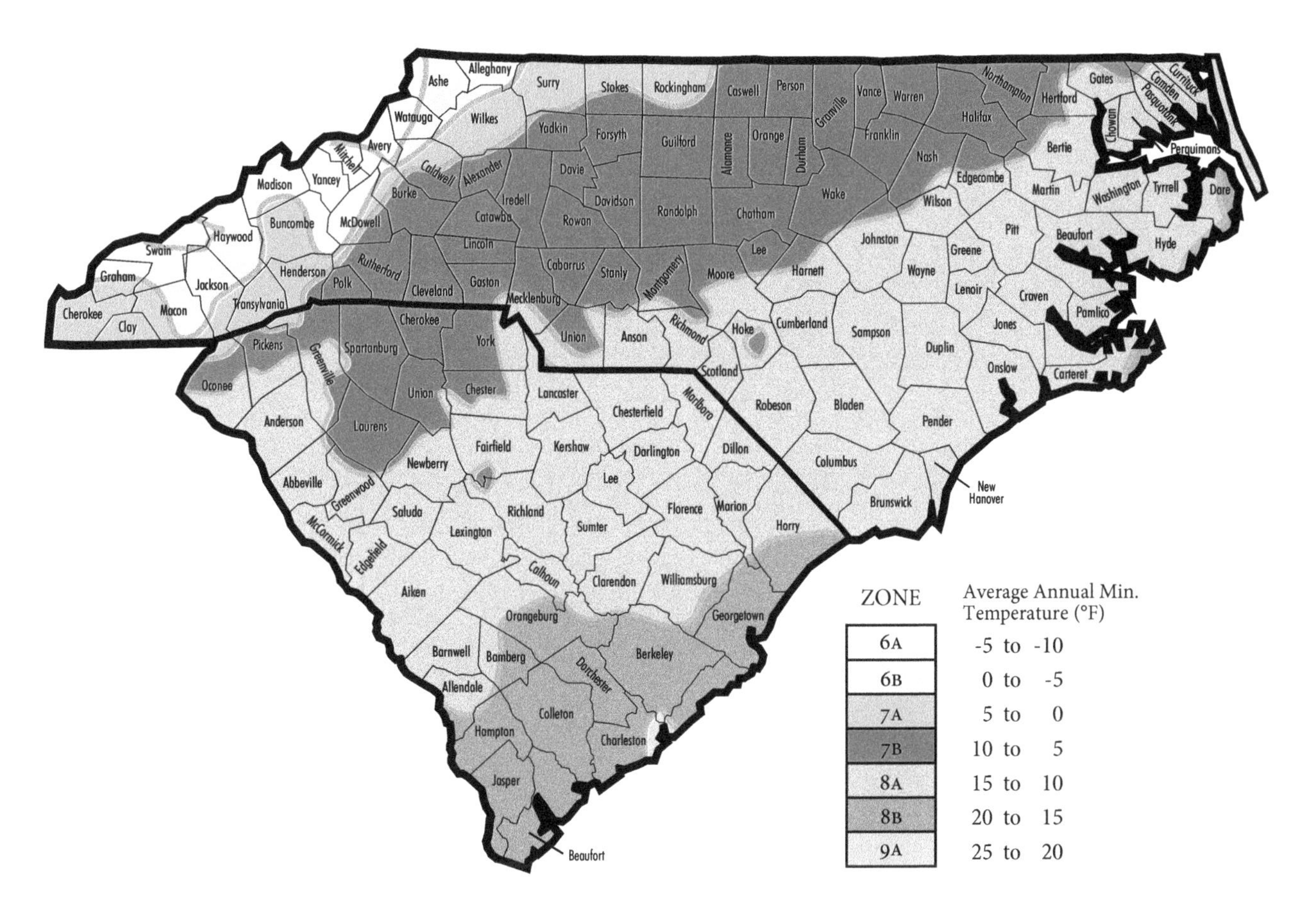

The United States Department of Agriculture (USDA) developed the cold-hardiness zone designations. They are based on the minimum average temperatures all over the country. Each variation of 10 degrees Fahrenheit represents a different zone, indicated by colored bands on a zone map. Because perennial plants, whose roots survive winter, vary in their tolerance for cold, it is important to choose those plants that are suitable for the zone of your region. Consult this map to learn in which zone you live. Most of the plants in this book will perform well throughout the area. Though a plant may grow in zones other than its recommended cold-hardiness zone, it is best to select plants labeled for your zone, or warmer.

ANNUALS

for the Carolinas

Annual flowers are garden plants that complete their life cycle in one growing season. These jewels, also called bedding plants, are the cheerful workhorses of the landscape. They can transform uninteresting spaces into colorful flower beds, and many will bloom continuously from spring until a hard frost in autumn blackens their foliage and terminates the bedding plant season.

Annuals are the backbone of the summer garden and are important for supplying color during the late summer "bloom gap" in perennial beds. This bloom gap is the period of time after the main-season summer perennials like phlox and daylilies have finished flowering and before the autumn-blooming varieties like asters, chrysanthemums, and Japanese anemones started. Most annuals are sun lovers, though a few are appropriate for lightly shaded landscapes. Petunias, pansies, dianthus, and wax begonias dazzle your eye with lovely color. Annuals are easy to plug into otherwise bleak gardens that are just waking up from their winter dormancy.

THE VERSATILITY OF ANNUALS

Most gardeners buy seedlings in pots or cell packs from local garden centers for planting after the danger of frost has passed. Annuals can be massed in beds for color impact or mixed into perennial beds and borders to help fill the gaps between other plants. Some annuals, like many varieties of cosmos, salvia, verbena, and angelonia, lend themselves particularly well to the perennial bed because of their less formal growth habit, which allows them to weave themselves in between nearby plants. Others, like most wax begonias, marigolds, and periwinkles, have a compact habit, which makes them better suited for bedding schemes or more formal plantings.

PROVING THE WINNERS

The South has a dynamic plant evaluation network in place. Most annuals on the market today are evaluated for several years before they are made available to gardeners at local nurseries and garden centers. These evaluations are conducted by horticulturists at both North Carolina State University and Clemson University, as well as the J. C. Raulston Arboretum in Raleigh. These programs benefit both commercial flower growers, who must select the best varieties to grow and sell for the upcoming season, and home gardeners, who can be assured that the varieties they are choosing from have been thoroughly tested and proven to grow well in a given area.

The garden seed and plant industry also operates a number of programs to evaluate and promote promising new annual and perennial varieties. The oldest (established in 1932) is All-America Selections. Newer marketing consortiums include Proven Winners, Flower Fields, and Simply Beautiful. The many field trials in the Carolinas and across the country are valuable tools in evaluating new garden plants under a wide variety of soil and climatic conditions to help determine which varieties are going to perform best in a given region.

FROM CONTAINER TO GARDEN

Annual flowers may be purchased in any number of ways in spring and early summer. Some are grown by the flat in tiny, 2-inch cells, while others may be in 3- or 4-inch pots. A few larger growing varieties may be for sale in 6-inch or even 8-inch pots and provide some degree of "instant gratification" when the need arises. No matter what size plants you are transplanting, and regardless of whether you will be planting them in the garden or in larger containers, consider what veteran gardeners call "butterflying" the rootballs.

Because annuals may be confined to small pots for several weeks to a few months, root systems can become so congested that they encase the rootball in a solid mat of rootlets that are reluctant to strike out into the surrounding soil in flower beds or containers. This condition is described as being "potbound." Butterflying the rootball consists of pushing or tapping the rootball out of the cell or pot, grasping it with both hands, and, with your fingertips across the bottom of the root system, gently cracking the rootball. New feeder roots will grow out of the crack and into the surrounding soil to take up water and nutrients.

Preparing Your Soil

Before transplanting annuals into the garden, be sure your soil is well prepared and ready to promote the lush growth you desire in your summer flowers. Ideally, you should have submitted a sample of your flower bed soil to your County Extension Service for testing. If you lack test results, liming is called for on all Carolina soil types, except for a few near the coast. As a general rule, topdress and work lime into the soil prior to planting. On sandy soils, apply ½ pound per 10 square feet. On clay soils (the heavy, sticky stuff), apply 1 pound per 10 square feet. Use pelletized dolomitic limestone that supplies both calcium and magnesium, and work it in thoroughly. Liming soils helps in two ways: It counteracts excessive acidity in the soil, and it supplies calcium and magnesium. Both elements are secondary but necessary plant nutrients.

Work up your soil by spading or tilling before spreading limestone. Remove roots of perennial grasses or weeds. For consistency of coverage, divide the recommended application of limestone into two parts. Broadcast half while walking in one direction and the other half while walking across your initial path. This is a good opportunity to add organic soil conditioner as well; such as aged pine bark, mushroom compost, peanut compost, composted manures, and so on. Spread these in a 2- to 3-inch layer over the existing soil. Finally, spread fertilizer to add the major plant nutrients: nitrogen, phosphorus, and potassium. One of the controlled-release fertilizers will do the best job; it will feed your annuals through most of the growing season. Thoroughly till all amendments and fertilizers into the soil prior to planting.

Read the descriptive labels that came with your plants. Sun-loving annuals will thrive in all-day sun, but some will need more frequent watering than others to keep them looking their best. If the label calls for shade, set your plants where they will get light shade or high shade during much of the day. Few flowering annuals will do well in moderate to deep shade; foliage plants fare better because their broad leaves can trap the limited light that bounces into shaded areas. The spacing recommendations on the labels are usually quite accurate and should be followed if you want your plants to develop, grow, and flower to their fullest potential.

NOW WHAT?

Keeping your flower beds free of weeds is most important. If you build a flower bed, weeds will come. The best way to minimize weeding is to spread a 2-inch layer of mulch. Pine or hardwood bark works well. Don't pull the mulch up close to the stems of annuals; it can hold moisture and cause plants to rot. Pine straw is difficult to work in between annual plants and is usually reserved for larger perennials and shrubs.

Broadleaf weeds and grass will find a way to emerge. Take a dandelion digger with you to pry out the entire root system with minimum soil disturbance. Collect the weeds and dump them in your compost heap. If you recognize the terrible weed called Florida betony, take a spray bottle of a nonselective herbicide with you. Set a tin can (bottom removed) over the weed before spraying, to avoid spray drift. This tough customer may try to regrow. Spray it again in three or four weeks. Any of the aggressive spreaders such as chameleon plant or culinary mint can be eradicated in this way.

Rigging a drip irrigation system is the easiest, most responsible, and most efficient way to water a flower bed during dry periods. Most annuals need at least 1 inch of rainfall or irrigation per week, and twice that in sandy soils, which tend to dry out faster. A "leaky hose" or soaker hose is the simplest drip irrigation system. Arrange the porous hose in a serpentine fashion throughout the flower bed so that no plant is more than 9 to 12 inches from the hose. Connect the soaker hose to a water faucet and let it run for an hour twice a week during dry weather. Some gardeners object to the industrial look of soaker hoses snaking among their flowers and conceal them beneath mulch, and while this may look nicer in the short term, it can lead to the hose being damaged with a hoe or dandelion digger. If you leave the hose on the surface, the annuals will soon spread and hide it, but you'll still be able to see it when working around it.

Deadheading annual flowers can be a dreaded task or a way to calm your turbulent mind while doing no-brainer work. Either way, deadheading leads to season-long color and to neater-looking flower beds. A few annuals such as coreopsis, cosmos, sunflowers, and the annual varieties of black-eyed Susan can provide food for finches and are often allowed to go to seed.

ALTERNANTHERA

Alternanthera ficoidea

Why It's Special—Grown for its beautiful foliage, ranging from green with red, pink, and white variegation to solid chartreuse, shrimp pink, orange, red, or burgundy, alternanthera, sometimes known as Joseph's coat, is a brightly colored addition to beds, borders, and containers. It is often used in Victorian-style pattern plantings or flower topiaries.

How to Plant & Grow—Alternanthera is available in cell packs or individual pots and can be planted in the garden after the danger of frost has passed. Different varieties require different spacing, so be sure to check the label. Rich, well-drained soil will promote lush growth and beautifully colored foliage.

Care & Problems—Alternanthera will grow in full sun to part shade, but the best color will develop in brighter light. Rabbits love this plant, especially when it's young and tender, so it may be prudent to spray with rabbit repellent when planting.

Bloom Color—Grown for foliage

Peak Season—Spring to frost

Mature Size (H x W)—6 in. to 2 ft. x 6 in. to 2 ft.

Water Needs—Evenly moist soil

Good in Containers? Yes, excellent in mixed pots

ANGELONIA

Angelonia angustifolia

Why It's Special—Angelonia is an indispensible annual for beds, borders, and containers. Heat and humidity don't faze it and it is virtually pest free. Color choices include cobalt blue, purple, pastel shades, bicolors, and white.

How to Plant & Grow—Angelonia likes it warm, so wait until at least two weeks after the last frost to plant it in the garden. It will grow very quickly once the soil and air temperatures have warmed. Drip irrigation works best, since constant overhead watering can beat down the delicate flower spikes.

Care & Problems—Deadhead spent flower spikes when they begin to look shabby by cutting two to three sets of leaves below the base of the spike. This will encourage multiple branching and profuse flowering. Angelonia expends a lot of energy on flowers, so feed it with water-soluble fertilizers and/or slow-release granules.

Bloom Color—Cobalt blue, purple, lavender, pink, white, bicolors

Peak Season—Spring to fall

Mature Size (H x W)—10 in. to 2 ft. x 1 ft. to 1½ ft.

Water Needs—Evenly moist soil

Good in Containers? Yes, excellent in containers

BLUE SALVIA

Salvia farinacea

Why It's Special—Blue salvia can be mixed into the perennial border, where its violet-blue spires of bloom will add color all summer. In warm climates, it may even act as a perennial for a few seasons! The variety 'Victoria' is most commonly available, and a bicolor blue-and-white form called 'Strata' is a beauty.

How to Plant & Grow—Blue salvia can be planted from spring to fall. Loosen the roots and set the transplants about 15 inches apart. Flowering is best in full, all-day sun, but plants will tolerate light afternoon shade with only a slight reduction in flowering.

Care & Problems—Salvias will languish if planted where the soil is poorly drained. In heavy clay soils, spade in 3 inches of pine bark soil conditioner to help loosen the soil and improve drainage. Feed regularly to promote continual new growth and flowering, deadheading old flower spikes as they fade.

Bloom Color—Violet-blue, white, bicolors

Peak Season—Spring to fall

Mature Size (H x W)—1½ to 2 ft. x 1 to 1½ ft.

Water Needs—Drought tolerant, once established

Good in Containers? Yes, as an upright filler

COPPERLEAF

Acalypha wilkesiana

Why It's Special—From summer to frost, this care-free tropical provides brilliant foliage in shades of bronzy green, coppery red, purple, pink, crimson, orange, and cream. Foliage can range from narrow and willowy to broad, bold, and twisted or contorted. The hotter and more humid it gets, the more spectacular copper leaf becomes.

How to Plant & Grow—Wait until all danger of frost has passed and the soil has warmed significantly before planting out in spring. Once in the ground, copper leaf will grow quickly. It prefers rich, well-amended soil with good drainage.

Care & Problems—Water thoroughly and deeply at planting time to encourage roots to grow deep into the soil. Copperleaf will respond to feeding by putting out lush growth throughout the summer. Smaller varieties are good in containers, but will be very thirsty by summer's end as plants become potbound.

Bloom Color—Red foilage; very showy in some varieties

Peak Season—Spring to fall

Mature Size (H x W)—2 to 6 ft. x 2 to 4 ft.

Water Needs—Evenly moist soil

Good in Containers? Yes, smaller varieties are excellent

COSMOS

Cosmos bipinnatus

Why It's Special—Its ferny, airy leaves give cosmos a delicate look, but it can endure all kinds of weather while continuing to open its candy-colored blossoms. Long stems make it perfect for cut flowers and hungry finches adore the seeds. A sister species, *Cosmos sulphureus*, is slightly smaller, just as tough, and blooms in shades of golden yellow, orange, and scarlet.

How to Plant & Grow—Cosmos plants can be found in garden centers in spring, but seeds can also be direct sown in the garden. If you purchase plants, be sure to gently break the rootball so the roots will grow deep into the soil.

Care & Problems—When plants reach 18 to 24 inches tall, it may be helpful to pinch them hard to encourage them to branch and remain slightly shorter, which helps to prevent them from blowing over during rain and windstorms. Cosmos are rugged and basically pest free.

Bloom Color—Pink, magenta, crimson, white, lavender

Peak Season—Mid- to late summer

Mature Size (H x W)—4 to 6 ft. x 2 to 3 ft.

Water Needs—Drought tolerant, once established

Good in Containers? No, best in the garden

DRAGON WING™ BEGONIA

Begonia x hybrida Dragon Wing™

Why It's Special—This relatively new begonia provides more bang for your buck in a part-sun to part-shade location than almost any other shade-tolerant annual. Large clusters of red or pink blooms appear throughout the summer.

How to Plant & Grow—Plants are available in pots in spring and should be planted after the danger of frost has passed. Dragon Wing™ begonias prefer rich, moist, well-drained soil and will grow to near-shrublike proportions by summer's end, so give them room. They make excellent space fillers in partly shaded beds and borders.

Care & Problems—Plants won't develop and flower fully in deep shade, so be sure that plants receive at least some sun during the day—morning sun or high, dappled shade is best. Water regularly and feed every two weeks with a water-soluble fertilizer. Slugs and snails can be a problem in damp shade.

Bloom Color—Red or pink

Peak Season—Spring to fall

Mature Size (H x W)—2 to 2½ ft. x 2½ to 3 ft.

Water Needs—Evenly moist soil

Good in Containers? Yes, excellent in large containers

FANFLOWER

Scaevola aemula

Why It's Special—Fanflower is a low-growing, trailing annual that produces a profusion of small, purple-blue, fan-shaped flowers from spring to frost. For a long season of bloom with minimal care, fanflower can't be beat. New varieties feature pink or white flowers, as well as more compact forms.

How to Plant & Grow—Plants are available in spring and should be planted after the danger of frost has passed. Fanflower needs full to part sun and well-drained soil. Water as needed to keep plants from wilting for the first month after planting. Once established, plants are quite drought tolerant.

Care & Problems—Fertilize fanflower with a water-soluble, bloom-promoting fertilizer once a month. Plants may be leggy when they are first planted. Trimming back by half when they go in the ground will promote branching, luxuriant growth, and flowering. In containers, regular watering and fertilizing is essential.

Bloom Color—Violet-blue, pink, white

Peak Season—Spring to fall

Mature Size (H x W)—6 to 8 in. x 24 to 36 in.

Water Needs—Average to slightly dry soil

Good in Containers? Yes, an excellent trailer

GLOBE AMARANTH

Gomphrena globosa

Why It's Special—Globe amaranth ranks near the top of the list of low-maintenance garden flowers, tolerating wind and searing sun. Shorter varieties are excellent for edgings and low borders, while taller varieties are perfect for filling gaps in perennial borders.

How to Plant & Grow—Plants are sold in cell packs or 4-inch pots in spring. Globe amaranth needs a sunny location and well-drained soil; even a dry spot in the garden will do. Don't set plants too deeply. Water regularly for the first two to three weeks.

Care & Problems—Globe amaranth thrives on neglect. Prune by one-third if plants get leggy, and feed very lightly to encourage new growth and flowering. Avoid poorly drained soils, which lead to root rot. To dry the flowers, cut when the flowers are half open and hang them upside down in a warm, dry garage or shed.

Bloom Color—White, lilac, purple, orange-red, salmon

Peak Season—Summer to fall

Mature Size (H x W)—10 to 24 in. x 10 to 24 in.

Water Needs—Drought tolerant

Good in Containers? No, better suited to beds

IMPATIENS

Impatiens walleriana

Why It's Special—Impatiens come in a wide range of colors and are among the most shade tolerant of annual flowers. They provide nonstop color until the first killing frost. Size ranges from 4-inch-tall miniatures to shrublike 3-foot specimens. Double-flowering forms have blossoms resembling miniature roses or camellias.

How to Plant & Grow—Set out transplants in spring after the danger of frost has passed. Impatiens thrive in rich, moist, well-drained soil that is thoroughly amended with organic matter such as compost. Keep plants well watered after transplanting. An organic granular fertilizer once a month will work wonders.

Care & Problems—For bushier plants, cut new transplants back by one-third about two weeks after planting. Fertilize lightly and they will recover in no time, producing fuller plants and more blooms. Slugs are occasionally a problem and can be treated with an iron-based, nontoxic bait.

Bloom Color—White, pink, fuchsia, orange, red

Peak Season—Early summer to fall

Mature Size (H x W)—10 to 24 in. x 15 to 30 in.

Water Needs—Evenly moist soil

Good in Containers? Yes, perfect for shady planters

INDIAN BLANKET

Gaillardia aristata

Why It's Special—Of the native annuals, Indian blanket may be the most tolerant of hostile surroundings. It grows along dry roadsides and in the dunes overlooking southern seacoasts, and its furry, gray-green foliage befits a drought-resistant species. It often drops seeds and volunteers the following year, but is not invasive.

How to Plant & Grow—Indian blanket grows quickly from late-spring planting. Unless you have heavy clay soil, amendments are rarely needed. Excellent drainage is essential; so in clay soils add a combination of pine bark soil conditioner and ¼-inch gravel. Water Indian blanket regularly until it is established.

Care & Problems—Deadheading, feeding, and watering late in the season can promote a second flush of bloom. Pests and diseases are generally not a problem, though root rot can strike plants in heavy clay soils. Leave a few seedheads to encourage reseeding.

Bloom Color—Red, orange, gold, bicolors

Peak Season—Midsummer to frost

Mature Size (H x W)—1 to 2 ft. x 1 to 1½ ft.

Water Needs—Very drought tolerant, once established

Good in Containers? No, best in the garden

LANTANA

Lantana camara

Why It's Special—Lantana's profusion of blooms last from spring to autumn. Happy plants can grow to shrublike proportions and in warm climates some varieties may be perennial. Lantana attracts butterflies, bees, and hummingbirds.

How to Plant & Grow—Plant in spring or early summer, when air and soil temperatures have warmed significantly. Lantana likes it hot and sunny, and even a few hours of shade will reduce flower production significantly. It is fabulous in containers but will need consistent watering.

Care & Problems—Lantana is a flowering powerhouse and uses a lot of water and energy for this purpose. The more you feed and water, the higher your reward. Deadheading is not necessary, but occasional light pruning will help control the size of the plants. Some people find that the tiny hairs on the leaves irritate their skin, but this is nothing serious.

Bloom Color—Yellow, orange, red, pink, peach

Peak Season—Early summer to frost

Mature Size (H x W)—1 to 4 ft. x 2½ to 4 ft.

Water Needs—Drought tolerant, once established

Good in Containers? Yes, excellent in containers

MARIGOLD

Tagetes spp. and hybrids

Why It's Special—Marigolds come in many heights and in various flower forms, from single to fully double. The bright flowers are sunny and warm, and the single and semidouble types attract butterflies. Dwarf varieties are excellent for edgings and borders.

How to Plant & Grow—Sow marigold seeds directly in the garden, or set out transplants after the danger of frost has passed. Plant in full sun in ordinary garden soil. Space the larger-growing African types 18 to 24 inches apart, and the dwarf French types 10 to 12 inches apart. Feed regularly to keep plants growing and blooming.

Care & Problems—Remove spent blooms to promote continuous flowering. Taller varieties may need to be staked. Spider mites can be a problem during dry weather and if plants become stressed. Keeping the soil evenly moist and the plants well fed will help combat this problem.

Bloom Color—Yellow, gold, orange, red, bicolors

Peak Season—Early summer to frost

Mature Size (H x W)—10 in. to 3 ft. x 10 in. to 2 ft.

Water Needs—Evenly moist soil

Good in Containers? Yes, dwarf varieties

MELAMPODIUM

Melampodium paludosum

Why It's Special—Melampodium, or "butter daisy," has impressive resistance to heat and humidity. It comes in only one color—yellow—but newer varieties have been bred for attractive foliage, compact forms, and profuse flowering.

How to Plant & Grow—Set out transplants after all danger of frost has passed and soil has begun to warm. Melampodium likes it hot and will languish if planted too early in the season. It is quite tolerant of unimproved soils, but grows lush and full when soils have been amended with compost and soil conditioner.

Care & Problems—Melampodium requires little in the way of maintenance. Deadheading is not necessary and the continual new growth covers spent blossoms, so plants always look clean and fresh. Though very drought tolerant, it grows and flowers best with a good, weekly soaking during dry periods. Liquid fertilizer once a month will keep plants healthy.

Bloom Color—Yellow

Peak Season—Early summer to frost

Mature Size (H x W)—1 to 2 ft. x 1 to 2 ft.

Water Needs—Drought tolerant, once established

Good in Containers? Yes, dwarf varieties

MEXICAN SUNFLOWER

Tithonia rotundifolia

Why It's Special—This tall annual has broad, fuzzy foliage and produces multitudes of brilliant orange daisies that attract butterflies and hummingbirds. The only drawback may be its size—5 to 7 feet tall—but it's worth finding a space for it!

How to Plant & Grow—Plants can be found in some garden centers in late spring, but Mexican sunflower is easy to grow from seed. Since it doesn't like to be potbound, you may have better results sowing seeds directly in the garden. It is not fussy about soil, but the better you treat it, the better it responds.

Care & Problems—Staking may be necessary for very tall plants. A light application of all-purpose fertilizer twice during the growing season will keep plants vigorous and blooming. A dwarf variety, 'Fiesta del Sol', grows only 2½ feet tall and is excellent for small gardens.

Bloom Color—Brilliant orange

Peak Season—Midsummer to frost

Mature Size (H x W)—2½ to 7 ft. x 2½ to 4 ft.

Water Needs—Thorough soaking once a week

Good in Containers? No, too large for containers

MILLION BELLS®

Calibrachoa spp. and hybrids

Why It's Special—Million Bells® are popular for container gardens and window boxes, from which they spread and trail. In garden beds, they remain low and spreading, covering the ground.

How to Plant & Grow—Most Million Bells® are generally only available in 4-inch pots; seeds are rarely, if ever, available. They grow quickly and will flower from planting time to hard frost in autumn. In heavy clay soils, plant high and mulch with 1 inch of sand to keep the soil surface dry and prevent stem rot.

Care & Problems—Million Bells® are nearly care free. They do not require deadheading, and occasional light pruning will keep them full. They are subject to root rot if planted in heavy clay soils, so amend thoroughly! Botrytis, or gray leaf mold, can be an occasional problem. Provide good air circulation and keep water off the leaves.

Bloom Color—Blue, pink, lavender, red, coral, yellow

Peak Season—Early summer to frost

Mature Size (H x W)—4 to 8 in. x 12 to 24 in.

Water Needs—Evenly moist soil

Good in Containers? Yes, outstanding container plants

NARROW-LEAF ZINNIA

Zinnia angustifolia

Why It's Special—A much smaller plant with a different form and habit than what most of us call "zinnias," this annual thrives with minimal care in heat and humidity. The blooms resemble miniature daisies and are produced in great quantity from summer to frost.

How to Plant & Grow—Plant transplants into the garden once the soil has warmed thoroughly—not before late April or early May. Zinnias despise cold, wet soil and will languish and sometimes rot if the soil is not sufficiently warm. They perform best in soils that are moist, well drained, and well amended with organic matter.

Care & Problems—In early summer, after plants are actively growing, a light shearing will produce bushier, more compact plants. Even though you'll be removing the flowers, plants will respond quickly. Apply a liquid fertilizer every two weeks during the growing season.

Bloom Color—Orange, yellow, white

Peak Season—Early summer to frost

Mature Size (H x W)—6 to 12 in. x 12 to 15 in.

Water Needs—Average to evenly moist soil

Good in Containers? Yes, a good filler plant

NASTURTIUM

Tropaeolum majus

Why It's Special—Nasturtiums are not a common choice among Southern gardeners because we have to "squeeze them in" during our cool spring and fall growing seasons, and their season of bloom is fairly short. That said, for bright, jewel-tone colors, few plants can beat nasturtiums and they're worth the extra effort.

How to Plant & Grow—Nasturtiums are cool-weather plants and while they can be grown in spring, the fall season may suit them best. If sown in early September, seeds germinate and grow quickly in the warm soil, and plants will thrive and bloom profusely during the cooler weather of October and November.

Care & Problems—Cabbage worms are occasionally a problem and can be controlled with a natural, nonpoisonous *Bt* spray. Aphids can also be a problem on tender new growth and can be removed with a gentle spray from a hose.

Bloom Color—Red, orange, gold, yellow, cream

Peak Season—Spring and fall

Mature Size (H x W)—12 to 14 in. x 12 to 14 in.

Water Needs—Keep on the dry side

Good in Containers? Yes, good fillers and trailers

NICOTIANA

Nicotiana spp. and hybrids

Why It's Special—Nicotiana, or flowering tobacco, is a first cousin to commercial tobacco. Recent advances in breeding have produced plants that are more compact, flower profusely, and keep their blossoms fully open all day. A few are even fragrant!

How to Plant & Grow—Nicotiana seed is dust-like and sometimes difficult to start indoors. Seed can be sown directly in the garden where you want it to grow or transplants can be purchased and planted anytime after the danger of frost is past. Light afternoon shade may prolong their flowering period for a week or two longer than full sun. Nicotiana likes alkaline soil, so be prepared to lime the area.

Care & Problems—Nicotiana needs little care. Aphids may collect on new growth and can be treated with a stream of water from the hose or, for particularly bad infestations, insecticidal soap. Root rot can occur in heavy clay soils that stay too wet.

Bloom Color—Red, pink, lavender, yellow, green, white

Peak Season—Late spring to late summer

Mature Size (H x W)—18 to 24 in. x 12 to 18 in.

Water Needs—Evenly moist soil

Good in Containers? Yes, but may be short-lived

PANSY

Viola x wittrockiana

Why It's Special—What would we plant for color in our winter landscapes if we didn't have pansies and violas? Their bright, cheerful jewel tones and cute faces are always welcome.

How to Plant & Grow—Pansies and violas can be planted from mid-September to late fall, as soon as nighttime temperatures begin to moderate. The earlier you can plant them and the better established they become, the more profuse the flowering will be through the winter. Many people wait until the last possible moment and plants sometimes struggle.

Care & Problems—If plants begin to grow leggy, pinch them back by one-third to encourage bushy new growth from the base. Deadhead regularly for the first few weeks to encourage plants to get into a healthy bloom cycle. Mixing a slow-release fertilizer into the soil at planting time is very beneficial.

Bloom Color—All colors, pastels to jewel tones

Peak Season—Fall, winter, early spring

Mature Size (H x W)—6 to 8 in. x 10 to 12 in.

Water Needs—Evenly moist soil

Good in Containers? Yes, outstanding in containers

PENTAS

Pentas lanceolata

Why It's Special—Southern gardeners love pentas for their durability in summer heat and humidity. Add to that their ability to attract multitudes of butterflies and hummingbirds and they become superstars!

How to Plant & Grow—Buy plants of pentas and set them into the garden or containers after the danger of frost has passed. Pentas prefer full sun, but may appreciate some light afternoon shade in the hottest coastal areas. Thoroughly amending your soil will prolong their span of bloom and help keep them in good condition.

Care & Problems—Rabbits can be a problem for young plants. Repellent sprays may be helpful. While deadheading is not an absolute requirement, it is very helpful. Pentas are heavy feeders and respond well to liquid fertilizer applied once every two weeks throughout the growing season. Water deeply and thoroughly during periods of drought and hot weather.

Bloom Color—Red, pink, lavender, white

Peak Season—Midsummer to frost

Mature Size (H x W)—1 to 2 ft. x 1 to 2 ft.

Water Needs—Evenly moist soil

Good in Containers? Yes, perfect in containers

PERIWINKLE

Catharanthus roseus

Why It's Special—Periwinkle is also sometimes called "vinca" because of the slight resemblance of its flower to the blue blooms of the vinca groundcover popular in shady gardens. Periwinkle, however, is an annual and is one of the most heat- and humidity-resistant plants a Southern gardener can grow. It is tough, adaptable, reasonably drought resistant, and troubled by few pests.

How to Plant & Grow—Do not plant periwinkle until the danger of frost is well past and the soil temperature has warmed significantly. Cold, wet soils spell almost certain death for periwinkle. Soil should be thoroughly amended and improved with at least 2 to 3 inches of pine bark soil conditioner to help with drainage and aeration.

Care & Problems—Periwinkle is virtually care free. Root rot can and will be a problem in cold and/or wet soils. Excellent drainage is really its only requirement. Liquid feed every two weeks during the growing season with a bloom-promoting, water-soluble fertilizer. Deadheading is not necessary.

Bloom Color—Red, plum, lavender, pink, coral, white

Peak Season—Early summer to frost

Mature Size (H x W)—12 to 14 in. x 18 to 24 in.

Water Needs—Moderately drought tolerant

Good in Containers? Yes, excellent fillers and trailers

PERSIAN SHIELD

Strobilanthes dyerianus

Why It's Special—Persian shield is a standout in container gardens and as a dramatic foliage plant in partly shaded flower beds. No other tropical plant has such exotic leaves: light purple overlaid on green, airbrushed with silver, and laced with dark veins.

How to Plant & Grow—Persian shield thrives in warm, tropical conditions. Hold plants until the air and soil temperatures have warmed significantly in late spring before planting out. Water and feed regularly to encourage plants to grow lush.

Care & Problems—While Persian shield may survive in full sun, it will develop its best color in part sun or very bright, dappled shade. Healthy plants should have leaves 6 to 8 inches long and 2 to 3 inches wide, with brilliant color. Pinch occasionally when young to encourage branching. Amend garden soils generously at planting time and apply liquid fertilizer every two weeks.

Bloom Color—Grown for foliage

Peak Season—Early summer to fall

Mature Size (H x W)—2 ft. x 2 ft. or larger

Water Needs—Evenly moist soil

Good in Containers? Yes, pinch to control height

PETUNIA

Petunia x hybrida

Why It's Special—These sturdy annuals come in myriad colors with masses of trumpet-shaped blooms. The most popular petunias today are the trailing or creeping varieties that produce hundreds of flowers at a time with no need for deadheading or extra care.

How to Plant & Grow—Petunias don't mind cool weather and can be planted as soon as the danger of frost has passed. Petunias need plenty of light to perform to their fullest potential, but will tolerate very light afternoon shade in the hottest areas. Good soil drainage is essential. Clay soils should be thoroughly amended.

Care & Problems—Petunias can have problems with leaf blight and stem rot. Water early in the morning to allow leaves and stems to dry off quickly. Pinch or shear back if they ramble too far. Liquid feed every two weeks.

Bloom Color—White, pink, red, purple, blue, yellow, bicolors

Peak Season—Early summer to frost

Mature Size (H x W)—6 in. to 1 ft. x 1 to 4 ft.

Water Needs—Evenly moist soil

Good in Containers? Yes, exceptional spillers and fillers

POLKA-DOT PLANT

Hypoestes phyllostachya

Why It's Special—Polka-dot plant features leaves with small white, pink, or red spots over a dark green background, and it is one of the few richly colored ornamentals that thrive in light to medium shade while standing up to heat and humidity. It is excellent in containers, beds, and borders.

How to Plant & Grow—Polka-dot plants are usually sold in six-packs or in small pots. After the danger of frost has passed, plant them in beds with morning sun or bright dappled shade throughout the day. Mix in a 2-inch layer of organic soil conditioner or compost and some granular, slow-release fertilizer.

Care & Problems—Be faithful in your watering, especially for new plantings. You may need to spritz plants twice a day for the first two weeks until you see active new growth. Polka-dot plants can be pinched to keep them compact.

Bloom Color—Grown for foliage

Peak Season—Early summer to frost

Mature Size (H x W)—1 to 1½ ft. x 1 to 1½ ft.

Water Needs—Evenly moist soil

Good in Containers? Yes, very good choice for containers

ROSE MOSS

Portulaca grandiflora

Why It's Special—Few flowers can match rose moss for sheer brilliance of color and the way its satiny petals reflect light. Modern varieties of this drought-resistant, resilient plant have been bred for fully double blossoms that remain open throughout the day.

How to Plant & Grow—Rose moss flourishes in heat, drought, and full sun, but will languish if planted in sticky, wet, clay soils. Transplants can be set out as soon as the danger of frost has passed and the soil feels warm to the touch.

Care & Problems—Grow with only the lightest applications of fertilizer when preparing the soil. Rose moss blooms so profusely that it often wears itself out by late July, but it can be sheared in half, lightly fed, and watered, and it will rebound beautifully. It will also politely reseed itself in the garden.

Bloom Color—Red, fuchsia, pink, yellow, peach, white

Peak Season—Early to mid summer; repeats in fall

Mature Size (H x W)—4 to 10 in. x 16 to 24 in.

Water Needs—Extremely drought tolerant, once established

Good in Containers? Yes, but finishes by late summer

SCARLET SAGE

Salvia splendens

Why It's Special—Recent hybrids feature more colors, longer bloom time, and flower spikes that stand well above the foliage. Few flowers offer blooms in this shade of blazing red and the hummingbirds will certainly take notice!

How to Plant & Grow—Plant salvias once all danger of frost has passed and soil is warm to the touch. The warm soil will get them off to the best possible start. Salvias prefer well-drained soil and benefit from the addition of soil conditioner and compost to the soil prior to planting.

Care & Problems—Regular deadheading is important to keep new growth coming and new flower spikes forming throughout the year. While scarlet sage will grow in full sun, a little light shade in the afternoons will often produce more robust plants with longer-lasting flowers that don't bleach and fade in the sun.

Bloom Color—Dark red, scarlet, purple, pink, coral, cream

Peak Season—Early summer to early fall

Mature Size (H x W)—1 to 2½ ft. x 1 to 2 ft.

Water Needs—Evenly moist soil

Good in Containers? Yes, a great focal point

SNAPDRAGON

Antirrhinum majus

Why It's Special—Snapdragons come in almost every color of the rainbow, and modern breeding has introduced more heat tolerance, though in the Carolinas, snapdragons are still best grown in early spring or fall, when the temperatures are milder. Tall varieties are excellent for cutting.

How to Plant & Grow—Transplants can be set early in the spring and will even tolerate very light frosts if they are hardened off. They thrive in cool temperatures and many gardeners like to plant them in early September. In the warmest coastal areas, "snaps" may bloom all winter.

Care & Problems—Aphids can be a problem on young plants or the tender new growth of older plants. Control with insecticidal soap. Rich soil and good drainage are all snapdragons really need to thrive. Staking may be necessary for tall varieties.

Bloom Color—Red, pink, yellow, purple, white

Peak Season—Spring to early summer, again in fall

Mature Size (H x W)—8 in. to 3 ft. x 8 in. to 1 ft.

Water Needs—Evenly moist soil

Good in Containers? Yes, dwarf or medium varieties

SPIDER FLOWER

Cleome hasslerana

Why It's Special—Spider flower gets its name from its long, threadlike flower stems and wispy blossoms. Seedpods add interest to the plant and ensure you'll have spider flower in the garden for many years.

How to Plant & Grow—Seeds germinate readily in sunny, warm flower beds. Plants can also be purchased in spring and planted in the garden once the danger of frost has passed. Spider flower needs to be well-watered for the first three to four weeks, but once it is established, it is quite drought tolerant.

Care & Problems—Little care is needed except for weed pulling. An occasional deep soaking may benefit the plants during periods of drought and will keep them from looking ragged. Spider mites occasionally attack, but can be controlled with insecticidal soap. A second sowing of seeds in mid-August will ensure a spectacular fall show.

Bloom Color—Pink, lavender-purple, white

Peak Season—Midsummer; fall with second sowing

Mature Size (H x W)—2 to 5 ft. x 1½ to 2 ft.

Water Needs—Drought tolerant, once established

Good in Containers? No, better in the garden

SUN COLEUS

Solenostemon scutellarioides

Why It's Special—Coleus has long been the backbone of annual shade gardens, but thanks to new introductions, coleus has come out of the shadows and into the light—literally. As long as you keep it well watered and well fed, sun coleus will offer up its vibrant, nonstop color from spring to fall.

How to Plant & Grow—Coleus can be planted anytime after the frost date has passed and soil has warmed. Moisture-retentive soil is essential, especially in full sun, and helpful even in part sun or dappled shade. In containers, use potting soil with moisture crystals mixed in.

Care & Problems—Occasional pinching will keep plants full and bushy. Remove any flower buds as they appear to keep new growth fresh and attractive. Slugs and snails can be a problem on young plants, but they can be controlled with a nontoxic, iron-based slug and snail bait.

Bloom Color—Grown for foliage

Peak Season—Late spring to fall

Mature Size (H x W)—2 to 4 ft. x 2 to 3 ft.

Water Needs—Evenly moist soil

Good in Containers? Yes, thrives in containers

SUNFLOWER

Helianthus annuus

Why It's Special—Many gardeners think that sunflowers come only in the giant, yellow-flowered types they grew as kids, but sunflowers can range from small single daisies to fluffy, fully double pompoms, in colors from creamy white to all shades of yellow, mahogany, bronze, and more.

How to Plant & Grow—Sunflowers resent being transplanted and are best grown by sowing seeds directly in the garden where you want them to grow. Ordinary garden soil is perfect, provided it is not heavy, sticky clay. All sunflowers really need is a good, deep watering twice a week and an occasional feeding with an all-purpose liquid fertilizer to keep the blooms coming for many weeks.

Care & Problems—Dwarf varieties are not usually good investments. They provide one nice flower and then usually play out quickly. The tallest varieties must be staked.

Bloom Color—White, yellow, burgundy, bronze, red

Peak Season—Mid- to late summer

Mature Size (H x W)—4 to 10 ft. x 2 to 4 ft.

Water Needs—Drought tolerant, once established

Good in Containers? No, for the garden only

SWEET POTATO VINE

Ipomoea batatas

Why It's Special—Few foliage plants can rival the brilliant color provided by sweet potato vine and it's the perfect companion plant for both flower beds and containers.

How to Plant & Grow—Sweet potato vine can be added to the garden anytime after the danger of frost has passed. Even small plants will grow quickly and prefer well-tilled, thoroughly amended soil to which some lime has been added. Allow plenty of room, as vines can spread 6 feet or more.

Care & Problems—Vines will need to be pruned occasionally to keep them in bounds, and the hotter it gets, the faster they grow! Potato weevils and slugs may chew holes in the leaves, and while unsightly, this is not life threatening. The fleshy roots can be dug and stored in a frost-free place to be replanted next spring.

Bloom Color—Grown for foliage

Peak Season—Early summer to frost

Mature Size (H x W)—6 to 10 in. x 3 to 6 ft.

Water Needs—Water deeply when plants wilt

Good in Containers? Yes, very good trailer and accent plant

TORENIA

Torenia fournieri

Why It's Special—The cool blue flowers of torenia blend well with almost any color scheme, and new cultivars have expanded the color range to gold, purple, white, and pink. Torenia comes in both mounding and spreading forms, so be sure to read the label.

How to Plant & Grow—Torenia thrives in any average garden soil, but responds particularly well to soil that has been thoroughly amended with compost and/or manure. It also thrives in commercial potting mixes, making it a great addition to containers.

Care & Problems—Water regularly during hot, dry weather and keep beds mulched to help conserve moisture and suppress weeds. In containers, water as needed to keep plants from wilting and be prepared to feed at least twice a month to keep new growth and flowers coming all summer long. Occasional deadheading will keep plants from looking tired.

Bloom Color—Blue, purple, pink, white, yellow

Peak Season—Early summer to frost

Mature Size (H x W)—8 to 12 in. x 12 to 18 in.

Water Needs—Evenly moist soil

Good in Containers? Yes, excellent in containers

VERBENA

Verbena hybrids

Why It's Special—Verbena makes a vivid groundcover in beds and borders and an outstanding trailing plant for pots and hanging baskets. It is well suited to edging paths, providing "feet" for taller-growing annuals and perennials, and is also right at home in the rock garden.

How to Plant & Grow—Plant in any sunny location in well-drained soil. Avoid heavy clay, where excess moisture can cause root rot. Verbena will root down as its stems trail across the ground, but the stems must come in contact with the soil, so mulch lightly.

Care & Problems—Deadhead on a regular basis and apply granular, organic fertilizer monthly to keep verbena lush and flowering. Supplemental feeding with a water-soluble liquid can also be done. Powdery mildew can sometimes be a problem during hot, humid weather.

Bloom Color—Purple, lavender, red, pink, white

Peak Season—Early summer to frost

Mature Size (H x W)—6 to 12 in. x 2 to 4 ft.

Water Needs—Evenly moist soil, not wet

Good in Containers? Yes, one of the best trailers for pots

WAX BEGONIA

Begonia semperflorens-cultorum

Why It's Special—Wax begonias have long been popular for shade gardens, edgings, and containers. Their profusion of flowers from spring until frost and their ability to thrive in heat and humidity make them a standout.

How to Plant & Grow—Plant wax begonias after the last frost date has passed and the soil has begun to warm. While some varieties will tolerate full sun, morning sun or bright dappled shade will keep the plants from looking burnt and crisp. A soil rich in organic matter is preferred, but begonias will tolerate almost any soil conditions except for constant wetness.

Care & Problems—Slugs occasionally bother begonias. Treat them with a nontoxic, iron-based slug bait. If plants become leggy, pinch them back to just above a leaf joint and they will become full again. Feed monthly and water at least twice weekly during dry spells.

Bloom Color—Pink, red, white, bicolors

Peak Season—Early summer to frost

Mature Size (H x W)—6 in. to 1 ft. x 1 ft.

Water Needs—Evenly moist soil, not wet

Good in Containers? Yes, very good container fillers

GARDENING WITH ANNUALS

Annuals are the workhorses of the garden. They can be relied on to deliver brilliant color and a long-lasting display of flowers all season long. Annuals do well in lead roles, planted *en masse* in sun or shade to produce a massive show of color. They can also do well as supporting cast members, serving as "fillers" to dress up open spaces that haven't yet been filled in by permanent plantings of perennials or shrubs. They work as screens too. Use them to keep the garden looking well dressed by hiding the fading leaves of bulbs that have finished flowering and are going dormant.

Some annuals are especially attractive to hummingbirds and butterflies; some specialize in providing exquisite fragrance; some are unequaled in colorful bouquets. Still others adapt readily to containers and hanging baskets to provide a spot of color. All of this from a group of plants whose entire life cycle lasts less than a year!

COLD TOLERANCE IN ANNUALS

Annuals differ in their ability to tolerate cold temperatures and are commonly categorized as hardy, half-hardy, or tender. These categories are a general guide to help you decide when to plant annuals. The two important dates to know in your area are the last expected freeze in spring and the first expected freeze in fall. Check with a local garden center or contact your local County Extension Service to find out what these dates are in your area.

Hardy annuals are the most cold tolerant of the group, sometimes withstanding freezing temperatures. In many cases, the seeds can be planted outdoors a few weeks before the last freeze in spring or in fall after freezing temperatures have arrived but while the soil can still be worked. Hardy annuals include calendula, larkspur, pansy, and stock. Most hardy annuals are not heat tolerant and usually decline and die with the onset of hot summer temperatures.

Half-hardy annuals can tolerate cool, wet weather but will be damaged, slowed down, or killed by freezing temperatures. The seeds of most half-hardy annuals can be sown after the last anticipated freeze in spring. Although most do not require warm soil temperatures to germinate, some do. Refer to the seed packet for specific information about optimum temperature ranges for good germination. Many half-hardy annuals decline in the midsummer heat but may bloom again in late summer or fall.

Tender annuals are generally native to tropical regions and cannot tolerate cold soils and air temperatures. They need warm soil temperatures for seeds to germinate and long, warm summers for plants to produce the best flower display. Typically, the seeds must be sown outdoors two to three weeks after the last spring freeze. But as we will discuss later, you can get ahead by starting the seeds indoors so that you can set out transplants when the time comes.

MORE PLANTING TIPS

When you're ready to transplant your annuals to the garden, these additional tips may be useful:

1 Moisten the potting medium before taking the plant out of the container. Moisten plants in peat pots before planting, pot and all.

2 Dig a hole a little wider than the rootball and the same depth as the rootball.

3 Hold your hand over the top of the pot with the plant stems between your fingers. Tip over the pot and tap the plant into your hand. Annuals growing in cell packs can be pushed out from the bottom.

4 Plant the rootball level with the soil surface.

5 Firm the soil around the plants and water them in, soaking them thoroughly. Apply a layer of mulch.

LONG-TERM CARE AND MAINTENANCE

You may have spent a lot of time raising, or a fair amount of money purchasing healthy transplants, and you may have selected and prepared appropriate sites, but you can still meet with disappointment if you do not continue to give your flowering annuals the care they need.

WATERING

Adequate water is necessary for annuals to grow vigorously and bloom continuously, especially during hot, dry summers. Some annuals require a continuous supply of water, while other, more drought-tolerant types can prosper with minimal regular watering.

Frequent watering, perhaps twice daily, is necessary when sowing seeds outdoors. Seedlings or newly planted annuals should be watered once a day.

Once established, you can gradually water annuals less frequently. Always water deeply to encourage deep rooting. Established plants may need to be watered once a week in clay soils that hold more water than sandy soils. Plants in sandy soils may need to be watered twice a week. Instead of following the calendar, water annuals when the top 2 or 3 inches of soil feels dry. You may want to consider using soaker hoses to water your annual beds. The "leaky" hoses that sweat and drip along their entire length are particularly effective. They can be placed in a serpentine pattern throughout the beds and can even be hooked to an automatic timer at the spigot, so all you have to do is check to make sure you don't have any dry spots that the soaker hose doesn't quite reach.

FERTILIZING

Annuals need adequate nutrients to sustain them during the growing season. Before making any supplemental fertilizer applications, let their growth rate, their leaf color, and a soil test be your guides. If the bed is already highly fertile, the soil test will save you from the undesirable results of overfertilizing. The rule of thumb for fertilizing is to apply a dry, granular, complete, fast-acting type of fertilizer such as 10-10-10 at a rate of 1 pound per 100 square feet monthly. That works out to approximately 2 cups per 100 square feet, or 4 tablespoons per 10 square feet. Keep this up throughout the growing season; stretch the intervals between feedings up to six weeks, based on your observations.

Water-soluble fertilizers usually call for shorter intervals between applications. They are not only quickly available, but also quickly used up. Most should be mixed with water and applied every two weeks, following label directions. These fertilizers can be absorbed by both leaves and roots.

Slow-release or controlled-release fertilizers deliver small amounts of nutrients gradually over an extended period. Depending on soil moisture and temperature, release of these nutrients may extend over several weeks or months. Typically, the first application is mixed into the bed just before planting. Some products will have to be applied a second time midway through the growing season. How much you apply and how often should be based on the manufacturer's instructions.

PEST CONTROL

Healthy, well-grown annuals that are watered and fed regularly will probably have few pest problems. If plants become stressed, either from too much or too little water, too much or too little fertilizer, improper planting, planting in the wrong place, or other factors, then problems may start to appear. Your local garden center or nursery professionals should be able to help you diagnose and control common disease and insect problems. Your local County Extension Service is also a valuable resource when it comes to diagnosing and dealing with common pest problems in your area.

JANUARY

- If you're growing annuals from seed indoors, organize your seed packets and create a sowing schedule. Different varieties will require different amounts of time between sowing the seeds and planting outdoors.

- Avoid sowing seeds too early because plants may be ready to transplant to the garden before outdoor conditions permit. This can lead to plants growing too tall and spindly before you can get them in the garden.

- When watering seedlings, determine the need for watering by squeezing the top one-half inch of soil between your thumb and forefinger. If water squeezes out easily, there's enough moisture.

- Seedlings will need to be fertilized to keep them healthy and growing before they're ready to transplant to the garden. Begin feeding at half the recommended strength when a seedling's first set of true leaves appear.

- Damping off disease can be a big problem with seedlings. This fungus causes a stem to look pinched and seedlings topple over at ground level. Avoid overwatering and excess humidity to help prevent damping off disease.

FEBRUARY

- When planning your garden, think in bold splashes of color instead of tiny drops. High-impact, traffic-stopping combinations are created when annuals are planted *en masse*.

- As you are growing seedlings for the garden and beginning to design and think about potential combinations, be sure to keep notes in your garden journal. You'll be happy you have them to refer back to!

- If you sowed seeds by scattering them in flats or larger pots instead of sowing them directly into individual containers, you'll need to transplant the seedlings once they have developed their first true set of leaves.

- Seedlings receiving inadequate light will become spindly and floppy. Supplement your natural light with grow lights or fluorescent tubes if this becomes a problem.

- Keep an eye out for damping off disease. It can attack young seedlings at any moment and is difficult to stop once it has started. Good air circulation is especially helpful.

MARCH

- Before visiting the garden center, make a list of the kinds and quantities of annuals you need. There are plenty of distractions, but a list can be very helpful in keeping you on track!

- Cool-season annuals such as alyssum, calendula, and snapdragons can be planted now, as well as any pansies or violas that might need to be replaced or filled in for the spring show.

- If seedlings growing indoors start to become spindly, pinch the growing tips to keep them more compact and encourage branching.

APRIL

- Hanging baskets and outdoor containers can be planted beginning in April. It is best to wait until after the last frost date to avoid having to haul heavy pots in and out if frost should threaten.

- Warm-season annuals such as cosmos, globe amaranth, marigolds, zinnias, and others can be planted in the garden beginning two to three weeks after the last frost date. Soil should feel warm to the touch before planting warm-season annuals.

- Tender annuals started indoors should gradually be "hardened off"—acclimated to the outdoors—before transplanting them to the garden. Gradually expose them to outdoor light and weather conditions for seven to ten days before transplanting.

- Watch for aphids on annuals that have just been transplanted to the garden. They love tender new growth, but can easily be washed away with a gentle spray from the garden hose.

MAY

- Warm-season annuals will thrive in the garden now that the soil temperature is getting warm. It is now safe to plant all summer-growing, summer-blooming annuals.

- If you sow seeds of annual flowers like zinnias, sunflowers, Mexican sunflowers, or cleome directly in the garden, be prepared to thin the seedlings once they come up. If you don't, plants will be crowded and spindly and will perform poorly.

- Newly planted transplants should not be allowed to dry out. Keep the soil moist and the leaves dry. Watering in the early morning gives the foliage time to dry before the heat of the day and helps prevent fungal diseases.

- Pests are out in force this month. Aphids, spider mites, whiteflies, slugs, and snails can all be problems. Seek advice from your local garden center about the best method of control.

JUNE

- It's not too late to plant annuals if you have spaces that still need filling up. Seeds are inexpensive and cosmos, cleome, Mexican sunflowers, portulaca, sunflowers, and zinnias can all be seeded directly into the garden if your budget is running low.

- If you haven't already, it's time to pull up and discard those weather-beaten pansies that are still hanging on and gasping their last breath!

- Fertilize your annuals this month, especially in sandy soils where nutrients leach out quickly. Annuals are heavy feeders and must have a continuous supply of nutrients to keep looking their best.

- Avoid overhead watering if at all possible and be on the lookout for fungal diseases such as powdery mildew and leaf spot. By keeping foliage dry, you can nearly eliminate many of these problems.

JULY

- If you're going on vacation this month, be sure to make arrangements to have someone look after your garden, and keep annuals and containers well watered. It doesn't take long for plants to dry out past the recovery point during hot summer days.

- In late July, consider sowing a second crop of warm-season annuals like cosmos, cleome, cutting zinnias, and others. Early crops will play out soon and a new crop will ensure flowers until frost.

- Deadheading is especially important this time of year to keep annuals growing and flowering. An extra shot of liquid fertilizer won't hurt, either, and will push annuals through the heat and into cooler autumn weather.

- July is spider mite season. When the weather turns hot and dry, the spider mites thrive. Unnoticed and uncontrolled, they can wipe out a planting in no time.

AUGUST

- The heat and humidity of August make this a good month to stay indoors and occasionally update your garden journal. Organize your notes so that they are useful when you need them.

- A final planting of marigold, zinnia, and cosmos seeds can still be made this month and have enough time to grow and bloom before frost.

- If you want to grow flowering cabbage and kale from seed for your fall garden, now is the time to get them started. It takes about eight to ten weeks for seeds to grow into plants that are ready to go in the ground.

- Fungal leaf spot and powdery mildew love the heat and humidity of August. Be on the lookout and treat as recommended by your local garden center. Keeping water off the foliage will help prevent these problems.

SEPTEMBER

- Be adventurous and try something new! Look for vegetable transplants at your local nursery or farmers' market and replace some of your fading summer annuals with beautiful leaf greens like purple mustard, Swiss chard, lettuces, and more.

- If you had any coleus that you were particularly smitten with, cuttings can be rooted in a glass of water and overwintered indoors in a sunny window to plant back out in the garden next spring.

- Fall is the driest season in the Carolinas. Be sure to keep newly planted transplants well watered until they are completely established.

- Summer annual weeds like crabgrass and goosegrass have matured and are going to seed. Stay on top of weeding so that these pernicious pests don't have the chance to drop thousands of seeds that you will have to contend with next year.

OCTOBER

- Early October is a great time to set out foxglove transplants if they can be found at a local nursery or garden center, or if you have grown your own from seeds sown in August. Days are warm and nights are cool and plants will become established quickly.

- Ornamental kale and cabbage and pansies need to be in the ground as soon as possible to give them at least six weeks to settle in and grow before cold temperatures arrive.

- Keep an eye on the watering of your annuals, especially emerging seedlings and newly planted transplants. It is easy to forget to water when the days become cooler.

- If you're planning to overwinter any annuals indoors, be sure to treat them thoroughly for spider mites and whiteflies before bringing them indoors. These pests can rapidly invade houseplants and are difficult to control indoors.

NOVEMBER

- As the season winds down, it's a great time to clean out the garden shed, clean up the tools, and make sure that everything is stored properly for the winter.

- In warmer areas of the Carolinas, foxgloves, pansies, forget-me-nots, sweet William, and other cool-weather annuals can still be planted.

- Garden cleanup should begin in earnest this month. Be sure to remove all fallen leaves, twigs, and other debris, as these may harbor insect eggs and diseases that can then reinfect the garden next season.

- When frost comes, pull dead plants from large containers and replace with winter annuals if you so desire. In cold mountain climates, containers may need to be emptied and stored for winter to prevent cracking.

DECEMBER

- December and January will be the slowest months for annuals in the garden in all but the very warmest areas of the Carolinas. Pansies may go through a semidormant phase during the coldest weather, but will perk up fast as soon as temperatures return to above freezing.

- This is a great time to catch up on those journal entries that you may not have had time to make during the busy months of autumn. Try to do this before you forget important information.

- Pansies and other winter annuals can be "heaved" out of the ground when the soil freezes and thaws. If this happens, gently press them back into the ground and they should be fine.

- You can lightly fertilize winter annuals such as pansies, violas and ornamental cabbage and kale between bouts of cold winter weather. Fertilize at half the recommended rate so that you don't force too much soft, new growth that could be damaged.

PERENNIALS

for the Carolinas

A perennial, in the broadest horticultural definition, is any plant that lives three or more years. Although trees, shrubs, and vines technically are perennials, gardeners typically use the term to refer to herbaceous perennial flowers. In autumn, the soft tops of most perennials will die to the ground, while the root system persists through the winter. In spring, the cycle begins anew with growth from a crown or modified roots.

Among the most rewarding traits of perennials is that they come up unprompted year after year to offer the garden masses of color in ever-changing patterns. They flower abundantly and multiply without being coaxed. Some will tolerate considerable neglect, and a few, like artemisia, prefer it that way. Perennial gardens are the rage all across the Carolinas. And while their primary season is April to November, with a little bit of planning and ingenuity on your part, you can find perennials that will offer beautiful foliage or flowers for all twelve months of the year.

Perennials are classified based on their hardiness. Hardy perennials will normally survive Carolina winters with little or no protection. Tender or half-hardy perennials will survive a mild winter in Zone 8 gardens but will need mulching in the mountain areas. Some, such as verbena and hardy ice plant, are usually grown as annuals in cold zones, where winter hardiness isn't a guarantee. One thing that the USDA hardiness zones do not take into account is the ability of a plant to withstand heat and drought, so while a certain perennial may be perfectly winter hardy in your area, the heat and humidity of the summer or particularly dry conditions may spell certain death. Microclimates and soil drainage are also important factors in determining how long-lived a perennial will be at any particular site.

HOW TO BE SUCCESSFUL

One distinction between annuals and perennials is their season of bloom. Many annuals will flower continuously for several months as they reproduce and set seed to carry on the next generation. Most perennials, on the other hand, bloom for only a few weeks each season in order to store energy in their roots to return next season. For this reason, it is important to consider what a perennial plant will look like throughout the year and how its foliage will work in the garden once its flowering season has passed. One of the basic goals of gardeners should be to obtain continuity of color by planting different varieties for bloom at different times. As one kind of perennial finishes, another begins to bloom. Perennials with colorful foliage, such as coral bells and purple heart, may be more valuable in the garden's design than those that only bloom and have foliage of marginal interest.

Site selection is very important for perennial gardens since the plants will be left in place for several years. There are plenty of choices both for sunny and shady locations. Soil pH requirements vary among perennials, but most prefer a pH between 5.5 and 6.5. For many perennials, a consistent, moderate level of soil moisture is important, but with a little research you can find varieties that are very drought tolerant and others that will thrive in wet areas. The one time of year that most perennials will not tolerate moisture at their feet is winter. Cold, wet conditions during the cold months of the year can easily lead to root and crown rot—a certain death sentence for many perennial plants. A 2- to 3-inch layer of finely ground pine bark, sold as "soil conditioner," can be tilled into beds before planting to improve soil drainage and aeration. Sedum, salvia, and other semiwoody perennials will benefit greatly from quick-draining soils where coarse soil amendments are incorporated as needed.

SHADY CHARACTERS

When growing perennial flowers, you are not limited to sunny borders, since many perennials flourish in the shade. Some of the best plants, such as lungwort, wild ginger, ferns, and hosta, can be used to create a showstopping garden where a majestic oak shadows the bed. Shaded sites can be problematic, however, in that tree roots forage for water in well-prepared sites. You may find it challenging to meet the water requirements of some perennials in shade gardens, but with some supplemental irrigation, success is easily within reach.

For native plant enthusiasts, shade gardens full of spring wildflowers are often the crown jewels of their gardens. The survival of many ephemeral wildflowers depends on their ability to bloom in early spring when light and moisture are plentiful; they phase into dormancy as the hot season advances. Many of our native woodland orchid species and trilliums flourish because of their resilience.

GARDEN AGGRESSORS

Another challenge with perennials is to keep certain species or varieties from overgrowing others in the same bed, becoming an unsightly jungle. And this problem is not limited to plants that are commonly labeled "invasive." Two good examples of native plants that can be very aggressive in a garden setting are obedient plant and pink showy primrose. (Ironically, the name of the former has nothing to with its land-grabbing proclivity.) Both of these native perennials will waste no time in dominating a border and should be planted with the full impact of their growth habits firmly in mind. Your success with perennials, as with so many other landscape ornamentals, involves selecting the right plants for a particular site.

PERENNIAL MAINTENANCE

Whoever said that perennials were low-maintenance plants was either an exceptional garden designer or one who moved across town before the garden matured. Maintenance is an inescapable part of gardening and will be required for any species of perennial flower.

Spacing plants so they produce a solid canopy and applying mulch are the best ways to minimize weed problems. Some plants will require staking and others deadheading to encourage repeat flowering. Gardens need water during dry periods and occasional fertilization for healthy foliage. While you can overdo it with fertilizer, you should not have problems if you amend beds based on a soil test report. Some gardeners fertilize every four to six weeks with a water-soluble bloom-booster fertilizer. An alternative is to use a slow-release product applied early at planting and again by midseason.

There has been much concern about the volume of water required to maintain horticultural plantings in the Carolinas. Many counties are experiencing water shortages and have set mandatory water restrictions to conserve this resource. In order to be good stewards, many gardeners in urban areas have elected to use perennials that are less dependent on supplemental irrigation. Since many perennials are water hogs, pay special attention to the ones that are drought tolerant. Your County Extension Service provides lists of these durable species. You will find many of these plants in the pages that follow.

While there is information about specific pests included in the "Care & Problems" section in each plant listing, consider these general guidelines for perennial gardening. First, don't apply excess fertilizers to these plants, as this leads to an open invitation to sucking insects, such as aphids or whiteflies. Insects feast on luscious new growth produced in abundance as a response to too much nitrogen. While beneficial insects found in flower gardens are usually sufficient to manage most pests, they need your help. Use a forceful stream of water from a garden hose to dislodge insect pests. To eliminate infestations, reach for nontoxic insecticides containing soap and horticultural oils. To thwart diseases, irrigate early in the day to keep foliage dry at night.

It is important to consult a horticulturist or other garden professional when diseases or insect infestations appear, especially before purchasing a curative fungicide or pesticide. Your County Extension Service and well-respected local garden centers are invaluable resources for identifying and treating problems in your garden.

THE BENEFITS OF PLANNING

Spend time planning your perennial garden, much as you would for a room addition. Perennials are traditionally planted in large beds 6 to 12 feet wide and are best displayed against backgrounds such as evergreens, a stone wall, or a fence. Consider using a walk or edging material in the foreground to reduce maintenance. Use color in bold groups, not spotted here and there. While it is commonly thought that plants should be arranged from tallest to shortest, back to front, it is often much more interesting to mix it up a bit. Never be afraid to challenge the "rules." Vertical interest can be achieved by incorporating ornamental grasses, accessories, and structures, and while perennials are not generally associated with formal design, they are versatile and will provide enjoyment in myriad locations. Be sure to explore plant catalogs and nursery websites to discover varieties you may not be familiar with and would like to try. You just might stumble across an exceptional performer and new garden favorite!

ARTEMISIA 'POWIS CASTLE'

Artemisia 'Powis Castle'

Why It's Special—'Powis Castle' is a shrubby, non-spreading artemisia that thrives in the heat and humidity of the South. Its silver foliage helps to blend and unify colors in the perennial border. In the milder climates of most of the Carolinas, it is nearly evergreen.

How to Plant & Grow—'Powis Castle' is best planted when soil temperatures begin to warm in late April or early May. Site in a full-sun location and give it some room, as it will grow 2 to 3 feet high and wide. The soil should be well drained, particularly in winter, when cold, wet conditions may lead to root rot.

Care & Problems—You can pinch or lightly prune at any time during the summer months if it begins to elbow other plants out of the way. However, reserve hard pruning for spring, just as new growth begins.

Hardiness—Zones 6a to 9a

Bloom Color—Grown for silvery foliage

Peak Season—April to November

Mature Size (H x W)—2 to 3 ft. x 2 to 3 ft.

Water Needs—Moderately drought tolerant, once established

ASTER

Aster spp. and hybrids

Why It's Special—Many asters are tough, resilient plants and while some varieties bloom earlier in the season, the most popular are those that put on an astounding show in late summer and autumn.

How to Plant & Grow—Plant in full sun or light afternoon shade any time from early spring through the early summer. Space plants according to the ultimate size listed on the plant label, understanding that asters sold in garden centers are often pinched hard to keep them much more compact than they will be in the garden.

Care & Problems—In early spring, cut perennial asters back to 4 to 6 inches in height. New growth will come from the base. Pinching the growing tips once or twice between May and July will make for bushier plants and more blooms on late-summer- and fall-flowering varieties. Stake the tallest varieties early in the season.

Hardiness—Zones 3a to 8b

Bloom Color—Crimson, pink, lavender, violet-blue, white

Peak Season—Early summer to late fall

Mature Size (H x W)—1 to 4 ft. x 1 to 4 ft.

Water Needs—Moderately moist to slightly dry soil

BAPTISIA

Baptisia spp. and hybrids

Why It's Special—Baptisia, or false indigo, is one of our toughest native perennials. Breeders have introduced new forms and colors, ranging from soft lavender to midnight blue, creamy yellow, white, and even some new bronze bicolors and blends.

How to Plant & Grow—Set out plants in spring, handling carefully as new growth is very brittle. Baptisia are notoriously slow to become established, so splurge and purchase the largest size you can afford. The flip side to this slow establishment is that baptisia will frequently live in the garden for twenty years or more with little to no care.

Care & Problems—Be sure to site baptisia where you want them the first time, as they resent being moved. Foliage is attractive throughout the growing season and should not be trimmed back until late fall. Seedpods remain ornamental through winter if allowed to stand.

Hardiness—Zones 3a to 8b

Bloom Color—Violet-blue, yellow, white, bronze

Peak Season—Spring to early summer

Mature Size (H x W)—1½ to 4 ft. x 1½ to 4 ft.

Water Needs—Very drought tolerant, once established

BEE BALM

Monarda didyma

Why It's Special—Bee balm is a hive of activity for hummingbirds, bees, and butterflies. Breeders have introduced new varieties with resistance to powdery mildew, and in the process have also greatly increased the color range.

How to Plant & Grow—Potted plants can be planted in full sun or afternoon shade anytime the ground can be worked. The more sun you can give them, the stronger your plants will be and the more blooms you will have. Though many consider bee balm tough and drought tolerant, the truth is that moist, well-drained soil suits it best.

Care & Problems—Bee balm can be aggressive: It performs well with other large plants like ornamental grasses, asters, and perennial sunflowers, but may overrun smaller plants if it isn't controlled. But it is still a welcome addition to the garden and is easy to pull where it isn't wanted.

Hardiness—Zones 4a to 9a

Bloom Color—Red, purple, lavender, pink, white

Peak Season—Early to midsummer

Mature Size (H x W)—1½ to 4 ft. x 1½ to 4 ft.

Water Needs—Evenly moist soil

BLACK-EYED SUSAN

Rudbeckia fulgida var. *sullivantii* 'Goldsturm'

Why It's Special—This durable favorite produces unmistakable, rich yellow flowers with protruding black cones in July. Its flowering time fills an important bloom gap in the perennial border when early-summer perennials have finished flowering and fall bloomers have yet to begin.

How to Plant & Grow—Plant black-eyed Susan anytime the soil can be worked, though the preferred season is spring. Purchase vigorously growing plants in 1-gallon pots if you want to be assured of having flowers the first season. It adapts to most conditions and soil types, but is ideal in well-drained, moisture-retentive soils.

Care & Problems—Black-eyed Susans are durable once established and are virtually maintenance free. After several years, clumps will have spread considerably and may begin to thin toward the center. Dig vigorous plants from the edges of the clump and transplant back to the middle, discarding any unwanted plants.

Hardiness—Zones 4a to 9a

Bloom Color—Brilliant, golden yellow

Peak Season—Mid- to late summer

Mature Size (H x W)—1½ to 2 ft. x 2 to 2½ ft.

Water Needs—Adaptable, but evenly moist soil is best

BUTTERFLY WEED

Asclepias tuberosa

Why It's Special—Butterfly weed is a tough roadside native that thrives on neglect. Its brilliant orange flowers light up the midsummer garden, attracting bees and butterflies. It also plays host to the caterpillars of the monarch butterfly, so if you see something munching on the leaves, don't spray!

How to Plant & Grow—Plant butterfly weed in spring to early summer in full sun and well-drained soil. It will tolerate both clay and sandy soils, but does not like wet feet. Butterfly weed has an extremely deep taproot that makes it difficult both to transplant and to divide. Once planted, it is best to leave it in place.

Care & Problems—Hot temperatures and dry soils are all this plant needs. Deadheading after the first flush of bloom and a light application of organic fertilizer may encourage it to flower a second time later in the season.

Hardiness—Zones 3a to 8b

Bloom Color—Deep orange; occasionally red or gold

Peak Season—Midsummer

Mature Size (H x W)—1½ to 2 ft. x 1½ to 2 ft.

Water Needs—Extremely drought tolerant, once established

CARYOPTERIS

Caryopteris x clandonensis

Why It's Special—Sometimes doubling as a shrub, caryopteris (also called blue mist shrub) has long, wispy branches that sport rich blue flower clusters in late summer. Most varieties have grayish green foliage that complements the blue flowers.

How to Plant & Grow—Plant container-grown plants in spring to get them well established during the warm summer months. Occasionally, plants will die to the base during winter. Wait until spring to do any pruning and then cut back to where the most vigorous new growth is sprouting. Plants will recover quickly and be full flowering size by midsummer.

Care & Problems—Plants can be lost in winter if planted in cold, wet soils. Good drainage is essential and drier conditions suit the plant best. Hard pruning should not be done until spring, when new growth begins to sprout. Pruning in fall or winter can lead to cold damage and dieback.

Hardiness—Zones 5b to 8b

Bloom Color—Blue

Peak Season—Late summer to early fall

Mature Size (H x W)—2 to 4 ft. x 2 to 4 ft.

Water Needs—Moderate to slightly dry, well-drained soil

CHRISTMAS FERN

Polystichum acrostichoides

Why It's Special—Christmas ferns are easy to transplant and will brighten up dark corners where almost nothing else will grow. These compact, clump-forming plants with delicate fronds add perpetual interest to the shade garden. Their evergreen qualities make them the perfect year-round addition to any shady nook.

How to Plant & Grow—Christmas fern is truly a low-maintenance and resilient plant once established. Watering is essential during the first season but is only needed in dry spells in the following years. An organic mulch of compost is the best fertilizer.

Care & Problems—Essentially pest free, Christmas fern requires little care. In late winter or early spring, last year's foliage should be trimmed off before new fronds begin to unfurl. Occasionally slugs attack new growth in early spring. Diatomaceous earth or a nontoxic slug bait will correct this problem.

Hardiness—Zones 3a to 9a

Bloom Color—Grown for evergreen foliage

Peak Season—Year-round

Mature Size (H x W)—1½ to 2 ft. x 1½ to 2 ft.

Water Needs—Moderately drought tolerant, once established

COLUMBINE

Aquilegia x hybrida

Why It's Special—The delicate and beautiful foliage of columbine resembles that of a maidenhair fern, and the spectacular blooms light up the spring shade garden. This nearly effortless perennial reseeds itself where it's happy.

How to Plant & Grow—Transplant potted columbine anytime from spring to fall. The ideal location is in morning sun with afternoon shade or in high dappled shade throughout the day. The plants prefer good, rich, loose soil, but will grow in less-than-ideal locations. Water twice a week for the first three to four weeks after planting. Once established, plants will be quite drought tolerant.

Care & Problems—This short-lived perennial typically lasts three to four years, possibly less in the warmest climates. Purchase new plants or transplant seedlings to keep new, robust plants coming along continually. Leafminers may burrow between the leaves; they are unsightly but not generally life threatening.

Hardiness—Zones 3a to 8a

Bloom Color—White, pink, yellow, red, purple, blue

Peak Season—Spring

Mature Size (H x W)—1 to 3 ft. x 1 to 1½ ft.

Water Needs—Average to moist soil

CORAL BELLS

Heuchera spp. and hybrids

Why It's Special—Today's generation of coral bells boasts tall flowers, evergreen foliage in an array of color combinations, and tolerance of hot, humid weather. By using our two Southern native species in their breeding programs, breeders have developed one of the best perennial plants for dry shade.

How to Plant & Grow—Plant container-grown coral bells in spring or fall. Most prefer dappled light and are happiest in partial shade. They are extremely adaptable and are tolerant of less-than-ideal soils and even some degree of drought, but plant them in good garden soil that is rich and well drained and their growth and beauty will be dramatic.

Care & Problems—Water deeply twice a week until well established. Rabbits, slugs, and snails can quickly disfigure young growth in spring. Diatomaceous earth or a nontoxic slug bait sprinkled on the ground will help eliminate slugs and snails.

Hardiness—Zones 4a to 8a

Bloom Color—White, pink, red

Peak Season—Spring to fall, depending on species

Mature Size (H x W)—Foliage, 8 to 10 in. x 1½ to 2 ft.

Water Needs—Moderately drought tolerant

COREOPSIS

Coreopsis lanceolata

Why It's Special—A tried-and-true native perennial, coreopsis is one of our toughest wildflowers. Its brilliant, golden yellow flowers make outstanding cut flowers.

How to Plant & Grow—Plant container-grown plants anytime from spring to fall. Keep well watered for the first three to four weeks. Once established, the plants are quite drought tolerant, but blooms will last longer and continue to appear for many weeks if they receive some irrigation and an occasional application of liquid "bloom booster"-type fertilizer.

Care & Problems—As with many perennial garden flowers that bloom for very long periods of time, coreopsis can sometimes be short-lived. Fortunately, if you allow a few seedpods to develop, they will politely seed themselves around the garden and you will have a continual supply of fresh plants, even as older ones begin to decline. Slugs and snails can attack during periods of wet weather.

Hardiness—Zones 3a to 9a

Bloom Color—Bright, golden yellow

Peak Season—Late spring to summer

Mature Size (H x W)—1 to 2 ft. x 1 to 2 ft.

Water Needs—Moderately drought tolerant, once established

COTTAGE PINK

Dianthus gratianapolitanus

Why It's Special—The cottage pink is a classic European garden flower that Southern gardeners struggled to grow for many years. 'Bath's Pink' and 'Firewitch', changed all that and allowed us to share in the joy and intoxicating fragrance that cottage pinks provide each spring. It makes an outstanding groundcover in full sun.

How to Plant & Grow—Container-grown plants can be planted in the garden in spring or fall. Choose a location in full sun with excellent drainage. 'Bath's Pink' is especially beautiful planted at the edge of a wall, where its blue-green foliage and pink flowers can cascade and soften the wall.

Care & Problems—Good drainage is essential. Stem and crown rot can occur in cold, wet soils in winter. Only a few varieties are well suited to growing in the South since heat and humidity take a quick toll on the plants. Deadhead by shearing old blooms all at once when flowering is finished.

Hardiness—Zones 3a to 8a

Bloom Color—Pink

Peak Season—Spring

Mature Size (H x W)—6 in. x 3 ft.

Water Needs—Moderately drought tolerant, once established

DAYLILY

Hemerocallis spp. and hybrids

Why It's Special—Daylilies are available in more than twenty-five thousand registered varieties. The old-fashioned orange "ditch lily" no longer reigns supreme—today's magnificent hybrids come in almost every size, shape, and color.

How to Plant & Grow—Plant in full sun in early spring or late fall. They will tolerate part shade conditions, but flower production will be sparse. In heavy clay, they require generous quantities of organic matter for best growth, but otherwise daylilies are nearly carefree.

Care & Problems—Deer can be a serious problem. Daylilies, along with hostas, are at the top of their "preferred foods" list, and in areas where deer are a problem, fencing is a must if you ever want to see a flower. Other than deer, daylilies are more or less pest free. For reblooming varieties, deadheading and evenly moist soil is important to keep new scapes and buds forming.

Hardiness—Zones 3a to 9b

Bloom Color—All colors, bicolors, and blends

Peak Season—Mid-spring to early fall

Mature Size (H x W)—1 to 6 ft. x 1 to 3 ft.

Water Needs—Even moisture for lush growth and flowers

FERN-LEAF YARROW

Achillea millefolium

Why It's Special—This showy perennial is favored by gardeners who enjoy good cutting and drying flowers. Yarrow is one tough plant and thrives in the dry gardens of the Southwest to the hard-baked clays, heat, and humidity of the Southeast.

How to Plant & Grow—Plant yarrow in spring or fall in full sun and average to poor soil. In heavy clay, amend with soil conditioner or gravel to help improve drainage. For drying, cut flowers just as they begin to show good color.

Care & Problems—The biggest problem with yarrow comes from soil that is poorly drained and remains wet. This can lead to crown rot. Plants growing in too much shade will flower sparsely and will likely need staking to keep them upright. Weak stems and flopping plants can also be caused by overfertilization or soil that is too rich; staking will be necessary in these cases.

Hardiness—Zones 3a to 8b

Bloom Color—Pink, white, and red

Peak Season—Early to midsummer

Mature Size (H x W)—3 ft. x 2 ft.

Water Needs—Drought tolerant, once established

FERNS

Many Genera

Why It's Special—While most people associate ferns with damp, shady, woodland sites, they can be found almost anywhere. Ferns are one of the most diverse groups of plants, and there is a fern for almost every garden setting imaginable.

How to Plant & Grow—Ferns transplant best in early spring or fall. Some ferns that are particularly well suited to the Carolinas are the Christmas fern (*Polystichum acrostichoides*), which has its own entry in this chapter, the Japanese painted fern (*Athyrium niponicum* 'Pictum' and many other improved cultivars), the autumn fern (*Dryopteris erythrosora*), and an unusual native hybrid called log fern (*Dryopteris celsa*).

Care & Problems—The key to growing ferns is to site them in an area similar to their native location—shade lovers in the shade and sun lovers in the sun, dry-growing forms where it's dry, and moisture lovers where it's damp.

Hardiness—Zones 3a to 9b

Bloom Color—Grown for foliage

Peak Season—Depends on the species

Mature Size (H x W)—6 in. to 5 ft. x 6 in. to 5 ft.

Water Needs—Dry to wet soil, depending on species

FOXGLOVE

Digitalis purpurea

Why It's Special—Foxgloves can substitute for tall delphiniums, which are difficult for gardeners in the Carolinas to grow. In soils rich in organic matter and afternoon shade, foxgloves can produce 4- to 6-foot spires of blooms. While technically perennial, in warm climates they are best treated as biennials.

How to Plant & Grow—Foxgloves purchased in full bloom often have difficulty adjusting to the garden. It is best to purchase small green plants in early spring. The first year, plants will grow large, leafy rosettes but most will not flower. These rosettes will overwinter and produce tall, sturdy flower stalks the following spring.

Care & Problems—Foxgloves like rich, well-amended, well-drained soil. The first season, feed every two to four weeks with water-soluble liquid fertilizer. When flower stalks begin to emerge the following spring, loosely tie to bamboo stakes when they are approximately 3 feet tall.

Hardiness—Zones 4a to 8a

Bloom Color—Pastel purple, pink, yellow, white

Peak Season—Mid- to late spring

Mature Size (H x W)—4 to 6 ft. x 1 to 1½ ft.

Water Needs—Consistently moist soil

GARDEN PHLOX

Phlox paniculata

Why It's Special—This old-fashioned, easy-to-grow perennial remains a garden standby. New breeding programs have introduced disease-resistant varieties ('David' was the first), new colors, and sturdier, more compact plants.

How to Plant & Grow—Phlox can be planted in either the spring or fall, and flowers best in full to partial sun. Rich, evenly moist soil and good air circulation are essential. For the ambiance of an English cottage garden, use phlox as a companion plant for other sun-loving perennials such as purple coneflower.

Care & Problems—Divide garden phlox every two to three years to keep it growing vigorously. In spring, thin the clumps to the strongest four to six stems by pinching out the others to increase air circulation. Highly refined horticultural oil mixed with 1 teaspoon of baking soda per gallon of water can be used as an effective mildew preventer.

Hardiness—Zones 4a to 8b

Bloom Color—Purple, magenta, orange, pink, white

Peak Season—Mid- to late summer

Mature Size (H x W)—1½ to 4 ft. x 1½ to 2½ ft.

Water Needs—Evenly moist soil

GAURA

Gaura lindheimeri

Why It's Special—Designers like gaura for its wispy, see-through blooms and its tough-as-nails constitution. Its wandlike stems make it a perfect companion for ornamental grasses. Newer selections are more compact, live longer, and produce more flowers; some have colored foliage.

How to Plant & Grow—Gaura thrives in the sunniest, hottest, driest corner of the garden. Rich, highly amended soils and too much fertilizer cause it to grow rampantly, becoming weak stemmed and floppy.

Care & Problems—In heavy clay, plants are often short-lived because the soil stays cold and wet during winter and then dries to a bricklike consistency in summer. Gaura does like to be dry, but sand or gravel is better than clay. If plants get leggy in midsummer, shear back to 8 to 10 inches, feed lightly, and water deeply once a week to encourage a second flush of growth and bloom.

Hardiness—Zones 6a to 9b

Bloom Color—Pink or white

Peak Season—Midsummer to fall

Mature Size (H x W)—2 to 4 ft. x 2 to 4 ft.

Water Needs—Extremely drought tolerant, once established

GOLDENROD

Solidago spp. and hybrids

Why It's Special—Goldenrod often gets a bad rap for causing hay fever and allergies, which is simply not the case. Goldenrod pollen is heavy and is carried by insects and not by the wind. Unfortunately, it is in full bloom at the same time that airborne ragweed pollen is at its peak and because goldenrod is more conspicuous, it gets the blame. It is an excellent ornamental, though some species can be aggressive.

How to Plant & Grow—Plant goldenrod in ordinary garden soil in spring or fall. Soils that are slightly dry and a little on the lean side will help to keep the more aggressive varieties under control. 'Fireworks' is one of the best varieties for Southern gardens.

Care & Problems—Downy mildew can be a problem if plants are highly stressed, but goldenrod is generally tough and carefree. Some woodland species are well adapted to shade.

Hardiness—Zones 3a to 9a

Bloom Color—Golden yellow

Peak Season—Late summer to fall

Mature Size (H x W)—1½ to 6 ft. x 2 to 4 ft.

Water Needs—Evenly moist soil

HARDY HIBISCUS

Hibiscus moscheutos and hybrids

Why It's Special—Several species of hardy hibiscus, including *H. moscheutos*, grow in damp sites from Texas to New England. With blooms up to 10 inches across, they're a showy addition to the summer perennial border that thrives even in drier conditions with minimal care.

How to Plant & Grow—Plant in spring as soil begins to warm. Plants are late to break dormancy, often not appearing until late April. A sunny garden and moist, average soil will encourage growth. Plants are shrublike, so allow plenty of room.

Care & Problems—Hardy hibiscus is a low-maintenance plant with few pests, though Japanese beetles can be a problem in early summer. Pick them off by hand and drop them in a jar of soapy water. For severe infestations, control with liquid Sevin. Another common pest is the hibiscus sawfly. The remedy is spinosad spray, a bacterial derivative that's nontoxic to nearly everything else. When clumps grow too large, dig and divide in early spring before new growth.

Hardiness—Zones 5a to 9a

Bloom Color—Red, pink, rose-red, and white

Peak Season—Midsummer

Mature Size (H x W)—2 to 5 ft. x 2 to 5 ft.

Water Needs—Average to moist soil

HELLEBORE

Helleborus spp. and hybrids

Why It's Special—With glossy, evergreen foliage and flowers that appear at a surprising time of year, hellebores, also known as Lenten roses, stand out when everything else is winter-weary. Depending on the species, flowers can appear as early as December and continue throughout the winter.

How to Plant & Grow—Fall is the best time to plant, as plants are making new roots at that time and become established easily. Hellebores perform best in rich, well-drained soil with plenty of compost added at planting time. A general, all-purpose fertilizer applied in very early spring is highly beneficial.

Care & Problems—Hellebores grow slowly during their first season or two, but once established will "fatten up" quickly and get bigger and more beautiful as the seasons progress. Mature clumps can have literally hundreds of blooms over a period of several months from winter to spring.

Hardiness—Zones 5b to 8b

Bloom Color—White, pink, green, deep purple

Peak Season—Winter to spring

Mature Size (H x W)—1 to 1½ ft. x 2 to 2½ ft.

Water Needs—Moderately drought tolerant, once established

HOSTA

Hosta spp. and hybrids

Why It's Special—With more than two thousand varieties available, hostas may be the ultimate shade plant for ease of culture, colorful foliage, resilience, and low maintenance. With sizes ranging from 4-inch-tall miniatures to 7-foot-wide giants, there is a hosta for every garden.

How to Plant & Grow—Hostas can be planted anytime the ground is not frozen, but they become particularly well established if planted in September and October, as they are going dormant. Root growth will continue through late fall and early winter, and plants will begin growing immediately the following spring. Hostas prefer well-drained soils that are rich in organic matter.

Care & Problems—Unfortunately, hostas are favorites of deer, and voles can also be a real problem, especially in winter and very early spring. Most garden centers will be able to offer suggestions for control methods that have been successful in your area.

Hardiness—Zones 3a to 8a

Bloom Color—White or lavender

Peak Season—April to October

Mature Size (H x W)—4 in. to 2½ ft. x 4 in. to 7 ft.

Water Needs—Average to moist soil

IRIS

Iris spp. and hybrids

Why It's Special—The bearded iris is probably the most familiar type, but *Iris* is actually one of the most diverse genera of garden plants and includes other spectacular perennials such as the Siberian iris, Japanese iris, Louisiana iris, and the almost orchidlike Spuria iris. These are all hardy and reliable in much of the Carolinas.

How to Plant & Grow—Iris can be found in most garden centers in spring, when they are in active growth and will become established quickly. Read the labels, as some grow in drier locations and others prefer near-constant moisture. While most species require full sun, some are woodland dwellers.

Care & Problems—Most iris are easy to grow and relatively carefree. Some of the more vigorous species benefit from being divided every three years to help maintain good vigor and prevent overcrowding.

Hardiness—Zones 3a to 9b, depending on species

Bloom Color—Nearly every color and combination

Peak Season—Late winter to early summer

Mature Size (H x W)—6 in. to 4 ft. x 1 ft. to 4 ft.

Water Needs—Varies greatly, depending on species

JAPANESE ANEMONE

Anemone x hybrida

Why It's Special—While most herbaceous perennials reach their zenith during the summer months, Japanese anemones make their debut around Labor Day. These clump-forming plants are wonderful for partially shaded gardens, where they will produce large but delicate poppylike blooms on long stalks from late summer until frost.

How to Plant & Grow—Japanese anemones are best planted in spring so that they can become well established before winter. Soil should be well prepared and thoroughly amended. Morning sun is ideal, though plants that are very well irrigated will take nearly full sun, with just a little shade during the hottest part of the day. They do like moisture and will not perform well in particularly dry sites.

Care & Problems—Some varieties may spread aggressively where they are happy. One of the most well behaved is the stunning, pure white variety 'Honorine Jobert'.

Hardiness—Zones 5b to 8b

Bloom Color—Pink or white

Peak Season—Late summer to fall

Mature Size (H x W)—2½ ft. to 4 ft. x 2½ ft.

Water Needs—Evenly moist soil

LAMB'S EARS

Stachys byzantina

Why It's Special—These vigorous, drought-tolerant plants with soft, silvery white leaves are sparsely flowered, and the long, furry flower stems can be cut for arrangements. The best variety for the South is 'Helene von Stein', also known as 'Big Ears'.

How to Plant & Grow—Plant potted specimens any time from spring to fall. They perform best in full sun in average soil with excellent drainage. The addition of sand to the soil when planting is helpful for improving drainage. Lamb's ears like alkaline soils, so if your soil is on the acidic side, add a handful of lime when planting.

Care & Problems—Overhead irrigation can be a problem during the heat of summer, causing plants to "melt" in the heat and humidity. Once established, plants are extremely drought tolerant and very little additional water is required. A light feeding in early spring will encourage lush growth.

Hardiness—Zones 4a to 8b

Bloom Color—Grown for silvery foliage

Peak Season—Year-round

Mature Size (H x W)—10 to 12 in. x 2 to 3 ft.

Water Needs—Drought tolerant, once established

LUNGWORT

Pulmonaria spp. and hybrids

Why It's Special—Lungwort is a durable early-spring bloomer that mixes extremely well with our native wildflowers in the shade garden. The small cup-shaped blooms, usually pink or cobalt blue, are spangled on short stalks that reach just above the spotted foliage.

How to Plant & Grow—Lungwort can be planted in spring or fall and will tolerate deeper shade than many perennials because it does most of its growing in the earliest part of spring before the trees leaf out. It thrives in moist, rich soil with morning sun or high dappled shade throughout the day.

Care & Problems—By midsummer, the heat may have taken its toll on some varieties. These plants can be cut to the ground, lightly fertilized, and thoroughly watered for a few weeks, and they will grow new foliage. Some varieties are extremely susceptible to powdery mildew. Many new hybrids are more mildew resistant.

Hardiness—Zones 4a to 8b

Bloom Color—Pink or cobalt blue, grown for foliage

Peak Season—Early spring

Mature Size (H x W)—8 to 12 in. x 1 to 2 ft.

Water Needs—Evenly moist soil

PURPLE CONEFLOWER

Echinacea purpurea

Why It's Special—This tough native perennial has been widely introduced as a garden plant around the world. It is easy to grow, loves sun, and produces long-lasting flowers from early summer to late fall, which make outstanding cut flowers.

How to Plant & Grow—Purple coneflowers can be planted from spring to fall. They are tolerant of a wide range of soils, provided the soil is well drained and is not waterlogged in winter. The root system can grow quite large, so a generous planting hole will help.

Care & Problems—In areas with long growing seasons, purple coneflower can be encouraged to rebloom at least once and sometimes twice after its initial flowering in late spring to early summer. Once all of the flowers have faded, cut the bloom stalks to the ground, leaving the basal foliage. New stalks will likely appear in a few weeks.

Hardiness—Zones 3a to 8b

Bloom Color—Pink, purple, white

Peak Season—Early summer to fall

Mature Size (H x W)—1 to 3 ft. x 1 to 1½ ft.

Water Needs—Well-drained, average to moist soil

PURPLE HEART

Setcreasea pallida

Why It's Special—This tough plant flourishes in heat and humidity and will overwinter readily throughout Zone 7b, and in Zones 7a and 6b with protection. It has extremely deep roots and is excellent for helping to stabilize difficult banks, but its royal purple foliage also makes a wonderful addition to perennial borders or containers.

How to Plant & Grow—Plant after the danger of frost has passed. Purple heart will thrive in the most challenging full sun and driest areas of the garden, but will also perform will in part shade, as well as moist areas. It is truly a versatile plant.

Care & Problems—If plants look ratty, cut them to the ground, feed, and water; they will respond with lush new growth in a matter of weeks. Keep in mind that they may not resprout in spring until the soil is thoroughly warm—possibly as late as May.

Hardiness—Zones 7a to 10

Bloom Color—Lavender, grown for colorful foliage

Peak Season—Spring to fall

Mature Size (H x W)—10 in. x 2 to 3 ft.

Water Needs—Very drought tolerant, once established

RED-HOT POKER

Kniphofia hybrids

Why It's Special—The glowing spires of red-hot poker tower above the garden. Though it comes in a range of colors from creamy white to yellow and coral, the vibrant orange-red varieties are best loved. In many varieties, the buds are a different or deeper color than the open flowers, giving the illusion of a flame.

How to Plant & Grow—Plant in spring in full sun and very well-drained soil. Excellent winter drainage is important to avoid crown rot or the freezing of the crown during cold weather.

Care & Problems—Some sources recommend cutting the foliage to the ground during winter, but the foliage actually helps protect and shed water from the crown. Tattered foliage can be cut off at the end of winter, but cutting back beyond 12 inches is not recommended, even in spring.

Hardiness—Zones 5b to 9a

Bloom Color—Cream, yellow, pink, coral, orange

Peak Season—Early summer to fall, depending on species

Mature Size (H x W)—1½ to 5 ft. x 1½ to 5 ft.

Water Needs—Very well-drained soil; moist in summer, drier in winter

RUSSIAN SAGE

Perovskia atriplicifolia

Why It's Special—One of the best "see-through" plants for the perennial border, Russian sage provides color all season long, from its silver-white leaves or its lavender-blue flower spikes. In well-drained soils, it can persist for many years.

How to Plant & Grow—Russian sage is available in spring in 1-gallon pots. It thrives in summer heat and its only real requirement is excellent drainage. It will grow in heavier clay soils, but may not survive the winter because of its intolerance of cold, wet roots. Clay soils should be thoroughly amended when planting.

Care & Problems—Outer stems of older plants become woody and may flop. Trim them off and others will grow. Allow the plant's semiwoody structure to stand through winter, both for visual interest and because the plants usually experience some dieback and pruning is best done in spring. Flowering stems can be cut for bouquets.

Hardiness—Zones 4b to 9a

Bloom Color—Lavender-blue

Peak Season—Midsummer to fall

Mature Size (H x W)—3 to 4 ft. x 3 to 4 ft.

Water Needs—Drought tolerant, once established

SALVIA

Salvia spp. and hybrids

Why It's Special—*Salvia* is another genus with enormous variation among species and suitable plants for almost any garden. While the best-known varieties typically flower in shades of blue, purple, or red, there are also pinks, yellows, whites, and more. Some species thrive in dry, desert-like conditions and others flourish in bogs.

How to Plant & Grow—Salvias can be planted from spring to fall. Most varieties love heat and will establish best during the warmer months. Water all types regularly until well established, and then reduce water for more drought-tolerant species. Very well-drained, fertile soil suits most species best.

Care & Problems—Regular deadheading will keep plants blooming. Some popular varieties, such as *Salvia guaranitica* and its cultivar 'Black and Blue', will flower from late spring to frost when well cared for. Texas sage (*Salvia greggii*) and its hybrids thrive in heat and humidity.

Hardiness—Zones 4a to 9b

Bloom Color—Purple, blue, red, pink, white, yellow

Peak Season—Late spring to fall

Mature Size (H x W)—1½ to 5 ft. to 1½ to 5 ft.

Water Needs—Varies with the species

SEDUM 'AUTUMN JOY'

Hylotelephium 'Autumn Joy'

Why It's Special—A garden favorite, 'Autumn Joy' sedum thrives in the hot and often dry Southern summers. It goes through several phases from gray-green early spring foliage to the broccoli-like midsummer buds, to brilliant reddish carmine flowers in late summer that transform to a coppery red by autumn.

How to Plant & Grow—Plant nursery-grown plants in spring after the danger of frost has passed. Tender new growth can be nipped by late frosts if set out too early. Once established, this is not a concern. Excellent drainage is very important to keep plants from rotting out during winter.

Care & Problems—Faded flower heads can be left for winter interest. Cut old stems back to the ground once they have begun to fall apart in midwinter. New growth will come from the base of the plant in spring. Do not mulch in winter.

Hardiness—Zones 3a to 9a

Bloom Color—Deep pink fading to coppery red

Peak Season—Late summer to fall

Mature Size (H x W)—1½ to 2 ft. x 1½ to 2 ft.

Water Needs—Drought tolerant, once established

SHASTA DAISY

Leucanthemum x superbum

Why It's Special—Many varieties of this traditional white daisy had the reputation of being poorly suited to Southern gardens until a few years ago, when the variety 'Becky' was discovered in Georgia. 'Becky' thrives in the heat and humidity of the South!

How to Plant & Grow—Shasta daisies are best planted in spring, allowing them to become established before blooming. They need loose, well-drained soil, and planting holes should be dug at least twice the width of the rootball. Shasta daisies form a crown right at the surface of the soil and should not be planted too deeply to ensure that crown rot does not set in during winter.

Care & Problems—Shasta daisies generally have few problems and no serious insect pests. Deer may browse the flower buds. Don't overfertilize, as this may encourage weak growth and floppy stems.

Hardiness—Zones 5a to 9a

Bloom Color—White

Peak Season—Early to late summer

Mature Size (H x W)—1 to 3 ft. x 1 to 3 ft.

Water Needs—Evenly moist soil, as plants are shallow rooted

SPIDERWORT

Tradescantia x andersoniana

Why It's Special—A tough native perennial, spiderwort can withstand heavy clay soils and wet conditions. Give it good garden soil and an occasional feeding and you will be amazed at its beauty from late spring to frost!

How to Plant & Grow—Plant in fall or spring. Fertilize once each spring, just as new growth appears. When plants begin to look ratty in midsummer, cut them all the way to the ground, foliage and all. Feed them thoroughly and keep them well watered during dry periods and you will get a spectacular repeat show from late summer until frost.

Care & Problems—Some varieties reseed readily and can be a problem in smaller gardens. Roots run deep and babies are difficult to pull without the aid of a trowel. The variety 'Sweet Kate' has spectacular golden foliage with cobalt blue flowers.

Hardiness—Zones 4b to 9b

Bloom Color—Blue, purple, white

Peak Season—Late spring to late fall

Mature Size (H x W)—1 to 3 ft. x 1 to 2 ft.

Water Needs—Average to very moist soil; tolerant of wet areas

STOKES' ASTER

Stokesia laevis

Why It's Special—One of the bluest of the blues when it comes to flower color, this daisy relative is welcome in any garden. Even the taller varieties are a manageable size and will not overwhelm smaller spaces. The varieties 'Omega Skyrocket' and 'Peachie's Pick' are exceptional. White and soft yellow varieties are not always the most robust selections for Southern gardens.

How to Plant & Grow—Plant in full sun and well-drained soil. Fertilize in spring and again in midsummer to encourage a late flush of bloom. You can leave the old flower stalks, as the seedpods can be ornamental, but this will discourage later flowering.

Care & Problems—Stokes' aster is relatively pest free. Divide in early spring, just as new growth begins, and plants will reestablish themselves and bloom by midsummer. Rabbits can occasionally be a problem early in the season.

Hardiness—Zones 5a to 8b

Bloom Color—Blue

Peak Season—Early to midsummer

Mature Size (H x W)—1 to 2½ ft. x 1 to 1½ ft.

Water Needs—Evenly moist soil, especially when in bloom

THREADLEAF COREOPSIS

Coreopsis verticillata

Why It's Special—Another outstanding American native, threadleaf coreopsis is a drought-resistant, low-maintenance perennial. The compact plants weave between other plants without being garden thugs. 'Moonbeam' is a popular cultivar, with pale yellow flowers from late spring to fall.

How to Plant & Grow—Potted threadleaf coreopsis can be planted from spring to fall. They will thrive in full sun and in any good, well-drained garden soil. Water thoroughly twice each week for the first month after planting—perhaps more if it is particularly dry. Once established, plants are fairly drought tolerant.

Care & Problems—Because the plants produce so many flowers, individual deadheading is nearly impossible; wait until the plants begin to look unkempt and then shear them back in midsummer to encourage a new flush of growth and bloom for late summer and fall. Powdery mildew can be a problem, but is not life threatening.

Hardiness—Zones 4a to 8b

Bloom Color—Yellow

Peak Season—Early to midsummer; some repeat

Mature Size (H x W)—1 to 1½ ft. x 1½ to 2 ft.

Water Needs—Evenly moist to slightly dry soil

YARROW

Achillea filipendulina

Why It's Special—Yarrow's fragrant, fernlike foliage adds texture to perennial gardens, and its golden yellow blooms are well suited to bright summer borders. As a cut flower, it is extremely long lasting and also dries beautifully. Butterflies and bees find yarrow irresistible!

How to Plant & Grow—Planted in spring or fall, yarrow thrives in very well-drained soils and tolerates thin, rocky, or lean soils better than many perennials. Yarrow needs some room, so space plants 24 inches apart. Avoid overfeeding, as this may cause excessive growth and weak stems that will fall over and need staking.

Care & Problems—Water well for the first few weeks after planting, but once the plants show signs of vigorous growth, they should survive on their own. Some water may be beneficial during extremely dry periods. Deadheading is not necessary, but will encourage more blooms to appear from dormant buds.

Hardiness—Zones 3a to 8a

Bloom Color—Golden yellow

Peak Season—Early to midsummer

Mature Size (H x W)—2½ to 3 ft. x 2½ to 3 ft.

Water Needs—Drought tolerant, once established

YUCCA

Yucca filamentosa

Why It's Special—Many gardeners have a love-hate relationship with yuccas, but for year-round architectural form, yuccas have few equals. Their spiky, swordlike foliage is a welcome addition to any garden. 'Colorguard' is a newer variety with beautiful green-and-yellow variegated leaves.

How to Plant & Grow—Plant in spring so that plants can become well established in summer. Yuccas (also called Adam's needle) will take two to three seasons to settle in and begin blooming, but their foliage value is worth it even before any flowers appear. In fact, some gardeners cut the bloom stalks off and just enjoy the foliage.

Care & Problems—Yuccas are extremely low maintenance. They also make excellent groundcovers for difficult sites, especially steep slopes in full sun. Once a plant flowers, that portion of the plant will die, but the many pups that are produced fill in quickly and you will never know that one is gone.

Hardiness—Zones 5a to 10

Bloom Color—White

Peak Season—Year-round

Mature Size (H x W)—2½ ft. x 3 ft.

Water Needs—Extremely drought tolerant

YOUR PERENNIAL GARDEN

PLANNING YOUR GARDEN

Picking the right perennials requires planning. Educate yourself before you buy and plant perennials:

1. Know the growing conditions in your landscape. Know the soil type and its pH, as well as how many hours of sun each area receives on a given day. For areas that are not in full sun all day long, it's also important to know whether they receive morning sun or afternoon sun. If you have shade, is it high dappled shade that is bright and open? Is it dense, deep shade where no sunlight reaches the plants? Another important consideration is whether you have areas that are particularly wet or dry in your landscape. All of these factors are key in selecting the right plant for the right place.

2. Once you know the growing conditions in your landscape, you need to know the growing requirements of your perennials. Match your plants' needs to the growing conditions you have and you're already well on your way to success. Use these criteria to winnow the list of candidates to some really worthwhile selections:

   Hardiness: Select perennials that are cold hardy in your area—able to survive the winter with little or no protection. See the cold-hardiness map in the introduction to this book to determine your hardiness zone. Remember that these hardiness zones are only guidelines, since microclimates and soil drainage often determine how hardy and long-lived a perennial will be in any given landscape. Heat hardiness is also important. Plants native to climates that have cool summers will not tolerate hot, dry summers. Attempting to grow them in a landscape outside their "comfort zone" will result in disappointment.

   Soil conditions: Generally, most perennials prefer soil that is well drained. In fact, more perennials are killed during the winter by wet, poorly drained soil than by cold temperatures. If the site is naturally wet and improving drainage would be prohibitively expensive, then by all means, cultivate moisture-loving perennials in that part of the garden.

   Sun exposure: Determine the amount of sunlight an area receives and match perennials to these light levels. Generally speaking, most shade-loving perennials will tolerate some morning sun and most sun-loving perennials will tolerate a bit of afternoon shade, but it is important that a plant's overall sun requirements be met in order to be successful.

3. Learn about the ornamental attributes of various perennials. Here are a few characteristics to look for:

   Eye-catching flowers, fruits, and leaves: Perennials are dynamic, ever-changing plants that are capable of offering more than one season of interest. In most cases, many cultivars of a given species are available, greatly extending the size and/or color range of the species.

   Time and length of bloom: To create a season-long display of color, know when your perennials will flower and you will be able to create a parade of color from a variety of perennials throughout the season. If you're looking for long-flowering perennials, there's usually a catch: in order for them to bloom continuously, you'll have to deadhead them (remove the spent flowers) repeatedly or cut them back.

   Height and size of mature plants: Knowing their eventual height and spread will help you select the right number of plants and space them strategically to avoid an overcrowded or overplanted look.

4. Learn about the maintenance requirements of your perennials. If you prefer a low-maintenance approach, avoid perennials that require staking, frequent dividing, and regular deadheading, as well as those that are invasive.

5. Whenever possible, select plants that are resistant to, or at least not bothered by, serious pests that may wreak havoc in the garden. Refer to mail-order catalogs, perennial plant encyclopedias, and gardening magazines to help you research your perennials.

SOIL PREPARATION

Because of the plants' perennial nature, prepare the planting bed right the first time. Deep and thorough soil preparation is essential to growing great perennials, especially in areas where heavy clay soils are the norm. Clay soils bake in summer, becoming bricklike and completely devoid of water, and in the winter, tend to be cold and constantly wet. This can lead to various forms of crown and root rot. It is essential, in clay soils, to add copious quantities of organic matter to help break the clay particles apart to create a looser, richer, and more friable soil. The opposite problem exists in sandy soils, where particles are so loose that water runs right through and nutrients have nothing to bind to, which causes them to leach out of the soil very quickly. Sandy soils are usually dry and nearly devoid of any nutrients. Organic matter in the form of composted leaves, composted manures, and garden compost are invaluable for improving a sandy soil's ability to retain water and nutrients. Just as organic matter helps to break down and loosen clay soils, by increasing water, nutrients, and airflow, it also helps to bind the particles together in sandy soils, retaining soil moisture and nutrients that can then be used by your plants.

PLANTING

Purchase perennials in containers or as dormant bare-root plants. You can grow them from seed, but starting with established plants will give you quicker satisfaction. In the Carolinas, you can plant container-grown perennials year-round. Fall is the best time to plant, as it gives the perennials sufficient time to become established before the onset of hot, dry summer weather. However, you'll usually find the best selection of perennials in spring. Gardeners faced with the prospect of a hot summer following closely on the heels of spring should plant early and be prepared to coddle the plants with regular watering during the summer months for the first year.

Here's how to plant a container-grown perennial:

1. Hold your hand over the top of the pot with the plant stems between your fingers. Tip the pot over and gently tap the plant into your hand. If the roots are circling around the rootball, loosen them to encourage growth into the surrounding soil. The tangled roots of large-rooted hostas and daylilies can be teased apart with your fingers. Use a knife, pruning shears, or a sharp spade to score the sides of the rootballs of fine-rooted perennials; make three or four shallow cuts to encourage root growth along the length of the ball.

2. Dig a hole the same depth as the rootball and slightly wider.

3. Set the plant in the hole so the plant's crown is at or slightly above ground level.

4. Cover the roots and firm the soil lightly around the plant.

5. Water thoroughly to settle the soil around the roots. Depending on the weather and rainfall, you may need to water daily for the first few weeks. Mulch with a 2- to 3-inch layer of compost to save moisture and suppress weeds, spreading a ½-inch layer near the crown but not covering it.

6. During the next few weeks, keep the plants well watered to help them become quickly established. After that, begin cutting back on water, eventually watering on an "as-needed" basis. Test the soil and rootball to see if they're moist.

FERTILIZING

If the soil is properly prepared at the start, supplemental fertilization may not be necessary for several years after planting. Let the perennial's growth rate and leaf color guide you in your fertilizing decisions—and rely on soil-test results. If the bed is already highly fertile, a soil test will save you from the undesirable results of overfertilizing, which leads to a lot of leafy growth at the expense of flowers. In the absence of a soil test, use a complete balanced fertilizer that contains nitrogen, phosphorus, and potassium, such as 10-10-10. Most fertilizer recommendations are based on nitrogen, which is an important element in plant growth and is often the nutrient most likely to be deficient in the soil. Apply 1 pound of nitrogen per 1,000 square feet (up to 2 pounds can be applied if you use a slow-release fertilizer).

Apply the fertilizer when the new shoots emerge and, if necessary, once or twice again during the growing season. Water the bed after application so the fertilizer enters the soil and is available to the plants. Try to avoid getting fertilizer on the leaves of the plants in the first place and be sure to wash any fertilizer off the foliage to prevent fertilizer burn.

WATERING

Perennials vary in their watering needs, but most require an ample moisture supply, at least when they are actively growing. Seedlings or newly planted perennials should be watered daily for the first few weeks, depending on the weather and rainfall. After that, begin cutting back, eventually watering only on an "as-needed" basis. Once plants are established, less frequent watering is required. Established plants may need to be watered once a week in clay soils that hold more water than sandy soils. Sandy soils may need to be watered twice a week. Instead of following the calendar, water when the top 2 or 3 inches of soil feels dry. When you do water, water deeply and thoroughly to encourage deep rooting, rather than just sprinkling the top of the soil. Shallow watering will lead to shallow roots and less hardiness, both in summer heat and drought, as well as winter cold.

DIVIDING

Perennials are divided to control their size, invigorate them, and to increase their numbers. Short-lived perennials or old perennials that are in decline can be kept vigorous and blooming through division. After dividing, the vigorous younger sections are replanted so they'll flower more prolifically.

A general rule of thumb is to divide spring- and summer-blooming perennials in the fall, and fall-flowering perennials in early spring when the new shoots have emerged. Exceptions to this rule are fleshy-rooted perennials such as peony (*Paeonia*) and Oriental poppy (*Papaver orientale*), which should be divided in the fall.

Mountain gardeners in the higher elevations can wait until spring to divide, since the rigors of winter may kill the young divisions before they have time to become established. Gardeners in the milder areas of the Carolinas can divide through fall and into early winter. It is important to divide the plants when they're not flowering.

PRUNING

Pruning is not often associated with herbaceous perennials, but deadheading to remove spent flowers, pinching stems or buds, and cutting back leggy plants are all aspects of pruning. Pruning improves the appearance of the plants, extends their bloom period or encourages repeat flowering, controls diseases by improving air movement, and increases the size and number of flowers.

PEST CONTROL

To manage pests, practice Integrated Pest Management, or IPM. This commonsense method focuses on establishing and maintaining healthy plants and understanding pests. When pest control is necessary, start with the least toxic solutions, such as handpicking the pests or dislodging them from the plant with a strong spray of water. Consider potent chemical pesticides only as a last resort, when the pest populations cause unacceptable levels of damage. You must decide if the plant should be saved with a pesticide application, or composted. Follow this IPM approach to reduce or avoid pest damage:

- Select and properly plant well-adapted species and cultivars, especially those that have disease resistance.
- Maintain them properly by meeting their needs for light, water, and nutrients.
- Inspect for pests regularly. It's easier to control small outbreaks than to be surprised by full-scale attacks. If you have to, prune out affected plant parts or completely remove the plant from the bed.

DISEASE PREVENTION

- Provide good soil drainage to prevent and control soilborne diseases that cause root and stem rots.
- To help reduce disease outbreaks, keep the leaves dry when watering and maintain enough room between plants for good air circulation.
- Clean up any fallen leaves and remove any spent flowers. They can harbor pests.

JANUARY

- As you design your garden, consider creating "island beds" that can be viewed from all sides and help to separate large expanses of lawn, giving seasonal color and interest—as well as texture and height variation—to what might be a less interesting part of the yard.
- If you wish to grow perennials from seed, January is a good month to start. You don't have to have a greenhouse, but fluorescent lights can be very helpful. Cold treatment may improve germination of some perennial seeds and will be noted in the instructions on the seed packet.
- If you do choose to start seeds indoors, watch out for damping off, a fungal disease that commonly attacks newly sprouted seedlings. Good air circulation and a light hand with the watering can will help to prevent this problem.

FEBRUARY

- Design your perennial beds on graph paper before planting. If you use ¼-inch graph paper, you can easily draw a plant to scale, where ¼ inch equals 1 foot. This generally produces a plan that is easy to read and follow when you're ready to begin.
- Some perennials will begin emerging by the end of this month. Be prepared to divide and replant summer- and fall-flowering perennials just as their new growth emerges. Most perennials won't need to be divided more than every three years and some can wait even longer.
- Cut back ornamental grasses in mid- to late February to clear the way for new growth that will begin emerging in March. Shorter ornamental grasses can be cut back to 6 inches, while larger specimens, such as pampas grass or some of the large *Miscanthus* species, should be cut back to 12 inches.
- Winter weeds such as chickweed and henbit are at their most active and robust right now. Control as necessary by pulling and then remulching where necessary.

MARCH

- Planting can begin in earnest this month. Wait for new shipments of plants to begin arriving at local garden centers to be sure that you are getting fresh, new stock and not plants that are leftovers from last year.
- Check again for any perennials that may have heaved out of the soil during winter freezing and thawing. If necessary, gently lift and replant these to make sure their roots are firmly in the ground.
- Most perennials benefit from a boost with fertilizer just as new growth begins to emerge in the spring. Slow release and/or

organic or all-natural fertilizers are generally best, as they last the longest in the soil and are less likely to burn tender new growth.

APRIL

- Some taller-growing perennials may become top-heavy and require support to prevent them from bending or toppling over. Plan to stake these plants or place supports around them early in the season.
- If you started seeds indoors, now is the time to harden them off to acclimate them to the outdoors. Gradually expose them to outdoor conditions by first moving them to a cold frame or covered porch for at least a week before planting in the garden.
- Keep newly planted perennials well watered during the first few weeks to help them get quickly established. Water deeply and thoroughly to encourage roots to grow deep into the soil in search of water.
- Watch for aphids and whiteflies on tender new growth. A strong spray of water or application of insecticidal soap will help with control.

MAY

- If you're serious about being successful in your gardening endeavors, now is a great time to start a garden journal. It will document your observations, thoughts, and plans for the future.
- Taller-growing perennials should be staked when they reach one-third of their mature height. Place the stakes close to the plant, but take care to avoid damaging the root system and secure the stems to the stakes with loosely tied twine so that they will not cut into the stems.
- When watering, apply sufficient water to soak the soil deeply, wetting the entire root zone of the plant. Instead of following the calendar, water when the top 2 to 3 inches of soil feels dry.
- Avoid leaf spot diseases by watering your perennials from below and limiting water on the leaves. Proper spacing with plenty of air movement will also reduce fungal infections.

JUNE

- Regularly water recently planted perennials, which are especially vulnerable to heat and drought stress. Water thoroughly to encourage deep rooting.
- If you used a slow-release fertilizer early in the season, check the label and evaluate the growth and appearance of your perennials to see if a second application is warranted.
- Many perennials will benefit from a light pinching of the growing tips at this time of year—especially late-blooming species like the various chrysanthemums, 'Autumn Joy' sedum, asters, Joe-Pye weed, and perennial sunflowers.
- Slugs and snails will be out in force this month, especially in highly irrigated sections of the garden or during periods of wet weather. Use a slug and snail bait whose active ingredient is iron phosphate, as it is nontoxic to children and pets.

JULY

- Be sure to keep up with regular journal entries. A lot is happening in the garden right now and it is important to have notes about how various plants are performing and what needs to be done in the coming weeks and months.
- Many nurseries and garden centers will be running deep discount sales this month in order to clear out spring stock. This can be a great way to expand your garden, but be aware that these plants will need some extra coddling to thrive.
- If you have tall perennials that still haven't been staked, do it as soon as possible. Trying to prop up plants that have already toppled over can be a daunting task.
- Keep an eye to the sky and be sure to provide supplemental water to the garden anytime you haven't received regular rainfall within a week's time.
- If you have been pinching any late-blooming perennials such as mums and asters to keep them more compact, you should stop all pinching this month so that buds will set for fall.

AUGUST

- If you're planning a vacation this month, be sure to have someone keep an eye on flower beds and especially on containers while you're away. It doesn't take long for plants to dry out during hot weather!
- Keep up with deadheading to encourage fall rebloom.
- Avoid irrigating perennial beds with overhead sprinklers. Wet foliage can lead to powdery mildew and various other fungal diseases. If overhead watering is your only option, do it as early in the morning as possible to allow foliage to dry during the day.
- Spider mites love the heat and humidity of late summer. Plants infested with spider mites have faded, stippled leaves.

SEPTEMBER

- Fall-flowering perennials begin coming into their own this month. Keep up with your journal, making notes about plants that perform well and others that may need some attention.

- Ornamental grasses shine at this time of year. If you don't have ornamental grasses in your garden, make a trip to a nearby public garden where you can see them at their peak and learn which ones might make great additions to your beds and borders.

- Fall is the driest season in the Carolinas. Keep new plantings and established beds thoroughly watered so that plants go into their winter dormancy healthy and happy.

- As leaves begin to fall, regular cleanup helps to ensure that insect eggs and disease spores do not overwinter in fallen debris.

OCTOBER

- With the onset of cooler weather, it's time to emerge from our air-conditioned houses and return in earnest to the garden. If you have plans to expand and rearrange old beds or create new ones, now is the perfect time.

- When starting new beds, be sure to have your soil tested. The results of your soil test will tell you what the pH of your soil is, as well as its nutrient content. This will let you know whether or not you need to add lime to raise the pH, and it also will tell you how you need to fertilize to achieve maximum performance from your plants.

- Autumn is the perfect time to dig, divide, and replant crowded perennials. Check your garden journal notes and if there were any underperformers in the summer garden; it may be time to divide.

- Don't fertilize perennials this late in the season. Allow them to go dormant so they are well prepared for the coming winter.

NOVEMBER

- The latest-flowering perennials like aster and sunflowers may just be finishing up their bloom. Leave seedheads in place for the birds to enjoy. Goldfinches are particularly attracted to the seeds of perennial sunflowers and other daisylike blooms.

- Planting can continue to within four to six weeks of the onset of winter. Just be sure plants have enough time to root in before the ground begins to freeze and thaw.

- Be sure to cut back and clear away the foliage of peonies, bee balm, phlox, and other plants that are known to have problems with fungal diseases like botrytis and powdery mildew. Spores can overwinter in old foliage and debris.

- Winter weeds will be appearing now. Henbit, chickweed, and others can be pulled and removed most easily while they are young.

DECEMBER

- As winter weather sets in, now is a good time to catch up on reading those gardening magazines that you may not have gotten around to in the past couple of months. Make notes of good plant combinations or plants you haven't grown that you may want to try.

- If you planted new perennials or divided old ones this fall, be sure to mulch them well before cold winter weather arrives. Mulch will conserve moisture and help to keep plants from heaving during periods of freezing and thawing.

- Garden cleanup should be finished this month, except for perennials such as purple coneflower, black-eyed Susan, and perennial sunflowers, whose seedheads offer food for the birds.

BULBS
for the Carolinas

A passion for flowers often begins with a handful of bulbs. Many gardeners have gotten their start with a plump amaryllis bulb or a few daffodils. Most garden shops offer a good selection of bulbs at the appropriate time to plant each species—some in spring and even more in the fall. During the holidays, amaryllis and paperwhite narcissus are popular gifts among gardeners, and tulips, daffodils, crocus, and others can be forced for winter blooms indoors.

Bulbs contain everything they need to grow and bloom—stored energy and dormant plants or buds that, given proper growing conditions, will spring to life with the guarantee of lovely flowers in a short period of time. Bulb culture opens up a whole new realm of possibilities in the garden and home, and you will get the greatest enjoyment from bulbs by planting a variety of different types and learning which ones will perform best in your particular location.

WHAT IS A BULB?

As gardeners, we tend to lump any plant that grows from an underground storage organ into the "bulb" category, but this isn't completely accurate. True bulbs, such as tulips and daffodils, have fleshy leaf scales that surround and protect a tiny and dormant—but completely formed—plant inside. Crocus and gladiolus grow from modified stems called corms, while the modified stems of bearded iris are called rhizomes. Tubers and tuberous roots are modified roots like you see on caladiums or dahlias. These storage organs are capable of holding food reserves from season to season, giving bulbs the ability to "perennialize" (come back year after year) in the garden or to be stored and replanted the following spring.

PLANTING SPRING-FLOWERING BULBS

Nothing beats tulips and daffodils when it comes to the popularity of spring-flowering bulbs. Running a close second would be bulbs such as the intoxicatingly fragrant Dutch hyacinths, crocus, grape hyacinths, various kinds of iris, fritillarias, anemones, and others. All of these bulbs, whose flowers grace our gardens from late winter to spring, must be planted in autumn in order to have blooms the following year. The reason is that these hardy, mostly perennial bulbs require a cold period of dormancy during the winter in order for their roots to grow and for certain things to happen within the bulb before they can grow and bloom in the spring. Without this cold period of at least three months, you'll likely see mixed results from your spring-flowering bulbs.

Planting depth can also affect how well your bulbs perform in the garden. As a very general rule of thumb, most bulbs should be planted at a depth that is equal to about three times their diameter. So a large daffodil bulb that might be as much as 2½ to 3 inches in diameter should be planted at

least 6 inches deep and could be placed closer to 8 or even 9 inches deep and still grow just fine. Smaller bulbs, such as crocus and muscari, may be planted anywhere from 2 to 4 inches deep, again depending on the size of the bulb.

Note that the planting depth for bulbs is measured from the top of the planting hole (ground level) to the bottom of the planting hole. That is, in a hole 8 inches deep, the *bottom* of the bulb sits at 8 inches while the top may only be covered with 6 inches of soil. Not planting bulbs deep enough can contribute to various problems: they may be eaten by voles and chipmunks, heave out of the ground during winter's freeze-thaw cycle, or emerge from the ground too early in the spring and get frozen in early-spring frosts.

NOT JUST FOR SPRING ANYMORE

While tulips and daffodils may still rank near the top in popularity, flower bulbs are not just spring bloomers. In the Carolinas, bulbs can flower twelve months of the year, depending on the species, extending the season well beyond Easter and into summer, autumn, and even winter! Indulge yourself with the wonderful woodland varieties like magic lilies, autumn crocus, and hardy cyclamen. For vertical accents, scatter a few gladiolus and crocosmia bulbs in a sunny perennial border. Oriental lilies produce exquisite, picture-perfect blooms for cutting, while their smaller Asiatic cousins are made for color beds.

With some bulbs, their foliage makes as big a statement as their flowers, and a few, like caladiums and elephant ears, are grown for their foliage alone. The bold leaves of cannas provide an exclamation point in open borders even when not in bloom, while caladiums brighten up the shadows under a majestic shade tree. If big leaves suit your fancy, gigantic elephant ears can be used judiciously as bold foliage accents in color beds and even in water gardens.

Dahlias flower repeatedly throughout the season and you'll find that the best blooms come during the cooler days of autumn, when colors intensify and the size of the blooms, especially on the dinner plate types, is truly astounding! A nice surprise in these late days of summer and autumn are the rain lilies, whose blooms will suddenly appear within just a day or two of a passing thunderstorm, after lying in wait for just a little moisture to spur them from their summer nap. Remontant, or reblooming, iris will also begin flowering again in early autumn and continue their show until almost Thanksgiving in mild climates.

The hardy cyclamen have a tough constitution that belies their diminutive size and delicate appearance. These bulbs begin emerging and flowering in autumn and, depending on the species, will continue to flower right through the winter months. Their beautiful silver-and-green mottled foliage is an added bonus and remains even through the coldest winter days. Cyclamen will also reseed where they are happy, creating magnificent carpets of color across the woodland floor.

CARE FOR BULBS

Successful gardeners prepare bulb beds for the long haul. Even if you're planting for one-season color, as with caladiums, you will want to amend the soil deeply. Studies at North Carolina State University (NCSU) revealed that many bulbs fail to thrive due to soil acidity, poor fertility, and poor drainage. Testing the soil should be a standard practice with new bed installations. Contact your County Extension Service for directions on taking and submitting soil samples. Bulbs will perform well in soils that have been limed to raise the pH to 6, and poorly drained clay soils must be well amended with organic matter such as pine bark soil conditioner, compost, and composted manures. Bulbs also thrive in raised beds, where drainage is excellent and the quality of the soil can be controlled from the outset.

"Bulb-booster" fertilizers supply balanced nutrition specifically for bulbs and encourage repeat flowering. Gardeners have commonly used bonemeal at planting time, but this is no longer recommended since bonemeal attracts vermin to the garden and may be a health hazard. The appropriate times for fertilizing spring-flowering

bulbs are in late summer and again in winter just as new growth begins to emerge, and the tiny green leaf tips can be seen just breaking the soil surface. These application times correlate to the periods of highest absorption of nutrients.

Summer-flowering bulbs can be fertilized with the bulb boosters either at planting time (for newly planted bulbs) or in spring as they emerge from their winter rest (for established plantings), but during their summer growth period, use water-soluble flower fertilizer every six weeks to keep the plants actively growing and blooming. Most of these summer bloomers are vigorous, fast growers and the slow-release fertilizers don't act quickly enough to provide all of the nutrients the plants can use.

THOSE PESKY CRITTERS

Wildlife in the garden can be a blessing and a curse. Though squirrels and other animals will leave your daffodil bulbs alone (they are toxic to critters), they will nibble at tulip flowers. Browsing deer rummaging through a bulb bed at peak bloom can certainly cause distress, and voles, also known as pine mice, can wipe out beds of plants before you even know you have them. Fortunately, there are legal ways to control voles, including snap traps and rodenticides. For the average homeowner in suburbia, a good cat or the amendment of the soil with gravel or VoleBloc goes a long way. Local garden centers or animal control professionals may also be able to make recommendations for controlling nuisance animals in the garden.

Specialty bulb catalogs and garden centers offer many bulb options for gardening year-round. For every sunny garden or shady nook, you can find just the right bulb. Some bulbs may be left in the ground for years, producing flowers for your enjoyment. Others will need to be lifted following the first frosts of autumn. Many of them are capable of surviving harsh storage conditions because they naturally go dormant until the environment becomes conducive to a normal growth cycle. You won't be disappointed with your bulb choices when you find the perfect places for them in your garden.

AMARYLLIS

Hippeastrum spp. and hybrids

Why It's Special—Known for its Christmastime blooms, the amaryllis also makes an excellent perennial garden bulb in Zone 8 and warmer, where it will produce extraordinary clusters of flowers each year. Christmas amaryllis are forced to flower out of season and will return to their normal spring routine when planted in the garden.

How to Plant & Grow—In Zones 8 and warmer, amaryllis bulbs can be planted outdoors in fall. Plant in full sun in rich, well-drained soil where the plants will not be disturbed. Prepare the soil deeply and amend thoroughly with compost or other organic matter. Plant bulbs so that the tip is at or just below the soil surface.

Care & Problems—When bloom stalks emerge and active growth begins, apply compost or fertilizer. Water regularly during dry spells to keep the bulbs growing throughout the summer.

Hardiness—Zones 7 (with protection) to 10

Bloom Color—White, pink, red, salmon, orange, striped

Peak Season—Flowers in spring and early summer

Mature Size (H x W)—2 ft. x 1 ft.

Water Needs—Water regularly during dry periods

AUTUMN CROCUS

Colchicum autumnale

Why It's Special—Called autumn crocus because its flowers look similar to crocus, this plant provides a spectacular fall display in September and October!

How to Plant & Grow—Bulbs will be shipped or available in garden centers in late summer at the proper time to plant. It is not uncommon for the flowers to emerge from the bulbs before they are even planted. Autumn crocus should be planted 2 to 3 inches deep and 6 inches apart in thoroughly amended garden soil. They are perfect for woodland gardens, where winter and early spring sunshine will reach their leaves and drier summers will help to cure the bulbs.

Care & Problems—The leaves will begin to emerge immediately after the bulbs flower and will remain green throughout the winter and spring. Foliage should not be removed until it has turned yellow and begun to die in late spring or early summer.

Hardiness—Zones 4 to 8

Bloom Color—White, pink, rose, lilac, purple

Peak Season—September to November

Mature Size (H x W)—6 in. x 10 in.

Water Needs—Drought tolerant, once established

BEARDED IRIS

Iris x hybrida

Why It's Special—Bearded iris are among the easiest, toughest, and showiest of perennials and come in a rainbow of colors. They range in height from 36- to 40-inch-tall standards to 6- to 8-inch miniatures.

How to Plant & Grow—Plant the thick rhizomes just at the surface of the soil. Bearded iris prefer neutral to alkaline soils, and lime may be necessary for acidic soils. They are heavy feeders—feed in spring and again in early to midsummer.

Care & Problems—Overcrowded clumps bloom poorly, so divide every three to four years to keep plants blooming profusely. Iris borers can be a problem, but can be treated by spraying the foliage and the exposed rhizomes at regular intervals in early spring. Division and transplanting is done in late summer, when plants are dormant.

Hardiness—Zones 3 to 8

Bloom Color—White, yellow, apricot, rose, maroon, blue, lavender, purple, bicolors

Peak Season—Spring to early summer; some varieties rebloom in autumn

Mature Size (H x W)—6 to 40 in. x 15 to 40 in.

Water Needs—Drought tolerant, once established

CALADIUM

Caladium bicolor

Why It's Special—Caladiums put most other bulbous plants to shame with their large, flamboyant leaves. They can be loosely grouped into "fancy-leaved" varieties, with heart-shaped leaves; and "strap-leaved" varieties, with more arrow-shaped leaves that are often thicker and more leathery. The strap-leaved varieties are more sun tolerant.

How to Plant & Grow—Caladiums can be started early in pots indoors and planted out when warm weather arrives. They will also grow from fleshy tubers planted directly into the garden in late spring, but only when soil is warm to the touch. Tubers vary greatly in size and their planting depth should be equal to their diameter. In late fall, after frost has killed the leaves, the tubers can be dug and stored in a cool, dry place until time to plant next spring.

Care & Problems—Deer can be a problem. Slugs and snails can be controlled with slug bait, if they're troublesome.

Hardiness—Zones 9 to 11, grown as annuals

Bloom Color—Green, white, pink, rose, red

Peak Season—Late spring to fall

Mature Size (H x W)—10 to 24 in. x 10 to 24 in.

Water Needs—Evenly moist soil

CANNA

Canna x generalis

Why It's Special—Once relegated to mass plantings along roadsides and in city parks, cannas have now become stars in the garden with their bold, often colorful tropical foliage and showy flowers that appear from early summer until frost.

How to Plant & Grow—Cannas grow quickly from thick, fleshy, deeply rooted rhizomes, which can spread to form large clumps over time. Divide every three years to keep them from outgrowing their space. Dormant rhizomes can be planted in spring, 3 to 4 inches deep, in rich, moist garden soil. Plants can also be purchased, potted and growing, in spring and summer for immediate planting.

Care & Problems—Cannas are thirsty, hungry plants. Consistent moisture and regular feeding will help keep them looking their best. Japanese beetles and leaf rollers can be problems in some areas, but are treatable.

Hardiness—Zones 7 to 10

Bloom Color—Red, yellow, orange, pink, bicolors

Peak Season—Early summer to frost

Mature Size (H x W)—2 to 6 ft. x 2 to 4 ft.

Water Needs—Evenly moist soil

CRINUM

Crinum spp. and hybrids

Why It's Special—Old-fashioned, Southern pass-along plants, crinum lilies have graced gardens throughout the South for generations. They have experienced a recent renaissance and the conservation of antique varieties along with the introduction of hardier hybrids has only helped their cause.

How to Plant & Grow—Crinum bulbs are large and require a deeply dug planting hole, at least 1 foot deep by 1½ feet wide. Thoroughly amend the soil with compost or other organic matter. Space the bulbs 2 feet apart, planting each with its long neck visible aboveground. Once planted, they can remain undisturbed for many years.

Care & Problems—Crinums have no serious pests or diseases. New plants will need a season or two to become established and begin flowering regularly. Fertilize established clumps with a "bulb booster" in mid-May of each year. Deadhead as flowers fade to keep plants blooming.

Hardiness—Zones 7b to 10 (some are hardier)

Bloom Color—White, pink, bicolors

Peak Season—Summer

Mature Size (H x W)—1½ to 3 ft. x 1½ to 3 ft.

Water Needs—Drought tolerant, but regular water is best

CROCOSMIA

Crocosmia spp. and hybrids

Why It's Special—Crocosmia provides a brilliant display of color in midsummer with showy flowers atop tall, wandlike stems. The spearlike foliage, in shades of green to slightly bronze, offers an excellent vertical accent in the garden. Fiery red 'Lucifer' is the most popular cultivar, but new hybrids will soon expand the range of colors into even more sunset shades of glowing apricots, pinks, and bronzes, as well as bicolors and others.

How to Plant & Grow—Like crocus, crocosmia grows from small corms. Dormant corms can be planted in spring about 3 inches deep and 5 inches apart. Growing plants can be purchased at garden centers for planting any time during the growing season. They prefer well-drained, humusy, fertile soil in full sun.

Care & Problems—Spider mites can be a problem, especially in hot, dry weather. Spraying may be necessary for control. Regular summer watering is a must.

Hardiness—Zones 6 to 10

Bloom Color—Red, orange, yellow, apricot, blends

Peak Season—Mid- to late summer

Mature Size (H x W)—1½ to 3 ft. x 1½ to 3 ft

Water Needs—Evenly moist soil

CYCLAMEN

Cyclamen hederifolium

Why It's Special—Cyclamen bring color and interest to the garden at a time of year when it's needed most. *Cyclamen hederifolium* flowers in mid to late autumn and its beautiful silver and green mottled foliage provides interest from winter into spring. Another species, *Cyclamen coum*, flowers from November to February.

How to Plant & Grow—Cyclamen are the perfect companions for woodland wildflowers and other shade-loving plants. Because they are dormant in summer, be sure to mark their locations so you don't accidentally dig them up. Plant them in humusy, woodland soils with the tops of their tubers right at soil level, just barely covered, if at all.

Care & Problems—Cyclamen will reseed themselves where they are happy and may eventually form spectacular carpets of color. Chipmunks and voles may dig and/or eat the tubers.

Hardiness—Zones 5 to 8

Bloom Color—White, or pale pink to deep fuchsia

Peak Season—Fall and winter

Mature Size (H x W)—4 to 6 in. x 8 to 12 in.

Water Needs—Water only if dry while blooming and growing

DAHLIA

Dahlia x hybrida

Why It's Special—This spectacular tender perennial has flowers in more colors, sizes, and forms than almost any other garden plant. Dahlias come in nearly every color but true blue, and the flowers can be as small as a nickel or a large as a dinner plate.

How to Plant & Grow—Dormant tubers may be planted in April, 2 to 3 inches deep, in rich, well-amended garden soil. Potted plants can be transplanted when the danger of frost has passed. Dahlias need regular water and fertilizer throughout the growing season. If plants begin to look ratty during the hottest summer months, they can be cut nearly to the ground, fertilized, and watered well, and they will resprout and rebloom in autumn.

Care & Problems—Taller varieties require staking. While dahlias do like moisture, waterlogged soils may cause stem rot.

Hardiness—Zones 7 to 9

Bloom Color—Every color except true blue, as well as bicolors and blends

Peak Season—Summer to fall

Mature Size (H x W)—1 to 7 ft. x 1 to 4 ft.

Water Needs—Water regularly throughout growing season

ELEPHANT EARS

Colocasia esculenta

Why It's Special—The bold, tropical foliage of elephant ears provides the perfect foil for many of our favorite annual and perennial garden plants. New selections include black-leaved varieties and bright golden yellow and variegated forms. Several new varieties are also more compact, making them suitable for smaller gardens.

How to Plant & Grow—Plant tubers or plants in late spring or early summer in rich, moist, organic soil. Varieties with colored leaves need full sun for best color. Elephant ears grow perfectly well in regular garden soil, but do need adequate moisture to thrive. They respond amazingly well to regular feeding, and some varieties can become massive if well fed and watered.

Care & Problems—There are no serious pests or diseases. Division every two to three years will help keep the size of the clumps in check.

Hardiness—Zones 7 to 10

Bloom Color—Grown for foliage; green, black, purple, chartreuse, variegated

Peak Season—Summer

Mature Size (H x W)—3 ft. x 3 ft. to 8 ft. x 8 ft., depending on variety

Water Needs—Damp to wet soil in summer, drier in winter

GLADIOLUS

Gladiolus hybrids

Why It's Special—The bright colors and tall stems of gladiolus make them perfect for cut flowers. Some varieties have been pass-along plants in Southern gardens for years, and a few are perennial. These include *Gladiolus* x *gandevensis* 'Boone' and a variety called 'Carolina Primrose', both discovered in North Carolina.

How to Plant & Grow—Most gladiolus are planted beginning in late spring, and then plantings are staggered every two weeks to provide a continuous show from midsummer on. They prefer well-drained soil and full sun. Plant the corms 3 to 5 inches deep for larger varieties, and 2 to 3 inches deep for smaller varieties.

Care & Problems—Thrips can be a problem, causing streaking of the flowers. Taller varieties need staking. Shorter and smaller-flowered varieties need less staking. In Zone 7, dig and store nonhardy varieties in winter.

Hardiness—Zones 8 to 10

Bloom Color—All colors but true blue, plus bicolors and blends

Peak Season—Mid- to late summer

Mature Size (H x W)—1½ to 6 ft. x 1 to 1½ ft.

Water Needs—Evenly moist soil, especially when in bloom

LILY

Lilium spp. and hybrids

Why It's Special—Grown for their exquisite flowers and heavenly fragrance, lilies come in many sizes, shapes, and colors. Most hybrids are easy to grow.

How to Plant & Grow—Bulbs should be firm and plump; plant them as soon as acquired. Soil should be deeply dug and generously amended. Planting depth is two to three times the diameter of the bulbs, so large bulbs may go 10 to 12 inches deep. Most varieties form spectacular clumps after two to three seasons.

Care & Problems—Lilies like their "head in the sun and feet in the shade;" mix them into perennial borders where surrounding plants will shade their roots. Deer love lilies. Voles can be a problem, but deep planting helps deter them. Staking may be necessary for taller varieties. Feed lily bulbs in early spring and again in fall.

Hardiness—Zones 4 to 9

Bloom Color—White, pink, red, yellow, orange, blends

Peak Season—Early summer to early fall

Mature Size (H x W)—1½ to 7 ft. x 1½ to 4 ft.

Water Needs—Evenly moist soil during active growth

LYCORIS

Lycoris spp. and hybrids

Why It's Special—Lycoris are also commonly known as surprise lilies, magic lilies, spider lilies, and naked ladies. These common names come from the fact that their blooms emerge suddenly and without warning in late summer and fall, and are borne atop bare stems.

How to Plant & Grow—Plant in well-amended garden soil, 3 to 5 inches deep, depending on the size of the bulb. Leaves of some species may emerge in fall, after flowers have faded, and will remain green throughout the winter and into the following spring, while others wait and emerge in spring. Some species grow their leaves in fall. Lycoris perform well in woodland gardens, but they also mingle well in perennial borders.

Care & Problems—Lycoris are generally pest free. Bulbs can rot if the soil stays excessively wet. Over time they will slowly form offsets and the clumps will grow larger and more spectacular with each passing year.

Hardiness—Zones 5 to 9

Bloom Color—Pink, white, lavender, yellow, orange, red

Peak Season—Late summer to fall

Mature Size (H x W)—15 to 24 in. x 12 to 24 in.

Water Needs—Drought tolerant, once established

MUSCARI

Muscari spp. and hybrids

Why It's Special—Muscari, or grape hyacinths, are favorite old-fashioned perennial bulbs that will multiply quickly and put on a beautiful show for many years in the garden. They are tough, easy and perfect for naturalizing in large drifts into lawns and woodlands.

How to Plant & Grow—Plant in fall in well-tilled, amended garden soil. Bulbs may vary in size and should be planted 2 to 4 inches deep; larger ones deeper, smaller ones shallower. Fertilize after flowering to encourage the bulbs to multiply and form clumps. A useful "trick" is to plant a few grape hyacinths where you plant tulips, daffodils, and other dormant bulbs. The grape hyacinths will sprout almost immediately and their leaves will remind you where you have planted other bulbs.

Care & Problems—Voles, squirrels, and chipmunks can be occasional problems.

Hardiness—Zones 3 to 8

Bloom Color—Purple, blue, yellow, white

Peak Season—Early to mid-spring

Mature Size (H x W)—6 to 8 in. x 6 to 8 in.

Water Needs—Evenly moist soil while growing, drier when dormant

NARCISSUS

Narcissus spp. and hybrids

Why It's Special—Perhaps no garden bulbs are as tried and true as narcissus. Also known as daffodils, jonquils, and—in the South—buttercups, the narcissus is a perennial performer that blooms at winter's end. By planting early-, mid-, and late-season varieties you can have narcissus of various sizes, shapes, and colors in flower from February to April.

How to Plant & Grow—Narcissus have a reputation for being tough, but generous holes and well-amended soil will gets new bulbs off to the best start. Planting depth varies with bulb size, and groups of ten bulbs or more will produce the best effect.

Care & Problems—Narcissus bulbs will be untouched by deer, voles, and chipmunks. Allow foliage to yellow completely after flowering before cutting it back, or you will weaken the bulb for next year. Fertilize yearly in early spring just as growth begins.

Hardiness—Zones 3 to 8

Bloom Color—White, yellow, gold, orange, combinations

Peak Season—Spring

Mature Size (H x W)—4 to 20 in. x 6 to 18 in.

Water Needs—Drought tolerant, once established

ORNAMENTAL ONION

Allium spp. and hybrids

Why It's Special—The ornamental onions, or alliums, bring a certain level of sophistication to the garden. They are easy to grow and can provide stunning architectural form and color from early spring to fall.

How to Plant & Grow—There is tremendous variation in size, shape, and color. Some grow from bulbs no larger than a lima bean, while others grow from bulbs almost as big as a softball. Almost all of them prefer full sun and very well-drained soil. Spring-flowering varieties, like the giant alliums and others that go dormant after flowering, need a good, hot, summer baking to mature their bulbs for next year. Many thrive on neglect!

Care & Problems—There are no serious pests or diseases.

Hardiness—Zones 4 to 8

Bloom Color—Blue, purple, pink, white, yellow

Peak Season—Spring to summer, depending on variety

Mature Size (H x W)—6 to 48 in. x 10 to 20 in.

Water Needs—Evenly moist soil while growing, drier when dormant

RAIN LILY

Zephyranthes spp. and hybrids

Why It's Special—The durable rain lily provides a surprising show in late summer and early fall. While the leaves sprout in spring at the same time as many other bulbs, the rain lily waits to flower until the end of summer. Then, just when you've given up hope, a passing thunderstorm provides just enough moisture to cause the rain lilies to burst into bloom.

How to Plant & Grow—Many rain lilies are native to Mexico and Central America, where the soils are arid, gritty, and very well drained. They will benefit from the addition of coarse sand, turkey grit, or small crushed gravel to help improve drainage, especially in clay soils. Once established, they require little care.

Care & Problems—Rain lilies have few pest or disease problems. A topdressing of compost once a year will help keep them healthy.

Hardiness—Zones 7 to 10

Bloom Color—White, pink, yellow, with new hybrids in sunset colors

Peak Season—Late summer to early autumn

Mature Size (H x W)—8 to 14 in. x 8 to 14 in.

Water Needs—Drought tolerant, once established

SPANISH BLUEBELLS

Hyacinthoides hispanica

Why It's Special—Spanish bluebells thrive in a woodland setting, tolerating the shade of overhead trees or competition from roots. In April, the tall spires are laden with up to twenty bell-shaped, hyacinth-like blossoms in shades of blue, white, or occasionally pink. Where they are happy, they will self-sow and naturalize.

How to Plant & Grow—Plant bulbs in autumn in moist, well-prepared soil that is at least moderately fertile. Topdress with slow-release bulb fertilizer each fall. Once flowering has finished in spring, deadheading is not necessary, especially if reseeding is desired, and the foliage should be allowed to die down naturally. Cutting the leaves prematurely will weaken the bulbs for the following season.

Care & Problems—There are no serious pests or diseases, though deer may nibble. They usually stop after a bite or two.

Hardiness—Zones 5 to 8

Bloom Color—Blue, purple, white, pink

Peak Season—Mid-spring

Mature Size (H x W)—12 to 16 in. x 12 to 16 in.

Water Needs—Evenly moist soil while growing, drier when dormant

SUMMER SNOWFLAKE

Leucojum aestivum

Why It's Special—Summer snowflake is a great choice for the shadier parts of the garden. It also thrives in full sun and is one of the few bulbs that will tolerate considerable moisture, even growing at the edges of ponds or streams.

How to Plant & Grow—After the soil has begun to cool in November and December, plant bulbs 3 to 4 inches deep. For best effect, plant fairly close together, as many as five to six bulbs per square foot. They will multiply and "clump up" quickly, providing a bigger and better show each year.

Care & Problems—They are generally not bothered by rodents or other pests. If blooming diminishes after several seasons, divide clumps right after flowering or in the fall when dormant. Allow foliage to yellow naturally before cutting the plants back after blooming. Cutting too early will affect the following season's display.

Hardiness—Zones 3 to 8

Bloom Color—White

Peak Season—Mid- to late spring

Mature Size (H x W)—12 to 18 in. x 12 in.

Water Needs—Evenly moist soil while growing, drier when dormant

TULIP

Tulipa spp. and hybrids

Why It's Special—In Southern climates, tulips are commonly grown as annuals, since our hot, humid summers and wet winters are not to their liking. Even so, tulips blooming in the garden are a sure sign that spring is at its peak!

How to Plant & Grow—Prechilling of tulip bulbs is not necessary in most areas of the Carolinas. Plant bulbs after the first frost and before Thanksgiving at least 6 to 8 inches deep in order to get them down into cooler soil and encourage the best root development, growth, and flowering. Deep planting also keeps the bulbs drier in summer and encourages them to be more perennial.

Care & Problems—Voles are particularly enamored of tulip bulbs. Deep planting helps protect the bulbs. Deer are also destructive to tulips when they emerge in spring.

Hardiness—Zones 3 to 7

Bloom Color—Nearly every color, blend, and pattern imaginable

Peak Season—Early to late spring

Mature Size (H x W)—6 to 30 in. x 6 to 10 in.

Water Needs—Evenly moist soil while growing, drier when dormant

FORCING BULBS

Making bulbs flower outside their normal season is a wonderful way of ushering spring into your home. Bulbs that can be easily forced include daffodils, hyacinths, and tulips. Smaller bulbs good for forcing include crocus, glory-of-the-snow (*Chionodoxa* spp.), grape hyacinth (*Muscari* spp.), netted iris (*Iris reticulata*), Siberian squill (*Scilla siberica*), spring snowflake (*Leucojum vernum*), snowdrop (*Galanthus nivalis*), winter aconite (*Eranthis hyemalis*), and wood hyacinth (*Hyacinthoides nonscripta*).

Follow these steps to force bulbs: Buy bulb cultivars that are recommended for forcing. Pot up the bulbs anytime from mid-September to December in a well-drained potting medium. Use commercial potting soil or make your own mix composed of equal parts potting soil, sphagnum peat moss, and perlite. Since the bulbs already contain enough food for the developing flowers and roots, fertilizing is unnecessary. Select a shallow pot or bulb pan that is at least twice the height of the bulbs. Fill it three-quarters full of mix and set the bulbs in place. Have at least 1 to 2 inches of soil beneath large bulbs. Tulips and daffodils can be left with their tips showing; completely cover smaller bulbs such as crocus, snowdrops, and grape hyacinths. When planting tulips, position the flat side of the bulb toward the outside of the pot; when the first and lowest leaf emerges, it will gracefully arch over the rim to give a balanced look.

Fill the pot with soil to within ¼ to ½ inch of the rim. Add water until it seeps through the drainage hole in the bottom of the pot. Label each pot, marking the name of the cultivar, the planting date, and the date to be brought into the house.

Cool the bulbs by exposing them to temperatures between 35 and 50 degrees F for twelve to sixteen weeks. Store them in an old refrigerator, an unheated basement, or a cold frame, or in the ground buried up to the pot rims. Protect the potted bulbs from freezing outdoors by covering them with sawdust, straw, leaves, or peat moss. After twelve weeks of chilling, check the pots. When you wiggle the bulb in the pot and it stays in place and roots can be seen through the drainage holes, bring the pot indoors for forcing.

Gradually expose the pots to light and warm temperatures. Start with a cool 60- to 65-degree F room in indirect sunlight. When the shoots turn green, expose the pots to warmer temperatures and more light to stimulate flowering. Rotate the pots regularly so that all the leaves receive an equal amount of light. After a week, move the pots to warmer temperatures and more light to encourage flowering. Keep the soil moist. The flowers will last longer if you move the pots to a cool room at night.

If you wait until after the last freeze, most forced bulbs can be planted in the garden. During their time indoors, keep them in bright sunlight and fertilize them with a water-soluble houseplant fertilizer. Once spring arrives, plant hardy bulbs that have been forced into bloom in the garden, or allow them to go dormant in their pots and then plant them in the fall. Daffodils, crocus, squills, and other hardy bulbs can be transplanted into the garden in spring and will flower normally the following year. Other bulbs, such as tulips and hyacinths, are best discarded after forcing.

JANUARY

- Check the condition of your stored bulbs such as caladiums, dahlias, and tuberous begonias. Discard any that show signs of rot, which attacks improperly stored tubers in warm, humid conditions.

- When preparing new beds for bulbs, mix compost, lime, and other amendments into the soil. Beds should be tilled deeply and thoroughly to make planting easier and allow roots to spread deep into the soil.

- Maintain a blanket of mulch at the feet of your bulbs, especially in the mountains, where freezing and thawing can lift the bulbs out of the ground, leaving them to dry out or be harmed by cold.

- If you are chilling potted tulips, daffodils, or other bulbs to force for indoor blooms, be sure to water occasionally to maintain moisture at their roots. Once the green shoots are 2 to 3 inches tall, you can begin bringing pots in a few at a time to flower indoors.

FEBRUARY

Resist spring-flowering bulbs at local garden centers that have been put on clearance. Tulips, daffodils, and crocus are unlikely to do well planted this late.

- It is still safe to purchase paperwhite narcissus and amaryllis bulbs for forcing indoors if retailers still have them for sale. Bulbs should be firm and plump with no mushy spots. If they're not, avoid them.

- The earliest daffodils and other bulbs will be flowering this month. Be sure to leave their foliage up for at least six weeks after they finish flowering to feed the bulbs for next year's display.

- Daffodils make nice tabletop bouquets, but their sap can be harmful to other cut flowers, causing them to lose their petals prematurely. Condition daffodils in a separate container of water for a day before adding them to bouquets.

MARCH

- When the leaves of spring-flowering bulbs emerge, apply a complete fertilizer to ensure quality blooms next year. Do not fertilize them after they've bloomed; these bulbs are going dormant.

- Snip off the spent blooms of spring-flowering bulbs to prevent seedpods from forming. If you expect them to repeat their show next spring, allow leaves to mature and die down naturally before removing.

- If weeds occur in bulb beds, do not remove them by cultivation. Pull them by hand so the bulbs and roots will not be disturbed.

- To control botrytis (gray mold), collect and discard faded flowers. Fungicides can be applied at the first sign of disease. Provide good air movement by not overcrowding the plants.

APRIL

- Evaluate your spring-flowering bulbs. Note in your gardening journal which bulbs and cultivars met or exceeded your expectations and which ones need further evaluation or possible removal.

- Summer-flowering bulbs such as crocosmias, dahlias, and gladiolus can be planted after the threat of freezing temperatures has passed. Mountain gardeners can wait until next month to plant.

- In the warmer parts of the Carolinas, dig, divide, and replant cannas and dahlias. The best time to do this is after the eyes have sprouted but before they have grown more than an inch. Stake dahlia tubers as you are replanting so you can insert the stake without skewering the tuber.

- Plant gladiolus corms every two weeks until July to create a continuous succession of flowers. Plant the corms at least 4 inches deep to stabilize them as they produce their long flower stalks. Insert stakes as you plant to avoid skewering corms later.

MAY

- As spring-flowering bulbs begin to fade, make plans to fill their voids with flowering annuals that are either direct sown as seed, or planted from transplants. Avoid injuring bulbs when planting over them.

- After the last freeze, plant tender summer bulbs such as cannas, dahlias, ginger lilies, and tuberoses that have been stored over the winter or purchased from mail-order companies or garden centers.

- Plant caladium bulbs when the soil temperature reaches 70 degrees F or warmer. Tubers may rot in cold soil if planted too early.

- Lightly fertilize newly planted summer-flowering bulbs such as cannas and dahlias when their shoots emerge, using a slow-release fertilizer. Water in thoroughly afterwards.

JUNE

- The leaves of most spring bulbs have finished maturing by now or have died back and can be cut back to ground level. Dig, divide, and replant any crowded bulbs that have declined and produced few, if any, flowers.

- Pests to watch for include aphids, spider mites, thrips, and Japanese beetles. Handpick Japanese beetles and discard them in a jar of soapy water. Neem oil can be applied to the leaves to reduce feeding by the adults.

- Watch for powdery mildew and leaf spot diseases on susceptible plants. Proper spacing and good air circulation will help to prevent fungal infestations, but spraying may be necessary for severe outbreaks.

- Hand pull weeds when they are young and easier to remove. Suppress them with a shallow layer of compost. Another way of handling weeds is to plant companion plants among your bulbs whose leaves will shade the soil and deprive the young weeds of sunlight.

JULY

- Now is the time to take advantage of early-order discounts from mail-order bulb distributors. Some bulbs may be available in limited quantities and you want to be first in line to ensure that you get the varieties you want.

- Watch for leaf roller larvae on cannas. These caterpillars will chew and roll the leaves, making plants unsightly, and occasionally will curb growth and flowering. *Bt* (*Bacillus thuringiensis*) sprays are safe and effective.

- If you have bulbs such as caladiums or tuberous begonias growing in pots, don't forget to feed them. Constant watering leaches nutrients from the soil, and container plants rely on you to replenish those nutrients.

- Continue securing and tying tall dahlias, lilies, and gladiolus to the stakes you have already provided them.

AUGUST

- Divide bearded iris so the plants will have plenty of time to become established before cooler weather arrives.

- Iris rhizomes may be infested with borers. Discard heavily infested rhizomes and salvage others by digging out the pinkish larvae with a pocketknife and trimming away any damaged tissue. Dust with sulfur before replanting to help prevent fungal diseases.

- Spider mites are especially troublesome during the hot, dry weather of this month. Regular applications of highly refined horticultural oils (applied only during the coolest parts of the day) will help to smother them.

- Don't let the weeds get the best of you this month. They're thriving while we're wilting in the heat, but be persistent and your efforts will pay off.

SEPTEMBER

- As you make plans to visit a garden center to purchase spring-flowering bulbs, remember that "bigger is better" when it comes to bulbs. Bigger bulbs produce bigger blossoms. Stay away from soft, mushy, moldy, or heavily bruised bulbs.

- Some bulbs such as tulips and daffodils have a brown, papery "tunic" covering the bulbs. This often comes off, especially with tulips, but is of no concern as long as the bulb underneath is plump, white, and free from bruising or damage.

- If bulbs need to be stored after you get them home or when they arrive in the mail, a cool garage, cellar, or basement is ideal. Avoid storing bulbs in the refrigerator, as the natural ethylene gas that is given off by fruits and vegetables as they ripen can be detrimental to flower bulbs.

- If you have purchased or ordered fall-flowering bulbs such as saffron crocus, colchicum, autumn crocus, or lycoris, be sure to plant them as soon as possible after their arrival. They will begin growing almost immediately.

OCTOBER

- Cut back lily stalks to soil level after they have turned yellow. The same applies to other summer-flowering bulbs once their foliage has yellowed or withered.

- Mountain gardeners should lift cannas, dahlias, gladiolus, and tuberous begonias after their foliage is killed by frost. Because they won't survive the winter outdoors, they need to be cleansed of soil and stored indoors in a cool but frost-free location.

- Watch out for storage diseases, including fusarium bulb rot and botrytis. Avoid damaging bulbs and tubers when lifting them out of the ground to be stored.

- Weeds, especially weedy grasses, may be in beds. Hand pull or hoe out the clumps. Also, spring weeds such as dandelions, henbit, and chickweed begin germinating now, so be on the lookout.

NOVEMBER

- "Minor" bulbs are excellent for naturalizing in lawns and natural areas around your property. Randomly scatter crocus, miniature daffodils, grape hyacinths, snowdrops, and anemones and plant them where they fall. Over time, they will create magnificent drifts.

- November is the time to plant spring-blooming anemones, crocus, daffodils, scillas, snowdrops, and others. In cooler areas, tulips can also be planted now. Use a time-release bulb fertilizer at planting time.

- Clean up and remove old, dried iris leaves, stems, and other debris in the fall to help eliminate overwintering eggs or iris borers. General cleanup of garden debris is a good idea at this time to prevent overwintering of insects and diseases from this year's garden.

- Fertilize new and established beds with a slow-release nitrogen fertilizer. Don't wait until spring, because the bulbs are producing roots and foraging for nutrients now.

DECEMBER

- Have soil samples from your beds tested if you haven't done so in the past two or three years. Since lime can take up to six months to react and increase the soil pH, the sooner you have your soil tested, the sooner you can apply lime to your beds if necessary.

- Mice may get into outdoor bulb beds or cold frames. Use hardware cloth to keep them out. Voles, also called meadow or field mice, can feed on a wide variety of plants, including your bulbs. Two kinds of voles, pine voles and meadow voles, reside in the Carolinas.

- Paperwhite narcissus are winter-blooming tender bulbs that you can force without having to expose them to cool temperatures. They are great fun for children to grow because they are easy and fast. Once they begin to sprout,you can even measure how much they've grown overnight!

EDIBLES: VEGETABLES, HERBS & FRUIT

for the Carolinas

Vegetable gardening is one of the most rewarding types of gardening you can do. From a tiny seed or a small transplant you reap great harvests in just a few weeks' or months' time, and we all know that nothing compares to that first homegrown tomato of the season or that sweet, succulent corn picked fresh off the stalk and dropped immediately into a pot of boiling water. While vegetable gardens are often thought of as being "utilitarian" in nature, today's gardeners have found many ways to make them both beautiful and functional, and there is no reason to relegate the vegetable garden to the back corner of the yard anymore. Let your veggies shine!

In addition to vegetables, many gardeners choose to include herbs, small fruits, and, if space allows, even fruit trees in their gardens and landscapes. For that reason, we chose to call this chapter "Edibles" and have included as many kinds of plants as possible that will provide you with nearly year-round harvests of luscious fruits, vegetables, and herbs fresh, from the garden.

LOCATION

Generally speaking, fruits, herbs, and vegetables love sun and will produce the most abundant harvest when they receive eight to ten hours of direct sun each day. Some crops can be grown in less than full sun, but the result may be less than a full crop. Avoid locations next to large trees or shrubs that will shade the garden and send roots into it; try to plant your garden a distance from trees and shrubs that is at least equal to the height of the plants. Choosing a site with a nearby water source will also make gardening easier for you in those inevitable dry spells.

SOIL PREPARATION

The most important step in creating any garden, especially when growing herbs, vegetables, and fruits, is proper soil preparation. Every dollar you invest and every hour you spend on plowing, amending, and tilling the soil will reward you ten times over when harvest time arrives.

The first step when building a new garden from scratch is to kill existing grasses and weeds. Plenty of new weeds will appear on their own, so you might as well start with a clean slate! You may choose to plow the weeds under and then till the ground thoroughly, hoe them out, or kill them with herbicides. Apply Roundup, which kills underground parts as well as tops, to perennial grasses such as quackgrass and Kentucky bluegrass, as well as existing annual weeds. Roundup is deactivated as soon as it hits the ground or is absorbed by the weeds, so there is no danger to plants later on. Keep it off of nearby perennial garden plants or any other plants that you want to save, however.

Most people will choose to spray and kill the weeds and then plow them under, but if you want to take a more organic approach, plowing alone will suffice. There is some debate about plowing the garden versus just tilling it, but the truth is that plowing will break the soil much deeper than most rototillers are able to go and vegetable roots need plenty of deep, rich soil to work their way into. Given the choice, plowing deeply and then tilling to break up the clods and smooth the soil will ultimately give you the best results.

Add as much organic matter as you can acquire, such as compost, well-rotted manure (aged a year or so), old plant tops, or leaves. Usually, about 2 inches evenly spread over the area is as much as a gardener can acquire or handle at one time. Spread a complete fertilizer such as 1 pound of 10-10-10 per 100 square feet of garden and thoroughly till the area to incorporate all of the organic matter and fertilizer into the soil.

WHEN TO PLANT

The timing of planting depends on the kinds of plants and the average date of the last frost (also called the frost-free date) in your area. Some vegetables are completely hardy and can withstand winter weather. Perennial vegetables and herbs such as asparagus and thyme are in this category. Annual vegetables are classified as either cool-season or warm season vegetables and which category they fall into will help to determine when

you plant. Cool-season vegetables such as cabbage, broccoli, peas, and others can stand chilly weather and even some light frost, while warm-season vegetables like peppers, tomatoes, corn, and eggplant love summer's heat and warm soil around their roots. Planting warm-season vegetables too early in the season may mean replanting if they get nipped by a late freeze, or stunted growth if the plants have to sit in cold, wet soil for several weeks before the soil temperature begins to rise.

HOW TO PLANT

For your method of planting, you may choose rows or hills. Plants may be set in rows, spaced evenly, or in hills, with several plants in one place at widely spaced intervals. Vegetables such as beans, corn, peas, and okra are more often grown in rows, while vining plants like cucumbers, squash, pumpkins, and melons are grown in hills spaced widely enough to allow them to spread across the ground. Some plants, like tomatoes, peppers, and eggplants, are commonly planted from transplants that gardeners have either started from seed indoors earlier in the year or purchased at their local garden center; while others, like beans, corn, cucumbers, and melons, are best sown directly into the garden where you want them to grow.

Set transplants you grow or buy into well-prepared soil. *If you have properly prepared the soil,* you can set the plants without using any tools. Dig your hand into the soil, pull open a hole big enough for the ball of soil on the plant, and set the plant in the hole at the same depth at which it was growing. Push the soil back around the plant and firm it down, using your thumb and forefingers to push the soil down next to the plant. Apply a transplant starter fertilizer in solution, and water the soil to settle it. For seeds, create rows or hills with a hoe and then plant the seeds at the depth indicated on the seed packet. You will need to keep newly planted seeds moist until they have germinated, which means you may have to water daily, or even twice a day if you have a warm spell, until the seedlings break the soil surface.

WATERING

Garden plants need about 1 inch of water per week. If rain does not fall, or if the plants begin to wilt, apply a measured inch of water. For a reliable way to determine when 1 inch has been applied with a sprinkler, set coffee cans in the garden and run the water until there is 1 inch of water in each can. As summer progresses and plants grow larger, more than 1 inch of water each week will probably be required to keep plants healthy and growing. It is important not to let plants wilt severely once fruit has begun to set or the plants may "shed" some of their crop in order to protect themselves and reduce the stress from drying out. This is as true for fruit crops as it is for vegetables, and some fruits, such as apples and peaches, will naturally shed part of their crop each year so that the tree only has as much fruit on it as it can reasonably support. This is Mother Nature's way of taking care of the plants and ensuring good crops each year.

MULCHING

Mulches help control weeds, conserve water, warm the soil in the spring, cool the soil in the summer, and keep the produce off the ground. Organic mulches consist of plant residues, such as straw, hay, leaves, crushed corncobs, grass clippings, or compost. These materials also decompose over the season, adding needed organic matter to the soil and recycling the nutrients. Organic matter addition is the primary means of improving soil tilth (physical condition of the soil). The recommended application is 2 to 4 inches deep on weed-free soil. Since organic mulches tend to keep the soil cool, apply them after the soil has warmed sufficiently in spring and the plants are growing well. Later in the season, some plants benefit from the cooling effects of the mulch. Organic mulches can simply be plowed under or rototilled in at the end of the season and then reapplied when new crops are planted.

FERTILIZING

Apply fertilizer according to soil test recommendations. Or, if you did not have a soil test done, apply 1 pound of complete balanced fertilizer such as 10-10-10 per 100 square feet of garden. About midseason, after the plants have become well developed, another application of fertilizer may be beneficial. Sidedress the plants with the same fertilizer at half the recommended rate, then water in thoroughly after application to wash the fertilizer off the plants and to activate the fertilizer. Water-soluble fertilizers can be applied according to the directions on the container.

ASPARAGUS

Asparagus officinalis

Why It's Special—Asparagus is a perennial garden vegetable that is well adapted to the Southern climate. Its tender spears, which arise from the crowns in spring, make it an appetizing product of the home garden.

How to Plant & Grow—Plant asparagus as soon as the ground can be worked in spring in a full-sun location. Dig the beds deeply and incorporate a generous amount of compost. Open a trench 6 inches deep and 15 inches wide, the length of the bed. Set the plants in the trench about 1 foot apart with the buds pointing up, then spread the roots in a uniform pattern around each crown. Replace 2 inches of the soil from the trench over the crowns, and water the plants thoroughly to settle the soil. Reserve the remaining soil to gradually cover the crowns as the plants grow during their first year; all of the soil should be used in the first year.

Care & Problems—In the first year, the plants will produce weak, spindly growth. As the root system develops, the spears will become larger each year, but the spears will not be ready for harvesting until the third season. When harvest is finished, apply fertilizer such as 10-10-10 at the rate of 2 to 3 pounds per 100 square feet of bed.

Harvest & Best Selections—'Jersey Giant', 'Jersey Knight', and 'Jersey Prince' are male selections that are extremely productive.

BEANS

Phaseolus vulgaris

Why It's Special—Beans may be the most diverse garden vegetable, ranking second only to tomatoes in popularity. Common beans are probably native to South America and were grown there for centuries before Europeans began growing them. All beans are members of the legume family and can extract and use nitrogen from the air.

How to Plant & Grow—Beans require full sun and warm, well-drained soil. Sow seeds of bush beans 2 to 3 inches apart, and cover them with 1 inch of soil. Sow seeds of pole beans 6 inches apart in rows along a fence or trellis, or sow them in hills of 6 seeds around poles set 3 feet apart; then cover the seeds with 1 inch of soil.

Care & Problems—Beans require little care except regular weeding and adequate water in dry weather. Applying Sevin insecticide will control numerous bean leaf beetles, which will eat holes in the leaves. Plant disease-resistant varieties and avoid working in the beans when they are wet to help prevent disease outbreaks.

Harvest & Best Selections—Popular snap beans include 'Blue Lake', 'Contender', and 'Kentucky Wonder'. Harvest snap beans when they are no thicker than a pencil to ensure that they are crisp and tender. 'Fordhook 242' is a popular lima bean, harvested when the seeds begin to fill the pods. Dry beans are allowed to mature on the plant, then harvested, and stored dry for use in soups and stews.

BEETS

Beta vulgaris

Why It's Special—Beets originated in the maritime regions of Europe, and gardeners hybridized them in Germany and England in the middle of the sixteenth century. People love beets both for their globe-shaped roots and their leafy tops. Beets are the main ingredients in borscht.

How to Plant & Grow—Because beets will stand a frost, you may sow them one month before the frost-free date (the average date of last frost). Beets need full sun and well-prepared loamy soil that is slightly alkaline (pH above 7). Good drainage is important, especially if you desire to start the plants early, so that the soil is dry enough to work.

Care & Problems—These plants require little care. Hoe or pull any weeds. If no rain falls for seven to ten days, apply 1 inch of water; beets that develop in dry weather will be fibrous and woody.

Harvest & Best Selections—Harvest tops when they are 6 inches high, and use them as you would use spinach. Harvest roots when they are 1½ to 2 inches in diameter. Beets allowed to grow more than 3 inches in diameter will be tough and woody. Dig late-season beets and store them in pits of sand or in boxes of sand in a cool place, such as a garage. Or store them in plastic bags with air holes. 'Detroit Dark Red' and 'Bull's Blood' are both popular varieties.

BROCCOLI

Brassica oleracea var. *italica*

Why It's Special—Although it has been cultivated for five thousand years, broccoli was developed from other cole crops as a specific crop quite late and has been popular in this country only since the 1930s. Grown for its compact cluster of flower buds, or head, this vegetable is picked before the flower buds begin to open. Secondary heads that develop in the leaf axils (between the bases of the leaves and the stem) can be harvested for several weeks after the central head is cut.

How to Plant & Grow—Broccoli loves cool weather and should be planted early and harvested before hot weather arrives. For the earliest production, start with transplants. Since broccoli will be harvested and out of the garden by midsummer, plan to replace it with a second crop. For a fall crop, set transplants in the garden between mid-August and early September. In mild fall weather, broccoli may last beyond Thanksgiving.

Care & Problems—Broccoli requires very little care. Water as necessary to keep the plants vigorous and growing. Cabbage looper larvae can be a problem, but are easily controlled by applying Sevin dust to the leaves.

Harvest & Best Selections—Harvest the heads with a sharp knife, leaving about 6 inches of stem attached, while they are still compact and before any of the flower buds open. Allow side shoots to develop for continuous production. 'Green Comet', 'Premium Crop', and 'Romanesque' are popular varieties.

BRUSSELS SPROUTS

Brassica oleracea var. *gemmifera*

Why It's Special—Named for the city in Belgium where they first attained popularity, Brussels sprouts have been grown there since the early 1300s. Brussels sprouts are grown for the cabbagelike buds that develop around the stems at the bases of the leaves.

How to Plant & Grow—This cool-weather crop takes a long time to mature and the best sprouts will be harvested in fall. Seeds started in midsummer can be transplanted to the garden in late August and harvested in November and December. Good garden centers will also carry transplants at the proper time for planting.

Care & Problems—With such a lengthy time to maturity, Brussels sprouts require careful attention. Apply sufficient water to keep the plants actively growing throughout the late summer. Sidedress the plants with a complete fertilizer when they are about 1 foot tall. Sprouts develop in the leaf axils starting at the bottom of the plant, and many growers remove the leaves a few at a time as the sprouts develop.

Harvest & Best Selections—Harvesting begins after the first frost. Pick or cut the sprouts when they are 1 to 1½ inches in diameter. There is no need to pick all the sprouts at one time; you can store them on the plants until needed. These very cold-hardy plants can last all winter when the weather is mild or there is sufficient snow to cover them. 'Jade Cross' is a popular variety.

CABBAGE

Brassica oleracea var. *capitata*

Why It's Special—Cabbage is one of the oldest recorded vegetables; it was mentioned in literature three thousand years ago and was in general use two thousand years ago throughout Europe and the Middle East.

How to Plant & Grow—This cool-weather plant produces best in spring. Transplants will be available at garden centers at the right time to plant and should have a good color, be short and compact, and have no pests. Since the cabbage will be harvested and out of the garden by midsummer, plan to replace it with a second crop, such as beans, that will thrive in summer weather.

Care & Problems—In rows, space the transplants 12 to 18 inches apart, with 24 inches between rows. In beds, space the plants 16 to 18 inches apart, which will allow two or three plants across the bed. Set the plants at the same depth they were growing. Water in the plants with transplant-starter fertilizer, such as 10-52-17 or 10-30-10, mixed according to directions on the label, and apply approximately 1 cup per plant. Water as necessary to keep plants growing vigorously and fertilize with a general-purpose 10-10-10 fertilizer when plants are about half-grown.

Harvest & Best Selections—When heads are full size, harvest by cutting just below them with a sharp knife. Remove and discard the plants once the heads are harvested. Popular varieties include 'Ruby Perfection', 'Savoy King', and 'Early Jersey Wakefield'.

CARROTS

Daucus carota var. *sativus*

Why It's Special—Ancient peoples probably cultivated carrots but not as a common food plant. They were originally used primarily for medicinal purposes. Carrots have managed to gain popularity since those early days, and most of the modern varieties come from those developed in France in the early 1800s.

How to Plant & Grow—Sow seeds as soon as the soil is workable in the spring; a freeze will not harm them. To provide a continuous supply of carrots, sow seeds every two to three weeks. To produce carrots in the fall, sow seeds in midsummer. These roots require deeply prepared, well-drained soil. The long varieties of carrots prefer sandy soils, and the shorter or half-long varieties produce the best quality in most Southern areas with heavy soils.

Care & Problems—A little hoeing or pulling of weeds, especially while the seedlings are small, will prevent weeds from competing with the carrots for water and nutrients. If no rain falls for seven to ten days, apply 1 inch of water. Carrots that develop in dry weather will be fibrous and woody.

Harvest & Best Selections—Harvest carrots when they are ½ to ¾ inch in diameter. Carrots left in the ground will continue to increase in size. Under normal conditions, expect a spring seeding to produce for three or four weeks. Summer seedings for fall crops may be left in the ground until a killing frost or even later if you mulch them to keep the ground from freezing.

CAULIFLOWER

Brassica oleracea var. *botrytis*

Why It's Special—Although it has been cultivated for five thousand years, cauliflower was developed from other cole crops quite late and has been popular in this country only since the 1930s. Cauliflower requires the best conditions and most care of all the members of the cabbage family.

How to Plant & Grow—Cauliflower is less tolerant of either heat or cold than its close relation broccoli, and will not grow as well in dry weather both spring and fall harvests. For the best success, use transplants instead of sowing seeds. Cauliflower prefers deeply prepared, well-drained soil; good drainage is essential. In rows, space the transplants about 18 inches apart, with 36 inches between rows.

Care & Problems—Cauliflower must grow vigorously from seeding to harvest. Water cauliflower as needed to provide 1 inch per week. When plants are about half-grown (8 to 12 inches tall), fertilize with nitrogen to stimulate continuing growth. Blanching is required for creamy white heads. When heads are about 3 inches in diameter, lift the leaves over the heads to shade them, and tie them with twine, rubber bands, or a couple of clothespins. Self-blanching varieties produce upright leaves that shade the heads and require no tying.

Harvest & Best Selections—Cut heads, leaving a few green leaves to protect them. Cauliflower deteriorates quickly after harvest, so use immediately or freeze. 'Snow Crown' and 'Self Blanch' are popular varieties.

CHARD

Beta vulgaris var. *cicla*

Why It's Special—Chard, or Swiss chard, is actually a beet that has been bred for leaves at the expense of the bulbous roots. Grown as a summer green, it is prepared like spinach. The attractive, colorful stalks of red and yellow also can be prepared and used like asparagus; they can be eaten raw or cooked.

How to Plant & Grow—Sow seeds directly in the garden or set out transplants at the frost-free date. A spring planting will produce all summer if it is kept picked. As soon as the seedlings are large enough to handle, thin them to 4 to 6 inches apart. If you wait until the seedlings are about 6 inches tall, you can cook the thinned seedlings as greens.

Care & Problems—Chard needs 1 inch of water per week to develop tender leaves. These plants are very susceptible to leafminer damage. Covering the planting with cheesecloth or commercial row covers is the only way to protect the plants. To help prevent diseases, do not go in the garden when leaves are wet in order to avoid spreading fungal spores from plant to plant.

Harvest & Best Selections—Harvest leaves when they are young and tender, about 12 inches long. Cut individual leaves 1 inch above the ground, being careful not to injure the remaining leaves. Or cut the entire bunch just below the ground. 'Bright Lights', 'Ruby', and 'Fordhook' are popular varieties.

COLLARDS

Brassica oleracea var. *acephala*

Why It's Special—A cool-season leafy vegetable, collards are a member of the cabbage family. Collards tolerate both warm and cold temperatures better than cabbage does. It is an important vegetable in traditional Southern cooking, where it is served as a leafy table green.

How to Plant & Grow—The best collards grow during the mild days and cool nights of autumn. Seeds can be sown directly in the garden in late summer, and with mild fall weather you can harvest collards until well after Thanksgiving. In the warmest parts of the Carolinas, collards will grow all winter long.

Care & Problems—These plants need adequate water, especially in hot weather, so you should provide 1 inch per week if rainfall is insufficient. Pests and diseases may affect the plantings. Prevent infestation of cabbage worms with *BtK* (*Bacillus thuringiensis* var. *kurstaki*) and use a copper-based fungicide to help prevent leaf spot diseases.

Harvest & Best Selections—Thin seedlings from a planting to about 6 inches apart and allow them to grow to 12 inches tall. Harvest them, leaving one plant every 18 inches. Allow these remaining plants to mature. Harvest collards either by cutting outer leaves as they reach full size or by cutting the entire plant at the soil line. 'HiCrop' and 'Champion Long Standing' are popular varieties. Some gardeners like to blanch the inner leaves by tying the outermost leaves together at the top of the plant.

CUCUMBER

Cucumis sativus

Why It's Special—Cucumbers are warm-season vine crops that are closely related to squashes, pumpkins, and melons. They are known for their refreshingly mild fruit. In the past twenty-five years, bush types have been developed that occupy less space and can even be grown in pots.

How to Plant & Grow—Cucumbers need warm weather to develop and may rot if the weather is cool and wet, so don't be in a hurry to plant them. Cucumbers resent root disturbance and will grow best when seeds are sown directly in the garden. Grow vining types on supports to save space and make harvesting easier; grow bush types in beds or containers.

Care & Problems—Water as needed to make sure plants get about 1 inch of water per week. Cucumber beetles are serious threats that not only eat the plants but also infect them with bacterial wilt that will kill them at about the time they begin to produce fruit. As soon as seeds germinate in the garden, apply Sevin insecticide or use row covers over the plants, being sure to tuck in the edges and ends to keep the beetles out. Remove the covers when the plants begin to vine.

Harvest & Best Selections—Harvest cucumbers when they reach a mature size. Standard cucumbers are 6 to 8 inches long. Burpless types are up to 1 foot long and pickling types are 2 to 6 inches long at maturity.

EGGPLANT

Solanum melongena var. esculentum

Why It's Special—Eggplant is a member of the same family as tomatoes, potatoes, and peppers. The cultivation of eggplants is very similar to that of bell peppers. Neither plant requires support, although eggplants are bigger than peppers. Both of these warm-weather crops thrive where the summer is long and hot, making them perfect for the Carolinas.

How to Plant & Grow—Eggplants are much more sensitive to cold than tomatoes are. They need warm weather to develop and may rot off when the weather is cool and wet. Transplants are the easiest way to start and can be planted out around May 1. Earlier planting is possible in the warmest areas of the Carolinas.

Care & Problems—After they are established, eggplants can stand dry weather. For best production, however, water them as needed to provide at least 1 inch per week. When the plants are half-grown (about 12 inches high), sidedress them with a high-nitrogen fertilizer. Flea beetles will make small holes in the leaves, and a severe infestation can reduce yield; control the pests with Sevin insecticide.

Harvest & Best Selections—Harvest the fruit when it reaches full size and is still glossy. Overly mature fruit will be spongy, seedy, and bitter. Cut the stem with shears or a sharp knife instead of trying to tear the fruit off. Watch out! The stems may be thorny. 'Black Beauty' and 'Rosa Bianca' are two of the best varieties.

GARLIC

Allium sativum

Why It's Special—Garlic is a hardy perennial bulb that consists of a cluster of small bulblets called cloves or toes, covered in a papery wrapper. Garlic is used primarily as a flavoring in European and Asian dishes. Roasted garlic, which loses much of its pungency, is a tasty appetizer, especially with Italian or Greek cuisine.

How to Plant & Grow—Plant garlic in autumn to harvest the following summer. Garlic prefers a location in full sun with well-prepared, well-drained soil. Planting in compacted soil will result in small, misshapen bulbs. Start garlic from cloves that you have separated from bulbs. Plant individual cloves 2 inches deep and 4 inches apart in rows 1 foot apart.

Care & Problems—Make sure garlic has plenty of water if the weather turns dry; it requires about 1 inch of water per week. Keeping weeds under control is an ongoing task. Since garlic does not provide complete cover, weeds will germinate all season. If thrips become troublesome, treat them with insecticidal soap.

Harvest & Best Selections—Garlic begins to bulb when the days are longest in June. The larger the plants are at that time, the larger the bulbs will be, so it is important to keep the plants growing. Harvest the garlic as soon as most of the leaves have turned yellow, usually in midsummer. There are many varieties of garlic. Try several to experience the wide range of types and flavors.

HOT PEPPER

Capsicum spp. and hybrids

Why It's Special—Hot peppers are the special ingredients in foods from many cultures that impart smoky flavor and heat. Be aware that some that the oils in some hot peppers are so volatile that they can burn tender skin around the mouth and eyes, so use some caution when harvesting and working with the fruit.

How to Plant & Grow—Peppers are warm-weather plants. There is no sense getting them in the garden before the soils warm up because the plants will just sit there. Plant peppers in a well-drained part of the garden that receives full sun. Remove the plants from the containers, and set the plants at the same depth they grew at in the containers. Firm the soil gently around each plant, and water in with 1 cup of transplant-starter fertilizer mixed according to directions on the package.

Care & Problems—Use insecticidal soap to combat aphids and mites; apply Sevin to cope with caterpillars and beetles.

Harvest & Best Selections—Hot peppers can be harvested green or allowed to ripen and turn color. After ripening, the flavors improve and the amount of heat may change, depending on the variety. Cutting the peppers with a sharp knife or shears is a better method than pulling them off, which may break the plants. 'Ancho', 'Habanero', 'Hungarian Wax', and 'Tam Jalapeno' are all popular selections with varying degrees of heat.

LEEK

Allium ampeloprasum

Why It's Special—Leeks are relatives of onions and chives. They have a milder, smoother flavor than onions, whose sharp, pungent taste many people find objectionable. The edible portion is the cylindrical base of the leaves instead of the bulb, unlike an onion. Native to the Mediterranean, leeks have been cultivated since prehistoric times.

How to Plant & Grow—For the earliest production, start with transplants purchased in early spring. Leeks require deeply prepared, thoroughly amended, well-drained soil and usually require one hundred or more days to mature. Spade or rototill the soil to a depth of at least 6 inches, more if possible. In rows, space transplants 4 inches apart, with 12 to 18 inches between rows.

Care & Problems—As the plants begin to grow, blanch the lower parts of the stems. Cultivate lightly, hilling soil up on the plants. Be careful not to bury the plants too deeply or too soon, or they will rot. When the plants approach full size, bank them with several inches of soil.

Harvest & Best Selections—Harvest leeks when the bases of the stems are about 1 inch in diameter. Dig only what you need because the plants store well in the ground and continue to increase in size. 'Alaska', 'Broad London', and 'Titan' are popular varieties.

LETTUCE

Lactuca sativa

Why It's Special—No other salad crop is grown or used in such large quantities as lettuce. This cool-weather crop that can be grown in spring or fall. Hot weather causes it to become bitter and to develop a tall seed stalk.

How to Plant & Grow—Sow seeds of leaf lettuce varieties directly in the garden as early as the soil can be worked. Since the lettuce will be harvested and out of the garden by midsummer, plan to replace it with a second crop. Bibb or head lettuces can be started from transplants purchased at the garden center in early spring.

Care & Problems—Excellent drainage is beneficial, because these plants need lots of water for vigorous growth but resent being in waterlogged soil. To keep the plants growing, water them as needed, about 1 inch of water per week. Control weeds while the plants are small by careful hoeing or pulling. Be careful; lettuce plants are shallowly rooted and easily uprooted.

Harvest & Best Selections—Harvest leaf lettuce by snipping off the outer leaves as soon as they are large enough for your use. When plants are large enough, harvest every other one, leaving more room for the others. Harvest head, Bibb, and romaine lettuce when the heads are full size. 'Butter Crunch' and 'Black-Seeded Simpson' are two of the most popular and easily grown varieties.

MUSKMELON

Cucumis melo var. *reticulatus*

Why It's Special—Muskmelons are vine crops, closely related to cucumbers, squashes, and pumpkins. These hot-weather plants with sweet, juicy fruit are commonly called cantaloupes. Like most vine crops, muskmelons can occupy a lot of room. One way to use less space is to grow them on trellises.

How to Plant & Grow—Don't be in a hurry to get muskmelons into the garden early. They need warm soil to develop and may rot if weather is cool and wet. Sow seeds 1 inch deep in hills about 36 inches apart. Muskmelon resents transplanting and grows best if sown directly in the garden where you want it to grow.

Care & Problems—As soon as muskmelon seedlings are planted in the garden, protect them from cucumber beetles. Cucumber beetles not only eat the plants but also infect them with bacterial wilt that will kill them at about the time they begin to produce fruit. Apply Sevin insecticide, or use row covers on the plants, being sure to tuck in the edges and ends, to keep the beetles out.

Harvest & Best Selections—For the best quality and sweetness, harvest melons when they are ripe. The rind will change from green to tan between the netting, and a ripe melon will smell sweet. Muskmelons do not continue to ripen once they are picked. They will become softer, but not sweeter. 'Jenny Lind' and 'Honeybush' are both tried-and-true varieties.

OKRA

Abelmoschus esculentus

Why It's Special—Okra is a relative of hollyhock and hibiscus. Gardeners grow it for the immature fruit pods, or seedpods, that they use to thicken soups and stews and to cook as vegetables. Okra is what makes gumbo . . . gumbo!

How to Plant & Grow—A warm-weather crop, okra should be planted after soil is warm to the touch. There is no need to get an early start because seeds will not germinate in cool soils. Sow seed directly in the garden a week or so after the last frost date. Stagger two to three sowings about two weeks apart to harvest well into fall.

Care & Problems—Okra needs little care to produce a good crop. Provide 1 inch of water per week, and remove the weeds by hoeing or pulling. Grasshoppers may nibble the foliage, but are generally not destructive.

Harvest & Best Selections—Harvest the pods when they are about 3 inches long and still tender. Use a knife or shears, and cut them every two days so they won't become woody. Okra plants have irritating hairs that cause some people to break out in a rash, so wear gloves and long sleeves when working with them. Be sure to remove any overripe pods to stimulate continuing production. The plants will produce until damaged by the cold. Popular selections include 'Clemson Spineless', 'Dwarf Green Longpod', and 'Burgundy'.

ONION

Allium cepa

Why It's Special—Gardeners grow these members of the lily family for the immature green bunching onions, often called scallions, or for the mature dry bulbs. Onions seem to have originated in the eastern Mediterranean from Palestine to India and are so easy to grow and so useful in the kitchen that they should be part of every garden.

How to Plant & Grow—Onions are completely hardy; put them out as soon as the soil can be worked in spring. Start them from seeds sown directly in the garden, from seedling transplants, or from onion sets. For transplants and sets, place plants about 2 inches deep. Sow seeds according to packet instructions.

Care & Problems—Onions are shallowly rooted, so be careful as you hoe or pull weeds. Try to get as much top growth as possible by the first day of summer. Bulbs begin to form when the days reach about fifteen hours in length, and the size of the dry onions is determined by the size of the tops.

Harvest & Best Selections—Harvest green onions when the stems are pencil sized. Pull any dry onions that form flower stalks, and use them immediately because they will not store well as dry onions. As tops begin to yellow in midsummer, allow the plants to die completely down before harvesting. 'Sweet Spanish' and 'White Portugal' are two of the most popular varieties.

PEAS

Pisum sativum var. *sativum* (English, Garden, and Snap)

Pisum sativum var. *macrocarpon* (Sugar, Snow, and Bush)

Why It's Special—Peas are decidedly cool-weather plants, intolerant of hot weather. As soon as the weather warms up, production ceases, much to the dismay of many pea-loving gardeners. Peas lose their flavor quickly after harvest and are a good choice for growing in the home garden to get the absolute best quality.

How to Plant & Grow—Sow seeds in the garden as soon as the soil can be worked in spring. In the South, planting between Valentine's Day and St. Patrick's Day is common. The seeds germinate when the soil temperature reaches about 45 degrees F. By preparing the soil in the fall, you can sow the seeds at the earliest opportunity in the spring without having to wait to till the soil. To produce a fall crop, sow in early fall and harvest during the cool weather of late fall and early winter.

Care & Problems—Bush peas are self-supporting. Placing vining types on a support of some kind conserves space, makes picking easier, and keeps the peas from getting muddy every time it rains.

Harvest & Best Selections—Harvest English or garden peas (*P. sativum* var. *sativum*) when they are full-size and before the seeds begin to dry. Pods should be green. Harvest snap peas (*P. sativum* var. *sativum*) when the pods are full-size for the variety and before the seeds are mature. Harvest sugar peas (*P. sativum* var. *macrocarpon*) when the pods are fully formed, but before the seeds begin to develop.

POTATO

Solanum tuberosum

Why It's Special—The potato ranks with rice and wheat as one of the world's leading food crops and is grown in nearly every country of the world. Potatoes originated in the high country of South America and were cultivated by the Incas.

How to Plant & Grow—Potatoes are started from seed pieces, not from actual seeds. The seed pieces should be 1½- to 2-ounce sections of tuber; this size gives the sprouts enough energy for a good start. Plant them 2 to 3 inches deep with the eyes up, and cover them gently to avoid breaking off any sprouts. Do not try to grow plants from store-bought potatoes, which have been treated with sprouting inhibitors.

Care & Problems—When sprouts are 6 inches high, begin hilling soil around them, being careful not to dig too deeply and injure roots. The hills eventually should be about 6 inches high and 1 foot wide. Hilling keeps the potatoes covered, loosens and aerates the soil, and eliminates weeds.

Harvest & Best Selections—Harvest new potatoes about ten weeks after planting. When the first flowers on the potatoes appear, small tubers are usually ready. When vines begin to yellow, mature potatoes are ready to harvest. Carefully lift them with a fork or spade. Spread the potatoes on the ground for a couple of hours to dry off before collecting them. Do not wash them or they will not keep.

PUMPKIN
Cucurbita pepo

Why It's Special—Pumpkins are much-loved decorations for the fall, but many people grow these warm-season vine crops for their flavorful flesh and for their seeds too. Actually, pumpkins are winter squashes, picked when they are fully colored and mature.

How to Plant & Grow—There is no need to get pumpkins into the garden very early. They need warm weather to develop and may rot off if the weather is cool and wet. Pumpkins prefer full sun and need a location with well-drained soil. Expect the pumpkins to make huge vines and allow them plenty of room to spread.

Care & Problems—After they set fruit, pumpkins need lots of water and fertilizer. Apply 1 inch of water per week when nature does not cooperate. Sidedress with nitrogen at half the normal rate when the vines have almost covered the ground, being careful to rinse with a hose if fertilizer gets on the leaves. All squashes are susceptible to attacks by squash vine borers, which are the larvae of red bee-like moths that lay eggs on the bases of the plants. Control these insects by applying Sevin insecticide to the stems of the plants every two weeks during the season.

Harvest & Best Selections—Harvest pumpkins when they have developed full color (no green on them). Cut the handles 3 to 4 inches long, using shears to avoid breaking them. 'Howden', 'Connecticut Field', and 'Jack-Be-Little' are proven performers.

RADISH
Raphanus sativus

Why It's Special—Radishes are fast-growing, cool-weather vegetables. They grow any place they can have some sun and moist, fertile soil. They do well in gardens, pots, planters, flower beds, and cold frames. Some people grow them in boxes of sand on high-rise balconies. Fresh radishes make tasty garnishes, hors d'oeuvres, or additions to salads.

How to Plant & Grow—Sow seeds as soon as the soil is dry enough to work for a spring crop. The soil is ready when you can squeeze a handful into a ball and it crumbles. Sow seeds in late summer or fall for a fall or winter crop. Sow seeds thinly and cover very lightly, keeping moist until they germinate. Thin seedlings to 2 to 3 inches apart as plants mature.

Care & Problems—Radishes are not labor-intensive plants. Hoe or pull the weeds, especially while the seedlings are small, so they don't compete with the radishes for water and nutrients. Keep the plants growing because radishes that develop slowly will be hot and pithy (soft and mealy).

Harvest & Best Selections—Harvest spring radishes at about 1 inch in size and winter radishes at 3 inches. Radishes stop developing in hot weather and send up seed stalks. Radishes come in both round and long forms. Popular round varieties include 'Cherry Belle', 'Easter Egg', and 'Early Scarlet Globe'. Long varieties are 'French Breakfast' and 'Icicle'.

SPINACH
Spinacia oleracea

Why It's Special—Spinach is probably native to southwest Asia. Gardeners have cultivated it for centuries as a salad green and cooked vegetable. Even though many youngsters are dissuaded by early experiences with boiled spinach, most adults eventually appreciate its versatility in such treats as salads, quiches, pizzas, crepes, and omelets. Spinach is a cool-weather crop that can produce in spring or fall.

How to Plant & Grow—Sow seeds in the garden as early as the soil can be worked. Spinach must be planted early and harvested before hot weather arrives. In hot weather, spinach bolts (sends up a seed stalks) and the quality quickly deteriorates. Unless you want lots of spinach at one time, however, make several seedings to spread out the harvest.

Care & Problems—Keep the plants actively growing by watering as needed to provide about 1 inch per week. Spinach plants are shallowly rooted and easily uprooted, so weed by careful hoeing or pulling while the plants are small. Pests and diseases may affect plantings. Control aphids with insecticidal soap.

Harvest & Best Selections—Harvest spinach by snipping off outer leaves as soon as they are large enough to use. When plants are large enough to harvest, cut every other one, leaving more room for the others. As soon as the plants begin to bolt, harvest all that remain before they are spoiled. 'Bloomsdale' is still the standard against which all other spinach is judged.

SQUASH

Cucurbita spp.

Why It's Special—Squashes are warm-season vine crops with flavorful flesh. The many types are divided into summer squash, grown for the immature fruit; and winter squash, which is harvested mature. Squash can take a lot of room, so be prepared. Summer squash are often more compact plants and better suited to smaller gardens.

How to Plant & Grow—Don't hurry to get squash into the garden very early. The plants need warm weather to develop and may rot off if weather is cool and wet. Sow seeds directly in the garden where you want them to grow, as they resent transplanting, and thin hills to the three strongest seedlings once the first true leaves appear.

Care & Problems—After setting fruit, apply 1 inch of water per week if nature does not cooperate. Fertilize with nitrogen when the vines have almost covered the ground, but be sure to rinse the fertilizer off the leaves. All squash are susceptible to attack by squash vine borers. Control these insects by applying Sevin insecticide to the stems when the plants begin to vine and then every two weeks during the season. Squash, especially summer squash, can be decimated by powdery mildew and/or squash bugs.

Harvest & Best Selections—Harvest summer squash while they are still immature for immediate use, and winter squash after they have completely matured for fall and winter storage. 'Yellow Crookneck' and 'Pattypan' are popular summer squash. Winter varieties include 'Butternut', 'Acorn', and 'Hubbard'.

SWEET CORN

Zea mays var. *rugosa*

Why It's Special—Who can resist a steaming-hot ear of corn on the cob? Sweet corn was developed from common field corn, which is harvested after it has matured and is used for innumerable products. Sweet corn is harvested before it matures, while it is tender and the sugar content is at its highest.

How to Plant & Grow—Begin planting once the soil feels warm to the touch. Make additional plantings until the first week of July if you desire. Sweet corn needs full sun, good drainage, and lots of room. Sow seeds ½ inch deep in cool soils or 1½ inches deep in warm soils. Space the seeds 9 inches apart in the rows, with 24 to 36 inches between rows. Plant two or more rows of each variety side by side to ensure good pollination.

Care & Problems—Water is important as the plants are tasseling and making silk. Pollination takes place then and will be poor if the plants are wilted. Kernel development takes water too. Once the silks begin to dry, be sure to keep the plants from wilting by providing about 1 inch of water per week. Flooding or soaking the rows is the easiest method of watering.

Harvest & Best Selections—Harvest sweet corn as soon as the ears are filled out and the kernels are milky inside, usually about sixteen days after silks appear. 'Silver Queen' is a popular variety. Explore supersweet varieties too.

SWEET PEPPER

Capsicum annuum

Why It's Special—Peppers are available in so many types and varieties that most gardeners stick to a few types that they use in cooking. The most familiar peppers are the bells: green-red, yellow, purple-lilac, and orange. These are mild and can be used as green peppers or allowed to ripen.

How to Plant & Grow—Peppers are warm-weather plants. Don't bother planting them before the soil warms up because they will just sit there. Plant peppers in a well-drained location that receives full sun. Remove the plants from the containers, and set the plants at the same depth they grew at in the containers. Firm the soil gently around each plant, and water in with 1 cup of transplant-starter fertilizer mixed according to directions on the package.

Care & Problems—To prevent sun scald, space peppers so that plants just touch when mature. The foliage from one plant will shade the peppers on neighboring plants. Reduce bacterial speck by soaking the soil at the base of the plants with soaker hoses or a slow trickle of water to avoid splashing water onto the fruit as it develops. Caused by cold or wet weather, not disease, blossom-end rot appears as a leathery brown spot on a pepper. Control aphids and mites with insecticidal soap and caterpillars and beetles with Sevin.

Harvest & Best Selections—Bell peppers can be harvested green or allowed to ripen and turn color. After ripening, the flavors improve. Cutting the peppers with a sharp knife or shears is a better method than pulling them off, which may break the plants. 'California Wonder' is still one of the best.

TOMATO

Lycopersicon lycopersicum

Why It's Special—Tomatoes are unquestionably the most popular garden vegetable in the United States. The flavor of a newly picked red tomato from your garden is second to none.

How to Plant & Grow—Tomatoes are tender plants that should not be planted out until all danger of frost has passed and the soil is warm to the touch. Plants may rot in cold soil or be hit by a late frost if planted too early in the season. Full sun and rich, well-prepared soil will give you vigorous growth and large quantities of tomatoes. Feed monthly with tomato fertilizer.

Care & Problems—Sturdy cages can easily be made from concrete reinforcing wire and will support plants throughout the season. Plants can also be staked, but this is much more labor intensive, as continuous "tying in" is required to keep the plants from sprawling on the ground and the fruit from rotting. Plant disease-resistant varieties to eliminate verticillium and fusarium wilts, and yellows. Control foliar diseases with maneb fungicide. Use insecticidal soap on aphids and mites; apply Sevin to take care of caterpillars and beetles.

Harvest & Best Selections—Selecting varieties to grow in your garden can be challenging. Tomatoes are offered in a wide range of sizes, shapes, colors, growth habits, and maturity dates. Garden centers carry varieties that are best suited to your area. 'Better Boy', 'Burpee's Big Boy', and 'Beefsteak' are time-tested winners in most climates.

WATERMELON

Citrullus lanatus

Why It's Special—Summertime celebrations would be incomplete without watermelons. Children of all ages love the sweet, juicy fruit of these hot-weather plants. As is the case with other summer melons, watermelons need a long, hot season to develop. If you are reluctant to plant them because your garden has restricted space, look for smaller-growing bush types.

How to Plant & Grow—Do not plant watermelons too early because they cannot stand a frost. They need warm soil to develop and may rot off if weather is cool and wet. It is best to sow watermelon seeds directly in the garden where you want them to grow. Seedlings resent disturbance once they have germinated.

Care & Problems—Cucumber beetles can damage the leaves and scar the stems. Apply Sevin insecticide to eliminate the beetles, or cover the plants with cloth row covers. When flowers appear, remove the covers so that bees may pollinate them.

Harvest & Best Selections—The most reliable way to check for ripeness is to look at the color of the bottom where the melon is lying on the ground: it should be a good yellow color. The little curlicue where the melon attaches to the stem dries up as the melon ripens. The skin becomes dull looking, rough, and so hard that you cannot cut into it with your fingernail. Popular varieties include 'Sugar Baby', 'Crimson Sweet', and 'Charleston Grey'.

ZUCCHINI

Cucurbita spp.

Why It's Special—Zucchini is one of the most prolific of all of the summer squash. A few hills will produce more than enough for a family of four and most of their friends and neighbors! Zucchini also makes a great choice for a child's garden because it is easy to grow, easy to harvest, and an almost guaranteed success.

How to Plant & Grow—Like all squash, zucchini likes it warm. Don't get in a hurry to plant your zucchini in the spring. Wait until the soil is comfortably warm to the touch. The easiest way to plant is to create a low mound (hill) and then plant three to five seeds about 6 inches apart in the top of the mound. Allow at least 5 feet of space per hill at maturity.

Care & Problems—Zucchini requires plenty of water while it is actively growing. Squash beetles can be a problem, as they can on all squash, and can be controlled with applications of Sevin every two weeks from the time the seeds germinate. Plants that suddenly collapse should be removed immediately to keep wilt diseases from passing from plant to plant.

Harvest & Best Selections—A common mistake is to leave zucchini on the vine too long. Harvest when they are 6 to 8 inches long and not more than 1½ to 2 inches in diameter. This will keep the vines producing throughout the summer.

BASIL

Ocimum basilicum

Why It's Special—Common sweet basil, the most popular culinary herb, is a vigorous annual with bright green, wrinkled leaves. Fresh basil is wonderful in Italian dishes, pesto, soups, and sauces. Several varieties are available, including lemon, cinnamon, licorice, and purple. All are easy to grow.

How to Plant & Grow—Basil loves the heat and will struggle in cold, damp soils. Be sure to wait until soil is warm to the touch before planting out. One to three plants will supply all the fresh basil needed by a small family, so most gardeners buy potted plants and set them out in sunny garden beds or containers. Site basil in well-drained soil to avoid stem, crown, and root diseases.

Care & Problems—Basil needs plenty of water at the beginning of summer when plants are developing rapidly. Irrigate at least twice a week; more if the basil is in containers. Do not allow the soil to become dry. Broadcast a granular flower fertilizer around plants when they are knee high. Snip off developing flowers weekly to stimulate new foliage.

Harvest & Best Selections—Harvest the tender young leaves with a quick snip of the scissors, and the plant will send out new growth at the cut points. Basils are frost-tender annuals; harvest the entire plant before the first killing frost. Freeze the tip growth and dry the older leaves. 'Genovese', 'Lettuce Leaf', and 'Purple Ruffles' are popular varieties.

CHIVES

Allium schoenoprasum

Why It's Special—Garden chives grow in bunches like slender scallions. Flowering stems topped with pink blossoms shoot up in April and last for about a month. In the kitchen, chives are used for their very mild onion flavor. The blooms can also be eaten. Chives are perennial and will return for many years.

How to Plant & Grow—Provide at least a half-day of sunlight and well-drained soil. Chives can tolerate a variety of soils and various moisture levels, but perform best in moderately moist garden sites that are high in organic matter. Set plants in holes twice the size of the rootball. Water well to settle the soil.

Care & Problems—Plants should dry slightly between waterings. The first year, water at least once every two weeks during spring and fall, more often during drought. Water outdoor container plants every third day. Chives do not need much fertilizer if they are planted in good soil.
A water-soluble transplant-starter fertilizer can be used every four weeks if you just want the foliage for cutting. There are no pests that bother chives.

Harvest & Best Selections—Chives are easily harvested by snipping the leaves about an inch from the base of the plant, as needed. Harvest a few entire leaves rather than just snipping the tips. The plants will look nicer and will continue producing fresh new leaves throughout the season.

CILANTRO/ CORIANDER

Coriandrum sativum

Why It's Special—When you plant coriander seeds, cilantro comes up. Coriander is the name given the dried seeds—cilantro describes the green leaves. The surging interest in Mexican and Asian cuisine has focused interest on fresh cilantro. Cilantro looks a lot like flat-leaf parsley but has a strong, distinctive flavor.

How to Plant & Grow—Cilantro can withstand light frosts and, in the Carolinas, it grows best when direct seeded in early spring and again in late summer for a fall and winter crop. During summer months, sow seeds of coriander every three weeks; harvest the seedlings, roots and all, and use the entire plant in guacamole, salsa, soups, and ceviche. An August sowing will give you plants that can be harvested well into fall.

Care & Problems—With cilantro genetically programmed to go to seed quickly during summer, you need fertile soil and abundant water for fast growth. Cilantro prefers weekly watering, twice weekly in extreme heat. Fertilize with 20-20-20 water-soluble fertilizer every two weeks to encourage vigorous vegetative growth.

Harvest & Best Selections—Harvest cilantro as often as needed. When cilantro is abundant, purée with a small amount of water and freeze in mini ice cube trays for near-fresh flavor. Coriander seeds can be gathered, toasted lightly, and stored in jars. If you are growing the plant for foliage, trim the lengthening seed stalks to delay seed production. If you want seeds, let the plants bloom.

DILL

Anethum graveolens

Why It's Special—Dill is a rather tender annual that grows best during short spring or fall days. During long summer days, you need to direct seed dill every three weeks to keep a supply of fresh foliage coming. Dill can be chopped and added to potato salad, sprinkled over green salads, or added to pickles.

How to Plant & Grow—Dill grows rapidly from seeds sown in the garden two weeks before the last spring frost date. Germinate dill seeds by planting them in shallow furrows and covering with ½ inch of play sand. Late summer is best for producing plants to transplant during cool, moist fall weather, but early spring sowings are also very successful. Be sure to plant enough for your needs and those of swallowtail butterflies that feed on the foliage of dill; they are a welcome addition to the garden.

Care & Problems—Dill does not require mulching, but a light layer of mulch will help to conserve soil moisture and keep weeds at bay. It can be fertilized with cottonseed meal or bloodmeal to promote lush foliage growth. Water dill weekly during dry weather.

Harvest & Best Selections—Drying the foliage of dill isn't worth the effort; instead, chop or puree it with a small amount of water and freeze it in mini ice cube trays to preserve its fresh flavor. Fresh stems of dill are also used in summer pickle making.

ENGLISH LAVENDER

Lavandula angustifolia

Why It's Special—Lavender has been called the Queen of the Scented Garden and has been a major player in the perfume and soap industry for decades. Horticulturists recognize this wonderful herb as a durable landscape ornamental. It has fine-textured foliage that can be a dull green or a pleasant silver-gray, with spikes of lavender-colored flowers that are the iconic image of southern France.

How to Plant & Grow—Lavender thrives in full sun and alkaline soil. Incorporate limestone thoroughly into the planting bed at the rate of 1 pound per 10 square feet. Spread the roots horizontally to ensure that the plant is set high—or plant lavender in a raised bed, container, or berm. Good drainage is essential for its success.

Care & Problems—Water twice weekly the first month, then only in dry weather as needed to promote healthy growth. Fertilizing should be avoided, as it can cause the plants to produce weak, floppy growth. Shear lavender in early spring to clean up the plant. Trim off foliage burned from winter exposure by pruning the tips of stems by 2 to 3 inches. On clay soils, the best mulch for lavender is a 1-inch layer of white sand that reflects light and heat. There are no special problems that require routine care.

Harvest & Best Selections—If you want to cut the spikes for drying, harvest when the flower buds are just beginning to open. 'Provence' and 'Grosso' are two varieties that perform well in the Carolinas.

FENNEL

Foeniculum vulgare

Why It's Special—Fennel, with its bronzy green color and fernlike texture, is a welcome addition to the herb garden. This licorice-flavored herb can be used sparingly in certain dishes and is especially good when combined with pot roast and other beef dishes.

How to Plant & Grow—Fennel is much more heat tolerant than its cousin dill, and it will thrive during the summer months in the Carolinas. Sow seeds in early spring or set out transplants when you find them in the garden centers. Plants can reach 4 feet tall by the time they flower and are loved by the black swallowtail butterfly as a host plant for its larvae. Instead of drying fennel, purée the fresh leaves with a small amount of water and freeze in mini ice cube trays for summer-fresh flavor.

Care & Problems—Fennel is one of the most care-free herbs. A plant or two will provide more than enough leaves both for you and the caterpillars. Full sun and good drainage are its only real requirements, and in most areas of the Carolinas, it will be a reliable perennial. It will also reseed itself around the garden.

Harvest & Best Selections—Fennel comes in both green- and bronze-leaf forms. Both have the same scent and flavor with distinct licorice overtones. The bronze form is particularly attractive and ornamental. Snip young leaves for use in salads or meat dishes.

FRENCH TARRAGON

Artemisia dracunculus var. *sativa*

Why It's Special—Anise-scented French tarragon is essential for béarnaise sauce, tasty green beans, fish, and herbal oils and vinegars. It's not at all aggressive by nature, and its 2-inch-long, narrow, grayish green leaves are reminiscent of dianthus foliage. It is a slow-growing perennial that spreads by underground rhizomes. Gardeners in the hottest and most humid parts of the Carolinas may find it challenging to bring tarragon through the summer, but it will grow well during the cooler months of the year.

How to Plant & Grow—Set out potted plants during cooler months, from October to May. Divide in spring, or take stem or root cuttings in fall or spring. Plant French tarragon in full sun or afternoon shade in rich, well-drained soil. It does not take the heat well, so protection from the afternoon sun will increase its life expectancy.

Care & Problems—In the western Carolinas, French tarragon can freeze to the ground, but don't worry; it is quite winter hardy. However, on new fall plantings, mulch with pine straw to prevent heaving. Shear heavily in early spring to remove cold injury and to rejuvenate the plants. In Zone 8 gardens, Mexican mint marigold (*Tagetes lucida*) may be used as a substitute for French tarragon, but professional chefs decry its lack of "bite."

Harvest & Best Selections—Harvest young, tender new growth as needed for inclusion in béarnaise sauces, fish dishes, and green beans.

LEMON BALM

Melissa officinalis

Why It's Special—Lemon balm is a lemon-scented member of the mint family, but unlike spearmint or peppermint, it doesn't produce rampant rhizomes that take over azalea beds and threaten flowers. Watch it, however, because plants can spread from abundant seed crops. Lemon balm is perennial across the Carolinas but may be short-lived in coastal heat.

How to Plant & Grow—Lemon balm is easy to grow from seeds sown in spring or early fall, but pot-grown plants and root divisions are faster and easier. Moist, fertile soil is best, but lemon balm will grow fairly well in poor, dry soil. It thrives in full sun or dappled shade, but plants grown in shade will be larger and more succulent than those grown in direct light.

Care & Problems—Water seedlings daily and newly planted lemon balm plants twice a week until they are 6 to 10 inches tall. Established plants of lemon balm are drought tolerant and need very little care. Lemon balm self-sows freely and may become a weed in mild regions. Remove and dispose of any terminal growth that appears to be flowering in order to keep seedlings from taking over the garden.

Harvest & Best Selections—Use lemon balm fresh, frozen, or preserved in oil, wine, or vinegar to impart a fresh, lemony flavor to various dishes. There are few cultivars of lemon balm, but the variety 'Aurea' has beautiful golden yellow foliage.

MINT

Mentha spp.

Why It's Special—Spearmint is one of the most popular culinary species within the great mint family, with peppermint a distant second. Garden centers and catalogs offer scores of fancifully named cultivars. Confine mints in pots. Anyone can succeed with these aromatic, flavorful plants, but any one of them could run wild in garden soil and become a troublesome weed.

How to Plant & Grow—Mints are seldom grown from seed because seedlings can vary greatly in flavor and aroma. Set out potted plants in early spring or fall. Mints love damp areas, but certain species can survive in dry spots as well. Given plenty of water, mints will thrive in full sun, but they do better in afternoon shade. Five-gallon nursery containers work very well for growing mints and keeping them contained.

Care & Problems—Thin plants occasionally to prevent leaf diseases. Use a strong spray of water or botanical insecticide to remove aphids.

Harvest & Best Selections—Trim mints as needed for teas and culinary uses throughout the growing season. Just snip the stems with pruning shears or scissors, making a cut just above a leaf node. Cut back after a hard freeze and mulch lightly. Try chopping fresh sprigs to make "mint cubes" in mini ice cube trays for use in summer beverages. Flowering spikes of mint make good garnishes for fancy meals. 'Kentucky Colonel' is a favorite cultivar and is the number-one choice for mint juleps.

OREGANO

Origanum vulgare

Why It's Special—Two major culinary types of oregano are Italian and Greek. Italian oregano is preferred by most chefs. It has white flowers on erect plants and is not winter hardy in Zone 7. Greek oregano has purple flowers on spreading plants and is quite hardy. Oregano is easy to grow and can be used in many cooked dishes.

How to Plant & Grow—Plant potted oregano in spring and summer in full sun or afternoon shade. When setting out container-grown plants, remove a plant from the pot, loosen the roots a bit, and place the rootball at its original depth. Firm in the backfill and water thoroughly. Water weekly for the first month. Soil fertility and water needs are minimal, although some irrigation is recommended during a drought. Apply organic fertilizer in spring to invigorate established plantings.

Care & Problems—Replant Italian oregano each spring, as it rarely winters over. Divide old plants of Greek oregano or replace with newer plants. Once plants are established, fresh sprigs can be harvested at will. Harvest before flowers appear. To enhance production of green shoots, shear off the flowers.

Harvest & Best Selections—When the plant matures, stems can be cut near the soil level, bundled, and hung up to dry in a dark, airy place. Store the dry leaves intact until shortly before use, then rub the leaves through a fine screen to ready them for seasoning cooked dishes.

PARSLEY

Petroselinum crispum

Why It's Special—This bright green, biennial herb comes in several varieties, some with curly leaves, some with flat, or "plain," leaves. The flat-leaf variety is favored by many chefs because it retains its flavor longer in cooked dishes. Parsley is popular in Mediterranean cuisine and is used as a garnish to decorate dinner plates, salads, and cold meats. Parsley is a member of the same family as dill and fennel and, like them, attracts caterpillars of swallowtail butterflies.

How to Plant & Grow—Transplant potted plants from the nursery anytime during the growing season. Sow seeds outdoors in late February, or start indoors in late winter. Plant parsley in full sun and in fertile, well-drained soil. When setting out a potted plant, loosen the rootball carefully and place it in a hole that's a little larger than the ball. Cover the roots with soil and water well.

Care & Problems—No pruning is necessary other than the harvesting of fresh sprigs. Snip the outer stems with scissors, but don't cut the central bud. Handpick caterpillars if you don't want them to decimate the plant in a few short days. Remember, this herb will die naturally after it flowers.

Harvest & Best Selections—Both flat-leaf and curly-leaf varieties are popular in the garden. Well-grown plants will provide enough leaves for both you and the swallowtail caterpillars to which the plant plays host. Harvest by simply snipping leaves as needed.

ROSEMARY

Rosmarinus officinalis

Why It's Special—In the Carolinas, we are able to grow rosemary to a great size. In the Mountains, it may not overwinter during severe winters, but throughout most of the Carolinas, it will be perfectly perennial. What a treat to have big, evergreen rosemary shrubs ready year-round to contribute sprigs for seasoning meats, stews, soups, and chicken.

How to Plant & Grow—Plant container-grown rosemary from spring to fall. Rosemary is not the fastest growing of herbs, so it may be wise to start with larger 1-gallon or 2-gallon plants if you plan to start harvesting right away. In the Mountains, you may wish to grow it in a pot and bring it in to a sunny window for the winter. Rosemary is a true sun lover and will thrive in fast-draining alkaline soil. Rosemary is the plant to grow in hot sites, as it stands up well in heat and drought.

Care & Problems—Prune rosemary in early spring and snip sprigs routinely. It is not bothered by deer, drought, or pests.

Harvest & Best Selections—'Hill Hardy' and 'Arp' are two of the most cold-hardy selections and will often make it through the winter in a protected location, even in the Mountains. Gardeners have reported success with both varieties into Zone 6. Harvest the leaves of rosemary anytime, although its fragrant oil is at its peak before the flowers open. Dry sprigs in a paper bag indoors.

SAGE

Salvia officinalis

Why It's Special—Sage offers so much more than pungent leaves to flavor turkey stuffing, cheese dishes, and teas. Certain cultivars rate highly as ornamentals, sporting beautifully variegated leaves of cream, light yellow, and burgundy. Few other evergreen herbs can survive subzero weather or extended drought.

How to Plant & Grow—Quart-sized plants can be planted successfully anytime the soil is warm. Seeds can be direct seeded in late spring. All varieties love to be planted in well-drained, full-sun garden spots. Space 36 inches apart for air circulation, except for edgings or knot gardens. If a plant is potbound, use a trowel to loosen the roots so they can be spread out in a shallow hole. Sage prefers alkaline soil, so if your soil test indicates that your soil is acidic, add garden lime at the rate of 5 pounds per 100 square feet.

Care & Problems—Give sage plenty of room for necessary air circulation; this prevents foliar diseases in our humid summers. Avoid root and stem rot diseases by planting in fast-draining soil.

Harvest & Best Selections—Keep sage compact by pruning after flowering; use the prunings for cooking or in sage butter, or harvest individual leaves as needed. Flowers can be used fresh in salads or as a garnish. 'Berggarten' is an attractive variety with large leaves and 'Tricolor' is a beautiful cultivar with leaves of green, purple, and white.

THYME

Thymus vulgaris

Why It's Special—Thyme is one of the robust, full-flavored, "savory herbs" that will hold its potency through extended cooking. Some species, such as mother-of-thyme (*T. serpyllum*), make temporary groundcovers, while others are perfect for herb bowls. English thyme is vegetatively propagated and is preferred for cooking, but seed-grown French thyme is also flavorful.

How to Plant & Grow—Thyme can be planted anytime from containers. Plant in well-drained soil in a sunny location. Thyme can tolerate dry soil, but irrigate your plantings during dry periods in summer and fall to keep new growth coming. If the soil stays too moist, root rot may occur. Plantings in containers will require twice-weekly watering. An occasional handful of lime will be beneficial in gardens with acidic soil.

Care & Problems—Keep thyme productive by shearing after bloom time. Thyme thrives on neglect once the plants are established. For lush growth, apply an organic, nitrogen-rich fertilizer monthly. Heavy clay soils can be a problem for thyme, so be sure that your soil is well amended and drains freely.

Harvest & Best Selections—Harvest anytime for use in the kitchen; the best flavor is just before bloom time. There are many varieties of thyme. English thyme is the most popular for cooking, but lemon thyme, variegated cultivars, and golden varieties also add beauty to the garden. Lemon thyme is particularly useful in teas and in fish dishes.

APPLE

Malus domestica

Why It's Special—Everyone knows that picking fresh apples from your own trees give you fruit that is second to none in flavor. Growing apples at home can be very successful if recommended varieties are selected and attention is paid to pest management. Nearly every variety is now available in a dwarf or semidwarf form that makes maintenance and harvesting easy.

How to Plant & Grow—Apples are best planted in late winter and very early spring, from mid-January until the end of March. This is especially important for bare-root trees. Set the trees at the same depth they grew at in the nursery. A soil line is usually visible near the base of the tree. Remember that apple trees require cross-pollination in order to produce apples, so you must plant at least two trees and they must be different varieties.

Care & Problems—New trees will need regular pruning to train them. Dwarf trees will need less pruning; prune only to remove branches that are crossing or rubbing, and to keep the center of the tree open for good airflow. Apples do have pests, and a regular maintenance schedule will be necessary to keep your trees and its fruit healthy. Consult your County Extension Service for details.

Harvest & Best Selections—Harvest will occur between September and November, depending on the variety. Later-ripening varieties are often the best "keepers" and, when properly stored, will last well into the winter.

BLACKBERRY

Rubus spp.

Why It's Special—There is nothing like a fresh blackberry harvested right from the plant, but dealing with the thorny brambles can be discouraging, at best. Thornless varieties of blackberries were a real gift to gardeners and will produce luscious crops year after year, providing enough berries for many delicious cobblers.

How to Plant & Grow—Dormant blackberries can be planted in early spring, while potted plants can be put in the ground anytime that the soil can be worked. Full sun will give the most fruit production, though plants will tolerate some shade. Avoid high-nitrogen fertilizers, which cause the plants to grow foliage at the expense of flowers and berries.

Care & Problems—Cut two-year-old blackberry canes to the ground after the berries have been harvested. Leave the one-year-old canes to produce next year's berries. New canes will appear shortly and these will bear fruit in two years. When these new canes reach 3 feet tall, cut off the tips to encourage them to branch and support a heavier crop. By removing two-year-old canes and tipping back the newest growth, you will ensure heavy crops of delicious berries each and every year.

Harvest & Best Selections—Harvest will occur in July and August on two-year-old canes. It may be necessary to cover plants with bird netting as harvest nears. 'Navajo' is one of the best thornless varieties and is an upright grower, not requiring a trellis.

BLUEBERRY

Vaccinium spp. and cultivars

Why It's Special—Blueberries can be grown in gardens throughout the Carolinas. The wild berries that can be found growing in the woods bear only light crops, but cultivated plants can bear as many as 8 to 12 pounds of blueberries per bush. Highbush varieties are the most cold hardy and are better suited to the Mountains, while the rabbiteye types are perfectly suited to the Piedmont and other areas.

How to Plant & Grow—Plant two- to three-year-old container-grown plants in spring, using more than one variety to ensure cross-pollination and heavy fruit set. Blueberries require more acidic soil than most plants, so it is very important to obtain a soil test and adjust the pH accordingly. Blueberries like moisture, but will develop root rot in poorly drained soils.

Care & Problems—Provide a minimum of 1½ inches of water per week during the growing season, especially as the berries are developing on the plants. Do not fertilize new blueberry plants until the first new leaves have reached full size, and then use azalea food or other fertilizer for acid-loving plants. Repeat at six-week intervals through mid-August. At planting time, prune off half of the twiggy growth to encourage strong new growth. In succeeding years, prune in winter to increase fruit production.

Harvest & Best Selections—Bird netting will be required as the berries begin to ripen if you want any for yourself. Harvest berries individually as they ripen.

FIG

Ficus carica

Why It's Special—The fig is a true connoisseur's fruit. This temperate-zone plant is scattered throughout the Carolinas, where it bears at least one and often two crops of succulent fruit each year. In the mountainous parts of North Carolina, it will need the protection of a south-facing wall in winter, but harvesting fresh figs each summer is worth any amount of effort.

How to Plant & Grow—Plant figs in early spring when the soil begins to warm, or in summer if you're willing to water for several weeks. Figs prefer moist, well-drained, thoroughly tilled soil. Add superphosphate and a handful of lime to the soil before planting. Water thoroughly to settle the plant into its new home.

Care & Problems—Figs require no spraying and are not finicky about pruning. They do, however, bear fruit on the previous season's growth, so spring pruning should be limited to removal of dead wood and light pruning to control size. Additional water during the hottest and driest months of summer is beneficial, and fertilizer for flowering and fruiting plants will help ensure good fruit set. Avoid high-nitrogen fertilizers that cause growth instead of fruiting.

Harvest & Best Selections—Figs will begin ripening in mid- to late summer and will continue through early fall. 'Hardy Chicago' is one of the most cold-hardy varieties, 'Brown Turkey' is popular and widely available, and 'Celeste' is a connoisseur's "white" fig.

GRAPE

Vitis labrusca

Why It's Special—American bunch grapes are popular fruits for the home garden. They can be grown in the garden as ornamentals, or just for the fruit. Plants often become overgrown, fail to produce fruit, and eventually are considered strictly ornamentals. In nearly every case, severe pruning could have saved or resurrected the plantings, but too many gardeners are afraid to prune.

How to Plant & Grow—Plant grapes in spring as soon as the soil is dry enough to work. Well-drained soil is essential, but grapes do not do well in extremely fertile soils. Poorer soils tend to produce moderate crops of grapes with excellent flavor. Hillsides are particularly good sites for grapes because they promote air drainage (cooler air flows down the hill). Air drainage reduces the chance of late-season frosts and dries foliage more rapidly, lessening problems with diseases.

Care & Problems—Immediately after planting, prune the plants to a single stem with two buds. This will encourage two strong shoots that will become the main structure of your grape vines. Pruning of grapes is a somewhat involved process. To get the most from your vines, contact your County Extension Service and ask for a pamphlet that explains pruning in detail.

Harvest & Best Selections—There are literally thousands of grape varieties. For varieties that are commonly grown in your area, check with your local garden center. 'Concord' and 'Niagara' are the two most popular table grapes.

MUSCADINE

Vitis rotundifolia

Why It's Special—Muscadine grapes make excellent and distinctive jellies, preserves, and juices. Their flavor is rich, distinct, and more fruity and intense than common table grapes. A mature muscadine vine can yield 20 pounds of fruit or more in the home garden.

How to Plant & Grow—Plant in late winter, before the buds swell. Well-drained, moderately fertile soil is best. Muscadines will not tolerate wet feet. It is important to note that muscadines have male and female vines; if you only plant one vine, be sure to plant a self-fertile variety such as 'Carlos'.

Care & Problems—Be sure to provide a sturdy trellis to support your muscadine vines. They are vigorous growers and will become large and heavy with age. Watering is crucial during the first season to encourage vigorous growth and to get the plant well established. In early spring and early summer each year, apply 1 cup of 10-10-10 fertilizer in a ring about 12 inches out from the base of the plant. Light pruning to control size is best done in early spring, just before the plants leaf out.

Harvest & Best Selections—Muscadines ripen in late summer and early fall. Most have a tough outer skin that makes them less ideal for fresh eating, but perfect for preserving and juicing. If you don't mind the skins, they are excellent fresh. 'Sterling' is a great bronze muscadine and 'Nesbitt' is a cold-hardy black cultivar.

ORIENTAL PERSIMMON

Diospyros kaki

Why It's Special—Oriental persimmon has ornamental appeal and produces delicious fruit. It is an attractive landscape plant that will adapt to most climates in the Carolinas, though the coldest parts of the Mountains may test its limits. There are two types of Oriental persimmons—astringent and non-astringent—with the non-astringent types being best suited to home gardens since they can be eaten fresh, right from the tree.

How to Plant & Grow—Potted trees should be planted in late winter and early spring. Persimmons are deep rooted and are adaptable, but prefer loamy, well-drained soil. Two trees are often needed for cross-pollination. Persimmons have fragile root systems, so handle carefully to avoid doing unnecessary root damage during planting.

Care & Problems—Prune only to remove weak limbs and root suckers. Remove fruiting wood every two years to keep fruit production vigorous. As the trees grow, train to an open framework to develop strong limbs that will support heavy fruits. Most persimmons are grafted. Try to locate plants that have been grafted onto our native American persimmon to ensure additional drought tolerance. One problem with persimmons is that often they only produce good crop of fruit every other year.

Harvest & Best Selections—Harvest will generally occur in October, when the fruit is fully colored but still firm. 'Great Wall' is a good, cold-hardy, non-astringent cultivar. 'Kamagaki' is also known to be very cold hardy.

PAWPAW

Asimina triloba

Why It's Special—The pawpaw is a deciduous, native fruiting tree with attractive 8- to 12-inch-long leaves and a pyramidal shape reminiscent of magnolias. Pawpaws are found along stream banks and in moist woodlands throughout the eastern United States. They make excellent small ornamental landscape trees.

How to Plant & Grow—Pawpaws are known for being finicky about being transplanted. The highest survival rate is from container-grown trees planted in late winter. Plant in full to part sun in deep, moist, acidic soil for the best growth and the most fruit set. If you are growing pawpaws for fruit set, be sure to purchase named varieties.

Care & Problems—Pawpaws tend to be slow growing for the first two to three years, but once established, they are attractive small trees in the landscape. Prune out twiggy branches on the interior to encourage strong side branching and good fruit production along the length of these strong branches. If you are lucky enough to have a native stand of pawpaws on your property, encourage them by carefully opening the canopy above them to allow more light to reach their leaves and keep understory plants from competing directly with them.

Harvest & Best Selections—The fruit of the pawpaw generally ripens in August and is soft and smells fruity when ripe. Its texture is more custard-like than banana-like, which surprises many gardeners based on its outward appearance.

PEACH

Prunus persica

Why It's Special—Peach trees can be a challenge to grow, yet gardeners continue to defy the odds and grow peaches because the results are so gratifying. There is certainly nothing like a juicy, ripe peach, fresh from the tree on a warm summer day. Peaches are self-fruitful and do not need another variety for pollination.

How to Plant & Grow—To choose a site, take into account the full-grown size of the trees. Peaches on dwarfing rootstock will spread 12 to 15 feet; standard trees will be twice that size. Peach trees prefer well-drained soil in full sun (8 to 10 hours will suffice) in an area that has protection from winter winds. The trees themselves are hardy, but the flower buds are not. If the garden is on a slope, plant the peach trees on the side of the hill so they are protected from wind, but not at the bottom, where cold air will settle.

Care & Problems—Pruning is essential to peach trees, and the open center system is recommended. Ask your County Extension Service for a pamphlet that details the proper pruning methods for all your fruit trees, including peaches. A regular spraying regimen to prevent various fungal diseases is an absolute necessity. This is also outlined in many Extension Service pamphlets.

Harvest & Best Selections—Harvest will occur in mid- to late summer. Consult your County Extension Service for recommended varieties for your area.

PEAR

Pyrus spp. and cultivars

Why It's Special—Pears would be as plentiful as apples were it not for the bacterial disease called fire blight, but pears can be grown successfully in home gardens by selecting disease-resistant varieties and carefully pruning them to remove diseased branches. Store-bought pears pale in comparison to tree-ripened fruit.

How to Plant & Grow—To plant a pear tree, dig a hole twice as wide as the spread of the roots and deep enough that the plant will be at the same depth it grew at in the nursery. Trim off excessively long and damaged roots, then spread out the roots in the bottom of the hole. Supporting the tree, begin to backfill the hole with soil, and firm the soil with a blunt stick, such as a 2 x 4. When the hole is half-filled with soil, fill it with water. After the water has drained, replace the remaining soil and fill with water again.

Care & Problems—Pear trees require less attention than peach or apple trees, but still need annual pruning, ideally in mid- to late winter. Pear trees should be pruned to encourage a strong central leader and an open framework of side branches. Instructions can be found online through your County Extension Service or in Extension Service brochures. A regular spraying regimen will keep trees healthy and the fruit free from pests.

Harvest & Best Selections—'Moonglow', 'Seckel', and 'Starking Delicious' are all fireblight resistant and will cross-pollinate one another.

PECAN

Carya illinoensis

Why It's Special—The pecan tree is a large hardwood tree with dark green, compound leaves that have an odor characteristic of walnuts. The pecan is native to America and has been grown commercially for well over one hundred years in many Southern states. Newer cultivars make excellent shade trees and begin bearing sweet pecans at a young age.

How to Plant & Grow—Plant pecans during the dormant season from January to March. Two varieties are needed for cross-pollination and the best nut production. Pecans are shallow-rooted trees and will respond well to good soil preparation at planting time. Most pecans are grafted and the graft union, visible 8 to 10 inches above the roots, should not be buried.

Care & Problems—Pecans will not tolerate severe drought while they are getting established and it is important to keep them watered well for the first two to three seasons. Training and pruning are critical to good development of young trees. Insects such as pecan weevil and twig girdler can be problems, but unless infestations are bad, it may not be wise to use insecticides on crops you plan to eat.

Harvest & Best Selections—Most pecans will ripen in October and November and you'll have to race the squirrels if you plan to get most of the nuts on younger trees, but older trees will produce enough for everyone. 'Kiowa' and 'Stuart' are both excellent cultivars.

PLUM

Prunus spp. and cultivars

Why It's Special—Plums are usually divided into two classes: Japanese (*P. salicina* and *P. triflora*) and European (*P. domestica*). Japanese plums are grown for fresh eating. European plums are eaten fresh, too, but are often used for making jam or drying. Hybrids are usually classified with the Japanese types. Only fresh figs can compare with the sweet, succulent flesh of tree-ripened plums, which are worth any amount of effort to grow successfully.

How to Plant & Grow—Choose a planting site with well-drained soil and full sun. Be sure to allow enough room to walk around the tree when it matures. Don't let plum trees grow into each other or into nearby structures. A regular spraying routine will be necessary to maintain healthy trees and ensure that the fruit is not infested by pests.

Care & Problems—European plums should be pruned to a central leader, while Japanese plums should be pruned to an open center system. These are the same pruning methods used on other fruit trees; consult your County Extension Service for details.

Harvest & Best Selections—Japanese plums ripen in early to midsummer, usually in early July, depending on the climate. It could be slightly earlier or later in warmer or cooler areas. European plums ripen later, usually in August. Harvest plums when they are fully ripe. Plums do not all ripen at the same time, so it will be necessary to harvest several times.

RASPBERRY

Rubus spp.

Why It's Special—After strawberries, raspberries are second in popularity in home gardens. Fresh raspberries are nearly impossible to find in stores because they deteriorate quickly after picking and do not ship well. Growing them in your back yard is the best way to enjoy this delicious fruit. Other than the inconvenience of their thorns, raspberries are easy to grow, and they are the most productive of the small fruits you can plant in your garden.

How to Plant & Grow—Plant raspberries in the spring as soon as the ground can be worked. Plant black and purple raspberries as far away from red raspberries as you can; 500 feet is recommended. Red raspberries carry viral diseases that do not affect them, but will destroy black or purple raspberries. Red and yellow raspberries sucker extensively and will develop into a hedgerow on their own. Black and purple raspberries do not sucker and will remain in hills.

Care & Problems—Although the plants will grow and fruit without support, raspberries are much more attractive and easier to take care of when they are trained up in some manner on supports. Proper pruning is essential for fruit production; your County Extension Service can supply detailed information.

Harvest & Best Selections—Harvest the berries as they ripen. The berries will achieve full color when they are ready to pick. All summer-bearing raspberries mature in early to midsummer. Fall-bearing types mature in September.

STRAWBERRY

Fragaria cv.

Why It's Special—Growing your own strawberries means that you have the makings for a tasty treat, especially with shortcake and ice cream, on a hot summer evening. Strawberries respond to good treatment and reward your time and effort with plenty of high-quality fruit. To have sufficient berries at one time for freezing or preserves, grow June-bearing types. To have fresh berries all summer, choose everbearing or day-neutral varieties.

How to Plant & Grow—Plant strawberries in early spring as soon as the soil dries enough to be workable. Early planting allows the plants to become established before the arrival of hot weather. Well-drained soil and full sun are essential for growing strawberries, and good air circulation is critical. The bed will be in place for three years or more, so locate it where it will not be disturbed and will not interfere with other gardening operations. Planting rooted strawberry plugs (not bare-root starts) in autumn is gaining favor. You get to harvest berries the following spring rather than waiting a year.

Care & Problems—Do not allow strawberries to flower and fruit the first season. Any fruit that develops will sap the strength of the plants and reduce next year's crop.

Harvest & Best Selections—Strawberries are ready for harvest about thirty days after the first bloom. Harvest the berries when they are fully red. Do not allow fully ripened berries to remain on the plants. Excellent everbearing varieties are 'Ogallala' and 'Ozark Beauty'. Great June bearers include 'Earliglow' and 'Honeoye'.

YOUR VEGETABLE GARDEN

PLANNING

The most important decision you will make regarding your vegetable garden is where to site it. You should choose a location in your yard that has relatively good soil with as little clay and as few rocks as possible. Most important, though, is that the location for your vegetable garden must receive full sun—a minimum of six hours of sun each day—for your vegetables to grow and produce to the best of their ability.

In the warmer areas of the Carolinas, you can grow vegetables nearly year- round. Late fall, winter, and early spring will find you growing cool-season crops like cabbage and broccoli that thrive in the chilly evenings and moderate daytime temperatures of the season, while summer means growing heat-loving vegetables like peppers, tomatoes, okra, and others. In the colder regions of the Carolinas, you can still be successful growing vegetables from the earliest days of spring throughout summer and autumn, with winter being the only season when the vegetable garden has some down time.

Planning for each of these seasons will ensure that you get the most out of your vegetable garden. As you gain experience in the vegetable garden, you will learn which vegetables thrive and produce the best in each season and you will be able to schedule your planting so that you realize the most benefits and rewards from your garden each year.

PLANTING

In the vegetable garden, planting can take place at various times throughout the growing season. Cool season vegetables will be planted at different times of the year than those that like it warm. Most of these differences, as well as special planting tips for specific vegetables and where they apply, are featured in the individual vegetable entries.

FERTILIZING

Apply fertilizer according to soil test recommendations. Or, if you did not have a soil test done, apply 1 pound of complete balanced fertilizer such as 10-10-10 per 100 square feet of garden. About midseason, after the plants have become well-developed, another application of fertilizer may be beneficial. "Side-dress" the plants with the same fertilizer at half the recommended rate, then water in thoroughly after application to wash fertilizer off the plants and to activate the fertilizer. Side-dressing means to apply the fertilizer around the base of the plant at the outer perimeter of the leaves. Liquid fertilizers mixed with water can be applied according to the directions on the container.

WATERING

Watering is one of the most important activities you do, and proper watering will ensure bountiful harvests from the vegetable garden. The most important point to remember when watering is that you're not just watering to keep plants from being dry and wilting. You are also watering to encourage roots to grow deep into the soil in search of water that is already there. By watering deeply and thoroughly each time you water, you ensure that each of your crops grows to its fullest potential and that you get the most from your vegetable garden. When you have watered properly and your vegetables have grown roots deep into the soil, they will be better able to survive periods of drought and will fill your kitchen with fresh-from-the-garden produce.

COMPOSTING

Any organic matter resulting from the garden, such as grass clippings, fallen leaves in autumn, plant tops, spent plants, and kitchen scraps (but no meat scraps), can be recycled by composting. Naturally occurring organisms—bacteria, fungi, worms, and other creatures—digest the organic matter and turn it into a dark brown, crumbly, earthy-smelling material that is compost.

A compost heap must be large enough to heat internally. The most convenient size for the average garden is about 3 feet high, wide, and deep. A pile can be built up on the ground, but a container, such as a bin made of concrete blocks, fence wire, or boards, is usually easier to handle. Construct the compost pile starting with a 6- to 8-inch layer of coarse organic matter. Moisten the matter so that it is damp. Cover that with about 2 inches of garden soil, which will add the organisms needed to start the process. Repeat alternating layers of organic matter and soil until the pile is 3 feet high. Sprinkle each layer with a couple of handfuls of nitrogen fertilizer such as ammonium nitrate or urea, which will feed the beneficial organisms that break the material you've added to the pile into rich, black compost. Finally, level the top.

In a properly constructed compost pile, the internal temperature should reach 140 to 160 degrees F in a few days. You can tell when it is working because the pile will settle noticeably. After a month, turn the pile over with a pitch fork, turning the outside of the old pile to the middle of the new pile. Then moisten it if necessary. The compost should be ready for use in four to five months.

PEST CONTROL

The use of pest controls in the vegetable garden must remain the choice of each individual gardener. It may not always be necessary to use pesticides to control insects or diseases. A particular pest or disease may not be harmful to your particular plants.

If pest control does become necessary in the vegetable garden, it is especially important to consider the use of alternative means. These include the use of resistant varieties, the use of botanical and microbial insecticides or soaps, encouraging predators and parasites, mechanical means such as screening, hand picking, and improving cultural practices.

If you do find it necessary to use traditional chemical pest controls, first consult your local authorities such as your Extension Service office for correct pest identification and control recommendations. Once you have decided to use a specific pest control product, you must read and follow label directions carefully.

JANUARY

- Now is the time to plan this year's vegetable garden. In the warmest areas of the Carolinas, cool-season vegetables can be planted soon, and fruit trees and plants can be planted beginning in late January.

- To make the most of your space, consider growing vining and sprawling plants such as cucumbers, melons, pole beans, and indeterminate tomatoes on trellises, nets, strings, or poles. They will take up less garden space and the remaining space can be planted with low-growing vegetables.

- Coastal Plain and Piedmont gardeners can sow seeds of broccoli, cabbage, and cauliflower indoors for transplanting within six to eight weeks.

FEBRUARY

- When the soil can be worked, turn under the cover crops planted last fall. Till the soil to a depth of 8 to 12 inches. Never work the soil when it is wet—working wet soils destroys the structure and makes the soil hard, compacted, and unproductive.

- In the Coastal Plain, sow warm-season vegetables indoors in flats or trays—try plants like eggplant, pepper, and tomato.

- Piedmont gardeners can sow basil, chives, parsley, sage, summer savory, and sweet marjoram indoors. To encourage parsley seeds to sprout more rapidly, soften the seeds by soaking them overnight in warm water.

- Coastal Plain gardeners can plant hardened-off vegetable transplants of broccoli, cabbage, and lettuce. Potatoes can be planted near the end of the month.

MARCH

- If you are serious about growing herbs and vegetables, plan to start a journal this month. It will document your observations, thoughts, and plans for the future. List the herbs and vegetables you planted in the garden. Include the seed company name, plant name, variety, planting date, and harvest date.

- Indoors in the Mountains, sow basil, chives, parsley, summer savory, and sweet marjoram. To encourage parsley seeds to sprout more rapidly, soften the seeds by soaking them overnight in warm water.

- In the Coastal Plain after the last freeze, set out eggplant, onion, pepper, and tomato plants. Sow seeds of lima beans, pole beans, snap beans, sweet corn, summer squash, and watermelon directly in the garden where you want them to grow.

- In the Piedmont and Mountains, plant asparagus crowns before new growth emerges from the buds. Set out transplants of broccoli, cabbage, and cauliflower as well, up to four weeks beforethe last spring freeze. Sow seeds of carrots, lettuce (leaf and head), garden peas, mustard, radishes, rutabaga, and spinach. Mountain gardeners can sow mustard, garden peas, radishes, spinach, and turnips.

APRIL

- In the Coastal Plain and Piedmont after the last freeze, sow beans, corn, cucumbers, and Southern peas. Avoid planting okra seeds too early. The soil temperature should be above 75 degrees F; soak okra seeds overnight before planting in the garden.

- Plant determinate bush-type tomatoes for canning or preserving so the fruit will ripen all at once, all within a week or two of each other. For vine-ripened tomatoes, plant indeterminate tomatoes that have an extended fruiting period; they vine, flower, and fruit all the way up to the first frost.

- To keep the cauliflower curds pure white, loosely tie the long outside leaves over the flat, open head when the head is 1 to 2 inches across. Hold the leaves together with a rubber band until the head is ready for harvesting. This process is called blanching.

- Root crops must be thinned, no matter how ruthless this practice seems. Thin beets, carrots, onions, Swiss chard, and turnips so you can get three fingers between individual plants.

MAY

- Sow warm-weather vegetables such as beans, cucumber, okra, and Southern peas. Extend your sweet corn harvest by planting successive crops when the previous crop has three to four leaves, or plant early-, mid-, and late-maturing varieties all at the same time.

- Harvest broccoli when the florets are still tight and green. After harvesting the main head, broccoli will put out smaller heads from the side shoots. Pick cauliflower before the curds begin to separate, and cabbage before it bolts (blooms). Pick green, sugar snap, and snow peas every couple of days to keep more coming.

- Water deeply, keeping the leaves of your vegetables dry. Invest in soaker hoses or drip irrigation.

- Be on the lookout for pest and disease problems in your vegetable, herb, and fruit gardens as summer approaches. Consult your local garden center or your County Extension Service for effective and safe methods of control.

JUNE

- If you've planted more than you can use, share your bounty with friends and neighbors. What about your community? Make plans to share your vegetables and herbs with your community soup kitchen or food bank.

- Mountain gardeners still have time to plant summer crops such as beans, cucumbers, okra, pumpkins, Southern peas, and squash, plus a last planting of sweet corn. Also, set out transplants of pepper, tomatoes, and sweet potato slips.

- Harvest beans, cucumbers, okra, and squash daily to keep the plants producing. Pick cucumbers when the fruits are small and before they turn yellow.

JULY

- Start planning your fall garden. Choose early-maturing vegetables when you can. Sow beans, cucumbers, or even short-season corn. They will replace those early vegetables you harvested this month and will be ready to pick before freezing weather comes.

- Mountain and Piedmont gardeners can start seeds of Brussels sprouts, cabbage, and cauliflower for the fall garden. Sow seeds indoors or in a partly shaded area outdoors.

- Sow pumpkins for Halloween.

- A vegetable garden thrives on an inch of water each week of summer. When rain is sparse, water deeply once a week with clay soils and every three days with sandy soils to encourage deep rooting.

- Restore soil fertility before planting your fall crops by working in fertilizer or manure. Do not fertilize drought-stressed plants. Wait until after watering or rainfall and the plants' leaves have dried off.

AUGUST

- As you update your garden journal, note the vegetables and herbs that didn't live up to expectations, and those that exceeded them. Make a note of insect and disease problems. In your plans for next year's garden, focus on varieties that performed well for you or that you have noticed did well in other gardens.

- Set out cloves of garlic for a harvest early next summer.

- In the Piedmont and Coastal Plain, plant greens such as kale, mustard, and turnips in intervals now and next month to lengthen the harvest season.

- In the Mountains, plant the last fall garden vegetables. For hardy crops like cabbage, cauliflower, and collards, take your average first frost date and count back the number of days the particular variety requires to mature; plant at the appropriate time.

SEPTEMBER

- Whether you garden year-round or hang up your hoe at summer's end, start tidying up the garden and take steps to build up the soil for next spring. Certain insects and diseases overwinter in plant debris. Time spent now burying plant stalks, debris, and mulch will eliminate winter havens for pests.

- Consider the steps you will take to build the soil for next season. Planting a cover crop or "green manure" this fall that you will turn under in the spring is a great way to improve soil fertility and structure.

- Plant beets, carrots, kale, lettuce, radishes, spinach, and turnips for fall harvest.

- Dig sweet potatoes before frost, being careful to avoid bruises and scrapes. Cure them for two or three weeks in the warmest room of the house to toughen the skin. Store them where it is cool and dark.

OCTOBER

- Piedmont and Coastal Plain gardeners can divide chives, thyme, mint, and French tarragon when new growth emerges.

- Extend the gardening season well into the winter. Lettuce, radishes, and spinach can all be grown in cold frames.

- In the Coastal Plain, plant onion sets and garlic cloves now to mid-November for harvest next spring and summer. Plant spinach in October to do well this fall and winter.

- Listen for frost warnings and be prepared to cover tomatoes, eggplants, peppers, and other tender vegetables. The weather often warms up again after the first frost, so this protection can prolong the harvest for weeks.

- Harvest sweet potatoes before frost as well as gourds, pumpkins, and winter squash. To store pumpkins, pick only solid, mature pumpkins of a deep orange color.

NOVEMBER

- Bring in your rain gauge to avoid freeze damage.
- Drain and store water hoses to extend their lives.
- Protect the garden tools in which you invested. Clean them up. Repair or replace broken ones.
- Plan for spring. As soon as seed flats and pots are emptied of fall transplants, wash and sterilize them. Use a 10 percent solution of household bleach and dry them thoroughly before storing them.
- In warmer areas of the Carolinas, plant lettuce and hardy vegetables such as beets, cabbage, and spinach in cold frames for winter or early-spring crops. Grow leafy vegetables such as lettuce, Chinese cabbage, and spinach in a cold frame or beneath a row cover for harvesting all winter long.
- A light mulch of shredded leaves or straw on carrots, turnips, and other root vegetables will help protect against freezing. Pick tomatoes when frost is predicted and store in a single layer in a cool location.

DECEMBER

- Finish organizing all of your journal notes from your gardening year. This will be a valuable tool as you begin planning for next year's vegetable garden.
- Prune fruit trees while they are completely dormant. It is easier to see which limbs need to be removed and where to make your pruning cuts.
- Piedmont and Coastal Plain gardeners can sow lettuce and other greens in cold frames for winter use.
- Continue to harvest chives, cilantro, and parsley. In the Piedmont and Mountains, protect winter greens with a fabric row cover or with plastic tunnels—plastic stretched over metal hoops for protection from hard freezes. Broccoli, Brussels sprouts, cabbage, mustard, turnips, and most lettuces will be damaged by a hard freeze (more than six hours below 26 degrees F).

GROUND COVERS & ORNAMENTAL GRASSES

for the Carolinas

GROUND COVERS

At one time, only turfgrasses were used to prevent soil erosion and to provide green in the home landscape. In today's landscapes and gardens, ground covers are frequently used for these purposes. Often referred to as "living mulch," ground covers are what landscape designers use to carpet our outdoor rooms. A ground cover can be defined as any dense, spreading plant that covers the ground when planted *en masse*. It can transform a barren area into a blanket of lush foliage and, if you wish, flowers as well.

THE ADVANTAGES OF GROUND COVERS

Once established, ground covers choke out most unwanted weeds, reducing maintenance in the long run. Planted either in sun or shade, they will hide the ugly knees of some taller-growing plants. They are especially handsome when placed under small specimen trees or when used to edge a flower border. Flowering ground covers, such as 'Homestead Purple' verbena, hardy ice plant, and dianthus are spectacular used in groupings for seasonal color. Ground covers are excellent plants to naturalize over bulb plantings, including surprise lilies, spider lilies, and daffodils.

Many gardeners love ground covers because of the savings in "sweat equity." More and more, gardeners want to reduce the time they spend mowing their lawns. (Not only do the fumes from mowing machines affect air quality, but the annoying racket also creates noise pollution in suburban neighborhoods.) Ground covers can solve landscape design problems. The right ground cover can grow better in shaded areas than lawn grass. Ground covers are ideal for steep slopes and rocky sites that make mowing hazardous and for open areas where exposed tree roots make mowing or gardening difficult. They can help define shrub beds and add variety to woodland gardens. As a supplement to turf areas, ground covers help blend and unite the yard into a harmonious picture.

HOW GROUND COVERS WORK

Different species and varieties of ground covers have different methods of spreading, and knowing how a ground cover spreads can be help you determine which ones will work well for a given area, especially if you need a ground cover to help control water runoff and erosion or to stabilize a steep bank.

Ground covers can spread by several different methods. Some spread by growing underground roots or stolons that spread a few inches to a few feet away from the base of the parent plant and then send up a new plant. This forms a thick, dense network of roots under the surface of the soil that help to hold the ground cover firmly in place. Pachysandra and *Liriope spicata* both spread in this way. English ivy is the perfect example of a plant that can be grown either as a vine or as a ground cover. It will send long, creeping stems across the surface of the soil, rooting and branching as it goes, and forming a dense, evergreen ground cover. But if it reaches a tree or a wall, it will immediately begin climbing and become a potentially aggressive vine. Still others spread by aboveground runners—stems with a baby plant attached to the end that will root when they come into contact with the soil. Once they have rooted and matured, they in turn will send out more runners and your patch of ground cover will grow and spread as far as you allow the runners to reach. Ajuga spreads in this manner and so do the strawberries that you may grow in your vegetable garden.

Generally speaking, the more aggressive a ground cover is, the better it may be for helping to stabilize areas with erosion problems, such as steep banks or slopes or drainage areas that may carry running water after heavy rains but are otherwise relatively dry. Slower-growing ground covers or those that don't send a deep network of roots into the ground are better grown for their ornamental value and for covering flatter surfaces where erosion control isn't a primary concern.

ORNAMENTAL GRASSES

Older gardeners remember when pampas grass was it. With a few exceptions, it was the only ornamental grass in the Carolinas. Then plant explorers, nursery professionals, and landscape designers began to introduce and promote ornamental grasses for commercial and residential landscape installations. Adventurous home gardeners saw them and nagged garden centers to offer ornamental grasses, and now it seems that you see ornamental grasses in almost every home garden. This is especially true in the Midwest and Plains states, where the native landscape is comprised largely of grasses, but there are grasses that thrive in nearly every climate and the Carolinas are no exception.

A WORD ON BEHAVIOR

Many of the ornamental grasses that first caught the attention of gardeners and landscape designers are native to other countries. Ecologists call them "exotic" species. Along the way, a few bad visitors were brought in that have bullied their way into wildlands and are pushing out native species that are ill equipped to compete with these robust imports. For the most part, however, ornamental grasses are not aggressive invaders and represent little or no threat to the environment. Even within some problem species, there are excellent cultivars that pose no problems at all.

Drive through certain parts of both North and South Carolina and you can see the straight species *Miscanthus sinensis* popping up everywhere along roadsides and in pastures and fields. However, the cultivars 'Cabaret', 'Morning Light', and 'Strictus' make excellent garden subjects and rarely, if ever, produce a single seedling. In a garden setting, even some native species can be problematic. Northern sea oats, for example, can quickly and aggressively choke out nearby garden plants. Near the coast,

Japanese blood grass, which spreads slowly by underground runners, can get out of control in moist, fertile soil. By being good stewards and responsible gardeners, we can still grow beautiful grasses and other plants from around the world that pose no threat to our native landscapes.

THE ADVANTAGES OF ORNAMENTAL GRASSES

Ornamental grasses come in many sizes, from small mounds of blue fescue to mighty clumps of pampas grass. Almost all prefer full sun, with just a small handful preferring shady locations. The size, texture, color, and flower heads of a given cultivar determine its best use in the landscape. For instance, many landscapes have sizable sunny areas where mowing is difficult, too expensive, or too time-consuming. Gardeners just want to fill up the space with something that looks good, isn't expensive, and requires little maintenance. Among the many ornamental grasses, they can find species that will meet those requirements.

CULTIVAR VERSATILITY

The variegated cultivars of ornamental grasses may carry cream or white stripes the length of their leaves or, in grasses like porcupine grass, may be banded in cream or yellow. All of these look especially good against dark green backgrounds, such as those provided by coniferous or broadleaf evergreen shrubs, and are equally as effective as tall backgrounds against which to display flowers or flowering shrubs of significant size, such as butterfly bush and rose of Sharon. Grasses may be at their finest, though, when backlit by morning or evening sun slanting low across the garden.

Certain ornamental grasses are an intense silvery blue color like lyme grass, or reddish purple like annual fountain grass or the All-America Selections winner 'Purple Majesty' millet. Others, like inland sea oats and rattlesnake grass, are grown more for their novel seeds than for their form or foliage.

Ornamental grasses change in size and appearance as they cycle through the seasons. Green, blue, and variegated leaves offer color and texture in the landscape. Their presentation varies from flowers and seedheads to blanched foliage caused by frost and winter rains. They also offer movement every time a gentle breeze blows through the garden. Many gardeners don't trim back their clumps of ornamental grasses until spring, preferring to let them stand to deliver strong architectural effect during the winter.

ORNAMENTAL GRASSES AS GROUND COVERS

Occasionally, ornamental grasses are used as very effective and beautiful ground covers. Some grasses and grasslike plants actually do spread by above- or below-ground stolons, and their deep, aggressive roots can be extremely helpful for stabilizing sandy soils in coastal areas or steep banks in other locales. Smaller, clump-forming grasses like blue fescue and fountain grass can also be used as "ground covers" by installing mass plantings on close spacing so that when the plants are mature, they touch and completely obscure the ground below. Because of their deep roots, even clumping grasses can be excellent candidates for erosion control.

THE TIP OF THE ICEBERG

Descriptions of some of the most popular ground covers and ornamental grasses follow. To see the actual plants and visualize how they might look in your garden, visit your nearest botanical garden or a well-stocked garden center. Please note that in the following descriptions for ornamental grasses and ground covers, "Peak Season" for ornamental grasses will refer to their "bloom," or "plume," time.

AJUGA

Ajuga reptans

Why It's Special—When spring bulbs are blooming, the deep blue flower spikes of ajuga, sometimes called bugleweed, come shining through, but it's the beautiful foliage that sets ajuga apart year-round. Leaves can range from deep—nearly black—purple to bronzy green, and variegated. For partly to fully shaded areas, ajuga is indispensible.

How to Plant & Grow—Ajuga plants are customarily sold in flats filled with small pots or six-packs. When planted anytime from late summer to December, ajuga gives good results, becoming well established during the warm days and cooler nights of autumn. Ajuga likes moisture and responds well to irrigation during the warmest months.

Care & Problems—Occasionally, ajuga suffers from a fungal disease called rhizoctonia that causes sudden browning and dying off in patches within the larger planting. Infected areas should be raked clean of dead plants and will usually fill in soon. If ajuga runners invade the lawn or nearby beds, they are easy to dig out and remove.

Foliage Color—Purple, bronze, variegated

Bloom Color—Blue, in spring

Hardiness—Zones 4b to 9a

Texture—Medium

Water Needs—Evenly moist soil

CAST-IRON PLANT

Aspidistra elatior

Why It's Special—For tough places in deep shade, the name "cast-iron plant" tells you almost everything you need to know. Though it is taller than a typical ground cover—it certainly doesn't hug the ground—it spreads by underground rhizomes and forms dense masses of foliage in the most challenging parts of the yard. Variegated forms can add even further interest and the plant is very competitive with tree roots.

How to Plant & Grow—Cast-iron plant can be planted anytime that it is actively growing, from spring to fall. Keep the soil evenly moist until plants are well established and they will be able to tolerate nearly anything that Mother Nature dishes out. Occasional water during a drought will keep plants from looking bedraggled.

Care & Problems—Fertilize with a slow-release fertilizer in early spring, just before new growth begins. If large stands become disheveled, they can be cut to the ground in early spring for complete rejuvenation.

Foliage Color—Green or variegated

Bloom Color—Cream to maroon, at ground level

Hardiness—Zones 7a to 10

Texture—Bold

Water Needs—Drought tolerant, once established

CREEPING JUNIPER

Juniperus horizontalis

Why It's Special—From Southern California to the coast of North Carolina and from as far north as Minnesota to as far south as Texas, creeping junipers provide sturdy, evergreen ground cover for slopes, banks, and other areas. Some varieties take on purplish coloration during winter months, giving them another layer of interest.

How to Plant & Grow—Water newly planted junipers for fifteen minutes twice a week for the first month, using a hose adjusted to low water flow. For the remainder of the first season, water once per week for the same time, especially during hot, dry weather. Fertilize in early spring with a slow-release or organic fertilizer.

Care & Problems—Prune creeping junipers only to contour the shape in early spring by selectively removing individual shoots. If runner-forming grasses, such as bermudagrass, invade your junipers, you may have a challenge. There are selective herbicides that will kill only grassy weeds and can be used effectively; consult a local garden center.

Foliage Color—Deep green to blue

Bloom Color—Insignificant

Hardiness—Zones 3a to Zone 9a

Texture—Fine

Water Needs—Drought tolerant, once established

CREEPING RASPBERRY

Rubus calycinoides

Why It's Special—This fast-growing, evergreen ground cover is a cousin to blackberries and strawberries. Creeping raspberry is thornless and its dark green, pebbly-textured foliage forms a dense mat. In winter, the leaves turn reddish purple. It is an excellent choice for suppressing weed and preventing erosion on slopes.

How to Plant & Grow—Creeping raspberry is available in the spring from garden centers. Partial shade is ideal, but it tolerates full morning sun as long as it has some shade by mid afternoon during the hottest months. Rich, well-drained soil is essential; do not plant in highly compacted or poorly drained soils.

Care & Problems—Trimming around the edges will be necessary if the plant is to be contained within a specific area. During periods of severe cold, some dieback may occur, but simply trim out the dead parts and it will rejuvenate itself very quickly. In poorly drained soils, bacterial leaf spot and root rot fungus can be problematic.

Foliage Color—Deep green, red in winter

Bloom Color—White, insignificant

Hardiness—Zones 6b to 9b

Texture—Medium

Water Needs—Fairly drought tolerant, once established

ENGLISH IVY

Hedera helix

Why It's Special—A popular ground cover in the Carolinas, English ivy does well in heavy shade, competing well with tree roots. It also adapts to sunnier locations, though full sun may burn the foliage or lead to leaf spot diseases. With over two hundred cultivars available, there are endless leaf shapes and foliage colors.

How to Plant & Grow—English ivy is commonly available in small pots or by the flat at garden centers. It can be planted year-round and is not particular as to soil, but rich, well-drained, and well-amended garden soil will encourage it to grow and fill in the fastest. Water regularly for the first four to six weeks and then during dry periods for the first season.

Care & Problems—The biggest challenge with ivy is containing it because it can also be a rampant vine. If it reaches a tree, wall, house façade, or other upright structure, it will shoot skyward and can become a nuisance.

Foliage Color—Green or variegated yellow/white

Bloom Color—Insignificant

Hardiness—Zones 5b to 9b, depending on variety

Texture—Medium

Water Needs—Drought tolerant, once established

HARDY ICE PLANT

Delosperma cooperi

Why It's Special—Thriving in heat and surviving winter cold, this wonderful plant belongs to a family of low-growing succulents from the deserts of South Africa. It is semievergreen with round, fleshy leaves, and its dense foliage quickly carpets the ground. Its hot pink blooms are showstopping in late spring and early summer.

How to Plant & Grow—Plant hardy ice plant from containers during the warmer months of spring and summer to get it well established before winter. It prefers full sun and very well-drained soil, especially in winter. It is excellent in the sandy soils of the coastal areas. Stems that are broken off will root and grow where they land.

Care & Problems—After a few hard freezes in late fall and early winter, the current year's foliage will "melt" and can be cleaned up with a rake. New growth will sprout in spring. It is almost pest free and pesticides will burn the foliage.

Foliage Color—Dark green to gray-green

Bloom Color—Hot pink, deep purple, or occasionally yellow

Hardiness—Zones 5b to 10

Texture—Fine

Water Needs—Extremely drought tolerant

HARDY VERBENA

Glandularia spp. and hybrids x hybrida

Why It's Special—The semievergreen verbenas have risen to stardom as flowering ground covers since the introduction of 'Homestead Purple'. Today, these hardy, heat- and humidity-loving perennial ground covers come in a wide range of varieties and colors.

How to Plant & Grow—Plant hardy verbena from early spring to early fall. Verbena likes a warm, sunny location where it will spread quickly and flower continuously. While good drainage is important, especially in winter, it is also important to keep plants well watered after planting until thoroughly established. Deadhead old flowers as needed.

Care & Problems—As cold weather sets in, leave foliage and stems intact even if they are frostbitten and brown. This helps to protect the crowns from winter's coldest weather and ensures that plants will resprout and grow quickly from the base when warm weather returns in spring. Spider mites can be a problem in hot, dry conditions and can be treated with highly refined horticultural oil sprays.

Foliage Color—Deep green, semievergreen

Bloom Color—Purple, lavender, pink, red, white

Hardiness—Zones 6a (with protection) to 9b

Texture—Fine

Water Needs—Drought tolerant, once established

LIRIOPE

Liriope muscari

Why It's Special—Liriope, or monkey grass, is extensively planted throughout the Carolinas. This grasslike member of the lily family is popular because it is easy to grow and thrives in almost any site from sun to shade, and sandy soils to clay. Purple or white blooms in late summer are an added bonus.

How to Plant & Grow—Potted plants can be set out anytime the ground is not frozen. Liriope will thrive in almost any soil conditions, but will respond with dramatic results when planted in good, well-amended garden soil. Transplants are frequently potbound; score roots with a sharp knife. Water thoroughly after planting.

Care & Problems—In late winter, before new spring growth emerges, trim foliage down to within 3 inches of the ground to remove last year's foliage. Within a few weeks, new growth will sprout and plants will look tidy. Voles can be a problem. Consult local garden centers for methods of control.

Foliage Color—Deep green or variegated yellow/white

Bloom Color—Purple or white

Hardiness—Zones 6a to 9b

Texture—Fine

Water Needs—Drought tolerant, once established

MONDO GRASS

Ophiopogon japonicus

Why It's Special—Mondo grass is similar to the ever-popular liriope, or monkey grass, but is generally finer and more grasslike in texture, and there are numerous varieties available that offer many more options in height, foliage color, and texture. *Ophiopogon planiscapus* 'Nigrescens' has almost solid black foliage and provides drama in part-shade areas.

How to Plant & Grow—Mondo grass is best planted in spring or summer, giving it ample time to settle in before winter. It prefers moist, well-amended soil in part sun to full shade. Most selections tolerate full sun if well irrigated, but may show some tip burn during the hottest, driest months.

Care & Problems—Once established, mondo grass is fairly carefree. Taller varieties can be cut back in late winter, but dwarf varieties require almost no maintenance. Voles can occasionally be a problem. Consult local garden centers for methods of control.

Foliage Color—Dark green, green and white, black

Bloom Color—Lavender

Hardiness—Zones 6b to 9b

Texture—Fine to very fine

Water Needs—Moderately moist soil; not as drought tolerant as liriope

PACHYSANDRA

Pachysandra terminalis

Why It's Special—This shade-loving evergreen ground cover features veined, oval leaves that are 2 to 4 inches in length and grow in whorled clusters at the top of upright stems. Pachysandra thrives in the shade of oaks and pine, where grass is nearly impossible to grow, and even tolerates the dense shade and root competition of Southern magnolia.

How to Plant & Grow—Set out potted pachysandra in spring or early fall, avoiding the hottest and driest months. Partial to full shade and rich, moist, organically enriched soils suit it best. A 1-inch layer of mulch over the soil after planting will help to conserve moisture and will encourage rapid growth of stolons and fast coverage.

Care & Problems—Pachysandra never needs pruning; just edge the beds occasionally to keep it from creeping out of bounds. Occasionally, dead circular patches occur on the leaves—a disease known as volutella. Contact your County Extension Service for advice. Too much sun can encourage this problem.

Foliage Color—Deep, lustrous green

Bloom Color—White

Hardiness—Zones 5b to 8b

Texture—Medium

Water Needs—Moderately moist to moist soil

ST. JOHN'S WORT

Hypericum calycinum

Why It's Special—There are over four hundred species of St. John's wort and several are native to the Southeast. Most are shrubby, but a few make excellent ground covers. Most hypericums are evergreen to semievergreen and all possess bright yellow flowers that last for several weeks in summer.

How to Plant & Grow—St. John's wort is best planted in fall to take advantage of winter moisture to get it established. Spring and summer planting is successful as long as adequate water is provided. Most species are tough and will even grow in thin, rocky soils once established. Fertilize in early spring as new growth begins.

Care & Problems—Most varieties bloom on the new season's growth, so hard pruning in late winter or early spring can be beneficial. You can cut ground cover types down to within 2 to 3 inches of the ground with a Weed Eater. Leaf spot, rust, and anthracnose can be problems in soils that are too wet.

Foliage Color—Olive green

Bloom Color—Bright yellow

Hardiness—Zones 5a to 7b

Texture—Medium

Water Needs—Well-drained, dry to moderately moist soil

VINCA

Vinca minor

Why It's Special—Whether you call it vinca or periwinkle, this spreading ground cover is popular for shaded gardens. Once established, it is one of the most drought-resistant evergreen ground covers available and is nearly indestructible. Blue flowers put on a show in the spring just as new growth appears.

How to Plant & Grow—Set out potted plants in spring or fall. Vinca prefers light shade and moist soil, but is tolerant of a wide range of less-than-ideal conditions. Vinca is shallow rooted and benefits from being planted high, with the top inch of the rootball above the soil line and then covered with a layer of loamy topsoil.

Care & Problems—Vinca is virtually maintenance free. The only trimming required is to keep it from creeping into beds or lawns where it isn't desired. Occasionally, stem blight can be a problem. This is most often seen in heavy clay soils that stay particularly wet. Vinca is considered invasive in some areas.

Foliage Color—Dark, lustrous green

Bloom Color—Lavender-blue

Hardiness—Zones 4a to 8b

Texture—Medium-fine

Water Needs—Drought tolerant, once established

BLUE FESCUE

Festuca glauca

Why It's Special—This densely tufted, silvery blue ornamental fescue is one of the most diminutive of the ornamental grasses and when planted *en masse*, on close centers, makes a near-perfect ground cover or alternative lawn. The tan seedheads are attractive in summer.

How to Plant & Grow—Set out container-grown plants in early spring. Blue fescue prefers leaner, drier soils and will not tolerate heavy, wet clay soil, especially in winter. If you desire a ground cover effect, plant on 18-inch centers so that plants will grow together and touch when they are mature. Water well to get new plants established, but then water only as needed during dry periods.

Care & Problems—Blue fescue is very low maintenance. Just cut back the plants in early spring, before new growth starts, to tidy them up and remove last year's old foliage. Clay soils that stay cold and wet in winter can lead to root and/or crown rot and the death of the plants.

Foliage Color—Silvery blue

Peak Season—Early summer

Hardiness—Zones 4a to 8a

Texture—Very fine

Water Needs—Drought tolerant, once established

FEATHER REED GRASS

Calamagrostis x acutiflora 'Karl Foerster'

Why It's Special—This erect, shoulder-high grass is suited to gardens of any size, because of its narrow, upright habit. Its deep green foliage is attractive from early spring until late fall, and the plumes that appear in early summer change from pinkish to golden tan.

How to Plant & Grow—Because it is a cool-season grass, it can be planted either in spring or fall. Plant in a sunny location with good air circulation. While it prefers well-drained, fertile soil with sufficient moisture, it will adapt to heavier clay soils and drier sites. Water thoroughly at least twice a week for the first month and then slowly reduce watering to an as-needed basis.

Care & Problems—Heavy rain or winds may bend the stems; they will usually right themselves. In Zone 8, heat, humidity, and poor air circulation can cause fungal leaf spot. Korean feather reed grass (*Calamagrostis brachytricha*) can tolerate hot, humid summers in the eastern Carolinas.

Foliage Color—Green or variegated

Peak Season—Early summer to fall

Hardiness—Zones 5a to 7b

Texture—Fine

Water Needs—Evenly moist to slightly dry soil

FOUNTAIN GRASS

Pennisetum alopecuroides

Why It's Special—Fountain grasses are well named, as their narrow leaves form graceful fountains of broadly arching foliage and their showy, foxtail plumes persist into early winter. They are easy to grow, adapting to nearly any type of soil. Smaller varieties can be used as sun-loving ground covers.

How to Plant & Grow—Fountain grass can be planted any time in spring through fall, but becomes best established during the warm months of late spring and early summer. Water thoroughly for the first month until it is rooted in, and then only as needed to keep the leaves from curling. Large varieties may need 5 feet between plants, while small varieties can be as close as 2 feet.

Care & Problems—Fountain grass is relatively pest free. In early spring, cut plants back to 8 to 12 inches to remove last season's growth. The variety 'Moudry', though beautiful, can reseed and become weedy. Divide every three to five years to maintain its vigor.

Foliage Color—Green

Peak Season—Midsummer to fall

Hardiness—Zones 5b to 8b

Texture—Fine

Water Needs—Moderately drought tolerant, once established

MAIDEN GRASS

Miscanthus sinensis 'Gracillimus'

Why It's Special—Maiden grass is hardy throughout the Carolinas and forms large clumps of finely textured, silver-green foliage. In autumn, it is topped with large, fan-shaped plumes that change from reddish tan to silvery white. Two other cultivars, 'Cabaret' and 'Morning Light', are variegated, beautiful, and noninvasive.

How to Plant & Grow—Maiden grass can be planted in spring through fall as long as the soil is workable. Grow in sun in any type of soil from wet areas to dry, rocky slopes. If potbound, be sure to loosen the roots. Water on a weekly basis until established. Avoid overfertilizing, which will cause stems to topple.

Care & Problems—Cut back clumps to 12 inches in early spring each year. Bundle the clumps together with twine and then cut below the twine to keep the dried leaves from creating a mess. You may need gas-powered hedge shears, but the ease of cleanup is worth it!

Foliage Color—Silver green or variegated

Peak Season—Late summer to fall

Hardiness—Zones 5a to 8b

Texture—Fine to medium

Water Needs—Moderately drought tolerant, once established

PAMPAS GRASS

Cortaderia selloana

Why It's Special—Pampas grass is the grandest of all the ornamental grasses. Gardeners in northern climates lust after it when they travel south in late autumn and see the magnificent plumes rising 10 to 12 feet into the air. The variety 'Pumila' is shorter, growing to 6 feet, and is at least one full zone hardier. The plumes last all winter, and in the Deep South, foliage remains semievergreen.

How to Plant & Grow—Container-grown pampas grass may be planted from spring to fall. It establishes itself best during the warmest months, and in the colder end of its hardiness range it is very important that it be well established before winter arrives. It grows best in rich, deep, well-drained soil but will flourish nearly anywhere.

Care & Problems—Plants should be cut back hard—to 6 to 8 inches, if possible—in early spring, but after the coldest weather has passed. Wear long sleeves and gloves. Pampas grass leaves are razor sharp and can inflict nasty cuts! Tie it up tightly with twine before cutting.

Foliage Color—Deep green or variegated

Peak Season—Fall

Hardiness—Zones 7a to 10a

Texture—Medium to coarse

Water Needs—Very drought tolerant, once established

PORCUPINE GRASS

Miscanthus sinensis 'Strictus'

Why It's Special—Porcupine grass is grown for its beautifully banded green-and-yellow foliage. Broomlike plumes appear in late summer and persist well into winter. It is more upright than many of the *Miscanthus* and adds structure to the garden. It is well suited to smaller gardens.

How to Plant & Grow—Plant container-grown porcupine grass from spring to fall. Like all of the warm-season ornamental grasses, it will establish itself best during the warmer months. Space plants at least 4 to 5 feet apart in the garden to allow them to reach their mature size without being crowded.

Care & Problems—Once it is well established, porcupine grass will thrive with a minimum of care. There are no insect pests that require spraying. In late winter or early spring, before new growth emerges, cut the foliage back to 1 foot to tidy the clump and allow fresh new growth to replace last year's foliage and plumes.

Foliage Color—Green with yellow banding

Peak Season—Late summer to fall

Hardiness—Zones 5a to 9a

Texture—Medium

Water Needs—Moderately drought tolerant, once established

PURPLE FOUNTAIN GRASS

Pennisetum setaceum 'Purpureum'

Why It's Special—This annual grass grows extremely fast and puts on a spectacular show in only one season. Purple fountain grass is beautiful either planted *en masse* or mixed in individually with colorful perennials and annuals. It also looks beautiful in containers. Foxtail plumes appear from midsummer to fall.

How to Plant & Grow—Plant in mid- to late spring after soil has warmed considerably. Purple fountain grass loves the heat and will not grow an inch if the soil is still too cold. Plant in well-amended, rich garden soil and provide plenty of moisture. Fertilize at planting time and once per month throughout the summer to encourage lush growth and lots of plumes.

Care & Problems—Purple fountain grass is not hardy and is grown as an annual. Even in climates where it is hardy, it can look pretty ratty in its second season and is usually replaced yearly. Other than having to be replaced, it is carefree.

Foliage Color—Deep burgundy-purple

Peak Season—Early summer to fall

Hardiness—Grown as an annual

Texture—Medium

Water Needs—Regular watering is necessary

PURPLE MUHLY GRASS
Muhlenbergia capillaris

Why It's Special—This native American grass is spectacular in its autumn plumage. Purple muhly grass is well suited to being planted in large masses, where the haze of purple flowers will be showstopping.

How to Plant & Grow—To enjoy the purple fog of muhly plumes in late summer, set out plants the previous fall in full sun and well-drained soil. Muhly can be a little finicky and prefers very well-aerated, rather dry soil, so amend thoroughly with finely ground pine bark (soil conditioner) that will help loosen the soil.

Care & Problems—Seedheads will stand until midwinter to extend the seasonal display. When plants begin to look unkempt, lightly shear them just enough to tidy up. Shearing too hard may not agree with them, so leave as much plant as possible. An application of 10-10-10 fertilizer in early summer when growth is well underway will encourage lush flowering in autumn.

Foliage Color—Gray-green

Peak Season—Fall

Hardiness—Zones 6b (with protection) to 9a

Texture—Fine

Water Needs—Very drought tolerant, once established

SWEET FLAG
Acorus gramineus

Why It's Special—Sweet flag is not a true grass, but a distant cousin of the iris. However, its grassy texture makes it useful as a dwarf grass in the landscape. It is native to boggy sites and is well suited to wet areas where many ornamental grasses would not thrive.

How to Plant & Grow—Plant sweet flag in spring at the edge of a pond or bog in a container with a soil mix recommended for water-loving plants. It will also adapt very well to a partially shaded spot in the garden. The varieties 'Ogon', with golden-striped foliage, and 'Minimus Aurea', a tiny gold form, are popular.

Care & Problems—Divide garden plants in early spring, just as new growth appears. At the edges of ponds, it can become invasive if not potted or kept in check with judicious removal. It can suffer from fungal leaf spot and rust if stressed, but these are rarely serious.

Foliage Color—Green, gold, variegated

Peak Season—Spring to fall

Hardiness—Zones 5a to 9a

Texture—Fine

Water Needs—Needs moisture, even shallow standing water

SWITCHGRASS
Panicum virgatum

Why It's Special—Along with native bluestems, switchgrass was a major component of the tallgrass prairies of the Great Plains. Before settlers arrived, it stretched in vast green oceans across the central United States. Now, many beautiful selections have been developed for inclusion in gardens.

How to Plant & Grow—Full sun is an absolute must. Switchgrass performs best when planted in spring; early rains will help it get established and the summer heat will encourage it to grow. Roots grow deeply, so switchgrass is excellent for erosion control. Do not overfertilize or growth will be weak and "floppy."

Care & Problems—Hard pruning back to 8 inches at the end of each winter will encourage lush growth from the base, and in two or three seasons, most switch-grasses will spread from 1-gallon pots to 4- to 5-foot-wide clumps. For smaller gardens where spread is a problem, try the very vertical and strictly clumping *Panicum virgatum* 'Northwind'.

Foliage Color—Green to blue-green

Peak Season—Midsummer to late fall

Hardiness—Zones 3a to 8b

Texture—Medium-fine

Water Needs—Very drought tolerant, once established

GROUND COVERS

ESTABLISHING GROUND COVER BEDS

Ground covers are beautiful and versatile plants that are commonly used in large masses to provide foreground interest for taller shrub and perennial plantings, to create alternative "lawns" in areas that are too shady to grow grass effectively, and to reduce the constant maintenance of weeding and mulching in open bed spaces throughout the landscape. Ground covers will take some time to become established and fill in, so a little preparation on the front end will help you get them off to a rollicking start.

Before digging your first hole, ground cover beds should be thoroughly and completely weeded so that you are starting with a clean, blank slate. Where possible, thoroughly till the soil, add soil amendments such as compost and soil conditioner, and retill to incorporate these into the planting bed. Under large trees, this may not be possible because you don't want to damage the roots of the tree by tilling. In that case, choose tough ground covers that are known to thrive with some shade and root competition, and be prepared to do a little extra feeding and watering to get your new ground covers off to the best possible start.

You may wish to use a pre-emergent herbicide on your newly planted ground cover beds when you have finished planting. This will help to prevent weed seeds from germinating. By applying a pre-emergent herbicide and then mulching with a light, 1-inch layer of mulch, you can nearly eliminate the chore of weeding. Keep in mind that pre-emergent herbicides are only effective for a certain period of time and will have to be reapplied at regular intervals. This is still easier than having to hand pull weeds in large ground cover beds. It will take most ground covers two to three seasons to completely fill in and start suppressing weeds on their own. Each year of growth will reduce the amount of weeding you have to do, and eventually, ground cover beds should be very low-maintenance areas of your landscape

STAGGERED PLANTING

When you're ready to plant, it's easiest to lay all of your plants out first, arranging them, as much as possible, in staggered rows. The easiest way to get a good stagger and even spacing is to start at the front edge of your bed and lay all of your plants out from front to back. Start your first row of plants at least 10 to 12 inches back from the front edge of the bed for small plants like pachysandra, and even farther back for large ground covers like creeping juniper. Ground covers will grow in every direction and you don't want them to crawl right out of the bed in the first month after they've been planted!

Once you have the first row spaced, move to the second row. The second-row plants will be set back at whatever spacing you have chosen, and instead of lining them up directly behind the plants in the first row, stagger them and line them up with the spaces in between those plants. When you move to the third row, the plants will line up with the plants in the first row, the fourth row will line up with the second row, and so on. By staggering in this way, your ground covers will actually fill in and cover the soil faster and more effectively. In curved beds, you'll have to adjust your spacing a bit as you round the curves, but it still works essentially the same way.

HOW MANY DO I BUY?

Questions that arise when buying ground covers are: How many do I purchase, and how much space do they require? Here is a handy guide to assist you in answering this question.

SPACE COVERED BY 100 GROUND COVER PLANTS

PLANTING DISTANCE APART (IN INCHES)	AREA COVERED (IN SQUARE FEET)
12	100
16	125
18	225
24	400
30	1625
36	1900
48	1600
60	2500

(Reprinted by permission from the *Tennessee Gardener's Guide*, Third Edition.)

ORNAMENTAL GRASSES

SOIL PREPARATION FOR ORNAMENTAL GRASSES

Most ornamental grasses will grow in unimproved soil. However, they will establish themselves more quickly and produce better-looking plants in amended soil. If you are among the fortunate few with clay loam soil, adding amendments will result in only marginal increases in performance. However, on red clay Piedmont soils, incorporating limestone and a 2-inch layer of organic soil conditioner or aged pine bark will improve drainage, water intake, and microbiological activity in the soil. On sandy soil near the coast and on the old sand dunes running southwest from Pinehurst to Columbia and Aiken, generous amounts of limestone and moistened peat moss or leaf compost worked into the soil will greatly improve its moisture retention. Aged pine bark generally works best on clay soils, and peat moss on sand. Initially and thereafter, yearly applications of organic mulch will help maintain a healthy organic content in your soil.

LONG-TERM CARE AND MAINTENANCE OF ORNAMENTAL GRASSES

Leaving large clumps of ornamental grasses to fend for themselves leads to their eventual failure. Even near the coast, clumps freeze back partway, and farther west some grasses may freeze essentially to ground level each winter. Emerging new blades are partially obscured by the old foliage and the visual effect is messy. Cutting old clumps to the ground each spring can be approached ritually or with trepidation, depending on your age and energy level. Even with electric or gas-powered hedge shears, the job isn't easy and you are left with large piles of hay. Fortunately, ornamental grasses make good raw material for composting.

If you find yourself needing to dig and divide large clumps of grasses, be prepared for a difficult job. Old clumps of *Miscanthus*, pampas grass, and other large-growing types have tremendous root systems that spread both deep and wide. In some instances, it may even take a truck or other piece of equipment to pull or dig grasses out. Division may have to be done with an ax or even a chain saw. Grasses are tough! These are extreme cases, though, and if you divide very fast-growing grasses every three years and slower ones every five years, on a regular schedule, they should remain manageable. Regular division will also keep large clumps from dying out in the center as they are sometimes known to do.

THE FOOLPROOF WAY TO SHEAR LARGE GRASSES

One trick of the trade that many professional landscapers use is to tie ornamental grasses up in tight bundles *before* cutting them. Starting at the base of the plant, wrap a piece of sturdy jute twine around the plant about 18 inches above ground level and tie it as tightly as you can. Then wrap the twine around the plant three to four times, working your way toward the top. Tie off again at the top, as tightly as possible. Now use your gas-powered hedge shears or a large pruning saw to cut through the stems about 6 inches *below* the first round of twine near the base of the plant. Once you've cut all the way through, the top of the grass will be neatly bundled and can easily be removed.

FURTHER NOTES ON INVASIVE PLANTS

"Invasive exotic" is certainly a hot buzzword in horticultural circles these days, and while this is a worthwhile concern, it's not always just the exotic species that can be troublesome in the garden. Potential problems with *Miscanthus* were mentioned at the beginning of the chapter. Near the coast, Japanese blood grass (*Imperata cylindrica*), which spreads by underground runners, can get out of control in moist, fertile soil.

But in a garden setting, even some of our native species can turn into aggressive thugs. Northern sea oats, or river oats, are a perfect example of a native grass that drops so many seeds that the phrase "like hair on a dog's back" accurately describes the crop of volunteer seedlings. Even though it is a native species, in a garden setting it can be very invasive and problematic. The same can be said for some of the switchgrasses, which can spread to form large clumps very quickly and run right over the tops of smaller plants that may be in their way. This does not make them any less garden worthy; it just means that you, the homeowner, need to educate yourself on the front end and know what to expect.

The more responsible garden centers and mail-order suppliers of ornamental grasses are sensitive to both environmental and garden issues and present the advantages and disadvantages of ornamental grasses in their descriptions.

GRASS LOOK-ALIKES

If you're interested in expanding your plant palette and learning even more about ornamental grasses and grasslike plants, be sure to take a look at the genus *Carex*, commonly known as the sedges. This is one of the most diverse groups of plants you can grow. There are forms with broad leaves an inch or more wide and forms with leaves so fine they look like mounds of hair. There are green forms, blue forms, golden forms, and beautiful variegated forms. There are also species that grow on dry, shady rock outcroppings in forests and others that grow in standing water in full sun at the edges of streams and ponds. In size, they can range anywhere from a diminutive 3 inches tall to over 3 feet tall when they are full grown. All of them have interesting and sometimes showy "flowers," and some have spectacular seedheads. No matter the site, soil, or amount of moisture, there is a sedge that will fit the bill.

Other grasslike plants include the sweet flags, one of which was described in the plant profiles, and the mondo grasses, of which there are many forms and varieties. For the true plant collectors, there is a "new" group of grasslike plants from South Africa, called restios. The restios are actually not new at all, but are ancient grass relatives and are extremely fascinating and beautiful. Not all of them are tolerant of hot, humid climates, but part of the fun in gardening is experimenting with new, unusual plants to learn how they grow and perform where we live.

JANUARY

- As the gardening catalogs arrive this month, scan them for new and unique ground covers and ornamental grasses that might make good additions to your garden or landscape. Think about some troublesome areas that might be improved by the addition of a tough ground cover or grass.
- In the warmer parts of the Carolinas, ground covers can be planted now, as long as the soil can be worked. For ornamental grasses, you should wait until the weather and soil warms just a little more.
- Water fall-planted ground covers, especially evergreen types, if the soil is dry. Winter desiccation can be very detrimental to newly planted ground covers.
- As ground covers are settling in, apply a 1-inch layer of mulch to help suppress weeds. Winter weeds are actively growing now and can quickly take over newly planted beds.

FEBRUARY

- For heavily shaded areas where grass won't grow, shade-loving ground covers are an excellent alternative.
- In warmer parts of the Carolinas, ornamental grasses can be dug and divided this month, just before they begin their new cycle of growth. In colder areas, wait until next month.
- Fertilize ground covers just as they begin growing. In warmer areas, February is a good month to do this, but in cooler areas, you'll need to wait until March. It's best to rely on the results of a soil test when determining what type of fertilizer you need to use.
- Cut liriope, or monkey grass, back to within 3 to 4 inches of the ground using a string trimmer or, for large areas, a push mower set as high as it will go. Beware that if your mower won't raise to *at least* 3 inches high, you run the risk of cutting into the crowns of the plants.

MARCH

- Strawberries can make an interesting and unusual ground cover in parts of the landscape that receive full sun. They'll pull double duty by covering the ground and rewarding you with fresh, sweet strawberries in spring and early summer—if you can beat the birds to them.
- Piedmont and Coastal Plain gardeners can plant container-grown ground covers and ornamental grasses this month. Look for healthy, robust plants that look fresh and new and not like they were left over from last fall.

- If you haven't cut your liriope yet, your window of time is closing very quickly. If you don't get it done by early March, you run the risk of cutting off new growth as it begins to sprout from within last year's growth.

APRIL

- For design purposes, consider the color of your home, fences, and paving and see if ground covers or ornamental grasses could be used to help unify your home and landscape.

- Now is the prime season for planting ornamental grasses throughout most of the Carolinas. Soil and air temperatures have warmed and grasses are actively growing and will become established quickly.

- Continue to keep weeds under control in ground cover beds that have not filled in completely. Ground covers are in their most active growth phase now and competition from weeds will be detrimental.

- If you haven't fertilized your ornamental grasses, a light feeding now will encourage robust summer growth. Don't overdo it, though, or the stems may become weak and plants may flop.

MAY

- Keep an eye out for troublesome spots in the landscape. If you have turf areas that are struggling in too much shade, consider replacing them with shade-loving evergreen ground covers.

- If you have borders of liriope around any of your landscape beds and it is beginning to encroach on the other plants, now is the perfect time to divide and replant to get it back in bounds.

- Be sure to keep mulch on areas where ground covers haven't completely filled in yet. Summer weeds are germinating quickly now and it won't take long for them to get out of hand if you don't stay on top of them.

- Leaf and stem blight can be a serious problem on pachysandra—brown blotches appear on the leaves and spread to the stems. Remove and discard infected plants. In autumn, remove fallen leaves from the top of pachysandra beds that may trap moisture and encourage disease.

JUNE

- You can still plant container-grown ornamental grasses and ground covers from nurseries and garden centers. Many of our most popular ornamental grasses are warm-season grasses and will become very well established during the warm days of early summer.

- Apply water as needed to keep newly planted ground covers and ornamental grasses from wilting or curling. It will only take a few weeks to get them established now that the soil and weather are consistently warm.

- Instead of using wood mulch on ground cover beds, consider using well-rotted horse manure if it is available in your area. It is relatively free from weed seeds and will quickly enrich your soil while suppressing weeds.

- Keep an eye out for crown rot in beds of ajuga and remove any infected plants. Bare patches will fill in quickly on their own.

JULY

- If you're planning a vacation, be sure to find someone to water any first-year ground cover beds and ornamental grasses that may not be established yet. You'll also need them to water any plants growing in containers.

- Fast-growing summer weeds seem to appear overnight. Be sure to keep them under control in ground cover beds until the ground covers are thick enough to choke out most weeds on their own.

- Aphids, spider mites, and Japanese beetles are very active this month. Most ornamental grasses are relatively pest free, but some ground covers can occasionally be attacked. Consult your local garden center for advice if you find yourself with an insect infestation.

AUGUST

- August is a stressful month for planting new plants. It is recommended that you wait until September or October to do any further planting. If you have plants that must get in the ground right away, be sure to keep them well watered during this hot, dry month.

- Watering will be at the top of your to-do list this month. Remember that you want to water deeply and less frequently to encourage roots to reach far into the soil searching for water and nutrients. This will greatly reduce how much you have to water in the future.

- August is a perfect time to walk your garden in the early morning, journal in hand, and make notes of which plans are performing well and which ones are not. You may want to add more of the ones that are proving themselves and replace those that aren't.

SEPTEMBER

- Fall is prime planting season for ground covers, and most ornamental grasses can still be planted through the month of September as well. Be sure that you can water new plantings in case September turns out to be dry.

- If established areas of ground cover have a few bare spots, try transplanting a few sprigs from the areas that are thick and lush into the bare spaces. Dig 3- to 4-inch plugs, making sure they have good roots attached. Keep them watered until established.

- Hold off on any fertilizing this month. Feeding now could spur your plants into growth and they may not have time to harden off before cold weather sets in later in the fall.

- Clean up fallen leaves in ground cover beds. If allowed to remain on the ground for the winter, they can harbor insects and diseases that can cause problems next growing season.

OCTOBER

- If you have a slope whose steepness makes mowing dangerous, consider planting ground covers or ornamental grasses as a low-maintenance solution. Their deep roots will also help to stabilize the ground.

- Interplant spring-flowering bulbs such as miniature daffodils, grape hyacinths, crocus, and others with your ground covers for splashes of color next spring. The smaller, earlier-flowering bulbs are best for this, as their foliage will be dying down by the time the ground covers begin growing actively.

- In the Mountains, consider doing your autumn mulching as soon as all the leaves have fallen and can be cleaned up. Mulching will help keep the soil from freezing and thawing in winter, which can heave plants out of the ground.

NOVEMBER

- In warmer areas, container-grown ground covers can still be planted. Avoid planting ornamental grasses now, though, since winter is just around the corner. They may not have time to become well established before cold weather sets in.

- Fall is usually a dry time of year in the Carolinas, so be sure to keep up with watering throughout the garden—especially for first-year plantings that are just getting well established.

- Winter and early spring weeds like chickweed, henbit, and dandelions will be germinating now. It is easiest to eradicate them while they are small. Be careful when hoeing or cultivating around shallow-rooted ground covers or landscape plants.

DECEMBER

- Update your gardening journal now, while the current season is still fresh in your mind. Your journal will be more meaningful and accurate if you don't have to reach too far back in your memory to recall how a particular plant or part of the garden performed this season.

- Don't forget to water beds of ground covers that were installed this fall. They probably haven't rooted in completely yet and will need some supplemental water, especially if late fall and early winter are dry.

- If you haven't removed leaves from ground cover beds yet, it is essential to get it done as soon as possible. Fallen leaves can harbor insects and diseases that will overwinter and cause problems come spring.

- Continue pulling winter weeds. They grow amazingly fast during the cool days and nights of late fall and early winter.

- If you had scale or spider mite problems on any ground covers this season, now is the time to spray with horticultural oil sprays to help smother the insects and their eggs that are overwintering.

LAWNS
for the Carolinas

The geographic and climatic conditions of the Carolinas are about as diverse as the number of turfgrass species that will thrive there. You'll find a wide range of soils, altitudes, rainfall, and temperatures, from north to south and east to west. In fact, the Carolinas have some of the greatest diversity of natural environments of any eastern states and as a result, the turfgrasses that can be grown here vary widely from one region to the next.

With such great diversity in land regions, including Coastal Plain, Piedmont, and Mountains, altitude is not the only factor that plays a part as you move from the cooler and more mountainous regions of the west into the Piedmont and coastal regions of the east; latitude also plays an important role as you move from the northern edge of North Carolina to the southern tip of South Carolina. Different grasses will perform better in different environments, and matching the appropriate lawn grass to its preferred growing conditions and region is essential. There are several species and numerous cultivars of turfgrass that can make showy and functional lawns in the various regions of both states, including both cool-season and warm-season types of turf.

SOILS

The Carolinas vary greatly in their soil makeup, from the sandy soil of the coasts, to the clay of the Piedmont and central regions, to rich, moist soil in the mountain woodlands. The structure of your soil has a lot to do with the types of turfgrasses that will grow successfully. Determining the soil texture (percentages of sand, silt, and clay) can tell you whether or not you need to add amendments, how much watering you will have to do, and what other maintenance might be required. A simple home test to help determine the texture of your soil is described near the end of this chapter.

Whether your soil is acid or alkaline also affects what types of turfgrasses will thrive in your area. The measurement of the acidity or alkalinity of the soil is called the soil's pH. While there are many home pH test kits available, it's a good idea, for accuracy's sake, to have your soil professionally tested by your County Extension Service before beginning any gardening project, including establishing a lawn. In addition to pH, a professional soil test will often tell you what amounts of nutrients are already present in your soil and which nutrients (nitrogen, phosphorous, or potassium) should be applied and in what quantities.

HARDINESS

A cold-hardiness zone is defined by the northernmost boundary in which plants can grow when the weather is at its coldest. In North Carolina, these zones vary more or less from west to east, from Zones 6a to 8a, with the majority of the state falling into Zones 7a and 7b. Some grasses are more cold tender than others and it is important to know which hardiness zone you're in when selecting a grass for your lawn. In South Carolina, the same holds true, with the hardiness zones varying more or less from west to east, getting warmer as you move toward the coast. The majority of South Carolina is covered by Zones 7b and 8a, with just the northwest corner being Zone 7a, and some areas along the coast falling into the warmer Zone 8b.

Many plants, lawn grasses included, are affected not only by average temperatures, but also by the range of extremes experienced throughout the year. So, in addition to cold, another temperature factor is heat, especially when coupled with humidity. If the cold of winter doesn't kill something, sometimes the heat of summer will. And while much of the Carolinas typically have very mild winters (although the Mountain region has colder winters and milder summers), the Coastal Plain and Piedmont regions can certainly be hot and humid.

It is important to note that there are many transitional areas in the Carolinas when it comes to lawn grasses, and while Kentucky bluegrass and fescues may thrive in the cooler, mountainous regions of western North Carolina, they will flounder in much of South Carolina. Similarly, St. Augustinegrass, bahiagrass, and the carpetgrasses will freeze out in colder areas. Still others, most notably bermudagrass and zoysiagrass, can be grown almost anywhere in either state.

PRECIPITATION

One of the most obvious factors affecting how well your lawn or garden grows is rainfall. It can determine what will thrive in your area and how much supplemental watering you may have to do. If you consult a yearly rainfall map, you will find that most of North Carolina receives over 50 inches of rainfall per year, with somewhat more along the coast and in the mountains in the southwest toe of the state, while South Carolina averages approximately 48 inches of rainfall a year, with the most rainfall occurring in the upper northwest corner and slightly less precipitation as you move toward the coast.

While the amount of annual precipitation is important, the other factor that comes into play is *when* the majority of the precipitation occurs. In both states, the rainy season for the coast is typically summer and early fall, and the farther inland you go, the more distributed through the year the rainfall is. But in all parts of the Carolinas, the precipitation can vary widely month to month. Knowing how much rain your area receives annually, when the rainy seasons are, and which months are the driest, will tell you when you need to be the most conscious of possible water needs in your yard.

If you live in parts of the state that receive less annual precipitation, you are more likely to be a candidate for installing irrigation, or you will at least need to set the sprinkler out during the driest times. And droughts can occur anywhere in the state. Know what to expect in your region and keep an eye on your lawn, especially if it is new. The grass will tell you when it needs water, but it's good to have some idea ahead of time when that might occur.

MAINTENANCE

To have a beautiful lawn, you need to take good care of it, and that means maintenance. Most homeowners already know that lawns require watering, fertilizing, and weed control, and they probably suspect there are other things they need to do as well. Having a schedule can make the task at hand seem easier and can prevent the sense of panic you feel when you think you've forgotten to do something. Fertilizing and weed control schedules for lawns will vary from region to region and from one type of grass to another, so it is best to consult a local authority who can speak directly to lawn maintenance in your area and specifically to the type of turf you have chosen to grow. Local garden centers and your County Extension Service are invaluable resources in helping you determine the best time of year and the best products for various lawn maintenance activities. In addition to watering, fertilizing, and weed control, proper mowing is crucial to maintaining a beautiful lawn. You will find suggestions for proper mowing heights for each type of turf listed in the plant profiles.

A WORD ON IRRIGATION

One of the most critical and costly mistakes when it comes to lawn care is improper watering. This is especially true for lawns with automatic irrigation systems, but 99 percent of the time it's not the fault of the system, but the fault of the homeowner. The typical line of thinking is that we have spent all of this money on automatic irrigation and now we want to see it run. The truth of the matter is this: If you run your irrigation for a brief period of time every day or, in some cases, even twice a day (people do that!), you are only saturating the uppermost surface of the soil. Roots only grow where they have to in order to get water, so if all of the water is in the upper 2 inches of soil, so are the roots. Then, when dry weather comes you'll find yourself watering constantly and paying exorbitant water bills trying to keep your lawn alive. Whether you water by hand or by automated system, the rule to follow is "deep and infrequent." The type of grass doesn't matter. The deeper you water and the deeper the roots have to go in search of that water, the better off your lawn will be in the long run.

Any aspect of gardening is seasonal, dependent on both the weather and the growth cycle of plants, and timing is everything. Having a healthy, green lawn is well worth the effort. Whether you use it as a practice soccer field, a complement to your flower beds, or a place to relax at the end of the day, once it's established, and once you're familiar with the routine that will keep it at its best, a lawn can offer years of enjoyment. Don't fight the lawn—learn how to work with it.

BERMUDAGRASS

Cynodon dactylon

Why It's Special—Bermudagrass is a tough, fast-growing, hardy turfgrass that quickly forms a lush, emerald green, carpetlike lawn. High traffic tolerance makes it a top choice for golf courses, and its toleration of both heat and cold means that it grows well in most regions of the Carolinas. Its adaptability to a wide range of soil types and pH and its moderate tolerance of salt (for coastal regions) are added benefits.

How to Plant & Grow—Bermudagrass can be be seeded, sprigged, or plugged with excellent results. Most commonly, 2-inch plugs are cut from sheets of sod, planted on 6- to 12-inch centers, and allowed to fill in during the first growing season.

Care & Problems—Bermudagrass's aggressiveness can be a double-edged sword if it begins to invade landscape beds, where it can be difficult to eradicate. It is intolerant of shade and will become thin and bare in shady corners, allowing weeds to take over.

Hardiness: Zones 6a to 9b, excellent heat tolerance

Type: Warm-season grass

Texture: Fine

Water Needs: Very drought tolerant, once established

Recommended Mowing Height: ½ inch to 2 inches

CARPETGRASS

Axonopus fissifolius

Why It's Special—Carpetgrass, while not one of the most popular lawn grasses, does have its place in poor, wet, acidic soils where it is difficult to grow other types of turf. It can be useful in the warmest coastal areas of the Carolinas.

How to Plant & Grow—Carpetgrass can be seeded, sprigged, or plugged, and since it is a warm-season grass, the optimum time to establish it is between the months of March and May, when the weather begins to warm and active growth begins. Overfertilization can lead to certain disease problems, as well as the abundant production of unsightly seedheads.

Care & Problems—Although carpetgrass is generally low maintenance, its biggest problem is that its seedheads grow quite tall very quickly, making frequent mowing necessary throughout the growing season to keep it looking its best. This may be a worthwhile tradeoff for extremely difficult areas in wet, acidic soils where no other turfgrasses will grow.

Hardiness: Zone 8b to 10

Type: Warm-season grass

Texture: Coarse

Water Needs: Tolerant of both wet and dry conditions

Recommended Mowing Height: 1 to 2 inches

CENTIPEDEGRASS

Eremochloa ophiuroides

Why It's Special—Centipedegrass is sometimes used as an alternative to bermudagrass in regions where it is hardy. The two are similar in appearance, but centipedegrass is slower growing and has shorter stolons, making it less invasive in flower beds and landscaped areas.

How to Plant & Grow—Centipedegrass is usually started by seeding between April and June, when the soil and air temperatures are warm and conducive to fast germination and establishment. It can also be sprigged or plugged, like many of the other warm-season grasses.

Care & Problems—Its slow growth can be a problem in areas prone to erosion. Centipedegrass also has a more yellow-green coloration that is less desirable in the eyes of some gardeners, though there are cultivars that have been selected for better green color. Salt tolerance is fairly low compared to some other species, so centipedegrass may not be the best choice for coastal areas where soil salinity may be a problem.

Hardiness: Zones 7a to 9b

Type: Warm-season grass

Texture: Medium

Water Needs: Medium, water during drought

Recommended Mowing Height: 1 to 2 inches

KENTUCKY BLUEGRASS

Poa pratensis

Why It's Special—Kentucky bluegrass is every homeowner's image of the "perfect" lawn—a thick, carpetlike, deep green grass. A word of caution: In the Carolinas, Kentucky bluegrass is best suited to higher elevations, where it receives some reprieve from heat and humidity.

How to Plant & Grow—The optimum time for planting is late September through October, while the soil is still warm but nighttime temperatures have begun to moderate. Thorough aeration prior to seeding or the use of a commercial seeder is beneficial, and the seeds must be kept constantly moist until they have germinated and the new grass is 2 to 3 inches tall.

Care & Problems—In the South, Kentucky bluegrass can be challenging. Deep, thorough watering during summer and regular fertilizing will help. Grub worms, brown patch, and rust can be problems in areas with high temperatures and humidity.

Hardiness: Zones 5a to 7a

Type: Cool-season grass

Texture: Fine

Water Needs: Deep, thorough watering throughout summer

Recommended Mowing Height: 2 to 2½ inches in spring and fall, 3 to 3½ inches in summer

RYEGRASS

Lolium spp.

Why It's Special—Ryegrass comes in two forms: annual and perennial. In the South, both are grown as annuals since neither tolerates summer's intense heat and high humidity. However, they are invaluable for overseeding warm-season grasses like bermudagrass and zoysiagrass to help maintain the green appearance of the lawn in winter when the warm- season grasses have gone dormant and turned brown.

How to Plant & Grow—Ryegrass is grown from seed and is commonly seeded into warm-season lawns in October and November, where it germinates quickly and becomes a green cover for the quickly browning warm-season turfgrasses. It can also be used in shadier areas of the landscape, where it will remain green throughout the winter and into late spring.

Care & Problems—Green winter color also means winter mowing. Ryegrass should be maintained at about 2½ inches through the winter. Take care not to use high-nitrogen fertilizers on ryegrass as they can cause problems for the dormant warm-season grass beneath it.

Hardiness: Grown as an annual

Type: Cool-season grass

Texture: Fine

Water Needs: Moderate, winter precipitation is usually adequate

Recommended Mowing Height: 2½ inches

ST. AUGUSTINEGRASS

Stenotaphrum secundatum

Why It's Special—St. Augustinegrass is one of the most shade tolerant of all the Southern turfgrasses, and this makes it worth considering for landscapes where pine, oak, and other trees eliminate the opportunities for growing less shade-tolerant species. It also thrives in heat and humidity and is fairly tolerant of saline soils, making it a good choice for coastal areas.

How to Plant & Grow—While St. Augustinegrass can be seeded, it is more commonly sprigged or plugged between the months of April and June, when soil and air temperatures are warm and sprigs or plugs will root and establish quickly. Regular watering is necessary until the lawn is well established.

Care & Problems—Because of its extremely dense growth habit, thick thatch can build up at the soil surface, harboring insects and fungal diseases. While the grass is rated hardy to Zone 7b, frequent or long drops in temperature below 20 degrees F can be damaging.

Hardiness: Zones 7b to 10

Type: Warm-season grass

Texture: Very coarse

Water Needs: Low, once established

Recommended Mowing Height: 2 to 3 inches or taller

TALL FESCUE

Festuca arundinacea

Why It's Special—Tall fescue is a cool-season grass that thrives in the upper and mid South as long as supplemental irrigation can be provided during summer. It is also one of the most shade tolerant of all turfgrasses.

How to Plant & Grow—Seeding is done from late September to October, when soil is still warm and seeds will germinate and grow quickly. Thorough and regular watering is a must to ensure that the seedbed does not dry out once germination has begun and while grass is young and tender.

Care & Problems—Tall fescue is not as drought tolerant as some species and summer irrigation is required to keep it from going dormant. Mowing at the highest possible mower setting will encourage tall fescue to push roots deep into the soil. Mowing too short will cause undue stress, opening the door to disease and insect problems when heat and humidity are high.

Hardiness: Zones 5a to 7b

Type: Cool-season grass

Texture: Medium to coarse, depending on variety

Water Needs: Medium, but higher in summer

Recommended Mowing Height: 3 to 3½ inches

ZOYSIAGRASS

Zoysia japonica

Why It's Special—Zoysia is cherished by many as the ideal lawn grass for the South because of its fine leaf blades and thick growth. It is one of the more shade-tolerant warm-season grasses, and its toleration of winter cold and summer heat and humidity makes it the near-perfect turfgrass.

How to Plant & Grow—Zoysiagrass is rarely seeded. Most commonly, it is either sprigged or plugged between April and June, when warm soil and air temperatures support root growth and establishment. Zoysia is a heavy feeder and your local garden center or County Extension Service can provide recommendations.

Care & Problems—Zoysia needs regular mowing to look and grow its best. It can be maintained at very short heights to give that "golf course"-like appearance, but this requires even more diligence. Thatch can be a problem with improper care, and zoysia is slower than other grasses to become established when planted and slower to recover if damaged.

Hardiness: Zones 6a to 9b

Type: Warm season grass

Texture: Fine

Water Needs: Drought tolerant, once established

Mowing Height: ¾ to 1½ inches

ALTERNATIVES TO LAWNS

In the age of more earth-friendly gardening practices, such as water conservation and the reduction of chemicals, many homeowners are actively working toward reducing the amount of traditional lawn they plant and maintain, and are turning to various ground covers, ornamental grasses, and other landscape plants to create beautiful alternatives to traditional lawns. This is not to say that turf should be eliminated entirely from the landscape, but to suggest that more thought should be given to where turf is truly useful and needed rather than carpeting the yard from property line to property line with thirsty, high-maintenance lawn.

One of the biggest obstacles homeowners face when deciding to pursue alternatives to a traditional lawn is changing their own viewpoints (and perhaps those of their neighbors) on just what a lawn "should" look like. The neatly manicured, deep green swath of lawn stretching from front to back and side to side of our urban and suburban lots has become a deeply ingrained part of the American psyche. Changing that expectation can sometimes be a challenge—for ourselves and for others. And if you live in a subdivision governed by a homeowner association (HOA), where rules and regulations apply to nearly every aspect of your home and its surroundings, having an alternative lawn may take a considerable amount of debate and convincing. However, if you are truly interested in this approach, the benefits may outweigh the potential challenges.

Today, the average American lawn ranges from 5,000 to 10,000 square feet. Did you know that by reducing a 10,000-square-foot lawn to 3,500 square feet and relandscaping the remaining area with ground covers and landscape plants, you can reduce your outdoor water usage (and your water bill!) by nearly 30 percent? This is a savings of over 150,000 gallons of water per year—water that you're conserving and, maybe just as importantly, not paying for! Of course, you have the initial expense of making a potentially dramatic change to your landscape, but depending on the size of your lot and how you're able to change your irrigation habits, you are looking at saving hundreds and potentially even thousands of dollars each year. In a few years' time, that initial investment may pay for itself several times over just through the savings in your monthly water bill, not to mention the beauty you bring to the neighborhood.

GROUND COVERS

One of the easiest changes you can make to eliminate high-maintenance turf from your landscape is to add beds of ground cover. This is a particularly useful tactic in shady areas where grass may struggle and you're frequently left with bare spots because the grass simply won't grow. Look for a natural boundary between where your lawn thrives and where it begins to look thin and bedraggled. Then consider where you can draw an attractive line to create a bed edge that will complement your existing landscape, and create a transitional ground cover bed in between. This could be an island around the base of existing trees in the lawn or perhaps a transitional area between existing lawn and landscape beds. There may be several possible scenarios. Use your creative eye to form and shape the beds in a pleasing way—don't blindly follow the shade line if there is a better alternative, even if it means removing a little bit of good turf or moving a few landscape plants around to get an attractive curve or line. For recommendations of specific ground covers, see the chapter on "Ground Covers & Ornamental Grasses."

ORNAMENTAL GRASSES AND SEDGES

If ground covers aren't for you, consider replacing your lawn with ornamental grasses and sedges (*Carex* spp.). By choosing drought-tolerant varieties of grasses and sedges that remain short and don't require mowing, not only can you reduce the need for excess irrigation, but you may be able to eliminate mowing and traditional lawn maintenance almost entirely! Native grasses and sedges that are already adapted to the region are particularly good choices for alternative lawns. Nurseries that specialize in native plants are invaluable resources for more information about transitioning from traditional lawns to native grass and sedge lawn alternatives.

If a true alternative lawn isn't an option for you, consider using ornamental grasses and sedges as ground covers or in mass plantings throughout your landscape. Their many beautiful forms, colors, and textures contrast well with other landscape plants and provide graceful movement in the garden each time a gentle breeze blows through. Wisely chosen, grasses and sedges can provide year-round beauty and interest in the landscape.

MEADOW AND PRAIRIE PLANTINGS

Other popular alternatives to traditional lawns are restored natural areas, often called "meadows" or "prairies" by the gardeners who grow and maintain them. These names may be a bit of a technical misnomer, but they do evoke a particular image that we can immediately associate with an area that has been returned to a mixture of grasses and flowering plants. Establishing a meadow or prairie planting is not difficult to do and, once established, it can be one of the lowest-maintenance type of gardens or landscapes to have. Keep in mind, though, that a prairie- or meadow-style garden involves more than just the plants. You are creating an ecosystem that, over time, will attract beneficial birds, insects, and other forms of wildlife. If you live in a neighborhood or subdivision, be proactive with neighbors and neighborhood associations, as well as honest about your intent, to head off potential misunderstandings about your endeavors.

HOME TEST TO DETERMINE SOIL MAKEUP

Your soil texture, along with other factors, affects the frequency and amount of water needed to maintain your lawn and landscape. The texture of a soil is determined by the proportions of the three main mineral components—sand, silt, and clay. Loamy soils are a mix of the three; they are ideal for most plants, including turf. A simple test to determine your soil texture is based on the weight of these particles when settled out of a water suspension. Sand is heavier than silt, and silt is heavier than clay, due to particle size. They will settle at various levels and times because of their differences in weight. This enables you to gauge the percentage of each in a soil sample. Here's how to do it:

1. Fill a quart jar two-thirds full of water, and add 1 teaspoon of liquid dishwashing detergent as a wetting agent.

2. Add soil until the water level reaches the neck of the jar, just below the cap threads, leaving some air space to allow for shaking. Remove any debris such as rocks, roots, or gravel. Break up any clods to help speed up the process. Shake the jar vigorously to make sure the soil and water are mixed thoroughly.

3. When the water and soil are completely mixed, vigorously shake the jar for a couple of minutes, and set it on a level surface. After about forty seconds the sand will settle. Mark the sand level with a permanent or waterproof marker on the outside of the jar. The time to mark the jar is when the settled sand particles are not moving, but the silt and clay are still in suspension, which can be hard to distinguish.

4. Wait another four hours without disturbing the jar; at this point most of the silt will be settled. Mark the silt level with the pen. The remainder that settles in the next twenty-four hours should be clay. Mark again to identify the clay level.

5. Observe the thickness of the three distinct sections. If all three layers are about equal, your soil is loamy; if the top layer is the deepest, your soil is mostly clay; and if the bottom layer is the deepest, your soil is sandy.

Looking at your jar of soil, assign a percentage to each layer with the percentages totaling 100. You can do this by using a ruler and first measuring the total depth of the soil in the jar and then measuring the depth of each individual layer. Next, divide the depth of each layer by the total depth of the soil in the jar. For example, when all of the soil has settled completely, let's say you measure and have 3 inches of soil, total. Then, when you measure the depth of the bottom layer (sand), you come up with 0.5 inches. Simply divide 0.5 by 3 and you get 0.166666, or 16.6 percent. This means that 16.6 percent of your sample is sand, and that silt and clay are each going to make up some portion of the remaining 83.4 percent of your soil sample. Next, measure each of the layers of silt and clay and perform the same calculation.

Now that you have some ballpark figures for your soil's makeup, what do you do with that information? In very general terms, consider the following:

- Sand is the least water retentive of the three particles and dries out the fastest. Soils with a large percentage of sand tend to dry out quickly and have little nutrient-holding capacity.

- Silt retains some moisture and although nutrients will bind and stick to silt particles, they are also easily released and made available to a plant's roots. Silty soils are moisture retentive, but rarely waterlogged and will readily exchange nutrients with the plants growing in them.

- Clay is the smallest particle of soil and binds very tightly to both water and nutrients, not wanting to let go of either. Clay soils tend to become sticky when wet and will not easily give up the nutrients that are bound to them.

- Given this information, you can understand that if your soil contains a large percentage of sand based on your calculations, it is likely that your soil will dry out quickly and that nutrients will rapidly leach from the soil, meaning that supplemental water and fertilizer will have to be provided at regular intervals throughout the growing season. If your soil contains a high percentage of clay, it will retain water for long periods of time, which can lead to roots being waterlogged and unable to breathe. Wet conditions can quickly lead to various root rot diseases for many plants. Additionally, plants growing in clay soils will often exhibit nutrient deficiencies, because while the nutrients are present in the soil, they are bound tightly to the clay particles and the plants are unable to absorb them.

So for soils that are either sandy or clay based in their makeup, how do we correct the associated problems? Organic matter—garden compost, composted manures, soil conditioners—is a must. It is organic matter that helps to increase the water- and nutrient-holding capacities of sandy soils, and it is organic matter that helps to break the tight bonds between clay particles and "loosen up" those sticky clay soils, allowing water and nutrients to pass through them more freely. In newly prepared beds that have yet to be planted, it is recommended that you add a minimum of 2 to 3 inches of good organic matter and till it thoroughly into the existing soil. In future years, a 1-inch topdressing of compost can be added to the beds in spring and fall to be incorporated by earthworms and other soil organisms. The same 1-inch topdressing can be applied on already-established beds or lawns where tilling around the plants is not an option. This treatment will help to keep your soil and your plants happy and healthy for years to come.

JANUARY

- If you're planning to hire a lawn service to care for your lawn, now is a good time to begin interviewing potential companies. Be realistic about your expectations and clear about exactly what services a company provides.

- Cool-season grasses can be sodded anytime the soil is not frozen, but planting of warm-season grasses should be delayed until the air temperature is consistently above 60 degrees F or even warmer.

- Cool-season lawns may need supplemental watering this month if it has been dry, warm, and windy. Newly planted fescue or bluegrass sod will need daily watering until it is thoroughly rooted in.

- If mowing is necessary on cool-season lawns, remove no more than one-third of the leaf blade at a time.

- January is the perfect time to perform mower maintenance: clean air filters, change spark plugs and oil, and sharpen mower blades for the upcoming season.

FEBRUARY

- Before you fertilize your lawn in the next few months, calibrate your spreader to make sure you are delivering the correct amount of fertilizer to your lawn. Instructions for proper calibration of both rotary and drop-type spreaders can be found online.

- New sod must be kept consistently moist for two to three weeks after it is installed. Roots grow quickly when moisture is present, so new sod should be thoroughly "knitted" to the soil within a few weeks; at this point, you can slowly reduce watering.

- If mowing is necessary, be sure your mower blades are good and sharp. Kentucky bluegrass should be maintained at 1½ to 2½ inches, fescue at 2 to 3 inches, and ryegrass overseeded into zoysia or bermuda should be maintained at about 1 inch.

MARCH

- Bagging your grass clippings keeps your lawn neat and clean, but it also removes valuable nutrients and organic matter. Returning your grass clippings to the soil also saves time and energy while mowing.

- Cool-season grasses can be fertilized this month according to the results of a soil test. If a soil test indicates that nutrient levels are sufficient in the soil and your lawn has good color and vigor, postpone fertilizing until fall.

- Dormant, warm-season lawns may need to be watered this month, as they will soon be waking up and beginning to grow. This is especially true if warm, windy weather prevails and soil dries out quickly.

- Brown patch attacks warm-season grasses in early spring as they emerge from dormancy. Avoid overfertilizing and apply fungicides if a serious outbreak occurs.

APRIL

- It is time to repair bare patches or replant large areas of warm-season grasses by seeding, plugging, or sprigging once average daytime temperatures are staying about 60 degrees F.

- Newly seeded, plugged, or sodded lawns will need frequent, thorough watering to keep the soil moist until germination and rooting have begun. Once established, slowly reduce the amount of water to encourage roots to grow deep into the soil.

- Water established lawns as needed. One inch of water per week is sufficient for clay and loam soils, but lawns growing on sandy soils may need 1½ to 2 inches per week, especially if the weather is dry.

- Lawn diseases will be rearing their ugly heads this month. Rust, dollar spot, brown patch, and spring dead spot can all be problems. Local garden centers or your County Extension Service are excellent resources for information about treatment.

MAY

- Encourage the development of a deep root system by reducing the frequency of watering and by watering thoroughly and deeply each time. Lawns with deep root systems will require less maintenance and will survive hot, dry periods with less stress and damage.

- Newly seeded, sprigged, or sodded lawns may still need frequent watering, but you should slowly reduce the amount of water they receive as they become established.

- Regular mowing of both warm- and cool-season grasses will encourage thick, lush growth and deep rooting.

- Southern chinch bugs can be problematic on all warm-season grasses, but are especially troublesome on St. Augustinegrass. The nymphs suck sap from the plants and inject a toxin that causes yellowing and death of the leaves.

- Pre-emergent herbicides that were applied earlier in the spring for control of crabgrass have probably lost their effectiveness by now. Reapplication may be necessary to prevent summer germination of grassy weeds.

JUNE

- The best way to determine fertilizer requirements for your lawn is to have your soil tested at least every three years through your local County Extension Service. Have your soil tested this month to make plans for fall.

- There is still time to renovate warm-season lawns by sodding, plugging, or sprigging.

- Water your lawn anytime that it shows signs of stress. These signs could include a bluish gray tint, footprints remaining in the lawn when you walk on it, and wilted, curled, or folded leaves.

- Brown patch can be a big problem in fescue and bluegrass lawns in June. A preventive application of fungicide may be advisable in areas where night temperatures and humidity remain high.

JULY

- Young lawns will need attention to watering until their root systems are thoroughly established and have grown deeply into the soil. During drought periods, apply at least 1 inch of water per week and ½ inch every third day in sandy soils.

- Newly sodded lawns can be mowed once they have firmly rooted into place. Raise the mowing height by one or two notches to decrease "pull" on the new sod as you cut. It may be a good idea to push mow new sod the first couple of times to avoid tearing tender roots with a heavy riding mower.

- Pythium blight is a hot-weather fungal disease that rapidly gobbles up lawns. Be on the lookout this month for leaves that appear water soaked or greasy looking, as this is a sure sign. Fungicides are available for prevention.

AUGUST

- It is too late for seeding, sprigging, or plugging warm-season grasses now. They will not have time to become established before autumn and may be killed by cold weather.

- Water dormant cool-season lawns thoroughly and deeply every two weeks in the absence of rain, knowing that they will soon be waking up with the onset of cooler fall weather.

- Overseeding may be necessary for bare spots once autumn arrives.

- Mow regularly and only remove one-third of the total leaf blade each time you mow. This reduces the stress on your lawn and keeps it healthy and looking its finest.

- White grubs are extremely active this month. If your lawn looks wilted even after watering, or if you have had particularly bad problems with digging skunks or moles, white grubs may be present. Milky spore disease can be used for grub control and is especially effective against Japanese beetle grubs.

SEPTEMBER

- Fall aeration can begin in earnest this month. For very small lawns, this can be done with a spading fork, but for larger lawns it is probably best to rent an aerator from a rental center. An aerator pulls a small core of soil from the ground and increases air, water, and nutrient penetration.
- In cooler areas, overseeding of cool-season lawns can begin in mid- to late September.
- Regular irrigation will be necessary once seed is down.
- Do not fertilize warm-season grasses at this time. Heavy amounts of nitrogen can force soft, lush growth that will be more susceptible to winterkill when cold temperatures arrive.
- Cool-season grasses can be fertilized now to encourage lush, thick growth during the cool days of autumn and early winter.

OCTOBER

- As you rake up the fallen leaves from your lawn, recycle them as mulch or compost. If possible, run them through a shredder first so they will break down more quickly and stay in place once they're spread through your beds.
- Reseeding of cool-season lawns can continue. Be sure to keep the seed consistently moist until it germinates, and then continue irrigating regularly until the new grass is well established.
- If you haven't fertilized your cool-season lawn already, it may be best to wait until late November and apply a "winterizer"-type fertilizer that will help carry your lawn through the winter.
- Mow cool-season grasses often and keep the mower height raised as high as recommended for the type of grass you're growing. Tall mowing encourages deep root systems.
- Henbit, chickweed, dandelions, and other broadleaf weeds begin germinating this month. Treat as necessary to reduce problems in winter and spring.

NOVEMBER

- Mosses growing in your lawn may indicate areas that are too shady or too wet, or soils that are too acidic, to support the good growth of turf. Before you eliminate moss, keep in mind that it may be very difficult to get a good stand of grass in these areas if the conditions are unsuitable for lawngrasses.
- November is the perfect month to install sod of cool-season grasses. Be sure that you can keep it thoroughly watered until it is well established.
- Warm-season grasses may need to be watered, even though they are going dormant.
- Wild garlic begins sprouting in earnest this month. It can be treated with a broadleaf herbicide when the air temperature is above 50 degrees F. You can hand pull wild garlic as long as you are sure to remove the entire plant, bulb and all.

DECEMBER

- Make plans to winterize your lawnmower before putting it away for the season to keep interior parts from rusting during the winter and to ensure that the mower will start when you need it in the spring.
- For cool-season grasses, if dry weather persists and the lawn shows signs of stress, apply 1 inch of water per week in the absence of precipitation.
- Cool-season lawns may need to be mowed through the month of December.
- Spot treat any chickweed, henbit, or dandelions by hand pulling or by using a broadleaf weed killer as they continue to germinate and grow.

ROSES

for the Carolinas

Perhaps no flower in the world is more popular than America's national flower: the rose. Its beautiful form, rich pleasing colors, delightful fragrances, and incredible versatility have made it a favorite of gardeners and flower lovers for generations. No wonder it is called the Queen of Flowers. The rose is a testament to human creativity. Once a wildflower, it has been cultivated and engineered to suit all types of gardens. There is a rose for every region of the Carolinas, a form for every location. Varieties are available for borders and for growing on arbors and trellises, and miniatures are even available for color beds. The unique tree roses grown as standards are ideal for container gardening, while the newer ground cover roses adapt well to small spaces. Of course, the hybrid teas are superb for cutting and are the rose of choice for millions of Americans.

FIRST THINGS FIRST

When researching roses, begin with the All-America Rose Selections (AARS). Winners of these awards will perform best and are most resistant to blackspot and mildew diseases. Several websites carry the AARS list and a handbook that rates varieties. The greatest challenge will be settling on a few plants to avoid crowding your garden bed—a *big* no-no in rose culture.

Not too long ago, we thought roses for cutting, like hybrid teas, were the only choice for gardeners. Nowadays, landscape roses are the best route for color and easy maintenance. In the past decade, the introduction of the Knock Out® series of roses and their kin has changed the way most of us think about roses in the garden. Their vibrant colors and exceptional disease resistance have lured homeowners with promises of nonstop blooms and easy maintenance. They have been successfully grown in beds and in containers for patio gardening. Their long blooming season and no-nonsense pruning requirements appeal to every homeowner. There are numerous roses entering the marketplace today with similar carefree characteristics and it is exciting to think that these will grow anywhere in the Carolinas.

WHAT DO ROSES REQUIRE?

Choose a site with good air circulation and six hours or more of daily sunshine. Morning sun is best for disease prevention, as it dries the foliage off early in the day. Be sure to do your homework in bed preparation too. The old adage that you should "plant a fifty-cent plant in a five-dollar hole" is a good one, especially for roses. Have the soil tested and amend as needed with organic amendments such as leaf compost, aged manure, and soil conditioner. Roses love water, but also need perfect drainage to carry surplus water away from their roots. In heavy clay soils, consider installing a drainage system or growing roses in raised beds or berms.

Regular care and maintenance for roses is just as important as site selection. They benefit from monthly fertilizing using either 10-10-10 or special rose fertilizers. Water-soluble fertilizers can be applied to supplement dry feeding, as can organic products ranging from alfalfa and cottonseed meal to Epsom salts and fish emulsion. Organic or all-natural fertilizers help reduce the risk of overfertilizing and burning tender roots, and they're better for the environment. All fertilizing should stop after August 1 so that plants have the chance to harden off and canes can ripen before the onset of cold winter weather.

Successful gardeners recognize rose pests and diseases and treat them with the appropriate substances. Apply a variety of garden fungicides weekly to prevent chronic diseases such as canker, mildew, and blackspot. The County Extension Service has current pesticide recommendations; these change occasionally. Some old pest-control recipes still circulate; they may or may not be effective (or legal) in some locales.

PRUNING YOUR ROSES

Pruning is a challenge for many people. It seems counterproductive to prune a plant as hard as you do some roses, but roses respond well to this treatment at certain times of year and will reward you many times over for a pruning job done well. Keep in mind that some roses, especially climbers and old-fashioned types, flower on the previous year's growth, so pruning too much or at the wrong time of year may mean that you're cutting off next year's blooms. To gain confidence, we suggest attending a rose-pruning clinic sponsored by a local rose society or Master Gardener program. You will find even more pruning tips at the end of this chapter.

- Use bypass-type hand shears. They cut cleanly. Anvil-type shears tend to crush stems.
- Pruning causes new growth, and pruning too early is risky. Generally speaking, early spring pruning should be carried out about two to three weeks before the last frost date. By the time new buds have begun growing actively, the frost date will have passed and tender new growth should be safe.
- Prune to an "outside" bud, meaning cut one-half inch beyond a bud on the outside of the branch or cane so that the new cane grows toward the outside of the shrub and not toward the interior.
- In order to avoid transferring disease from one plant to another, hand pruners should be cleaned in rubbing alcohol before moving on to another bush.
- Large wounds resulting from the hard pruning of canes or removal of side branches should be painted with a dab of white glue to prevent boring insects from entering the freshly cut canes.
- At times, you will need to use a pruning saw or loppers to remove woody old canes so that new canes can sprout from the crown. Prune flush with the crown to avoid leaving a stub. Be careful not to damage surrounding canes.

CHOOSE WISELY TO AVOID DISEASES

Disease resistance is usually noted in catalogs, rose books, or on the plant tags. Search for roses that have genetic resistance to blackspot and powdery mildew diseases. These plagues disfigure bushes and can weaken them to the point that they will gradually decline and die. The humid climate of the Carolinas—the rose grower's worst enemy—fosters serious foliar diseases. We must underscore the importance of good air circulation to ensure success with your roses. Plant pathologists periodically evaluate the cultivars for disease tolerance, and each class has something to offer. Experiment with these if your garden has less-than-ideal conditions for roses: 'Knock Out®', 'Playboy', 'Carefree Wonder™', 'Mary Rose®', 'New Dawn', 'Ice Meidiland®', and 'Sea Foam'.

PLANTING ROSES

- Soil preparation for roses is of utmost importance. Large quantities of organic matter such as compost, composted manures, and leaf mold (composted leaves) tilled into the soil all help to improve aeration, increase drainage, and retain nutrients.
- First and foremost, have your soil tested and amend as directed.
- For potted roses, dig planting holes to the depth of the rootball or root system and twice as wide.
- Look for the graft union, usually a swollen joint or "knot," near the base of the plant, and place the rose so that this union is just above soil level to help reduce the incidence of suckers growing up from the rootstock.
- For bare-root roses, shake off the packing material, soak the roots in a bucket of water overnight, and dig a planting hole to the depth of the root system. Amend the soil with limestone, superphosphate, and soil conditioner as recommended by soil tests.
- Make a cone of amended soil in the bottom of the hole and straddle it with the roots.
- The graft union of the plant should be 1 inch above the surface of surrounding soil.
- Pull in amended soil around the roots and firm it down with your hands; don't tamp it down.

- Spread 2 inches of mulch in a circle 2 feet in diameter.
- Settle the roses in place by trickling water over the dug area. For the next month, water twice weekly between rains.
- Wait two weeks, scatter granular rose fertilizer around the plant at the rate recommended on the package, and water it in. Fertilize monthly, but not past mid-August.

GRAFTED VERSUS OWN-ROOT ROSES

We have already mentioned the "graft" or "graft union" of a rose several times. Most roses today are bud grafted, or budded, with the desirable rose that you want to grow being grafted to a more vigorous set of roots that give it a better chance of thriving in the garden. The drawback to growing grafted roses is that if the graft dies for some reason, the rootstock is an entirely different rose than the desirable variety you originally purchased. Some growers are now growing the most vigorous varieties of roses on their own roots, without grafting, and this ensures that if the rose dies to ground level for any reason, the shoots that return from the roots will be the same as the rose you originally purchased. Less vigorous roses continue to be grafted to increase their survivability in the garden.

CLIMBING ROSE

Rosa spp. and hybrids

Why It's Special—Nothing is more picturesque than a climbing rose winding around an arbor. While roses have no tendrils to attach themselves to a support, they do produce long, rambling canes that can be tied and trained.

How to Plant & Grow—Plant bare-root roses from February to April. Potted roses can be planted anytime, but spring or early summer is best. Roses need at least six hours of full sun and plenty of air circulation to help prevent diseases such as blackspot and powdery mildew. Drip irrigation is the most effective way to water roses while keeping foliage dry.

Care & Problems—In the South, most roses require regular spraying with fungicide and insecticide. Proper pruning, fertilization, and irrigation are key. Some of the large, old-fashioned climbers are quite disease resistant.

Bloom Size—Small to medium, individually or in clusters

Bloom Color—White, yellow, orange, pink, red

Bloom Period—Heaviest in spring, but some varieties repeat

Fragrance—Depends on variety

Water Needs—1 inch or more per week while growing

Recommended Climbing Roses—'Cecile Brunner'; 'Climbing Pinkie'; 'Eden', a.k.a. 'Pierre de Ronsard'; Lady Banks (*Rosa banksiae* var. *lutea*); 'New Dawn'

FLORIBUNDA ROSE

Rosa hybrids

Why It's Special—During the early twentieth century, this class originated from a cross between hybrid tea and polyantha roses. Floribundas have smaller flowers than hybrid teas, borne in clusters, but they usually retain some of the classic tea rose shape.

How to Plant & Grow—Plant bare-root roses from February to April. Potted roses can be planted anytime, but spring or early summer is best. Roses need at least six hours of full sun and plenty of air circulation to help prevent diseases such as blackspot and powdery mildew. Drip irrigation is the most effective way to water roses while keeping foliage dry.

Care & Problems—In the South, most roses require regular spraying with fungicide and insecticide. Proper pruning, fertilization, and irrigation are key. Many varieties of floribunda roses are quite disease resistant.

Bloom Size—Small to medium, in clusters

Bloom Color—White, yellow, orange, pink, red; bicolors and blends

Bloom Period—Heaviest in spring, but many varieties repeat

Fragrance—Depends on the variety

Water Needs—1 inch or more per week while growing

Recommended Floribunda Roses—'Easy Does It™', 'Europeana', 'Iceberg', 'Julia Child', 'Livin' Easy™'

HYBRID TEA ROSE

Rosa hybrids

Why It's Special—Aristocratic hybrid tea roses are known for their elegant buds and heavenly scent. Their long stems and beautiful blooms make them perfect for cutting.

How to Plant & Grow—Plant bare-root roses from February to April. Potted roses can be planted anytime, but spring or early summer is best. Roses need at least six hours of full sun and plenty of air circulation to help prevent diseases such as blackspot and powdery mildew. Drip irrigation is the most effective way to water roses while keeping foliage dry.

Care & Problems—In the South, most roses require regular spraying with fungicide and insecticide. Proper pruning, fertilization, and irrigation are key. Hybrid tea roses require exacting care, but the rewards are the stuff gardening dreams are made of.

Bloom Size—Medium to large, borne singly on long stems

Bloom Color—White, yellow, orange, pink, red; bicolors and blends

Bloom Period—Heaviest in spring, but many varieties repeat

Fragrance—Light tea fragrance to rich, heady perfume

Water Needs—1 inch or more per week while growing

Recommended Hybrid Tea Roses—'Double Delight', 'Olympiad', 'Elle™', 'Tropicana', 'Peace'

MINIATURE ROSE

Rosa hybrids

Why It's Special—Miniature roses are true dwarf members of the rose family and can be grown with a minimum of care and space. Since they are not grafted and grow on their own rootstock, they handle our unpredictable winters well.

How to Plant & Grow—Plant bare-root roses from February to April. Potted roses can be planted anytime, but spring or early summer is best. Roses need a minimum of six hours of full sun and plenty of air circulation to help prevent diseases such as blackspot and powdery mildew. Drip irrigation is the most effective way to water roses while keeping foliage dry.

Care & Problems—In the South, most roses require regular spraying with fungicide and insecticide. Proper pruning, fertilization, and irrigation are key. Miniature roses are prone to spider mites during hot, dry weather, so spray accordingly.

Bloom Size—Small, borne singly or in small clusters

Bloom Color—White, yellow, orange, pink, red; bicolors and blends

Bloom Period—Reliably bloom from spring to frost

Fragrance—Limited fragrance in most miniatures

Water Needs—1 inch or more per week while growing

Recommended Miniature Roses—'Fairhope', 'Minnie Pearl', 'Pride 'n' Joy', 'Rise 'n' Shine', 'Starina®'

OLD GARDEN ROSES

Rosa spp. and hybrids

Why It's Special—Old garden roses are appreciated for their repeat flowering, disease resistance, and fragrant blooms. Most tolerate hot, dry summers and have few problems with pests. They make excellent additions to landscape beds, where they can reach their full, shrublike size.

How to Plant & Grow—Plant bare-root roses from February to April. Potted roses can be planted anytime, but spring or early summer is best. Roses need a minimum of six hours of full sun and plenty of air circulation to help prevent diseases such as blackspot and powdery mildew. Drip irrigation is the most effective way to water roses while keeping foliage dry.

Care & Problems—Old garden roses are the only roses that do not require a dedicated spray program, but proper pruning, fertilization, and irrigation are still key. Most old garden roses flower on the previous season's growth, so pruning is generally done after the first flush of spring blooms.

Bloom Size—Small to large, borne singly or in clusters

Bloom Color—White, pink, lavender, crimson; variegated

Bloom Period—Heaviest in spring, but some varieties repeat

Fragrance—Rich, heady aroma in many varieties

Water Needs—1 inch or more per week while growing

Recommended Old Garden Roses—'Mrs. B. R. Cant', 'Old Blush'

SHRUB ROSES

Rosa spp. and hybrids

Why It's Special—Shrub, or landscape, roses often fulfill a gardener's desire to enjoy the beauty and fragrance of roses without employing a crew of horticulturists. Easy-care shrub roses are a sure bet for hedges and informal plantings. *Rugosa* roses are especially good on the coast.

How to Plant & Grow—Plant bare-root roses from February to April. Potted roses can be planted anytime, but spring or early summer is best. Roses need a minimum of six hours of full sun and plenty of air circulation to prevent diseases such as blackspot and powdery mildew. Drip irrigation is the most effective way to water roses while keeping foliage dry.

Care & Problems—Shrub roses require the least amount of care in the rose "family," but they are not immune to disease. Some shrub roses flower on old wood and some on new wood, so be sure to know the flowering cycle before you prune to keep from pruning off the next cycle of flowers.

Bloom Size—Small to medium, borne singly or in clusters

Bloom Color—White, yellow, pink, red

Bloom Period—Near continuous, spring to fall

Fragrance—Most are not fragrant

Water Needs—1 inch or more per week while growing

Recommended Shrub Roses—Carefree, Flower Carpet™, Knock Out®, and Meidiland® series, *Rosa rugosa* and cultivars

THE KNOCK OUT® FAMILY OF ROSES

It seems hard to believe that the Knock Out® rose has only been a part of our lives for a decade. They're everywhere! In only a few years, they have become such a part of the fabric of our gardens that it's hard to remember a time when we didn't have the disease resistance and constant blooms of these beautiful roses.

An All-America Rose Selection in 2000, the original Knock Out® rose, with its vibrant, cherry red flowers and exceptional resistance to blackspot, quickly became a landscape favorite and has since broken all records for sales of a new rose. According to Conard-Pyle/Star® Roses, the company that introduced and distributes the Knock Out® family of roses, "Rose breeder Bill Radler has revolutionized the way we think about roses" by developing a group of plants with stunning flower power and no need to spray to control common rose diseases. Granted, Knock Out® roses are not the perfectly formed, high-centered, exquisitely fragrant hybrid teas that so many of us associate with the "perfect" rose, but their exceptional disease resistance and ability to flower nonstop from spring to frost with almost no intervention from the gardener has made them immensely popular.

Currently, there are seven members of the Knock Out® rose family, with more plants under evaluation for future introduction. The following helpful descriptions from Conard-Pyle will give you more information about each of the seven roses currently available in the line; the roses are listed in the order of their release:

KNOCK OUT® ROSE

Rosa 'Radrazz'

Mature Size (H x W): 3 to 4 ft. x 3 to 4 ft., with pruning

The original member of the Knock Out® family, this shrub rose set a new standard in disease resistance with little to no maintenance required. The bloom cycle produces rich, cherry red blooms that will continue until the first hard frost. Blackspot resistant, drought tolerant, and self-cleaning, this rose suits every garden and every lifestyle.

DOUBLE KNOCK OUT® ROSE

Rosa 'Radtko'

Mature Size (H x W): 4 ft x 4 ft.

From the same cross that produced the original Knock Out®, the Double Knock Out® rose represents the next generation in the family of Knock Out® roses. The double flowers look just like a classic rose. What it gained in beauty, it did not lose in performance. It is as resistant to blackspot as the original, has the same bloom cycle, and is slightly more winter hardy. This shrub rose has the look and the toughness that you expect from a member of the Knock Out® family.

PINK KNOCK OUT® ROSE

Rosa 'Radcon'

Mature Size (H x W): 3 to 4 ft. x 3 to 4 ft., with pruning

This rose has single petals just like the original Knock Out®, but in a beautiful shade of bright pink. And like the other members of the family, the Pink Knock Out® rose is blackspot resistant, drought tolerant, and self-cleaning. It is a perfect companion to other shrubs, roses, and perennials.

DOUBLE PINK KNOCK OUT® ROSE

Rosa 'Radtkopink'

Mature Size (H x W): 3 to 4 ft. x 3 to 4 ft.

This bright bubble-gum pink version of the Double Knock Out® rose is very stable and also unfazed by the heat. Classic-shaped flowers bloom from early spring to the first frost. With superior drought tolerance once established, it has the toughness and resistance for which the family is known. The vibrant color perks up any landscape.

RAINBOW KNOCK OUT® ROSE

Rosa 'Radcor'

Mature Size (H x W): 3 ft. x 3 ft.

Bearing uniquely colored, coral pink blooms with yellow centers, the Rainbow Knock Out® rose is more compact than the other members. It is rarely affected by blackspot. New foliage appears in deep burgundy, then ages to dark green.

BLUSHING KNOCK OUT® ROSE

Rosa 'Radyod'

Mature Size (H x W): 3 to 4 ft. x 3 to 4 ft., with pruning

With similar flowers to the Knock Out® rose, this variety has light pink blooms that, with age, fade to a delicate, subtle pink. This shrub rose will be a versatile addition to any landscape.

SUNNY KNOCK OUT® ROSE

Rosa 'Radsunny'

Mature Size (H x W): 3 to 5 ft. x 3 to 4 ft.

The newest release from rose breeder Bill Radler is the only fragrant member in the Knock Out® family of roses. It has a slightly more compact and upright habit than the Knock Out® rose, with bright yellow flowers that fade quickly to a pastel cream color. The yellow color stays more intense during cooler times of the year. The dark, semiglossy foliage contrasts nicely with the bright blooms.

Research and development continues within the Knock Out® family of roses, with plants being tested in various locations around the country and held to the exacting standards of the original Knock Out® rose. All varieties are tested in a wide range of climates and growing conditions, with only a small handful of plants actually making it to nurseries and garden centers around the country for homeowners and gardeners to grow and enjoy.

WHY ALL THE LETTERS? THE ARS AND THE AARS

The ARS—the American Rose Society—and the AARS—the All-America Rose Selections—are invaluable resources for information about growing roses and offer what seems like limitless information on recommended varieties, new varieties, disease resistance, garden performance, and much more.

Take a look at the *Handbook for Selecting Roses*, published yearly by the American Rose Society (American Rose Society, P.O. Box 30,000, Shreveport, Louisiana 71130-0030; 318-938-5402; www.ars.org). It covers both old garden and modern roses that are evaluated by rosarians across the country. The scores will give a clue to how your choices measure up against others in their class.

Consider All-America roses as well. All-America Rose Selections, Inc. (www.rose.org), is a nonprofit research organization founded in 1938 for the purpose of evaluating and identifying roses that stand head and shoulders above others. Six types of roses can vie for the All-America title each year: hybrid teas, floribundas, grandifloras, miniatures, climbers, and landscape roses. AARS roses are evaluated in test gardens throughout the United States by commercial rose producers. They are scored on such characteristics as vigor, growth habit, hardiness, disease resistance, and flower production.

You should also consider consulting your local chapter of the Rose Society or, if your city or town does not have a chapter, you may wish to contact the Carolina District Rose Society for more information about growing roses successfully in your area. If it turns out some varieties you have picked have not been tested by the rosarians in the Carolina District Rose Society, you may enjoy taking it upon yourself to give them a trial in your own garden.

PRUNING REVISITED

Roses must be pruned in order for them to thrive and reach their full growth and flowering potential. The following expanded lists of tips and suggestions will help you prune your roses properly. Why do your roses need pruning?

- *To keep them healthy.* Dead, damaged, or diseased growth should be removed when discovered, at any time of year.

- *To shape and direct their growth.* Climbing and rambling roses must be pruned so their canes can be secured to trellises or arbors. Roses with a bush-type habit benefit from having their shoots directed away from the center of the plant. Know whether your roses flower on new growth or old growth in order to avoid pruning off blooms before you get to enjoy them!

- *To encourage more blooms.* Pruning repeat-blooming roses such as hybrid teas that produce flowers on the current season's shoots encourages flushes of new growth on which flowers are produced.

- *To keep them confined to their allotted space.* Some roses can be given 3 feet, but in a short time they'll scramble for more room. Pruning keeps them in their place so they won't crowd their neighbors.

Pruning can be intimidating, not only because of the thorns but also because of the uncertainty of what and where to cut. It's really not a complicated process. Pruning roses involves three basic cuts:

- Thinning is the removal of a shoot at its point of origin on the stem or at the base. These cuts open up the plant to improve air movement and sunlight penetration.

- Cutting back, or heading back, is pruning back to a bud on the stem. This cut encourages branching by stimulating a few buds behind the cut to grow.

- Shearing is an intense form of heading back where multiple cuts are made to produce dense growth. Miniature roses and floribundas grown as hedges are commonly sheared.

Although pruning methods vary among different classes of roses, you should always follow these general rules:

- Use sharp tools to make clean cuts for rapid healing of wounds.

- Always begin by pruning out dead, damaged, and diseased wood (the "three Ds"). Head or cut back the canes to at least an inch below darkened or discolored areas, making sure you cut back to healthy green wood. Examine the pith or center of the cane. If it's brown, continue pruning back until the pith looks white.

- Angle each cut. Point your shears at a 45-degree angle toward the center of the shrub, sloping the cut downward from the bud. The dormant bud should be at the top of the angle.

- Make pruning cuts above a bud or branch that faces away from the center of the plant to keep new shoots from growing into the center of the plant and restricting air circulation.

- Eliminate any crisscrossing canes that rub together by removing the lower of the two canes. Rubbing produces wounds that are open invitations to pests.

- Prune out suckers—growths that emerge from below the bud union on grafted roses—at their attachment on the rootstock.

- Thin out any spindly, weak branches and any canes growing into the center of the bush.
- Allow the natural habit of the plant to guide your cuts.

HELPING ROSES SURVIVE WINTER

Gardeners, particularly in the Mountains, need to keep the following points in mind to ensure roses will last through winter:

- The plants should go into the winter in a vigorous state. Plants stressed by drought or lack of fertility, or those defoliated by pests, are more inclined to succumb to cold than robust plants are.
- Roses should be grown in a well-drained location. Roses will not tolerate wet feet, especially during the winter months.
- Winter winds can dry out the canes of exposed roses, loosen a rose's footing, or bruise canes as they're jostled by the wind. You can plant roses near walls or fences, erect temporary windbreaks of burlap, or stake or tie down canes.
- Mountain gardeners are faced with the freezing and thawing of the soil, resulting in frost heaving, which can lift up plants, causing them to dry out. Carefully push down any plants that heave, and maintain a mulch layer to moderate soil temperatures.

GET OUT AND GO!

As part of your summer vacation, find some time to visit private and public gardens that feature roses. It can be inspiring to see the extraordinary roses that you've glimpsed only in catalogs Some notable rose gardens are the All-America Rose Selections Public Gardens. These accredited gardens showcase the three or four exceptional roses selected from thousands each year. Here are the AARS gardens in the Carolinas:

- North Carolina Biltmore Estate in Asheville
- Fayetteville Rose Garden at Fayetteville Technical Community College
- Raleigh Municipal Rose Garden in Raleigh
- Reynolda Rose Gardens of Wake Forest University in Winston-Salem
- South Carolina Edisto Memorial Gardens in Orangeburg
- Witherspoon Rose Garden in Durham

Don't forget your camera and gardening journal. Enjoy!

JANUARY

- If you are planning to plant a new rose garden or expand an existing one in spring, now is the time to prepare the new site. Raised beds or berms provide excellent drainage.
- Coastal Plain gardeners can select and plant bare-root roses from mid-January to mid-March. Bare-root roses should have three or more sturdy canes, healthy-looking roots, and dormant, leafless canes. A bare-root rose that has leafed out could be in jeopardy.
- Mountain gardeners should check the winter protection on their roses to be sure that mulch has not been scattered or blown away to expose the crown or graft of the plant.
- Apply horticultural dormant oil in late winter, before new growth begins, to smother any overwintering insects and their eggs. Be sure to follow label directions carefully.
- If you're growing miniature roses indoors for winter blooms, be sure to keep an eye out for spider mites. Insecticidal soap is safe to use indoors and will help keep mites under control.

FEBRUARY

- Winter-blooming annuals and spring-flowering bulbs can fill in around the stark-looking canes of roses that are dormant.
- Continue planting bare-root roses if you haven't already done so. Be sure to amend soil thoroughly and deeply when planting.
- Old-fashioned roses that only flower once should be fertilized now, before new growth begins.
- Pruning will begin this month for roses that produce flowers on the current season's growth. Coastal Plain gardeners will prune first and Mountain gardeners will wait until early March.
- Remember to disinfect your pruners in between plants so that you don't transfer overwintering diseases from plant to plant.

MARCH

- Potted roses can be planted in most areas of the Carolinas, except for the North Carolina mountains. If frost threatens tender new growth, an old bed sheet makes a good cover.
- When pruning, be sure to clean out and open up the centers of your roses. Good air circulation is essential to maintain the health of your roses and reduce problems with blackspot and powdery mildew later in the season.
- Hand pull winter annuals such as henbit and common chickweed to prevent them from going to seed. Once beds are clean, pre-emergent herbicide granules will help to prevent more weed seeds from germinating.

- Watch for aphids on the very tender new growth that has just begun sprouting from recently pruned roses. A strong spray of water will dislodge them.

APRIL

- If you haven't already, start a garden journal this month. It can be especially helpful for recording bloom dates, overall health of plants, and notes on performance of different varieties

- If natural rainfall is sparse, be sure to water your roses thoroughly and deeply at least once a week—twice if it is particularly dry.

- If you haven't already, remove all of last year's old mulch, which may be harboring pests and diseases, and replace with fresh, clean mulch.

- Loosely tie new growth on climbing roses to their support structure. Broad strips of soft cloth or old pantyhose work very well for tying rose canes. Use a figure-eight tie between the rose cane and its support to avoid girdling the cane.

- Softwood cuttings can be taken this month if you would like to root some new roses of your own.

- One of the most common rose pests is the rose sawfly, the larvae of which skeletonize leaves. Rose gardeners should spray preventatively starting mid- to late April with spinosad, continuing through mid- to late June.

MAY

- Supplemental watering will be a must this month as hot summer weather arrives. Roses need 1 inch of water per week throughout the growing season.

- Don't forget Mom! A potted rose makes a great Mother's Day gift!

- Old-fashioned roses and once-blooming climbers that bloom on last year's growth have probably finished blooming by the end of May. After they finish flowering, prune as needed immediately.

- Blackspot and powdery mildew will be rearing their ugly heads this month. Spray on a regular basis and be diligent about removing infected leaves.

- Learn to evaluate the water needs of your plants just by looking at them. A change in leaf color or limpness in the flower will often precede a full-on wilt, which can be detrimental to the plant.

JUNE

- If you're vacationing, find time to visit some public rose gardens.

- Remember that roses growing in sandy soils will require more frequent watering and fertilizing than those growing in clay soils.

- Fungal diseases like blackspot rely on moisture to infect and spread. Keeping water off the leaves of your roses will help combat this problem.

- If you used a slow-release fertilizer in early spring, check the label and evaluate the growth and flowering of your roses to determine if a second application is needed.

- Japanese beetles will be out in full force this month. They will attack both the foliage and flowers of your roses. Pick them off and drop them in a jar of soapy water, or spray with liquid Sevin to help control them.

JULY

- Roses may take a rest from flowering as daytime temperatures reach into the 90s. Plants in full summer sun are especially affected.

- Prune off faded flowers and cut back any weak canes to prepare the plant for a long blooming spell in the fall.

- In the hotter parts of the Carolinas, avoid fertilizing this month and in August.

- Japanese beetles continue to be active this month, skeletonizing leaves and eating holes through the flower petals. Pick them off and drop them in a jar of soapy water.

- Root nematodes can be problematic in certain parts of the Carolinas, causing "knots" to develop in the roots and decreasing their ability to absorb water and nutrients efficiently. There is no easy treatment, but keeping plants healthy and growing as actively as possible will help.

AUGUST

- Mountain and Piedmont gardeners may be able to jump-start their roses by fertilizing now.

- Continue applying at least 1 to 2 inches of water per week, especially during dry periods of late summer and early fall.

- Japanese beetles, aphids, and spider mites can continue to be problems this month. Check regularly and treat accordingly.

- Rose mosaic disease is a problem in some roses. Symptoms include deformed new growth and irregular yellow blotches or yellow ring patterns on the leaves, but is mostly cosmetic and relatively harmless to the plant.

- Continue to hand pull weeds to keep competition with your roses at a minimum.

SEPTEMBER

- It's time to order roses this month! They will be delivered in December in coastal regions and just after the first of the year elsewhere, at the proper planting time.

- Climbing roses may show vigorous spurts of growth this month. Let the canes shoot up as tall as they want to go, and then gently tie them into their trellis, arbor, or pergola.

- Be sure to keep your roses deadheaded and do any pruning necessary to encourage a good flush of fall growth and bloom.

- Continue monitoring rose aphids and spider mites, treating as necessary. Highly refined horticultural oils or insecticidal soaps can be used to help smother soft-bodied insects like aphids and mites. Be sure to spray in early morning or late evening, when the sun is not shining directly on the foliage.

- Clean up any rose leaves as they fall to the ground. They can harbor diseases and insect pests if allowed to remain. Blackspot spores can splash from the ground to the plant when it rains.

OCTOBER

- Soil testing should be done in your rose garden every two to three years, and October is the perfect month to take samples.

- October is a good month for planting roses, especially in the milder areas of the Carolinas. Be sure to thoroughly amend your soil with organic matter, compost, or composted manure any time you are planting new roses.

- If you haven't already, be sure to tie up new canes on your climbing roses so that wind does not whip the canes around and break or damage them.

- In warmer parts of the Carolinas, gardeners still need to be diligent about spider mite and aphid control and treat accordingly.

- Fall can be a dry time in the Carolinas, so keep your eye to the sky and water accordingly if sufficient rainfall is not present.

NOVEMBER

- Update your garden journal and plan for improvements, additions, and replacements for next year. Make notes while the current growing season is fresh in your mind.

- Allow rose hips (seedpods) to develop to signal to the roses that it is time to go dormant and rest for the winter. Rose hips are also beautiful and will attract birds to the garden during the winter months.

- Do not prune late in the season. It may spur the plants into new growth, which will then be frozen in the first cold snap.

- Pull back on water, refrain from fertilizing, and encourage the plants to begin going dormant.

- Do not compost diseased rose leaves. If your compost pile does not get hot enough, the spores will not be killed and you will spread the disease back through the garden when you use the compost.

DECEMBER

- Weather permitting, Coastal Plain gardeners can plant bare-root roses or move roses to other parts of the garden. Be sure to thoroughly amend your soil with compost, composted manure, or other organic matter each time you plant.

- Roses that were newly planted in the fall will benefit from winter protection; place mounds of dry mulch or pine straw over their crowns.

- Trim the canes of hybrid tea roses down to 3 feet to keep canes from whipping in winter winds and doing potential damage to the crown of the plant.

- Hand pull any young winter annual weeds such as henbit and chickweed. Once beds are completely clean, a granular pre-emergent herbicide can help prevent further weed growth.

SHRUBS

for the Carolinas

If ground covers are the carpets of our outdoor rooms and trees are the walls, then shrubs can be likened to furniture. They shape and delineate space and soften corners. They are frequently placed just out from the walls of our homes, as you would place a sofa indoors. They can be colorful entities and collectively they can add beauty to a stark, unattractive yard. A landscape would not be complete without their seasonal interest. We use shrubs in so many ways that it is hard to list all their wonderful qualities and distinctive habits.

WHAT ARE SHRUBS?

By definition, shrubs are woody plants, usually with multiple stems, that mature at less than 15 feet in height. They come in every imaginable size and form—weeping, columnar, round, pyramidal, open, or compact. Some, like azaleas, burst into vivid color in springtime; others, like sasanqua camellias, bloom for weeks in autumn. Large shrubs can be "limbed up" to produce small specimen trees. Many are planted close together—and sometimes stair-stepped in ranks to create privacy hedges and to screen views. The most popular use of shrubs is to skirt foundations and emphasize corners, giving new homes a finished look.

TYPES OF SHRUBS

Evergreen shrubs—those that keep their leaves year-round—are the ones most sought after for screening purposes, landscape accents, and foundation plantings. They may be conifers with flattened, scalelike leaves—such as arborvitae or juniper—or broadleaf evergreens with broad, flattened leaves like rhododendron or hollies.

Conifers are seeing a surge in popularity in the landscape because of the wide range of colors, forms, and textures they offer in the landscape throughout the year. The limiting factor for many conifers is whether or not they will tolerate the intense heat and humidity of Southern summers, particularly nighttime temperatures that can stay above 80 degrees F for several weeks at a time in mid to late summer. Enterprising nurserymen and the more serious gardeners among us are really pushing the limits of conifers to determine which ones will thrive in our climate and which ones will struggle.

Deciduous shrubs are those that lose their leaves in the winter and include many of our most common landscape shrubs. Forsythia, oakleaf hydrangea, and spirea are all examples of popular deciduous shrubs. Even though they lose their leaves, don't discount the year-round interest of these shrubs. Many of them have interesting bark texture, twig color, or architectural value that can bring beauty to the winter landscape, even without leaves.

You might notice that many of our most popular deciduous shrubs also happen to be some of our most popular flowering shrubs. Quince, witch hazel, forsythia, and others flower while their branches are bare and leafless, their showy blooms taking center stage in the garden. Still others, like oakleaf hydrangea, butterfly bush, and rose of Sharon present their blooms later in the season against a cushion of green leaves.

GOING NATIVE

The Carolinas are blessed with many native woody ornamentals, both evergreen and deciduous, that thrive in our gardens and lift our spirits. Be sure to investigate these native species when planning your landscape or adding to existing beds and plantings. By choosing native plants that are already well adapted to the region, many trials and tribulations can be avoided. However, just because a shrub is native doesn't mean that it is automatically low or no maintenance, which is a common misconception. For instance, many shrubs native to the Mountains will not thrive in lowland areas. Compacted red clay, hot and humid summers, and wildly fluctuating winters put a lot of stress on plants. Conversely, native species with a coastal provenance have trouble surviving Piedmont winters and are hopeless at high elevations. Yet, if you plant a native species in an environment that simulates its native habitat, it can surpass most exotics in beauty and performance.

There is a debate brewing across the country about the use of native plants versus the use of introduced ornamentals. Carolinians garden in four hardiness zones, and there is no doubt that many "exotic" landscape shrubs are superior to our natives. The question is whether or not those exotics also have the potential to be invasive. This is where the trouble starts brewing. We certainly wouldn't have beautiful landscape plants like camellias or gardenias if it weren't for plant explorers and nurserymen discovering, propagating, and introducing species of all kinds. The opposite argument can be made that we also wouldn't have kudzu if someone hadn't imported it in the early twentieth century. This is a many-faceted argument that likely won't be settled anytime soon.

THE ROLE OF SHRUBS

Shrubs offer a variety of individual traits. Without shrubs such as Koreanspice viburnum, gardenia, osmanthus, and lilac, you would be deprived of wonderful fragrance in the garden. Many shrubs, such as rainbow leucothoe, aucuba, and dwarf nandina, boast interesting color from

variegated foliage. Deciduous holly is perfect for the winter garden since its red berries sparkle in sunlight, and the marvelous dwarf conifers offer myriad forms and foliage colors. Dwarf conifers, looking like tiny bonsai, are popular for rock gardens and toy railroad gardens. Another desirable feature of many shrubs is the attraction they hold for butterflies. What garden is complete without a butterfly bush or a bottlebrush buckeye?

Legend has it that foundation plantings were hatched to hide the crawlspaces under spacious farm porches that provided dry, shaded resting places for pets and chickens. But times are a-changin'! Recent design theories de-emphasize hiding foundations with closely spaced shrubs. Today, entrance plantings of evergreen shrubs are "in." They serve a dual function: They eliminate the stark look and barrenness of our houses' architectural features, and they deflect wind and reduce heat loss for energy conservation. Best of all, shrubs provide winter interest and color during the gray, often rainy days leading up to spring.

SOME ASSEMBLY REQUIRED

Before purchasing your shrubs, keep in mind that few are maintenance free. Almost all shrubs need light pruning during the year to open up dense growth and to remove weak or damaged twigs. Hedges require the most maintenance and are best sheared with sharp, hand-held hedge scissors. Power shears are popular because they make the job easier, but they can be hard on shrubs if not used properly. If they become dull, they are very difficult to sharpen and they will "chew" rather than cut, which can be damaging to your shrubs.

Hand pruning with loppers or bypass pruners maintains the natural form of individual shrubs. Some plants, such as azaleas and abelias, will produce long, vigorous shoots that extend well beyond the canopy. Prune back the shoots to a lateral branch within the plant canopy; this hides unsightly stubs. Conifers can be sheared in late winter or hand pruned in late spring by removing one third of the current season's growth.

Timing is critical to pruning success. If you're unsure about when to prune, take a close look at the flowering time of the shrub in need of pruning. If it is an early-spring bloomer like forsythia, camellia, or azalea, you will prune it after it flowers in spring. These shrubs formed their flower buds last summer, and if you prune them before they flower, you will be cutting the flowers off. Summer-blooming shrubs like butterfly bush and roses flower on their new growth of the current season and should be cut back hard in early spring to encourage lush new growth and profuse flowering. An exception to this rule, is hydrangeas. Most hydrangeas bloom in late spring to early summer, but they do flower on last year's growth, so they should not be pruned until *after* they flower. You will find additional pruning information at the end of this chapter.

LOOK BEFORE YOU LEAP

Paralleling the service provided by All America Selections annual flower trial gardens across the state, new woody ornamental introductions continue appearing in record numbers at public arboretums. The J. C. Raulston Arboretum at NCSU boasts a North Carolina Evaluation Network to test new plants in the different hardiness zones and microclimates of the state. The South Carolina State Botanical Garden at Clemson tests new species and introductions brought into the United States, mostly from Asia.

Of course, large domestic wholesale growers have a continuing program for developing and introducing improved shrubs. Prime examples of the new faces on well-known garden shrubs are 'Goshiki' osmanthus and the hybrid Chinese allspice shrub. (It is no surprise that larger blossoms and variegated foliage sell well at garden centers.) Take the time to experience the offerings in the marketplace, but stay focused on the ones that are not demanding or temperamental in your landscape. Public gardens are excellent places to visit to see plants in the landscape before adding them to your own.

ARBORVITAE

Thuja occidentalis

Why It's Special—Arborvitae make excellent screening plants and landscape accents. These conifers grow at a moderate to fast rate and are well suited to both small, urban lots and sprawling properties. They come in a wide array of forms and colors, from rounded to strictly upright, and from emerald green to golden yellow and variegated.

How to Plant & Grow—Plant balled-and-burlapped or container-grown arborvitae in fall, winter, or early spring. They are easy to establish during the dormant season. Arborvitae will grow in almost any soil as long as it is not waterlogged.

Care & Problems—Most arborvitae grow relatively fast. Even small, inexpensive 1-gallon potted plants can reach 6 feet or more in less than five years. Keep an eye out for bagworms and spider mites. Their populations can explode suddenly and damage can occur very quickly.

Hardiness—Zones 4b to 8b, depending on variety

Mature Size (H x W)—5 to 40 ft. x 5 to 20 ft.

Water Needs—Evenly moist to slightly dry soil

Bloom Color—No blooms

Special Features—Evergreen foliage; year-round color and form

AUCUBA

Aucuba japonica

Why It's Special—With its broad, evergreen leaves that are often patterned with yellow, aucuba looks as if it belongs in a tropical Florida garden. But no other shrub thrives in deeper shade than aucuba. The foliage also makes a beautiful filler for cutflower arrangements.

How to Plant & Grow—Plant from spring to early fall, before the ground turns cold in winter. Aucuba loves warm weather and is easiest to establish during summer. Aucuba's only two requirements are well-drained soil and plenty of shade. Its leaves will actually burn and blacken, even in winter, if it receives too much sun.

Care & Problems—Prune in spring to shape and to remove any winter-damaged stems. Aucuba's problems are generally limited to wind-damaged leaves and sunscald. Heavy clay soils that are poorly drained and stay cold and wet in winter may lead to root rot.

Hardiness—Zones 6b to 9b

Mature Size (H x W)—4 to 8 ft. x 4 to 8 ft.

Water Needs—Evenly moist soil

Bloom Color—Insignificant blooms; showy red berries on female plants

Special Features—Bold texture and brightly colored foliage

AZALEA

Rhododendron x hybridum

Why It's Special—Azaleas epitomize spring in the Carolinas; their wide range of sizes and colors make azaleas adaptable to most any landscape.

How to Plant & Grow—Plant hybrid azaleas any time from spring to fall. While they will tolerate both full sun and full shade, the best location is in morning sun or bright dappled shade throughout the day. A certain amount of sun is required to ensure a good floral display. Azaleas require very loose, well-drained garden soil that has been heavily amended with soil conditioner.

Care & Problems—Prune immediately after flowering in spring. In hot climates, lace bugs are sure to attack in mid to late summer. Consult your local garden center or County Extension Service for the best treatment. Fertilize immediately after flowering at the same time you prune, and again in early to mid summer.

Hardiness—Zones 6b to 9b

Mature Size (H x W)—4 to 6 ft. x 4 to 6 ft.

Water Needs—Evenly moist soil

Bloom Color—White, red, pink, fuchsia, bicolors

Special Features—One of the most spectacular floral displays of spring

BOXWOOD

Buxus sempervirens

Why It's Special—"American" boxwood is an aristocrat among shrubs. It is actually native to southern and western Europe, but its rich history here since Colonial times has allowed us to claim it as our own.

How to Plant & Grow—Boxwoods can be planted year-round, but it is best to avoid the hottest and driest months of the summer. They will grow in full sun, but the most beautiful specimens are usually found in part sun to part shade. Avoid sites that stay constantly wet, such as near a downspout or in a low area.

Care & Problems—Hard pruning or shearing should be done in February, just before new growth starts in spring. Leafminers can be a significant problem and cause the leaves to look blistered and off-color. Severe infestations can kill the plants and chemical treatment is required. This is best left to a landscape-care professional.

Hardiness—Zones 6a to 8b

Mature Size (H x W)—1½ to 15 ft. x 1½ to 15 ft., depending on variety

Water Needs—Average to slightly dry soil

Bloom Color—No blooms

Special Features—Evergreen foliage and aristocratic character

BUTTERFLY BUSH

Buddleia davidii

Why It's Special—This deciduous flowering shrub is highly attractive to butterflies, bees, and hummingbirds. Long, colorful spires of fragrant blooms remain on display all summer and into the fall if deadheading is done regularly.

How to Plant & Grow—Butterfly bush performs best in full sun and can be planted any time during spring or summer while it is actively growing. Plants are often potbound when grown in containers, so be sure to loosen the rootball.

Care & Problems—Prune hard in late winter, cutting the plants back to between 12 and 18 inches tall. This may sound extreme, but this will encourage vigorous growth and a spectacular display of blooms in early summer. Water and feed regularly during summer, and keep old blooms removed to encourage continual flowering from spring to frost. Do not prune in fall, as stems may freeze and die.

Hardiness—Zones 5a to 8b

Mature Size (H x W)—3 to 6 ft. x 3 to 6 ft.

Water Needs—Evenly moist to slightly dry soil

Bloom Color—White, purple, magenta, lavender-blue

Special Features—Attracts butterflies, bees, and hummingbirds

CAMELLIA

Camellia japonica

Why It's Special—Camellias are one of the signature plants of Southern gardens. Modern, cold-hardy hybrids have expanded the range of where camellias can be grown successfully. Their large blooms, resembling roses or peonies, are a welcome sight in late winter and early spring.

How to Plant & Grow—Camellias should be planted from March to October to take advantage of warm temperatures. Thoroughly amended soil that is well drained and high in organic matter is essential. Camellias love shade and will sunburn if planted in too much sun. Morning sun or high dappled shade is best.

Care & Problems—Pruning should be kept to a minimum and must occur at just the right time—usually immediately after camellias finish flowering. Prune camellias carefully with hand pruners, not with gas-powered or electric shears that tear stems and destroy the plant's appearance. Voles can be a problem.

Hardiness—Zones 6a to 9b

Mature Size (H x W)—6 to 15 ft. x 5 to 10 ft.

Water Needs—Moist, well-drained soil

Bloom Color—Pink, white, red, variegated

Special Features—Newer varieties are hardy to Zone 6

CHERRY LAUREL

Prunus laurocerasus

Why It's Special—This species includes some of the finest broadleaf evergreens for Carolina landscapes. Several cultivars can be planted as large privacy hedges or dense foundation shrubs. 'Otto Luyken' is excellent for foundation plantings and low borders.

How to Plant & Grow—Plant any time in spring or fall. In the western Carolinas, give cherry laurels a month or two to get established before cold weather arrives. They will grow in sun to filtered shade and prefer well-drained, moderately fertile soil. Mulch to conserve moisture and control weeds.

Care & Problems—Do not overwater in clay soils, as cherry laurels are prone to root rot. Lightly prune occasionally to control size and shape. Shearing with gas or electric hedge shears causes leaves to brown and makes plants unattractive. Borers can be a problem and treatment is essential. Control shot-hole fungus by applying fungicide regularly from early spring to early summer.

Hardiness—Zones 6a to 9b

Mature Size (H x W)—4 to 12 ft. x 4 to 10 ft.

Water Needs—Average to slightly dry

Bloom Color—White

Special Features—Evergreen foliage; easy to grow

CLEYERA

Ternstroemia gymnanthera

Why It's Special—This camellia cousin is a great choice for shade, though it doesn't have the showy flowers of its kin. It makes an excellent screening plant where soils are moist and deep. Dark green foliage is beautiful year-round and some cultivars have bronze-colored new growth.

How to Plant & Grow—Plant anytime the soil can be worked during fall, winter, or early spring. Prepare a planting hole twice the diameter of the rootball or wider, and amend the soil well, especially in clay or sandy soils. Apply an all-purpose fertilizer in early spring to encourage lush new growth each season.

Care & Problems—Mulch well and keep plants watered for the first two growing seasons. Once established, they are relatively carefree. Cleyera is pest and drought resistant. Some pruning will be required to remove occasional long, errant stems. Waterlogged soils can lead to root rot.

Hardiness—Zones 7a to 10b

Mature Size (H x W)—10 ft. x 6 ft.

Water Needs—Drought tolerant, once established

Bloom Color—White, insignificant blooms

Special Features—Some varieties have bronzy red new growth

CURLED LEAF PRIVET

Ligustrum japonicum 'Recurvifolium'

Why It's Special—This shrub is a handsome, low-maintenance choice for gardens in the Piedmont and low country, and is one of the best behaved privets. Its dark green leaves with wavy margins give it a distinctive appearance.

How to Plant & Grow—Container-grown curled leaf privet can be transplanted anytime the ground is not frozen, though fall or spring is best. It is pH adaptable and grows in full sun to part shade. Water weekly for the first month after planting, and then water thoroughly and deeply when soil is dry to the touch.

Care & Problems—Very little pruning is needed, though crowded branches can be removed. Shear as it matures to shape and control height. Overgrown plants can be pruned hard in late winter or can be limbed up to create architectural specimens. Curled leaf privet has no serious diseases or insect problems. Sunscald can occur in winter.

Hardiness—Zones 7a to 10b

Mature Size (H x W)—5 to 8 ft. x 3 to 6 ft.

Water Needs—Drought tolerant, once established

Bloom Color—Insignificant blooms

Special Features—Unique, contorted habit and architectural form

DECIDUOUS AZALEA

Rhododendron spp. and hybrids

Why It's Special—Many species are native to the southeastern United States; they provide spectacular spring and summer color throughout the forested coast and into the mountains, thriving from upland slopes to river bottoms. The Exbury hybrids have large flowers in bright pinks, oranges, and golds.

How to Plant & Grow—Plant azaleas anytime from spring to fall. (Note: There is a law against digging native azaleas from the wild.) Site in morning sun or filtered shade, in well-drained, moist, humusy soil. Compost-amended raised beds are perfect.

Care & Problems—Water every three days for the first two weeks, then weekly as needed until established. Feed azaleas as soon as they finish flowering and again six to eight weeks later. Pruning is rarely needed. If necessary, prune after flowering, trimming out branches to maintain a natural appearance. Water is essential during the hottest, driest months.

Hardiness—Zones 4a to 9b

Mature Size (H x W)—5 to 12 ft. x 5 to 10 ft.

Water Needs—Evenly moist soil

Bloom Color—White to deep pink, yellow, orange

Special Features—Beautiful, often fragrant flowers

FALSE CYPRESS

Chamaecyparis spp. and cultivars

Why It's Special—False cypress is truly a diverse group of evergreen conifers: shrubs range from tiny buns of congested foliage less than a foot tall to elegant specimens rising several feet, and colors range from silvery blue to yellow.

How to Plant & Grow—False cypress can be planted anytime soil conditions will permit. They will adapt to a wide range of soil types, but prefer moist, well-drained, slightly acidic soil. Light shade in the afternoon is beneficial if soil tends to be dry. With moisture, full sun is fine.

Care & Problems—False cypress are somewhat slow to establish and can suffer in dry soils during the first growing season. Keep plants well watered. Apply a slow-release fertilizer each spring. Prune in late spring by selectively removing branches or branch tips with hand shears.

Hardiness—Zones 5b to 8b

Mature Size (H x W)—6 to 10 ft. x 3 to 6 ft.

Water Needs—Evenly moist soil

Bloom Color—No blooms

Special Features—Color foliage and many interesting forms

FORSYTHIA

Forsythia x intermedia

Why It's Special—Forsythia heralds the coming of spring. By January in mild climates and February where it's a little colder, forsythia is raring to go. In a matter of days, it transforms from a leafless mass of twigs to a glowing, golden yellow mass of bloom.

How to Plant & Grow—Plant forsythia anytime the soil can be worked. Best flowering will occur in full-sun, but respectable specimens can be found in part sun. Forsythia will adapt to nearly any soil type and growing conditions and will grow very quickly, once established.

Care & Problems—Prune forsythias immediately after flowering. Remove one-third of the oldest growth each year to encourage new growth from the base. A second, light pruning can be done in early summer to shape, but next year's buds are set by July, so no late pruning should be done.

Hardiness—Zones 4b to 8a

Mature Size (H x W)—6 to 10 ft. x 6 to 10 ft.

Water Needs—Drought tolerant, once established

Bloom Color—Golden yellow

Special Features—Spectacular spring show; tough as nails

FOTHERGILLA

Fothergilla x intermedia

Why It's Special—This native, deciduous ornamental, sometimes known as witch alder, boasts showy, 2-inch, white "bottlebrush" flowers in spring and dazzling fall colors from yellow to orange-red. It is a relative of witch hazel and exhibits some of the same traits, particularly pest resistance, shade tolerance, and fall color, and deserves a place alongside your azaleas to brighten up the spring in the woodland garden.

How to Plant & Grow—Container-grown fothergilla can be planted in spring, fall, or late winter. It grows relatively fast in moist, acidic soils, tolerating full sun to partial shade. It is not particularly drought tolerant.

Care & Problems—Keep the soil moist but not soggy throughout the first growing season. In subsequent years, water in hot, dry weather. Thin selectively in the early years to train the shrubs into a pleasing, open form. Most pruning should be delayed until after flowering has finished.

Hardiness—Zones 5a to 8b

Mature Size (H x W)—4 ft. x 5 ft.

Water Needs—Evenly moist soil

Bloom Color—White

Special Features—White spring blooms and spectacular fall color

GARDENIA

Gardenia jasminoides

Why It's Special—Gardenias bloom in profusion in the Carolinas, emitting a sweet fragrance that evokes the ambiance of the Old South. Distinctive, silvery gray bark and glossy, evergreen foliage add to its charm. The pristine white flowers resemble the waxy blooms of Southern magnolia.

How to Plant & Grow—Plant gardenias in spring and early summer. They thrive in heat and humidity and need to be well established before winter. Moist, loamy, well-drained soils with a pH of 5 to 6 suit them best. Sunlight is important for flowering, but foliage may burn in full sun, and cold temperatures can cause winter burn.

Care & Problems—Gardenias prefer moist soil and benefit from drip irrigation or soaker hoses. Fertilize twice each year with a complete garden fertilizer. Apply once in early April and again in mid-June. Whitefly and scale can be a problem. Severe infestations can cause sooty mold.

Hardiness—Zones 7b to 9b

Mature Size (H x W)—3 to 6 ft. x 3 to 5 ft.

Water Needs—Evenly moist soil

Bloom Color—White

Special Features—Long season of fragrant white blossoms

GLOSSY ABELIA

Abelia x grandiflora

Why It's Special—Glossy abelia is a handsome plant with glossy green foliage in summer, which turns burgundy in winter. It flowers freely from early summer to fall, attracting honeybees and butterflies. Variegated and colored-foliage forms make beautiful accent plants.

How to Plant & Grow—Plant anytime the soil is not wet or frozen. Abelia is a sun lover, and though it will grow in some degree of shade, flowering will be sparse. It is not finicky about soil types and is quite drought tolerant, once established. Thoroughly loosen the roots when planting to encourage them to grow into the surrounding soil.

Care & Problems—Abelia is one of the most care-free landscape shrubs you can grow. Occasional trimming may be necessary on larger-growing varieties to control size and shape. More compact forms are available that require virtually no maintenance whatsoever.

Hardiness—Zones 6a to 9b

Mature Size (H x W)—4 to 8 ft. x 4 to 8 ft.

Water Needs—Drought tolerant, once established

Bloom Color—White to pale pink

Special Features—Glossy, evergreen foliage and fragrant blooms

HYDRANGEA

Hydrangea macrophylla

Why It's Special—Big, billowing, blue and pink mophead hydrangeas—there are only a few other shrubs that says "Southern garden" in the same way. Advances in breeding mean more cold hardiness and a wider range of colors. Check out the beautiful, delicate lacecap varieties.

How to Plant & Grow—Hydrangeas are generally available in 2-, 3-, and 5-gallon containers at nurseries from spring to fall. Most hydrangeas prefer a partial-shade situation with protection from the hottest afternoon sun. Soil should be rich, loose, and consistently moist.

Care & Problems—Irrigation is necessary during summer, either by automatic system or by you. Hydrangeas are water lovers. Pruning is done immediately after the first flush of bloom in early summer. Prune dead tips and branches after plants leaf out, but only dead tips and branches or you may cut off the flower buds.

Hardiness—Zones 5a to 9b

Mature Size (H x W)—5 to 7 ft. x 4 to 8 ft.

Water Needs—Evenly moist soil

Bloom Color—Pure white, pink, blue, red

Special Features—One of the most spectacular floral displays of summer

INDIAN HAWTHORN

Rhaphiolepis indica

Why It's Special—This tough shrub is best suited to milder-winter areas and is often used as a substitute for azaleas in coastal regions where the sandy soil and extreme heat are unsuitable for them. Indian hawthorn has rounded, dark green, leathery leaves and dense clusters of fragrant pink or white flowers.

How to Plant & Grow—In warm coastal regions, Indian hawthorn can be planted anytime. Further inland, where winters are colder, be sure to get shrubs planted and established before winter. Unlike azaleas, Indian hawthorn prefers slightly alkaline soil, so add lime if your soil pH is below 6.5. Fertile, fast-draining soils are best.

Care & Problems—Irrigate during dry periods until plants are well established, especially in sandy, coastal soils. Prune lightly in late winter to remove dead or damaged wood. Flowers appear on old growth. Indian hawthorn is generally pest and disease free in well-drained soil.

Hardiness—Zones 7b to 10a

Mature Size (H x W)—4 ft. x 4 ft.

Water Needs—Drought tolerant, once established

Bloom Color—Pink or white

Special Features—Salt tolerant; good for coastal gardens

JAPANESE HOLLY

Ilex crenata

Why It's Special—Many landscape professionals and gardeners have a love-hate relationship with Japanese holly, considering it an overused plant. The flip side is that a plant usually gains popularity because it is widely adaptable, easy to grow, and relatively low maintenance, and that is definitely the case with Japanese holly.

How to Plant & Grow—Look for the healthiest plants you can find at reputable garden centers. Plant anytime during the growing season, but allow several weeks for plants to get established before winter. Full sun to part sun is best to prevent plants from becoming leggy.

Care & Problems—Japanese holly prefers moisture. Irrigate during hot, dry months, even after it is established. Add 2 to 3 inches of mulch around the base of the plant to help conserve soil and reduce weeds. Shear in late winter or early summer, if necessary.

Hardiness—Zones 5b to 8b

Mature Size (H x W)—2 to 8 ft. x 2 to 8 ft.

Water Needs—Evenly moist soil; water during drought

Bloom Color—White, insignificant blooms

Special Features—Evergreen foliage and occasional black berries

JAPANESE PLUM YEW

Cephalotaxus harringtonia

Why It's Special—Its soft texture, dark green foliage, and low, spreading habit make Japanese plum yew incredibly versatile. This popular shrub is care free and perfectly happy in shady nooks or woodland gardens, foundation plantings, and shrub borders.

How to Plant & Grow—Plant in spring or fall. It will grow in full sun, given very good, well-drained soil and plenty of water, but the best location is in morning sun or very bright, dappled shade. It will not grow with wet feet, so drainage is a must! Water during drought.

Care & Problems—If a plant sprouts an upright shoot, remove it to retain the broad, spreading habit. Once established, specimens growing in shade are quite drought tolerant, but in sunnier locations irrigation is required. Browning foliage is a sign of winter damage or dry soil. Young plants are easily broken, so plant carefully.

Hardiness—Zones 6a to 9a

Mature Size (H x W)—2 to 6 ft. x 5 to 10 ft.

Water Needs—Evenly moist to slightly dry soil

Bloom Color—Green, insignificant blooms

Special Features—Feathery foliage provides year-round interest

KOREANSPICE VIBURNUM

Viburnum carlesii

Why It's Special—This outstanding large shrub thrives in the cooler areas of the Carolinas. In early spring, clusters of rosy pink buds open to 3-inch clusters of white flowers with a warm, spicy fragrance. One Koreanspice viburnum can perfume an entire back yard without being overwhelming.

How to Plant & Grow—Plant container-grown viburnums anytime the soil is not frozen; water late-summer plantings regularly. Plants prefer full morning sun with light afternoon shade and moist, well-drained soil. Nursery stock often looks thin, but plants fill out quickly once planted.

Care & Problems—Koreanspice viburnum needs little care. Pruning usually involves removing a few wild shoots here and there. A light pruning after flowering can help shape the shrub, but is usually not needed. During wet summer weather, leaf spot can occur, but is mostly cosmetic and not a problem.

Hardiness—Zones 5a to 8a

Mature Size (H x W)—6 to 10 ft. x 6 to 10 ft.

Water Needs—Evenly moist soil

Bloom Color—Pink buds and white blooms

Special Features—Semievergreen foliage and 3-inch clusters of fragrant white blooms

LOROPETALUM

Loropetalum chinense

Why It's Special—Loropetalum is a showy, semievergreen shrub with wide-spreading branches that light up in spring with feathery white or pink flowers. New forms range from very compact, ground-hugging plants to broad, open specimens that can be limbed up into small, multistemmed "trees." Foliage color ranges from olive green to deep, lustrous black-purple.

How to Plant & Grow—Loropetalum is best planted while the soil is warm. In the western Carolinas, protection from winter winds is needed. Foliage color develops best in full sun; the leaves take on bronze to purple-green tones in shade. Loropetalum will tolerate clay soils.

Care & Problems—Loropetalum may need light pruning after the second season to control shape and height. Prune in late spring or after flowering has finished. If shrubs become overgrown, hard pruning to within 1 foot of the ground will encourage robust new growth from ground level.

Hardiness—Zones 7a to 9b

Mature Size (H x W)—3 to 8 ft. x 3 to 8 ft.

Water Needs—Evenly moist soil

Bloom Color—Pink, burgundy, white

Special Features—Semievergreen leaves provide winter color

NANDINA

Nandina domestica

Why It's Special—Some gardeners look down their nose at nandina, but it's tough, easy to grow, pest free, and evergreen, and it produces showy red berries that shine in the winter landscape. Dwarf varieties don't produce as many berries, but often have excellent foliage color in winter.

How to Plant & Grow—Nandina can be planted any time the soil is not frozen. If you need to transplant established nandinas, do it in late fall or early spring, before growth begins. Water plants thoroughly and deeply for the first two months after planting.

Care & Problems—After nandinas are established, they will thrive perfectly well on their own, with little intervention on your part. The only time they struggle is in very heavy, sticky, wet clay where the roots are waterlogged and deprived of air. Fertilize in early spring.

Hardiness—Zones 6a to 9b

Mature Size (H x W)—2 to 8 ft. x 2 to 6 ft.

Water Needs—Drought tolerant, once established

Bloom Color—White

Special Features—Showy red berries in fall and winter

OAKLEAF HYDRANGEA

Hydrangea quercifolia

Why It's Special—Oakleaf hydrangea is a fine native shrub with large, deeply notched leaves resembling those of red oak. In June, it displays large panicles of showy white flowers that later fade to a soft rose color in the best varieties. 'Snowflake' is a double-flowered variety with enormous, cascading blooms.

How to Plant & Grow—Oakleaf hydrangea can be planted year-round, but summer-planted specimens require close attention to watering. In cooler climates, oakleaf hydrangea will tolerate full sun, but morning sun or very bright, dappled shade suits it best.

Care & Problems—Pruning can be tricky. Oakleaf hydrangea flowers on old wood, so should only be pruned after it flowers, but because it flowers late and looks good for so long, this often means pruning while the blooms are still present. Wait until the flowers have turned from their white "full bloom" stage to beige, then prune as needed.

Hardiness—Zones 5a to 8b

Mature Size (H x W)—4 to 10 ft. x 4 to 10 ft.

Water Needs—Evenly moist soil

Bloom Color—White

Special Features—Showy, long-lasting blooms in early summer

OLEANDER

Nerium oleander

Why It's Special—These gorgeous but tender evergreen shrubs are commonly seen in the coastal regions but rarely elsewhere in the Carolinas. Hardy throughout Zone 8, oleanders flower heavily in spring and summer, providing large clusters of blooms.

How to Plant & Grow—Oleanders are best planted in spring, so they can become established before winter. In areas colder than Zone 8, they may not survive outdoors unless they are planted in a protected area. They are quite salt tolerant, making them good coastal plants.

Care & Problems—In Zone 8, plants may need protection during their first two winters. Once established, they'll be fine. If pruning is necessary, do it in early spring before new growth begins. **Warning:** Oleander is extremely poisonous. Do not burn clippings, as even the smoke can be dangerous, and keep the plants away from areas where young children are present.

Hardiness—Zones 8a to 10b

Mature Size (H x W)—4 to 12 ft. x 6 to 12 ft.

Water Needs—Very drought tolerant

Bloom Color—White, pink, red, salmon, light yellow

Special Features—Superb for difficult seaside locations

PIERIS

Pieris japonica

Why It's Special—Pieris is an evergreen shrub whose spring display of lightly fragrant flowers cascades in ivory-colored chains off the plant's spreading branches. Its reddish-bronze new growth unfurls into lustrous evergreen foliage.

How to Plant & Grow—The ideal time to plant pieris is early fall, when the weather has cooled and rains are falling, but the soil is still warm enough to encourage ample rooting in. It grows best in soil that is well drained, rich in organic matter, and acidic, with a pH near 5.5. It is short-lived in wet sites and heavy clay soil.

Care & Problems—Irrigate pieris during drought. It is shallow rooted and should not be allowed to dry out. Water weekly during dry summer months. While moisture is essential, soggy soils will lead to root rot and death. Lace bugs can be a problem.

Hardiness—Zones 5b to 8b

Mature Size (H x W)—4 to 8 ft. x 4 to 8 ft.

Water Needs—Evenly moist soil

Bloom Color—White or pale pink

Special Features—Evergreen foliage and fragrant chains of flowers in late winter

PITTOSPORUM

Pittosporum tobira

Why It's Special—Pittosporum is hardy in the warmer regions of the Carolinas, from Raleigh and Columbia eastward, where its lustrous, leathery leaves and full, rounded appearance make it an important foundation plant. Small clusters of fragrant white flowers appear in spring.

How to Plant & Grow—Plant in late winter and early spring to get plants established before winter. Dwarf and variegated forms need part shade to shade to keep from burning, but standard varieties will grow in full sun if the soil is moist. Water weekly during the first growing season. For a dense hedge, begin shearing when plants are young to encourage growth from the inside out.

Care & Problems—Allow plenty of room for pittosporum to develop its natural rounded shape. It will need little to no pruning. Scale insects can be a problem near the coast. Consult your County Extension Service.

Hardiness—Zones 8a to 10b

Mature Size (H x W)—5 to 15 ft. x 5 to 12 ft.

Water Needs—Drought tolerant, once established

Bloom Color—Creamy white

Special Features—Evergreen, rhododendron-like foliage and fragrant white flowers

PYRACANTHA

Pyracantha coccinea

Why It's Special—Pyracantha (also called firethorn) is a tough, handsome evergreen whose brilliant orange berries provide one of autumn's most spectacular displays. Its stems are covered in long barbs that can make you dread pruning it, but they are useful where an impenetrable barrier is needed.

How to Plant & Grow—In colder areas, plant pyracantha in spring. In warmer climates, it can be planted any time the ground can be worked. Pyracantha can be finicky about transplanting and container-grown plants are superior to balled-and-burlapped specimens. Full sun will give the best flower and berry production.

Care & Problems—Prune wild shoots to train and shape the shrub. Prune in spring after it flowers and as berries are beginning to develop. This will keep you from pruning off the fall berry display. Lace bugs can be a problem. Consult your local garden center for treatment methods.

Hardiness—Zones 5b to 8b

Mature Size (H x W)—6 to 15 ft. x 6 to 10 ft.

Water Needs—Moderate to slightly dry soil

Bloom Color—White

Special Features—Spectacular display of brilliant orange berries in fall

RED TWIG DOGWOOD

Cornus sericea

Why It's Special—Winter is when the red twig dogwood truly shines, with blood red stalks providing interest from November to March. Yellow-twigged forms also exist, as well as varieties that combine both yellow and red on the same branches. This shrub is great for low areas where soil stays wet.

How to Plant & Grow—Plant anytime the soil is not frozen in fall, winter, or early spring. Full sun is best for development of winter twig color. Red twig dogwood is adaptable to wet soils and will thrive near stream banks or natural ponds.

Care & Problems—Red twig dogwood is very low maintenance. Each spring, remove one-third of the oldest stems to keep new growth coming from the base. Newer growth provides winter color, while older stems develop gray bark. Twig canker is an occasional problem. Prune out and discard any twigs with blackened sections.

Hardiness—Zones 3a to 8a

Mature Size (H x W)—4 to 8 ft. x 4 to 6 ft.

Water Needs—Evenly moist to wet soil

Bloom Color—White

Special Features—Colorful twigs add interest to the winter landscape

RHODODENDRON

Rhododendron spp. and hybrids

Why It's Special—Rhododendron provides a magnificent spring floral display. It is the standard by which other flowering shrubs are judged, which may be an unfair comparison, as few others can compete with a truly well-grown rhododendron specimen.

How to Plant & Grow—Rhododendrons are best suited to the Mountains and Piedmont. Plant container-grown plants in early spring, before they start flowering. Partial shade and very well-drained, loose soil that is acidic and evenly moist are ideal. Amend heavily with pine bark soil conditioner to help with drainage and maintain acidity.

Care & Problems—Rhododendrons can be finicky. Twig dieback is common and affected twigs should be pruned out. It can also be spread from plant to plant, so sterilize pruner blades with rubbing alcohol when moving from one shrub to another. Root rot is common in heavy clay soils and is difficult to control.

Hardiness—Zones 5b to 7b

Mature Size (H x W)—2 to 8 ft. x 2 to 8 ft.

Water Needs—Evenly moist soil

Bloom Color—Pink, red, white, magenta, and more

Special Features—Broad, evergreen leaves and showy spring blooms

ROSE OF SHARON

Hibiscus syriacus

Why It's Special—When most other garden shrubs are thinking about going dormant for the winter, rose of Sharon is at its peak. Beginning in late July to early August and continuing through September, it opens its hibiscus-like flowers when the garden needs them most.

How to Plant & Grow—Plant rose of Sharon anytime from late fall to spring. It will tolerate part shade conditions, but flowers best in full sun. It tolerates a wide range of soil types, but flourishes in moist, fertile soil. For hedges, space plants 5 feet apart so they will grow together when mature.

Care & Problems—Pruning is usually not necessary, but when it is, prune in early spring. Water is important during dry summers, especially when the plants are flowering. Japanese beetles may be a problem on foliage in June and July and should be treated.

Hardiness—Zones 5a to 8b

Mature Size (H x W)—8 to 12 ft. x 6 to 12 ft.

Water Needs—Drought tolerant, once established

Bloom Color—White, lavender, pink, red

Special Features—Showy blooms in late summer and early fall

SASANQUA

Camellia sasanqua

Why It's Special—Fall-flowering camellias usually go by the common name of sasanqua. They are vigorous and free-flowering and because they flower in autumn, there are no worries of flower buds freezing during winter.

How to Plant & Grow—Plant sasanquas from March to October to establish roots during warm weather. This species is more sun tolerant than the japonicas, but still performs best in partly sunny to partly shady conditions. Sasanquas need loose, well-drained soil that is high in organic matter.

Care & Problems—Sunscald can occur during winter months on plants in sunny, windswept sites. Prune in late winter or very early spring, before new growth begins. Keep an eye out for blighted shoots that die quickly and prune them out immediately. Scale is an occasional problem and can be controlled with horticultural oil sprays.

Hardiness—Zones 6b to 9b

Mature Size (H x W)—10 ft. x 5 to 10 ft.

Water Needs—Moderately drought tolerant, once established

Bloom Color—White, red, pink

Special Features—Very showy blooms in late fall and early winter

SUMMERSWEET

Clethra alnifolia

Why It's Special—Members of the genus *Clethra* are large shrubs to small trees with very beautiful, dark green foliage. They flower in summer, when few other shrubs are in bloom. White to soft pink, intensely fragrant spires are followed by black, peppercorn-like berries. The cultivar 'Ruby Spice' has rosy pink flowers that hold their color well.

How to Plant & Grow—Plant summersweet anytime soil conditions permit. It is very adaptable, thriving in full sun to part shade and also in damp to wet soils. It is completely hardy and surprisingly salt tolerant, making it a good choice for coastal gardens.

Care & Problems—Prune summersweet in late fall or early spring. It will flower on the season's new growth. In moist locations, it will sucker freely, forming sizable colonies. The plant is pest and disease free if moisture is adequate.

Hardiness—Zones 4b to 9a

Mature Size (H x W)—3 to 8 ft. x 4 to 6 ft.

Water Needs—Moist to wet soil

Bloom Color—White or soft pink

Special Features—Beautiful glossy foliage and intensely fragrant flowers

VIRGINIA SWEETSPIRE

Itea virginica

Why It's Special—Virginia sweetspire is the epitome of grace and character among native ornamentals. Drooping 6-inch spikes of sweetly fragrant flowers appear in midsummer, when few shrubs are showy. Crimson fall color adds to the show later in the season. The shrub is extremely adaptable as to site and climate.

How to Plant & Grow—Plant Virginia sweetspire in spring or fall in full sun to part shade. Deep shade reduces flower production, though the plant will survive. It grows best in fairly rich, moist soil, but is very adaptable and will tolerate drier conditions.

Care & Problems—Once established, sweetspire is low maintenance. It does spread by underground stolons and will become a dense, thick "ground cover" with time; it can choke out neighboring plants if not kept under control. Slugs and snails can chew holes in the leaves, but the damage is not life threatening.

Hardiness—Zones 5a to 9b

Mature Size (H x W)—2 to 5 ft. x 4 to 5 ft.

Water Needs—Moist to wet soil

Bloom Color—White

Special Features—A tough native that thrives in wet locations

WAX MYRTLE

Morella cerifera

Why It's Special—Wax myrtle, or bayberry, produces aromatic berries that are relished by birds and used in candle-making and potpourri. This tough evergreen native thrives in moist clay soils and dry, sandy coastal soils.

How to Plant & Grow—Plant container-grown wax myrtle in spring, summer, or fall. It tolerates full sun to partial shade in any type of soil. It enjoys moist soil, so water generously in dry weather, but it will not tolerate wet feet or standing water, especially in cold weather. It is a heavy feeder, so fertilize yearly.

Care & Problems—Wax myrtle will tolerate heavy pruning in early spring and will respond with vigorous new growth, but it will not take kindly to shearing. Twig dieback caused by a fungus is common during wet summers but is not serious. Suckers can be removed, if desired, but it isn't necessary.

Hardiness—Zones 7a to 10a

Mature Size (H x W)—5 to 20 ft. x 5 to 20 ft.

Water Needs—Evenly moist soil

Bloom Color—Insignificant blooms

Special Features—Fragrant, evergreen foliage and fragrant gray berries

WITCH HAZEL

Hamamelis virginiana

Why It's Special—One of the best plants for year-round interest is witch hazel. This sweet-scented native bears twisted, yellow flowers along naked stems in late fall and early winter. Other species and hybrids bloom in winter and early spring. 'Arnold Promise' is one of the best spring bloomers.

How to Plant & Grow—Witch hazel can be planted from late winter to spring or in early fall. It prefers evenly moist soils rich in organic matter in morning sun or bright, dappled shade. Amend the soil with copious quantities of compost and soil.

Care & Problems—Prune after blooming in late winter to open up the centers of the plants and to control size. Plants are best left to grow in their natural, upright to vase-shaped form. Good leaf mulch does wonders for stimulating root activity. Borers can be a problem in stressed plants.

Hardiness—Zones 4a to 8a

Mature Size (H x W)—8 to 12 ft. x 8 to 12 ft.

Water Needs—Average to evenly moist soil

Bloom Color—Yellow, orange, red

Special Features—Unique, ribbonlike blooms in fall and winter

YAUPON HOLLY

Ilex vomitoria

Why It's Special—Yaupon holly tolerates drought and neglect, survives in coastal conditions, and does not succumb to pests, root rot, or nematodes. This versatile shrub is available in a wide variety of shapes, sizes, and forms. In late fall and winter, the clear gray stems are adorned with bright red berries.

How to Plant & Grow—Plant year-round as soil conditions permit. In colder areas, install plants in spring to allow them to become well established before winter. This plant thrives in heat and humidity, so give it the hottest site you can dish out and watch it grow!

Care & Problems—Yaupon holly tolerates severe pruning and can even be sheared into topiary shapes. While tough, it is intolerant of extremely wet winter conditions and may suffer severe dieback if cold temperatures arrive before it hardens off.

Hardiness—Zones 7a to 10a

Mature Size (H x W)—3 to 16 ft. x 3 to 16 ft.

Water Needs—Dry to wet soil; very adaptable

Bloom Color—Insignificant blooms

Special Features—Bright red berries can be spectacular on good cultivars

SHRUBS IN THE LANDSCAPE

PLANNING

Once you've determined where you want your shrubs, select ones that match the conditions in your landscape. Pay attention to the following factors.

Light requirements: Does your site have full sun, partial sun, partial shade or shade? What do the shrubs prefer?

Drainage: In general, plants prefer well-drained soil. Plants like azaleas and boxwoods will wilt and die in a constantly damp low spot faster than you can say "phytophthora" (that's the root rot that preys on plants intolerant of wet feet). If you have such "hog wallows," choose shrubs that are adapted to boggy conditions. These include anise tree (*Illicium*), Virginia sweetspire (*Itea virginica*), and summersweet (*Clethra alnifolia*).

Temperature: Will the shrubs be exposed to freezing temperatures or extreme heat?

Space limitations: What is the eventual mature height and spread of the shrubs? How fast will they grow? In limited spaces, select smaller, more compact shrubs over the vigorous growers that soon engulf windows and porches.

PLANTING

Most shrubs are available either in pots or as field-grown, balled-and-burlapped plants. Follow these steps to ensure a good start for your new shrubs:

1. Match the shrub to its location. In addition to light levels, be aware of drainage, soil type, and other factors that can affect the shrub's growth.

2. Have your soil tested through your County Extension Service office.

3. Dig a wide, shallow hole at least two or three times larger than the diameter of the rootball, but no deeper than the height of the ball. By making the hole as wide as possible, the roots will grow quickly into the loosened soil, thereby speeding up the plant's establishment in its new home.

4. Slip the plant out of the pot and examine the rootball. Shrubs growing in containers may have roots circling around the outside of the rootball. If you plant it as is, roots will grow from the bottom of the rootball. You should encourage roots to grow along the entire length of the rootball. Take a knife, pruning shears, or the end of a sharp spade and score the rootball in three or four places. Make shallow cuts from the top to the bottom. Gently tease the sides of the rootball apart and the plant will produce new roots from these cuts all around the rootball.

5. Remove wire or twine from balled-and-burlapped plants. Cut away as much wrapping material as possible after placing it in the hole. Remove synthetic burlap entirely; it won't break down and will ultimately strangle the roots.

6. Plant evenly with or slightly above the surrounding soil. Place the shrub in the hole for fit. Lay your shovel across the hole. The rootball should be level with or slightly above the handle. If you've gone too deep, shovel some soil back in and gently compact it with your feet. You want a firm footing for the rootball so it won't later sink below the level of the surrounding grade, which can cause roots to suffocate. In slowly draining soils, set the rootball an inch or two higher than the surrounding soil. Cover it with mulch.

7. Start backfilling, returning the soil to the planting hole. Tamp the soil lightly as you go, but don't compact it. When half the rootball is covered, add some water to settle any air pockets and remoisten the rootball. Backfill and water again. Do not cover the top of the rootball with soil.

8. Apply 2 to 4 inches of organic mulch such as compost, leaf litter, shredded wood, or pine straw. Extend it to the outermost reaches of the branches (the drip line). Leave a space of 3 inches or more around the trunk to keep the bark dry.

9. Depending on weather and rainfall, you may need to water daily for the first few weeks. After that, begin cutting back, eventually reaching an "as needed" basis by testing the soil and rootball for moisture.

FERTILIZING

Newly planted shrubs can be fertilized after they've become established. That may take months or longer, depending on their size. Once established, fertilizer applications can stimulate growth and help shrubs fill their allotted space in the landscape. Shrubs that have already "filled in" won't have to be fertilized on a regular basis. Replenishing the mulch at their roots with compost or other "recyclable" organic materials will provide them with a steady diet of minerals. If your shrubs are growing in a lawn that is fertilized, do not add additional fertilizer.

Apply fertilizer when it will be readily absorbed by the roots of your shrubs and when the soil is moist, which can be anytime from late spring, after new growth emerges, up to early fall. However, if water is unavailable or when the shrubs are stressed by drought during the summer months, do not fertilize at all because their roots will be unable to absorb the nutrients.

Apply fertilizer to the shrub's root zone area (the area occupied by nutrient- and water-absorbing roots), which can extend beyond the drip line or outermost branches. Since most of a shrub's roots are in the top foot of soil, be sure to broadcast fertilizer evenly around the plant. Sweep any fertilizer off the branches and water afterwards to make the nutrients available to the roots.

WATERING

Watering is one of the most critical activities in the garden and proper watering will ensure success with the shrubs you've chosen. The most important point to remember when watering is that you're not just watering to keep plants from being dry and wilted. You are also watering to encourage roots to grow deep into the soil in search of water that is already there. By watering deeply and thoroughly each time you do water, you will actually reduce the amount of watering you will have to do as your shrubs grow and mature. When you have watered properly and your shrubs have grown roots deep into the soil, they will be better able to survive periods of drought because they will be able to access moisture that is locked away in the deeper layers of soil.

PRUNING

Pruning is a basic maintenance requirement for shrubs; it improves their health and appearance and keeps them inbounds. Not all shrubs have to be pruned, however. Barberry, cotoneaster, gardenia, mahonia, and pittosporum rarely need to be pruned if given enough space to develop their natural size. Some multistemmed shrubs, such as deutzia, forsythia, and nandina, must have their older stems removed entirely, a few at a time each year. This keeps them youthful and vigorous. Others, such as mountain laurel, rose of Sharon, and viburnum, already have an attractive natural shape that may require the occasional removal of wayward branches that detract from their beauty.

There are two basic pruning cuts: heading and thinning. Heading, or heading back, involves removing a portion of a branch back to a bud or branch. Heading stimulates a flush of new shoots just below the cut, making the plant look more dense. When you shear your yaupon holly or boxwood hedges, you're making a bunch of heading cuts. A thinning cut is the removal of a branch back to where it joins the limb or trunk. Thinning opens up the center of the shrub to sunlight and reduces the number of new shoots that sprout along the branches. A lot of growth can be removed by thinning without dramatically changing the shrub's natural appearance or growth habit and giving it that "just pruned" look.

When you prune, follow two basic rules:

1. Spring-flowering plants that bloom before June 1 can be pruned right after flowering; they bloom on last year's growth. So pruning shrubs such as forsythia, quince, and azalea at this stage will give them time to develop new flower buds for next year. There are a few exceptions to this rule, such as oakleaf hydrangea and certain azalea cultivars that bloom after June 1, or even into July, but on last year's wood.

2. Summer-flowering shrubs produce flower buds on the current season's shoots. They can be pruned in late winter before new growth emerges. A few of these summer-flowering shrubs are beautyberry, butterfly bush, panicle hydrangea, and glossy abelia. Prune out dead, damaged, or diseased wood at anytime of the year.

PEST CONTROL

Experts have developed a commonsense approach to pest management. It brings Mother Nature into the battle on the gardener's side by integrating smart plant selection with good planting and maintenance practices and an understanding of pests and their habits. This approach starts with growing strong, healthy plants that can prosper with minimal help from you. As in nature, an acceptable level of pests are tolerated. Control is the goal, rather than elimination. This system is called Integrated Pest Management, or IPM for short, and it can work for you.

IPM can be summarized in these steps:

1. Select shrubs that are adapted to your region and have few pest problems. Visit local nurseries and garden centers, and consult your County Extension Service.

2. Start with healthy, high-quality, pest-free plants.

3. Select the right location.

4. Properly plant, fertilize, mulch, and water the plants. Avoid overfertilizing, which encourages a lot of succulent growth that is attractive to insects and susceptible to disease. Overfertilization can also contaminate streams, lakes, and groundwater.

5. Watch for and learn to identify pests. At least once a week, walk through your landscape and examine your shrubs for problems. Inspect the undersides of the leaves and the shoots. If you spot a problem and can't identify it, take a sample to your garden center or County Extension Service for assistance.

6. When trouble strikes, turn to nonchemical controls first. Insects such as aphids can be hosed off with a strong spray of water; others such as Japanese beetles can be handpicked.

7. Sometimes it is necessary to resort to more potent but less toxic measures such as insecticidal soap and *Bt*.

8. You may have to occasionally resort to more potent pesticides, especially when you feel the damage is more than you or your shrubs can tolerate. Consider spot treating heavily infested plants instead of making a blanket application that can destroy beneficial insects such as ladybugs, predatory mites, and green lacewings. Use recommended pesticides and apply according to label directions. Foraging honeybees and other pollinators are sensitive to these insecticides, so treat the plants in early morning or late evening when no bees are present.

9. Keep your garden clean. Remove damaged, dead, or pest-ridden stems or branches. Clean up and discard any infected flowers and leaves.

JANUARY

- As the garden catalogs arrive this month, be on the lookout for new or unusual varieties of shrubs that you may want to add to your garden this year. Each catalog will have new introductions for the year.

- Container-grown and balled-and-burlapped shrubs can be planted in the warmer areas of the Carolinas as long as the soil is not frozen. If you have established shrubs that need to be transplanted, do it now.

- During winter thaws, water both newly planted and established evergreens, especially those on the south and west sides of a house, where sun and wind can be particularly drying. Evergreens continue to lose water through their leaves, even in winter.

- Apply dormant horticultural oil sprays on trees and shrubs to smother overwintering insect eggs, aphids, mites, and scale insects. Oil sprays should not be used on conifers, especially those with blue coloration, as it will affect their color.

FEBRUARY

- Branches from early-spring-flowering shrubs like quince and forsythia can easily be forced into bloom indoors. For four to six weeks before they begin blooming in the landscape, stems can be cut and placed in water indoors to flower in about a week's time.

- Don't be too hasty to fertilize your shrubs. Wait until you see the buds begin to swell before applying fertilizer. If you use slow-release organic fertilizers, you can fertilize a little early, as they will need a couple of weeks to "activate."

- In warmer areas, summer-flowering shrubs that flower on their new growth, such as roses and butterfly bush, can be pruned this month. Most can be pruned down to within 12 to 15 inches of the ground and will respond with lush new growth.

- If you grow spring-blooming camellias, be sure to keep fallen blooms picked up off of the ground. They can harbor fungal diseases, some serious enough to damage the plants.

MARCH

- Planting of both balled-and-burlapped and container-grown shrubs can begin in earnest this month. Air and soil temperatures have begun to warm and digging is easy to do. Spring rains will soon begin and will help plants get established quickly.

- Water newly planted shrubs regularly if spring turns out to be dry. Check the moisture in the rootball and surrounding soil before watering.

- Fertilizing can be done for most shrubs this month. Spring-flowering shrubs that have just finished flowering will be entering a stage of active growth, and summer-blooming shrubs that have just been pruned will use the nutrients to grow quickly and luxuriantly.

APRIL

- Don't be too quick to remove shrubs that have been damaged by cold. Cut back dead branches just above the ground, but leave the roots in place until June. They may resprout from the roots and will usually grow vigorously when they do.

- For blue flowers on your hydrangeas, fertilize with an acid-based fertilizer formulated specifically for hydrangeas, azaleas, hollies, and other acid-loving plants. This needs to be done on a regular basis to maintain the flowers' blue color.

- To prevent water from running off, create a temporary berm, or dike, around newly planted shrubs. Level the berm once the plants have become established and it is no longer needed.

- Aphids, whiteflies, and spider mites will be hatching this month as temperatures rise. Aphids may be present as early as March. Insecticidal soap will help to prevent severe infestations if you start spraying early in the season.

MAY

- Summer is just around the corner and you need to start considering irrigation options this month. If you don't have an automatic system, be sure that you are prepared with hoses, sprinklers, and soaker hoses to get the job done.

- Container-grown shrubs can still be planted as long as you pay careful attention to watering. Remember that roots are confined to a relatively small rootball and water needs to be put directly on the plant until roots begin to grow into surrounding soil.

- When azaleas finish flowering, it is time to prune. They may not need pruning every year, but when they do, the window of time runs from when flowering finishes until about June 15. Later than that, you may be damaging next year's buds.

JUNE

- As part of your summer vacation, why not plan to visit some private and public gardens in the Carolinas? Garden tours are popular this time of year and during organized weekends you may be able to see beautiful private gardens that you would not normally have access to.

- Be sure to water recently planted shrubs. The heat of summer is beginning to set in and weather may be dry. It doesn't take long for newly planted shrubs to dry out and begin to suffer.

- Spider mites and Japanese beetles are particularly active this month. Spider mites can be sprayed with insecticidal soap. Japanese beetles can be handpicked and dropped in a jar of soapy water; for severe infestations, spray with liquid Sevin. Bagworms can also be active, especially on conifers like arborvitae and juniper.

- Weeds will compete for water and nutrients. Be sure to keep them pulled.

JULY

- If you're going on vacation this month, be sure to have your automatic irrigation system adjusted accordingly. If you don't have an automatic system, don't forget to make plans for a friend or neighbor to water potted plants and newly planted landscape plants.

- Water needs will vary from plant to plant. Be sure to keep a close eye on newly planted shrubs. They can dry out very quickly and it doesn't take much time for permanent damage to occur when temperatures are high.

- Spider mites are at their worst this month. They can attack quickly and aggressively and do a lot of damage in a short amount of time.

- Root rots can also attack during warm weather if heavy clay soils remain waterlogged from overwatering. In clay soils, there is a fine line between enough water and too much.

AUGUST

- Take advantage of indoor air conditioning to catch up on writing in your garden journal. If you've been compiling notes about your summer garden, now is a great time to get them organized.

- When watering, remember to soak the rootballs thoroughly and deeply. This encourages roots to grow deep into the soil in search of water, increasing their ability to withstand drought once they're established.

- Red-headed azalea caterpillars are active this month and can completely defoliate branches if not detected early. You can identify this caterpillar by its red head and yellow stripes. Control with the natural insecticide *Bt* (*Bacillus thuringiensis*).

- Plants that wilt and die suddenly may be suffering from phytophthora root rot. It is most common in wet soils, but can attack stressed plants in drier locations. It can move from plant to plant. Phytophthora, if caught early, can be treated with a fungicide used as a soil drench. Check with a local garden center or your County Extension Office for a list of products that are recommended for homeowner use.

SEPTEMBER

- September usually means a break in the weather and is a good time to evaluate how the garden has survived the rigors of summer. Take notes to be added to your garden journal when you have time.

- Fall is prime planting season. Begin making plans for shrubs you want to add to your landscape during the months of October and November. Nurseries will have fresh plants in stock by the end of the month.

- If shrubs have suffered any kind of dieback during the heat and drought of summer, prune out dead branches. Any other pruning should be reserved for the proper time of year, usually late winter to early spring.

- Clean up falling leaves, which can harbor disease and insect pests over the winter.

- Cool-season weeds like henbit, chickweed, and dandelions will be germinating this month. Pre-emergent products will help control them.

OCTOBER

- Fall is the best time for planting shrubs and trees in the Carolina landscape. Warm soil temperatures encourage fast root growth and establishment, but cooler temperatures keep plants from being stressed.

- Fall is unusually dry in the Carolinas, so don't rely on Mother Nature to water newly planted shrubs. Water thoroughly and deeply, checking soil moisture and the rootball itself before watering.

- It is too late to do any shearing or pruning now. Shearing will leave you with brown-edged leaves all winter long and pruning may encourage new growth to sprout from pruning cuts that will then freeze when cold weather arrives.

NOVEMBER

- The fall planting season is still in full swing. In the mountains and colder areas of the Carolinas, mulch newly planted shrubs to keep soil from freezing right away and give roots time to grow into the surrounding soil.

- Rake up and compost fallen leaves and fruit around shrubs because this litter offers overwintering places for insects and diseases.

- Tender broadleaf evergreens exposed to drying winds and sun may need to be shaded on the south and southwest sides to reduce moisture loss and leaf injury.

- If fall rains have been scarce in the Mountains where the ground freezes, keep broadleaf evergreens such as hollies and rhododendrons well watered. Give them a deep and thorough watering every two weeks to ensure that there is consistent moisture at their roots.

- Spruce mites are cool-weather mites that are active this month on arborvitae, juniper, spruce, and other conifers. They attack in spring and fall, although at higher elevations they may be active all summer long.

DECEMBER

- In the Piedmont and Coastal Plain, you can continue to plant container-grown and balled-and-burlapped shrubs.

- If you are a more advanced gardener and like to grow your own plants from cuttings, December is the perfect time to take hardwood cuttings of boxwood, camellia, holly, and juniper. They can be rooted in a cold frame.

- In cold, dry, exposed sites, broadleaf evergreens, especially those that are more tender, may benefit from a winter windbreak that can be made from sturdy stakes with burlap stapled to them.

- When cutting braches from hollies or other evergreens for holiday decoration, be sure to maintain the natural form and beauty of the shrubs you're clipping from.

VINES

for the Carolinas

The popularity of vines continues to grow as rapidly as the plants themselves. Gardeners are always looking for a quick fix when they need instant shade or want to hide an unsightly view. Vines fit the bill in both cases. Beautiful vines, like the spring-flowering clematis, are the pride of seasoned gardeners. Others, like Confederate jasmine, provide exotic fragrance that will permeate the garden and send visitors searching for its source.

Being a resident of the Carolinas may affect your opinion of vines, since we are all too familiar with some of the more undesirable examples around us—namely, kudzu and poison ivy. These two vines aside, there are some fine native vines that can be found across the states. Carolina jessamine, the state flower of South Carolina, serves both as ground cover and an evergreen vine, with pure yellow flowers that are a welcome sight in late winter and early spring. Cross vine and trumpet honeysuckle attract hummingbirds and provide nesting sites for songbirds.

Vines can soften the architecture of a home or shade a patio from the harsh sun. Vines are a must on decorative arbors or trellises, where they add a vertical dimension as well as seasonal flowers. Lampposts and mailboxes serve as supports for a host of showy vines, such as the popular mandevilla, which is an annual in all but the warmest areas, but is still a welcome addition to any garden because of its rapid growth and near-continuous summer flowers. In fact, there are many annual vines that are worthwhile additions to the garden because of their brilliant color and flower power, and we've suggested several in the following pages that you may wish to try in your garden.

UP, UP, AND AWAY

When choosing to plant a vine, do your research and find the one that will suit your needs and grow within your space limitations. One of the biggest mistakes that gardeners and homeowners make is selecting a vine that will ultimately grow much larger than the space available for it. While it is possible to do some trimming and pruning to control a vine's ultimate size, this can turn into a nightmare scenario—not to mention a tremendous amount of near-constant work—if you choose a vine that is ultimately just not suited to the place where you want it to grow.

It seems that some vines have minds of their own, often taking several years to begin flowering on a regular basis. Wisteria and climbing hydrangea are two excellent examples of this. The Chinese and Japanese wisterias have long been popular in gardens; but can take as long as ten years to begin flowering regularly and putting on the spectacular display we see in gardening books and catalogs. The same is true for many of the climbing hydrangeas. They will grow rampantly and climb many feet in a short period of time, but it could be anywhere from five to ten years before you begin seeing flowers on a regular basis. This doesn't mean that these vines aren't garden worthy, but it is helpful to be informed on the front end so that your expectations will be appropriate.

Keep in mind that even though you may be planting a particular vine for a particular purpose and one or more of its ornamental qualities, vines can still be invasive. They can quickly outgrow their space, overgrow nearby plants, and even escape into nearby woodlands and natural areas and become pests. This isn't meant to scare you away or talk you out of growing vines—vines are wonderful!—but you do need to keep in mind that there is a certain amount of maintenance that goes along with some vines in order to keep them from making a nuisance of themselves.

PLANTING AND CARING FOR VINES

Vines are generally purchased and planted in the same way as shrubs, usually in 1-, 3-, or 5-gallon containers that are added to the garden during either the spring or fall planting seasons. Thoroughly loosen the roots of the plant after removing it from its pot; if a specimen is particularly potbound, you may wish to cut through several of the largest roots to encourage them to branch and grow outside of the confines of the rootball.

Dig a planting hole as deep as the depth of the rootball and three times as wide. Mix a 5-gallon bucket of an organic soil conditioner, such as dried cow manure, with the excavated soil. Mix in 2 cups of pelletized dolomitic limestone and 2 tablespoons of slow-release flower fertilizer. Backfill the hole with this blend of garden soil and soil conditioner and water thoroughly. Put down a 2-inch layer of compost or mulch to enrich the soil, conserve moisture, and suppress weeds. Be sure to keep your vines thoroughly watered during their first growing season—twice weekly for the first month after planting and at least once per week after that—to encourage them to root in deeply and grow actively so they can begin covering whatever structure you have chosen to grow them on or over.

Annual vines, such as morning glory or moon vine, grow best if direct seeded where the plants are to remain. There is no advantage to starting with young plants; in fact, annual vine seedlings are difficult to transplant. Soak seeds overnight in tepid water just before planting. In clay soils, make low mounds (hills) by mixing a 5-gallon bucket of play sand and a bucket of dried cow manure with an equal volume of clay, and plant seeds directly into this mixture. Provide strings for the vines to begin climbing on until they reach their intended structures and they will begin twining within a week of emerging from the soil.

SUPPORTS FOR VINES

Vines can be grown on or over any number of supports. Perhaps most commonly, they are grown on trellises or fences, but they can also be grown on walls, up trees, and over arches, arbors, or pergolas; they can even be grown on the ground as ground covers. Smaller vines can be grown successfully in pots and this is a good way to grow vines that may not be hardy in your area.

When choosing a vine to grow on or over a particular structure, give careful consideration to your ultimate goal, your expectations for the vine, and the amount of trimming and training you are willing to do in order to encourage the vine to grow how and where you want it to. Most vines either twine their stems around part of a structure or use a tendril (a modified stem that twists and curls) to attach themselves to whatever they are growing on, but some vines produce aerial roots or even small "suction cups" to stick themselves to the side of a wall, post, or other support. These aerial roots and suction cups literally glue themselves to whatever they are climbing and can leave unsightly marks and tracks if they need to be pruned to keep them in check or removed entirely.

Be sure to consider a vine's method of climbing and the structure it will be climbing on when you're deciding what types of vines you wish to plant and where. Pair vines with structures that can support their physical weight and will display them to their best advantage. An open pergola or arbor allows the pendulous flowers of wisteria to hang down through it, while a stone mailbox or a fence may be the perfect backdrop for morning glory flowers. Perhaps the ideal place to grow the vigorous sweet autumn clematis is the roof of a garden shed or the top of a gazebo, where its stunning floral display can be seen from across the garden and its exquisite fragrance can be carried on the breeze.

EXOTIC VINES

If commonplace ornamental vines do not excite you, consider a more exotic alternative. Tropical vines grow quickly and can add marvelous color while inviting bees and butterflies to the garden. The ever-popular mandevilla (*Mandevilla* hybrids), with its large pink, red, or white trumpets, is a foolproof place to start. Some of the more unusual tropical vines include the Giant Dutchman's pipe (*Aristolochea gigantea*), with blooms up to a foot wide, and the exotic-looking Spanish flag (*Mina lobata*), with fiery spikes of flowers in cream, yellow, and fire-engine red. If you want edible plants, kiwis (*Actinidia* spp.) will be right at home on a sturdy arbor in your garden and these will be perennial, returning for many years and only getting bigger and better with age.

Whether flowering or evergreen, vines are versatile ornamental plants that are still waiting to be discovered. They can be planted in so many wonderful locations. A vine may be just the thing that your garden needs as the "icing on the cake."

AMERICAN WISTERIA

Wisteria frutescens

Why It's Special—American wisteria is native to the Southeast and grows well over arbors and pergolas. It is much less aggressive than its more common Chinese and Japanese counterparts and doesn't have their invasive tendencies. Look for 'Amethyst Falls', which has purple blooms in spring and repeats up to two times during summer. 'Clara Mack' has white flowers.

How to Plant & Grow—Plant American wisteria in spring or fall in full to part sun. It flowers best in lean soil, so don't overamend the soil or overfertilize the plants once in the ground.

Care & Problems—Prune in mid- to late spring, after the first flush of bloom, to shape and train the vine. Second and third flushes of bloom will occur in summer on the new growth that appears after the initial spring flowering and trimming. Because the vines are much less rampant than the Asian wisterias, which are extremely invasive, less additional pruning is required.

Bloom Color—Lavender or white

Bloom Period—Spring, with summer repeat

Type/Hardiness—Deciduous, Zones 5b to 9a

Height—15 to 20 ft.

Water Needs—Moderately moist soil; water in summer to encourage rebloom

ARMAND CLEMATIS

Clematis armandii

Why It's Special—This vigorous vine is perfect for covering a large pergola, gazebo, or wall. Exquisitely fragrant white flowers appear in early spring and the long, leathery, evergreen leaves provide year-round interest. Songbirds nest in its foliage.

How to Plant & Grow—Plant in spring or fall in rich, well-drained, well-amended garden soil. Immediately after flowering in spring, prune and apply a slow-release fertilizer. It is a vigorous grower, but can be kept inbounds with occasional trimming of any errant shoots. Because the leaves are evergreen, winter water may be necessary during dry periods.

Care & Problems—Pruning and trimming can be an issue. This particular clematis is a vigorous grower and needs some elbow room. It flowers early in the spring and can be nipped by an early frost, though this is not as serious a problem in southern climates as it is toward the northern end of its hardiness range.

Bloom Color—White

Bloom Period—Late winter to early spring

Type/Hardiness—Evergreen, Zones 6b (with protection) to 9b

Height—25 ft.

Water Needs—Moderately moist soil; water during dry periods

CAROLINA JESSAMINE

Gelsemium sempervirens

Why It's Special—This native evergreen vine with bright yellow flowers is the perfect size for any garden. In late winter and early spring, small clusters of showy blooms are displayed against glossy green foliage. 'Pride of Augusta' is a double-flowered form with small, roselike blooms.

How to Plant & Grow—Plant in spring or summer to allow plants to become well established before winter. Although it is a fairly tough native vine, Carolina jessamine prefers rich, moist garden soil, where it will grow into a dense mass with hundreds or even thousands of blooms each spring. Fertilize once a year, just after flowering.

Care & Problems—Carolina jessamine may need help getting started on its support. Older growth may need to be tied to the support until vigorous new growth begins. The new growth will wind itself around the support. No serious pest problems are encountered.

Bloom Color—Yellow

Bloom Period—Late winter to early spring

Type/Hardiness—Evergreen, Zones 6 to 10

Height—15 to 20 ft., but can be kept smaller

Water Needs—Drought tolerant, but responds well to moisture

CLEMATIS

Clematis hybrids

Why It's Special—This entry focuses on the popular large-flowered clematis hybrids. Varieties such as 'Jackmanii' have been grown for more than a hundred years, and modern hybrids continue to expand the color range, flower forms, and bloom times.

How to Plant & Grow—Plant clematis in rich, deep, moist garden soil. Set plants deeply in the planting hole with the crown 2 to 3 inches below the soil level. This encourages deep root growth and the formation of a crown below the soil surface so that the plant can regrow if it is damaged.

Care & Problems—Clematis like their tops in the sun and their roots in the shade. Clematis wilt, a fungal disease, can be especially aggravating in southern states. It is usually not lethal, and as long as plants were planted deeply, new growth will sprout from the underground crown.

Color—Purple, lavender, pink, red, white

Bloom Period—Spring to fall

Type/Hardiness—Mostly deciduous, Zones 5a to 8b

Height—5 to 15 ft.

Water Needs—Moderately moist soil; water during extended drought

CLIMBING HYDRANGEA

Hydrangea anomala ssp. petiolaris

Why It's Special—Climbing hydrangea is an excellent clinging vine for softening a brick or stone wall or for growing up the trunk of a large tree. Large, white lacecap hydrangea blooms appear in June and July and are slightly fragrant. Bronze-colored exfoliating (peeling) bark becomes visible in the fall and provides winter interest.

How to Plant & Grow—Plants can be slow to establish, so keep the soil moist for the first year. Mulch to conserve moisture and enrich soil. If plants are in a sunny location, water regularly for at least the first two seasons. A slow-release flower fertilizer is helpful if applied in early spring.

Care & Problems—This will be a big vine, so site accordingly and on a structure that can support its bulk and weight. Climbing hydrangea may take three to five years to begin flowering, so be patient. Spider mites can be a problem when plants are young. Treat with insecticidal soap.

Bloom Color—White

Bloom Period—June and July

Type/Hardiness—Deciduous, Zones 5a to 7b

Height—40 to 60 ft.

Water Needs—Moisture is essential

CONFEDERATE JASMINE

Trachelospermum jasminoides

Why It's Special—Confederate jasmine is an excellent vine for the warmer areas of the Carolinas, where its fragrant, white flowers bloom for six to eight weeks each spring. As it grows, it can be sheared in summer and will almost become a dense, clinging shrub. It is the perfect choice for covering chain-link fences or screening unsightly views.

How to Plant & Grow—Plant container-grown plants in spring or fall. Water regularly until the plants are well established and then as needed during dry months. Hard pruning should be done immediately after flowering has finished in spring. Occasional pruning in summer will encourage the vine to become thick.

Care & Problems—Confederate jasmine can be sensitive to extreme cold, but can be grown throughout the Zone 8 areas of the Carolinas and in protected areas of Zone 7b. Scale insects can be a problem. Spray with horticultural oil sprays during winter.

Bloom Color—White

Bloom Period—Spring

Type/Hardiness—Evergreen, Zones 7b (with protection) to Zone 9b

Height—15 to 20 ft.

Water Needs—Moist soil until established, then moderately moist

CROSS VINE

Bignonia capreolata

Why It's Special—This popular Carolina native boasts beautiful, orange-red, trumpet-shaped blooms and evergreen or semievergreen foliage that turns deep purplish maroon in winter. Its fast growth rate makes it an excellent choice for growing on trellises, arbors or large tree trunks.

How to Plant & Grow—Cross vine tolerates a wide range of soil conditions, from dry clay to wetter coastal soils. Ideally, it should be planted in rich, well-drained garden soil in full to part sun. This will encourage lush growth and spectacular bloom. While drought tolerant, it benefits from watering in dry periods.

Care & Problems—Prune this vigorous vine immediately after it flowers and as often as necessary to train it to a structure. Cross vine attaches itself with tiny "suction cups" that glue themselves very tightly to its support. It is not recommended for covering clapboard or shingled structures, but stone or brick walls are excellent supports.

Bloom Color—Orange-red

Bloom Period—Spring

Type/Hardiness—Evergreen or semievergreen, Zones 6a to 9b

Height—Up to 30 ft. or more

Water Needs—Drought tolerant, once established

FIVE-LEAF AKEBIA

Akebia quinata

Why It's Special—Akebia is a tough vine that will scale walls, provide shade over arbors, or rapidly cover a trellis. In spring, clusters of small, fragrant, dark purple or white flowers appear. It is well suited to new home sites, where soils are often poor and compacted.

How to Plant & Grow—Akebia is not fussy about soil and will grow almost anywhere. It performs best in sun to part shade. Mulch as summer approaches and keep new plants evenly moist through their first growing season. Fertilize in early spring for the first two years and only as needed after that.

Care & Problems—Pruning immediately after the flowers drop in spring and then as needed through summer to control growth. Akebia is a large vine and should be planted on a sturdy, supportive structure. If you plant both the purple- and white-flowered forms, you may get large, sausage-like fruits in summer.

Bloom Color—Dark purple or white

Bloom Period—Spring

Type/Hardiness—Evergreen to semievergreen, Zones 5b to 9a

Height—20 to 40 ft.

Water Needs—Drought tolerant, once established

HYACINTH BEAN

Dolichos lablab

Why It's Special—This fast-growing annual vine with beautiful purple flowers and showy purple "beans" is an excellent choice for masking chain-link fences, screening unsightly views, or covering a trellis or small arbor. It attracts hummingbirds and is a perfect plant for children to grow since the large seeds are easy to handle and grow quickly.

How to Plant & Grow—Sow seeds outdoors after the soil has warmed in mid- to late spring. They will germinate within seven to ten days and grow rapidly, twining their way up a support. Flowers will appear from midsummer to frost.

Care & Problems—Japanese beetles can be a problem. Pick them off and drop them in a jar of soapy water or spray with liquid Sevin to control severe infestations. The showy purple "beans" are appreciated for their ornamental value only and should not be eaten. Harvest seeds when pods dry in autumn and plant next spring.

Bloom Color—Purple flowers and pods

Bloom Period—Midsummer to frost

Type/Hardiness—Grown as an annual

Height—Up to 10 ft.

Water Needs—Moist soil until established, then moderately moist

JAPANESE WISTERIA

Wisteria floribunda

Why It's Special—Under strict management, Japanese wisteria can be a showstopper in the spring garden. You can train it into "tree" form by staking it to the height you want the trunk to eventually be and keeping all suckers trimmed off, only allowing top growth.

How to Plant & Grow—Wisteria will grow almost anywhere, but full sun and lean, unamended soil are ideal. Water new plants regularly until well established, then leave them alone. They are extremely drought tolerant, once established, and if overfertilized or planted in overly rich soil, they will grow excessively fast and may produce foliage at the expense of flowers the following season.

Care & Problems—Hard pruning should be done immediately after flowering in spring. Prune as needed through summer by trimming the stems back to 8-inch-long stubs, or spurs. Stop all pruning and fertilizing by August 1 to preserve next spring's flower buds. Japanese wisteria can be very invasive.

Bloom Color—Purple or white

Bloom Period—Spring

Type/Hardiness—Deciduous, Zones 4b to 8a

Height—25 to 30 ft. or more

Water Needs—Drought tolerant, once established

MOON VINE

Ipomoea alba

Why It's Special—Perhaps no other annual vine is as intriguing as the moon vine. Its saucer-sized, pure white blooms unfurl each night as the sun sets and remain open until the following morning. On moonlit nights, they literally glow in the evening garden, attracting nighttime moths and other pollinators with their rich, heady fragrance.

How to Plant & Grow—Sow seeds directly in the garden after the soil has thoroughly warmed in spring. Moon vine resents being transplanted, so direct sowing is best. Plant in rich, deep, thoroughly amended garden soil. Keep the plants well watered throughout the growing season.

Care & Problems—These vines are fairly pest and disease free. They do grow large, so give them room to climb and spread on a fence, arbor, or large trellis. They can easily reach 20 feet by the end of the season and are difficult to prune, since the flowers appear continually as the vine grows.

Bloom Color—Pure white

Bloom Period—Midsummer to frost

Type/Hardiness—Annual, not hardy

Height—20 ft. or more

Water Needs—Evenly moist soil for best growth

SWEET AUTUMN CLEMATIS

Clematis terniflora

Why It's Special—Beginning in late August, this native vine becomes a fragrant white cloud of flowers, and later in the season, the silvery seedheads can be used in dried arrangements. Its rambling habit makes it perfect for covering an arbor, pergola, or sturdy shade tree.

How to Plant & Grow—Plant in spring when soil begins to warm. Sweet autumn clematis is not picky about soil, and you frequently see it growing on roadsides in areas with thin, lean, clayey soil. Full sun will give you the most flowers, but this vine is also quite shade tolerant and will still perform in part shade.

Care & Problems—Prune in early spring to neaten the plant and encourage healthy new growth. Flowers appear at the end of the growing season on the current season's growth; prune only if necessary as summer progresses. Training needs to begin in early spring to keep this vine from becoming a tangled mess.

Bloom Color—White

Bloom Period—August and September

Type/Hardiness—Deciduous, Zones 5a to 9b

Height—20 ft. or more

Water Needs—Drought tolerant, once established

TRUMPET HONEYSUCKLE

Lonicera sempervirens

Why It's Special—Perhaps no other vine attracts hummingbirds as well as our native trumpet, or coral, honeysuckle. This is not the invasive Japanese honeysuckle that has overtaken fields and woodlands throughout the Southeast, but a wonderful native vine that is an excellent addition to any garden.

How to Plant & Grow—Plant trumpet honeysuckle in spring or fall, when regular rainfall will help the plants get established. If your soil is well drained, there is no need to amend. If you have heavy clay, add soil conditioner and compost.

Care & Problems—Provide a sturdy structure for trumpet honeysuckle to grow on. In good soil, it can become quite large, though it can also be pruned and trained to stay within bounds in smaller spaces. Pruning should be done after the first flush of bloom in early to midsummer. Powdery mildew may be a problem but is not life threatening.

Bloom Color—Coral red or soft yellow

Bloom Period—Early summer, with some repeat

Type/Hardiness—Semievergreen, Zones 5b to 9a

Height—15 to 20 ft.

Water Needs—Moderately moist soil, once established

TRUMPET VINE

Campsis radicans

Why It's Special—This tough—some say indestructible—native flowering vine provides a spectacular display of tubular, deep orange flowers from late June to September. A magnet for hummingbirds, it thrives in hot, humid summers and in difficult, rocky, clay-based soils.

How to Plant & Grow—Trumpet vine can be planted in spring, summer, or fall as long as it is watered long enough to get it established. Flowering will be best in full sun, but it will also perform well in light shade.

Care & Problems—With vines, extremely tough can also mean extremely aggressive, and trumpet vine is no exception. Even though trumpet vine is native, it can still swallow an arbor, pergola, gazebo, or the side of a house in short order. Give careful consideration to the site. It sticks itself to its support with woody roots that sprout from the stem and are nearly impossible to remove once they're stuck.

Bloom Color—Orange to red, rarely yellow

Bloom Period—June to September

Type/Hardiness—Deciduous, Zones 4a to 9b

Height—20 to 30 ft.

Water Needs—Drought tolerant, once established

USING VINES IN THE LANDSCAPE

Before selecting vines for your landscape, become familiar with the environmental conditions of the site: Light exposure (full sun, partial sun, partial shade, or dense shade), soil moisture, and drainage. Most flowering vines perform best in full sunlight to partial shade. Coastal gardeners need to select vines that tolerate salt spray. Always match the plant to the site rather then attempting to change the environment to accommodate the plant. It is also wise to familiarize yourself with the method a vine uses to climb so you'll know the kind of support to select for it and how to maintain it. If you already have a support, select a vine that will be able to climb it with ease.

Twining vines twist their stems around supports. With a little coaxing, American wisteria (*Wisteria frutescens*), Confederate jasmine (*Trachelospermum jasminoides*), and Carolina jessamine (*Gelsemium sempervirens*) happily wrap themselves around mailbox posts, lampposts, and railings.

Some vines use tendrils to cling to objects. Clematis (*Clematis* spp. and hybrids), cross vine (*Bignonia capreolata*), and others have specialized structures called tendrils that quickly and tightly wrap themselves around their supports to pull the stems and leaves of the vine upright and into position.

Finally, some vines use specialized roots to give them a foothold. Climbing fig (*Ficus pumila*), Japanese hydrangea vine (*Schizophragma hydrangeoides*), climbing hydrangea (*Hydrangea anomala* ssp. *petiolaris*), English ivy (*Hedera helix*), and Virginia creeper (*Parthenocissus quinquefolia*) produce rootlets along their stems that have adhesive, suction cup–like disks at their tips for attaching to surfaces.

Keep vines off of wooden walls—they trap moisture and slow the drying of wood, which can encourage decay. When shading brick or masonry walls with clinging vines that have aerial rootlets or adhesive disks (like English and Boston ivies and climbing hydrangea), think twice before allowing them to cling to the walls. Once you allow them to climb on the walls, they're very difficult to remove. After you tear down the vine, you're left with rootlets and disks that can only be removed with a stiff scrub brush.

PREPARING THE SOIL AND PLANTING

Before planting, thoroughly amend the soil where your vines are going to grow. Many vines, once established, will need relatively little care other than pruning to keep them inbounds, and many have such extensive root systems at maturity that trying to work soil amendments in around them later on is an exercise in futility. Test the soil for pH and fertility levels. Add lime or sulfur and nutrients as recommended by soil-test results. To plant your vines, follow these steps:

1. Dig a wide, shallow hole, at least two to three times the diameter of the rootball, but no deeper than the height of the rootball. Roots will grow quickly into the loosened soil and will speed up the plant's establishment in its new home. In heavy clay soils, dig the hole so the rootball will be 1 to 2 inches higher than the surrounding soil to help ensure that the crown of the plant won't sit in wet clay soil.

2. Slip the plant out of the pot and examine the rootball. Vines growing in plastic or other hard-sided containers may have roots circling around the outside of the rootball. Encourage roots to grow along the entire length of the rootball by lightly scoring the rootball in three or four places with a knife, pruning shears, or the end of a sharp spade. Make shallow cuts from the top to the bottom of the rootball. Gently tease the sides apart. Now this "doctored" plant will produce new roots from the cuts all around the rootball. If any thick, ropelike roots have become knotted or contorted, cut through those as well.

3. Plant even with or, if you have clay soil, slightly above the surrounding soil. Place the vine into the hole and measure the height of the rootball against the surrounding soil. With large plants, lay your shovel across the hole to see that the rootball is even or slightly above the handle. If the hole is too deep, put some soil on the bottom of the hole, tamp it down with your feet to give the plant some solid footing, and put the plant back in the hole.

4. Loosen and break up any clods of soil before backfilling half the hole. Never add any organic matter or sand into the backfill soil when digging individual planting holes—doing so will create problems with water movement and root growth between the rootball and soil.

5. Lightly tamp down the soil with your feet or hands, but not so heavily that you compact the soil. Water when half the rootball is covered to settle out any air pockets and to remoisten the soil in the rootball. Finish backfilling and water again. Apply 2 to 3 inches of mulch around the base of the vine, keeping it clear of the stems so you don't invite insect or disease problems.

WATERING

Water newly planted vines frequently until they become established. Water—not fertilizer—is the most important ingredient for helping them get established in the landscape. Keep the soil moist, but not sopping wet.

PRUNING

Methods and timing of pruning will vary from vine to vine. Some vines, like sweet autumn clematis, flower on their current season's growth and can be pruned hard in early spring to encourage lush, vigorous growth that will bear flowers in the fall. Others, such as wisteria and Carolina jessamine, flower in spring on growth that was made the year before. These vines should be pruned in spring, immediately *after* they finish flowering and then only as needed to keep them shaped and in bounds for the remainder of the year.

TIPS AND TRICKS FOR PRUNING CLEMATIS

The key to determining when to prune your clematis is knowing whether it flowers on last year's growth, this year's growth, or both. Experts divide the genus into three groups.

Group I consists of the early-spring-flowering evergreen clematis and early- and mid-flowering species. This group includes Alpine clematis (*Clematis alpina*), Armand clematis (*C. armandii*), downy clematis (*C. macropetala*), and anemone clematis (*C. montana*). These clematis flower on last year's wood and should be pruned after the flowers fade but no later than July. The only pruning really needed is to remove weak or dead stems and to confine the plant to its allotted space.

Group II consists of clematis that also flower on last year's growth but will produce a second flush of bloom on new growth. Included are midseason large-flowered cultivars such as 'Bees' Jubilee', 'Henryi', 'Nelly Moser', and 'Vyvyan Pennell'. Remove all dead and weak stems in late winter or early spring, and cut the remaining stems back to a pair of strong buds that will produce the first blooms. Occasional pinching after flowering will stimulate branching.

Group III consists of late-flowering cultivars and species that flower on this season's growth, such as fragrant virgin's bower (*C. flammula*), solitary clematis (*C. integrifolia*), Sweet Autumn clematis (*C. terniflora*) *C.* 'Jackmanii', Italian clematis (*C. viticella*), golden clematis (*C. tangutica*), scarlet clematis (*C. texensis*), and the herbaceous species. These can also be pruned in late winter or early spring. For the first two or three years, they may be cut back to 1 foot from the ground. Later, cut them back to 2 feet. If not cut regularly, this group can become very leggy and overgrown.

The boundaries between these three groups are not absolute. Certain Group III clematis, for example, can be treated as Group II to produce early blooms on previous year's wood. Likewise, large-flowered hybrids that are technically in Group II, such as 'Nelly Moser', can be cut back hard in early spring to produce a strong flush of new growth from the base. They will still flower profusely on their new growth and the vines will have fewer tendencies to become leggy and bare at the base. The groups serve as a rough guide to keeping your clematis vines within bounds.

JANUARY

- As new plant catalogs begin arriving this month, scan them for unique and interesting vines that will complement your landscape. Pay special attention to new introductions that may be coming on to the market, as these will often be the most unique and unusual varieties and it's always fun to try something new!

- In the warmer parts of the Carolinas, vines can be planted now as long as the soil can be worked.

- Desiccation by cold weather and winter wind can be hard on evergreen vines if they are not yet fully established. Be sure to water evergreen vines during winter dry spells, especially if they were just planted the previous season.

- To control overwintering insects and spider mite eggs, apply a dormant oil spray before new growth emerges. Read the label and follow the directions regarding the limits of high and low temperatures for safe application.

FEBRUARY

- Keep newly planted vines well watered to help them get established quickly.
- An early-spring application of organic, slow-release fertilizer can be applied to vines now to get them off to a good start as they begin to grow in spring. Be careful not to overfertilize vines, especially the more aggressive growers, or you may find yourself spending a lot of time trimming to keep them under control.
- Vines that have outgrown their space can be cut back now, but avoid pruning vines such as wisteria that will be blooming in just a few weeks on the growth they made last year. Prune those vines immediately after they finish flowering.
- Once the coldest winter weather has passed, prune summer-flowering vines such as Confederate jasmine (*Trachelospermum jasminoides*) and trumpet creeper (*Campsis radicans*). They will flower on their new spring and summer growth.

MARCH

- Piedmont and Coastal Plain gardeners can begin planting vines this month, as temperatures begin to moderate.
- Spring is rarely dry, so newly planted vines may not need frequent watering, but check the soil at least once a week to be sure that the roots remain moist during the first six to eight weeks they are in the ground.
- Spring-flowering vines such as Carolina jessamine, Armand clematis, and cross vine should be pruned as necessary after flowering. Remove any dead or damaged shoots and cut back others to keep the vine in bounds.
- Fall-flowering vines such as sweet autumn clematis can also be pruned now and will flower on this season's new growth.

APRIL

- Take pictures of your landscape from various viewpoints and angles to help determine where vines can be used to bring color to nondescript areas.
- Seeds for moon vine and morning glory can be planted in the warmer areas of the Carolinas this month. Both have very hard seed coats, so it is helpful to knick them with a file or rub them between two pieces of coarse sandpaper and then soak them overnight to allow water to be absorbed before planting out.
- If you have overwintered tropical vines, such as mandevilla, indoors, they can be planted out this month to grow and bloom in the garden until frost threatens in late autumn.
- When wisteria, Carolina jessamine, Armand clematis, and other early-spring-flowering vines have finished flowering, it is time to prune.

MAY

- Continue planting seeds of summer-flowering annual vines such as moon vine, hyacinth bean, and morning glory. They will germinate and grow quickly as the soil warms in the late-spring sunshine.
- Mulch vines to suppress weeds and conserve moisture. Organic mulches such as composted leaves or soil conditioner will break down and help to enrich the soil.
- Create supports for annual vines before they become a tangled mess. Use strings, trellises, or other supports, making sure that they will support the weight of the full-grown vines later in the summer.
- Watch for signs of clematis wilt. Though it is rarely fatal, it can be devastating to vines that are just getting ready to flower. Carefully trim out any stems that wilt and die suddenly. Be sure to sterilize your pruner blades with rubbing alcohol to prevent passing the disease from plant to plant.

JUNE

- Take notes on your vines over the next few months and record your observations in your journal. Notes on bloom time, ornamental features, growth rates, and pest problems will be helpful in making plans to relocate or replace any poorly performing plants.
- Train rapidly growing vines to the trellis, arbor, or other structure they are meant to grow on. You may have to attach some temporary strings or wires to the structure to get the vines started.
- Japanese beetles are at their most active this month. They find climbing roses, wisteria, and climbing hydrangea particularly tasty! Pick them off by hand and drop them in a jar of soapy water, or spray with liquid Sevin for severe infestations.
- Hand pull weeds to prevent them from stealing water and nutrients from your vines.

JULY

- If you're planning a vacation this month, don't forget to find someone to check on the garden and water as necessary while you're gone.
- Japanese and Chinese wisteria may need to be pruned to encourage the production of flowering spurs, which will provide next year's floral display. Cut the lateral shoots back to

just beyond the sixth or seventh leaf up from the base of the stem. New shoots may break from buds behind the cut. Wait until they have developed two to three sets of leaves and cut them back to just above the first bud.

- Japanese beetles can still be active this month. Handpick them and drop them in a jar of soapy water, or spray with liquid Sevin for severe infestations. Spider mites love the hot summer months and are often recognized by the white speckling they cause on leaves.

AUGUST

- Collect seeds from annual vines such as morning glory, moon vine, and hyacinth bean, and store them in paper envelopes or small paper bags for planting next year. Paper is better than a plastic zip-top bag because paper breathes and doesn't trap moisture, which can be detrimental to dormant seeds.

- Be diligent about watering vines this month, especially if natural rainfall is scarce. Vines that will flower early next spring, such as wisteria and Carolina jessamine, are forming their flower buds now and drought stress could hinder this process and affect next spring's floral display.

- Continue inspecting your vines for spider mite and aphid infestations. Evaluate the extent of the injury and take action if the health of the vine is in jeopardy.

SEPTEMBER

- For a different approach, grow well-behaved vines on or through trees and shrubs. Draping vines over other plants allows you to create eye-catching combinations with contrasting foliage textures, as well as flower and foliage pairings.

- It is too late to do any major pruning now, especially for spring-flowering vines such as wisteria, Carolina Jessamine, and others. They have already set their flower buds for next spring's bloom, and pruning now means cutting off those buds and ruining the display.

- Vines should not be fertilized this time of year. Fertilizing can encourage tender new growth that may not have time to harden off before cold weather arrives.

- Winter weeds such as henbit and chickweed, as well as dandelions, begin germinating this month. Remove them now while they're young and easy to pull. Pre-emergent herbicides must be applied *before* weed seeds germinate.

OCTOBER

- Mountain gardeners need to get their planting finished this month so that newly planted vines will have a chance to get rooted in and established before cold weather arrives.

- If you grow the colorful-leaved ornamental sweet potato vines in your flower beds, you can dig the tubers now and store them in a cool, dry location for replanting next spring after the danger of frost has passed.

- Annual vines that have been killed with the first freeze should be cut back from their supports and composted.

- Spider mites may still be present in the warmest areas of the Carolinas. After vines have gone completely dormant in late fall or early winter, spraying with dormant horticultural oil will help smother spider mite eggs and reduce next year's population.

NOVEMBER

- If you're a do-it-yourselfer, make plans to build a new arbor, pergola, or trellis that can eventually support a vine. Winter is a great time to do these kinds of projects, which many of us are too busy to do during the hectic summer season.

- Fall is usually dry in the Carolinas, so don't rely on Mother Nature to water newly planted vines. Have the hose at the ready and give vines, especially newly planted ones, a thorough soaking at least once and maybe twice a week until winter precipitation begins to fall.

- Remember that evergreen vines such as Armand clematis and Carolina jessamine continue to lose water through their leaves, even though they are technically dormant. It is especially important to water evergreen vines during periods of winter dryness.

- Rake up fallen leaves from the ground under your vines and compost them. Fallen leaves can harbor insects and disease, which can then reinfect the plants next spring as they begin to grow.

DECEMBER

- Update your gardening journal this month—hopefully you have been taking notes throughout the growing season—and make plans for garden and landscape improvements next year.

- Now is also an excellent time to create a wish list for next year, since new plant catalogs may begin arriving as early as December and will definitely start arriving right after the first of the year.

- Remember to keep vines off wooden walls. They can trap moisture, slow the drying of the wood, and encourage decay.

- Dormant oil can be applied to vines this month to help control spider mites, scale insects, and mealybugs. Be sure to read the label for directions for proper mixing and for cautions regarding the limits of high and low temperatures at the time of application.

TREES

for the Carolinas

It is hard to imagine living in a neighborhood without trees. Trees make our environments more pleasant and add seasonal beauty. In the Carolinas, trees display unique arboreal interest through all four seasons. Autumn color in the Carolinas is spectacular, particularly in the Piedmont and Mountains, and winter snowstorms light up our evergreens on hillsides and mountain ridges. Our spring-flowering bulbs and wildflower gardens are enhanced by the beauty of a number of flowering tree companions. Trees produce berries that attract birds and wildlife to our home landscapes. Evergreen trees are important nesting sites for birds, doubling as windbreaks and privacy screens.

Spring announces its arrival in our states with a parade of redbuds, Japanese cherries, saucer magnolias, and, of course, dogwoods in full, resplendent bloom. In early summer, 'Royal Purple' smoke tree and 'Forest Pansy' redbuds steal the show with their fabulous burgundy leaf color. Fall echoes the floral display of spring with dazzling colors of other hues. The fall show that envelops the Carolinas begins in early October on the lofty peaks of the Blue Ridge and Great Smoky Mountains and gradually wends its way across the Piedmont to the Coastal Plain. The seasonal spectacle of our hardwood trees ensures that tourism will always contribute to the economy of the Carolinas.

THE VALUE OF TREES

In studies of residential real estate values, tree-filled building lots bring market prices 20 to 30 percent higher than similar lots without trees. Strategically placed trees can significantly reduce the cost of cooling a home by providing much-needed shade during the summer months. Trees are nature's air conditioners, reducing ambient heat as they shade homes and transpire moisture. In addition to the natural beauty they provide, shade trees can be a financial asset.

With increasing concerns for air quality, the public should recognize that trees provide a cost-effective way to clean the air in urban communities. Carbon dioxide production is a major factor in global warming. Depending on the species, a single mature tree can consume up to 48 pounds of carbon dioxide every year and may store up to 13 pounds of carbon. In return, it releases enough oxygen back into the atmosphere to support two human beings.

SELECTING A TREE

A tree should be selected not only for its form, but for a number of other characteristics as well. When it comes to form, some varieties grow broadly upright or rounded, like many of our native maples that provide the stunning fall color we see in the Mountain and Piedmont regions. Others may be more narrowly upright or columnar like cedar, pendulous like weeping cherry, or vase shaped like elm and zelkova. A tree's mature form is very important in determining how that tree will function for us in the landscape. Obviously, if you're looking for a shade tree, you don't want to plant a tree that grows in a narrowly upright fashion with no spreading branches to shade the ground below. Likewise, you may not want to plant a large, spreading oak on a tiny urban lot where it may eventually engulf your entire yard!

In addition to a tree's form, there are both deciduous and evergreen species to be considered. Deciduous trees, those that drop their leaves in autumn, are often selected because they offer summer shade and allow the winter sun to warm our houses. The largest specimens, like the oaks, are known for their long lives and majestic form, while others provide outstanding fall color and ornamental appeal. Still others, like the ginkgo, have an ancient history as well as a unique beauty all their own.

When it comes to evergreens, most of us are familiar with the many pines that grow in the Carolinas, but there are other beautiful evergreen options, too, including Southern magnolia and American holly. Even some of our oaks, like the amazing live oak, are evergreen. Keep in mind, however, that evergreens have their challenges too. One of those is that the ground beneath these trees is in the shade for twelve months of the year. Add to that the root competition created by trees, and this can present some stumbling blocks when it comes to growing lawns and landscaping these areas. While there are many options for plants that will thrive under shady conditions, it is important to consider all of these advantages and disadvantages from the start.

WHAT TREES OFFER

Shade trees can frame a house the way a beautiful frame enhances a lasting work of art. Evergreens block objectionable views and divert strong winds. As a group, evergreens can add color to an otherwise bleak winter landscape. Although they never lose all their leaves, pines shed some of their needles each year in spring or fall, gifting you with coveted "pine straw" mulch. People commonly plant evergreens too close to the house. Ask the question, "What is the mature spread?" and plant accordingly.

During the dreary winter months, many ornamental trees provide colorful berries for our enjoyment and sustenance for birds. The seedpods and berries that follow the handsome flowers are a special treat in the garden. Boughs laden with snow provide a "photo op" for gardeners anxious to capture a cardinal feasting near a window. *Prunus mume*, the Japanese flowering apricot, is a winter-flowering gem whose blossoms will emerge as early as January in warmer climates and February where it's a little colder. If you're lucky enough to avoid a late hard freeze, you'll even find small apricots on the trees later in the season that are very attractive to birds and wildlife.

One often-overlooked characteristic of deciduous trees is exfoliating bark, such as the bark of the river birch that flakes and peels in long cream, beige-and-salmon-colored strips. The cinnamon-colored, mottled bark of crape myrtle is most appreciated in the winter garden, but is a characteristic that is often overlooked when initial choices are being made. Research the subtle seasonal characteristics of landscape trees before you plant, and site them where their traits can be most appreciated.

BEAUTY CLOSE TO HOME

Many Carolina gardeners are passionate about dogwood, the North Carolina state flower. Dogwood is a native flowering tree whose spring, fall, and winter beauty is unsurpassed. A fungal disease, dogwood anthracnose, threatens the dogwood's survival in Mountain and upper Piedmont landscapes, but new disease-resistant dogwood hybrids offer hope that this deciduous tree will be found in our gardens for many decades to come. Researchers, nurserymen, and plant enthusiasts are also working tirelessly toward finding naturally occurring forms of the native dogwood that are resistant to anthracnose, powdery mildew, and dogwood borer. All of these would be important discoveries for ensuring the survival of these beautiful native trees.

THINKING AHEAD

Trees can be the biggest investment in landscape installations. From a purely monetary standpoint, trees are going to be one of the bigger financial investments you make in your landscape. Not only are they more expensive to buy, but eventually they are going to need occasional maintenance to keep them strong and healthy. With trees, you're not just planning for this season or even five or ten seasons from now. You are truly planning for the future and wise planning is essential. Ask yourself why you need a tree for a particular location. Is shade your primary goal? What about privacy? Are there height restrictions in the space? If a tree produces fruit or drops twigs, would it create a hazard or maintenance concern? Do you desire pretty flowers, or is a conifer acceptable? Many trees attract wildlife; are you prepared for the litter that accompanies critters?

You can consult with a county forester, city arborist, or a County Extension Service agent for lists of trees for special situations. This expert can guide your tree selection by considering your particular soil types and environment, as well as your lot's limitations. Remember, too, that many people living in modern-day subdivisions must abide by ordinances and rules. These ordinances may specify which tree species can be planted near streets or power lines and may also stipulate restrictions for protecting valuable, mature trees onsite.

VARIETY IS THE SPICE OF LIFE

Not all trees are created equal. There is as much variation among species of trees as there are among breeds of dogs, and selecting a tree for the home landscape requires thoughtful preparation. Architect Frank Lloyd Wright once said, "Form follows function." This is a good rule to remember when selecting a tree. Select the right form (size and shape) to complement the desired function and you will not only enhance the beauty of your landscape and home, but reduce the need and cost of long-term maintenance as well.

AMERICAN HOLLY

Ilex opaca

Why It's Special—Throughout the Carolinas and up the Eastern Seaboard, American hollies are found growing in the wild. This stately holly evokes memories of Christmas past with holly berries on the mantle, but its dark green foliage offers character and interest year-round.

How to Plant & Grow—Balled-and-burlapped specimens should be planted in late winter or early spring, before plants break dormancy. Container-grown specimens can be planted in spring or fall. Hollies have a broad-spreading, fibrous root system and need a generous planting hole twice as wide as the rootball.

Care & Problems—Hollies prefer well-drained, moist soil, but will tolerate drier sites if kept well watered until established. Prune in July when berries are visible. It may take two to three seasons after transplanting for berry production to start, and you must have both male and female plants nearby.

Hardiness—Zones 5b to 9a

Mature Size (H x W)—30 to 45 ft. x 15 to 25 ft.

Water Needs—Evenly moist to slightly dry soil

Flowers/Berries—Small white flowers, showy red berries

Fall Color—Evergreen

BALD CYPRESS

Taxodium distichum

Why It's Special—One of the few deciduous conifers, this native tree makes an imposing specimen in large landscapes. It has been typecast as a swamp citizen, but it adapts perfectly well to the drier landscape and in that setting rarely produces the "knees" that it is known for in wetlands.

How to Plant & Grow—Plant bald cypress in fall or winter, after the needles have dropped. It will grow in wet, difficult areas, but will also tolerate drier sites and does not require standing water.

Care & Problems—Be careful not to injure the growing tip of the upright central leader, as its loss can result in lopsided growth. The beauty of a cypress is its near-perfect symmetry, and carelessness or poor pruning can quickly ruin its form. Lower branches can be carefully limbed up as the tree ages.

Hardiness—Zones 5a to 10a

Mature Size (H x W)—50 to 75 ft. x 40 to 60 ft.

Water Needs—Average to wet soil

Flowers/Berries—Inconspicuous flowers, occasional small cones

Fall Color—Cinnamon or bronze before dropping

CAROLINA HORNBEAM

Carpinus caroliniana

Why It's Special—Carolina hornbeam is one of our most overlooked and underused small to medium native trees. New leaves are tinged with red in spring, and unique, bract-covered flowers appear in early summer. In autumn, leaves turn the color of parchment and hang delicately on the tree throughout winter.

How to Plant & Grow—Transplant only container-grown plants that have their entire root system intact. Balled-and-burlapped specimens rarely do well. The best seasons are late fall and early winter, when plants are dormant but their roots are still growing.

Care & Problems—Protect the smooth, sinewy bark from damage caused by antler-rubbing deer, lawnmowers, and weed trimmers. Remove any weeds around the base of the tree so that lawn services (or you) aren't tempted to weed eat right up to the base of the tree, girdling and killing the tree in the process. The hornbeam has very few insect or disease problems.

Hardiness—Zones 3a to 9b

Mature Size (H x W)—30 ft. x 30 ft.

Water Needs—Evenly moist to slightly dry soil

Flowers/Berries—None

Fall Color—Parchment beige, retained through winter

CAROLINA SILVERBELL

Halesia carolina

Why It's Special—This attractive understory tree is a native gem. The small deciduous tree is found growing in moist, rich soil along streams and in bottomland in the western regions of North Carolina. The name "silverbell" comes from the early spring cluster of white bell-shaped flowers.

How to Plant & Grow—Carolina silverbell can be planted most successfully between November and March, when winter moisture is readily available to help get the tree established before summer. Plant in rich, moist, well-drained soil. Silverbell will grow in full sun, but is at its best in part sun to part shade.

Care & Problems—Moisture is key. Silverbell is simply not drought tolerant. Newly planted trees should be watered twice weekly for the first month and once weekly for the remainder of their first year in the ground. Carolina silverbell is relatively pest and disease free.

Hardiness—Zones 5b to 8a

Mature Size (H x W)—25 to 35 ft. x 25 ft to 30 ft.

Water Needs—Evenly moist soil

Flowers/Berries—White flowers in early spring, winged fruit

Fall Color—Yellow, not always showy

COLORADO BLUE SPRUCE

Picea pungens 'Glauca'

Why It's Special—Although a slow grower, Colorado blue spruce is worth planting in large gardens across the Mountains and in the Foothill region of North Carolina. Unfortunately, the trees struggle in the heat and heavy clays soils of the Piedmont area and southward into South Carolina.

How to Plant & Grow—Plant field-grown or potted spruces during the dormant season, from November to March. Blue spruce needs a minimum of six hours of direct sun each day and appreciates moist, well-drained soil. It will flounder in heavy clay, where wet conditions and poor air circulation lead to root rot diseases.

Care & Problems—Water during the first two seasons. Even after it's established, irrigating may be necessary during drought. To maintain good color, use a slow-release nursery or tree fertilizer each March. In dry locations, spider mites can be a problem in summer heat.

Hardiness—Zones 3a to 7a

Mature Size (H x W)—50 to 60 ft. x 20 to 25 ft.

Water Needs—Evenly moist, very well-drained soil

Flowers/Berries—Cones may be present on old trees

Fall Color—Evergreen, year-round blue color

CRAPE MYRTLE

Lagerstroemia indica

Why It's Special—These striking small to medium trees are midsummer showstoppers. Few other flowering trees can match their colorful display or the length of their bloom period. Many varieties have beautiful flaking and peeling bark in shades of silver to cinnamon.

How to Plant & Grow—Crape myrtles thrive in heat and humidity and are best planted in early spring to take advantage of warm soil and air to get them established. They must have full sun. Even a few hours of daily shade will significantly reduce flowering and will invite problems with powdery mildew.

Care & Problems—Crape myrtles must be well watered during their first season. Once established, they are fairly drought tolerant, but will have a difficult time recovering from prolonged drought. Important note: The mutilation-style pruning of crape myrtles that has become common is unnecessary and detrimental. Please don't do it!

Hardiness—Zones 6a to 9b

Mature Size (H x W)—10 to 30 ft. x 10 to 25 ft.

Water Needs—Evenly moist soil

Flowers/Berries—Flowers in white, lavender, red, pink

Fall Color—Yellow to red, depending on variety

CRYPTOMERIA

Cryptomeria japonica

Why It's Special—Cryptomeria, or Japanese cedar, is a cousin to the giant sequoia of the West Coast and quite different from our native cedar. Soft sprays of foliage appear in spirals along drooping branches. Old specimens have attractive reddish brown bark that peels off in long shreds. Unusual variants include dwarf and globe-shaped forms.

How to Plant & Grow—Cryptomeria can be planted any time the ground can be worked and water can be provided to new plants. They thrive in sunny locations with deep, rich, moist soil. Once established, they grow quickly; larger varieties may grow 2 to 4 feet per year.

Care & Problems—Keep trees dense and full by shearing very lightly in early spring, just before new growth begins. Do not cut the central leader (trunk), as this will ruin the shape. Japanese cedars will not tolerate long periods of drought and must be kept mulched and well watered for the first two seasons.

Hardiness—Zones 6a to 9a

Mature Size (H x W)—5 to 50 ft. x 5 to 25 ft.

Water Needs—Evenly moist soil

Flowers/Berries—None significant

Fall Color—Evergreen

DOGWOOD

Cornus florida

Why It's Special—Dogwood blooms mean spring in the South, where the trees peek at us from the woods' edge as we drive the highways and byways. Dogwood's intense red fall color also contributes to our autumn majesty.

How to Plant & Grow—Unlike most deciduous trees, dogwood is best planted in spring rather than fall. This is particularly true of balled-and-burlapped plants. Dogwoods prefer well-drained, slightly acidic soil with plenty of organic matter. In heavier clay soils, amend deeply and thoroughly when planting.

Care & Problems—Avoid pruning during borer season in June and July, as this can invite borers into open pruning cuts. Leaf spot anthracnose is a common problem and is worse in years when we have wet, rainy springs. This is unsightly but not life threatening like the discula dogwood blight that can weaken and kill trees outright.

Hardiness—Zones 5b to 9a

Mature Size (H x W)—20 to 30 ft. x 20 to 30 ft.

Water Needs—Evenly moist to slightly dry soil

Flowers/Berries—Showy white flowers, red fruits

Fall Color—Deep, burning red in October to November

EASTERN REDBUD

Cercis canadensis

Why It's Special—Redbuds in full bloom are among the most striking sights of spring. A small, vase-shaped tree, redbud forms a rounded canopy of heart-shaped leaves by early summer, providing dappled shade for outdoor lounging.

How to Plant & Grow—Container-grown redbuds can be planted either in spring or fall. Balled-and-burlapped specimens are a little trickier, since redbuds have a deep taproot that does not like to be cut, but they can still be transplanted successfully. The best time is late fall and winter so that new root growth can begin while the tree is dormant.

Care & Problems—Redbuds will not tolerate waterlogged soil, so be sure that drainage is adequate. Other than that, this is one of our toughest native trees. After transplanting, soak thoroughly twice each week for the first six to eight weeks and then only as needed during dry weather.

Hardiness—Zones 4b to 8b

Mature Size (H x W)—20 to 25 ft. x 20 to 30 ft.

Water Needs—Average to dry soil

Flowers/Berries—Magenta flowers in early spring

Fall Color—Usually not showy, occasionally yellow

FLOWERING CRAB APPLE

Malus spp. and hybrids

Why It's Special—Noted for its beautiful spring flowers and attractive autumn fruit, the crab apple also takes its lumps for being disease prone and messy. Fortunately, disease-resistant cultivars are introduced every year and you can site the tree where fruit drop won't be a problem.

How to Plant & Grow—Crab apples can be planted any time the soil can be worked, but late fall through spring is ideal. Site in full sun with good air circulation. Water deeply once a week for the first month and then every other week for the first growing season.

Care & Problems—Lightly prune during the first few years. Most crab apples do not have a strong central leader and will be pruned to an "open center" form to allow good air circulation and help reduce leaf spot, cedar apple rust, and other fungal diseases.

Hardiness—Zones 4a to 8a

Mature Size (H x W)—10 to 30 ft. x 10 to 25 ft.

Water Needs—Average to slightly dry soil

Flowers/Berries—White, pink, red flowers; red or gold fruit

Fall Color—None

FRUITLESS SWEETGUM

Liquidambar styraciflua 'Rotundiloba'

Why It's Special—Many gardeners have a special dislike for the sweetgum because of the spiny round seedpods that drop from the trees in autumn, but in 1930 a discovery was made in North Carolina. 'Rotundiloba' is a special variety bearing round-lobed leaves instead of the typical pointed stars that produces very few fruits.

How to Plant & Grow—Plant in late winter or early spring to take advantage of spring rains for establishment. Sweetgums prefer a rich, moist, well-drained site, but will tolerate nearly any conditions, except for constantly wet soils. The best fall color will develop in full sun.

Care & Problems—Some sources list 'Rotundiloba' as being a smaller form of the tree, and while it is more compact, it is not a small tree. After the tree has been planted for one season, begin pruning to encourage a single, strong leader in the center.

Hardiness—Zones 5a to 8b

Mature Size (H x W)—50 ft. x 25 ft.

Water Needs—Average to evenly moist soil

Flowers/Berries—Inconspicuous flowers, few fruits

Fall Color—Spectacular burgundy, orange, gold

GINKGO

Ginkgo biloba

Why It's Special—Ginkgo is a native of China with ancestral ties to conifers. It is an excellent slow-growing landscape tree with brilliant golden yellow fall color. Its distinctive fan-shaped leaves bear a striking resemblance to those of the maidenhair fern.

How to Plant & Grow—Ginkgo is best planted in late winter through early spring, while trees are dormant. Full sun and rich, fertile soil will encourage relatively fast growth. Without a little extra care on the front end, ginkgos can be notoriously slow growing. Water thoroughly and deeply once a week after planting, more if weather is hot and dry.

Care & Problems—The ginkgo is virtually pest, disease, and maintenance free. When buying a ginkgo, consult with your local garden center and purchase a cultivar that is known to be a male variety. With age, the female tree produces copious quantities of messy, bad-smelling fruit.

Hardiness—Zones 4a to 9a

Mature Size (H x W)—60 ft. x 45 ft.

Water Needs—Average to slightly moist soil

Flowers/Berries—Undesirable fruits on female trees

Fall Color—Brilliant golden yellow

HOLLY 'NELLIE R. STEVENS'

Ilex 'Nellie R. Stevens'

Why It's Special—A large and fast-growing hybrid holly, 'Nellie R. Stevens' has become a favorite among landscape designers for formal hedges and screens. It is also an excellent specimen plant for larger landscapes, where it can be allowed to develop to its full size and natural shape.

How to Plant & Grow—Plant container-grown holly anytime the ground permits. Large balled-and-burlapped specimens should be planted in late winter or early spring, while they are still dormant, so they can get established before summer growth begins. 'Nellie R. Stevens' is tough and reasonably drought tolerant, once established.

Care & Problems—Water newly planted hollies regularly for the first two seasons. Use drip irrigation or set up a hose and sprinkler that can be turned on and off as needed. Prune in very late winter or early summer, immediately before or after the spring growth flush.

Hardiness—Zones 6a to 9a

Mature Size (H x W)—20 to 25 ft. x 10 to 15 ft.

Water Needs—Average to slightly dry soil

Flowers/Berries—Small white flowers, showy red berries

Fall Color—Evergreen

JAPANESE FLOWERING CHERRY

Prunus spp.

Why It's Special—Japanese flowering cherry dominates the spring landscape with a light pink wash of color. Popular varieties have either upright or weeping growth habits, and white or pink flowers. 'Kwanzan', the latest bloomer, has big pink pompom flowers.

How to Plant & Grow—Whether potted or balled-and-burlapped, cherries should be planted during the dormant season so that their roots can get established before summer. Flowering cherries need excellent drainage and will benefit from being planted on a low berm. Soil should be thoroughly amended with organic matter.

Care & Problems—Apply at least 1 inch of water per week for the first two years while the trees are actively growing. Fertilize with an all-purpose nursery fertilizer each spring right after flowering. Prune while dormant in winter, or in August when dead wood can be easily distinguished from live growth.

Hardiness—Zones 5a to 7b

Mature Size (H x W)—15 to 35 ft. x 20 to 25 ft.

Water Needs—Evenly moist soil, not waterlogged

Flowers/Berries—Pink or white flowers in early spring, no fruit

Fall Color—'Kwanzan' is best in glowing gold to orange

JAPANESE MAPLE

Acer palmatum

Why It's Special—Few ornamental trees are as useful in the landscape as the Japanese maple. Its outstanding features include its intricate foliage and varying leaf types, shapes, and colors. An old Japanese maple offers unmatched architectural form, with its gnarled and twisted trunks.

How to Plant & Grow—Plant Japanese maples any time from November to April, while they are dormant, so their roots can grow before summer heat arrives. Maples will grow well in a variety of soils, providing they are not waterlogged, but will perform best in rich, well-drained, woodsy, humus-rich soil.

Care & Problems—Water deeply and thoroughly in summer, especially during the first two seasons, to encourage roots to grow deep into the soil in search of water. This will help to keep foliage from burning and prevent trees from becoming stressed during the hot summer months.

Hardiness—Zones 5b to 8b

Mature Size (H x W)—4 to 30 ft. x 6 to 20 ft., depending on variety

Water Needs—Average to moist soil

Flowers/Berries—None

Fall Color—Spectacular red, orange, gold

LIVE OAK

Quercus virginiana

Why It's Special—This signature coastal evergreen tree has horizontal branches often festooned with Spanish moss and resurrection ferns. Near the coast in Charleston and other locations, the grandest and oldest live oaks bend their limbs to touch the ground, creating amazing living sculptures. In the lower Piedmont, however, they tend to grow a more upright, but still broad, canopy.

How to Plant & Grow—Oaks can be finicky when it comes to transplanting. Plant container-grown trees with intact roots rather than balled-and-burlapped specimens with compromised taproots. When planting container-grown trees, be sure to prune off any girdling roots.

Care & Problems—Oak wilt can affect live oaks, and chestnut blight can be a problem on live oaks growing near the coast. Call in a certified arborist at the first sign of decline. These diseases can spread from tree to tree through contaminated tools, so use professional arborists.

Hardiness—Zones 7b to 9b

Mature Size (H x W)—60 to 80 ft. x 70 to 100 ft.

Water Needs—Average to dry soil

Flowers/Berries—Acorns on older trees

Fall Color—Evergreen

LONGLEAF PINE

Pinus palustris

Why It's Special—This distinctive Southern pine has foot-long needles that provide the best pine straw mulch. Young trees tend to grow straight up with no side branches until they reach 8 to 12 feet tall. Until then, they look like giant bottlebrushes and can be unique architectural landscape features.

How to Plant & Grow—Plant container-grown longleaf pines anytime the soil is not frozen. Water weekly until the tree is firmly established. If your soil is particularly dry and sandy, water more often during the first growing season. Avoid overfertilizing, as this can encourage weak growth.

Care & Problems—Pines, in general, are notorious for blowing over during severe storms with high winds. Plant trees far enough from the house so as not to pose a threat. Trees may need staking once they reach 4 to 6 feet tall until trunks "firm up."

Hardiness—Zones 7a to 9b

Mature Size (H x W)—60 to 80 ft. x 25 to 40 ft.

Water Needs—Drought tolerant, once established

Flowers/Berries—Large cones on older trees

Fall Color—Evergreen

PALMETTO

Sabal palmetto

Why It's Special—This southeastern native is one of the hardiest palm species. Once established, it can withstand temperatures of 10 degrees F on a regular basis and possibly even lower for brief periods. The palmetto can be recognized by its single, straight trunk and compact, rounded crown.

How to Plant & Grow—Plant container-grown plants anytime in late spring or summer. They transplant easily from May to July in Zones 7 and 8, thriving in summer heat and humidity. Palmettos will grow in almost any well-drained soil, as long as they are not waterlogged in winter.

Care & Problems—Thoroughly soak newly planted palmettos once or twice a week for the first two summers. After that, they will thrive with little or no intervention. Old leaves do deteriorate and should be pruned away, as needed. Palmetto weevils and palm leaf skeletonizers may attack and may warrant some control. Consult your local garden center. Extremely cold temperatures may cause leaf burn.

Hardiness—Zones 7b to 9b

Mature Size (H x W)—20 to 50 ft. x 6 to 10 ft.

Water Needs—Evenly moist, well-drained soil

Flowers/Berries—Large fruit clusters on mature trees

Fall Color—Evergreen

RED BUCKEYE

Aesculus pavia

Why It's Special—Red buckeye is a graceful tree with broad, five-fingered leaves. Red flowers appear in mid-spring and usually signal the arrival of hummingbirds. In fact, the ruby-throated hummingbird follows the bloom season of the red buckeye from south to north.

How to Plant & Grow—Red buckeye transplants readily while dormant, in late fall or winter. Container-grown plants occasionally die if transplanted after they leaf out in spring. It is best planted as a specimen tree. It tolerates full sun, but is best suited to areas with moist soil and light afternoon shade.

Care & Problems—Few native trees are as adaptable or pest free as red buckeye. Prune only to shape the tree and remove any errant growth. Buckeyes are drought tolerant once established, but expect some leaf scorch in dry conditions. Leaves may drop as early as August. This is natural and harmless.

Hardiness—Zones 5a to 8a

Mature Size (H x W)—15 to 20 ft. x 15 to 20 ft.

Water Needs—Evenly moist to slightly dry soil

Flowers/Berries—Red flowers in spring

Fall Color—None, leaves fall early

RED MAPLE

Acer rubrum

Why It's Special—The star of Southern maples, red maple is relatively fast growing and has an upright growth habit when young and a broader, spreading crown as it ages, making it a perfect shade tree for the urban landscape. The fine variety 'October Glory' holds its brilliant red color late into fall.

How to Plant & Grow—Red maples are available as both container-grown and balled-and-burlapped specimens. Plant in winter or early spring so that the roots can begin to get established before hot weather arrives. Water regularly during the first two years; after this, trees will thrive on their own unless extreme heat and drought occur.

Care & Problems—Develop a strong framework with a single trunk and branches growing perpendicular to the trunk. As the tree matures, remove weak branches and limbs with narrow crotches at the trunk, as these will become weak.

Hardiness—Zones 4b to 9a

Mature Size (H x W)—40 to 60 ft. x 30 to 50 ft.

Water Needs—Drought tolerant, once established

Flowers/Berries—Red flowers in early spring

Fall Color—Brilliant, scarlet red in autumn

RIVER BIRCH

Betula nigra

Why It's Special—Many people think river birch needs a wet site, but if you allow enough space for this beautiful native tree, you can enjoy its marvelous features practically anywhere. 'Dura Heed®' is the best cultivar for the South and is especially tolerant of hot summers. It's salmon-colored inner bark is revealed as the older bark peels in long, shaggy strips.

How to Plant & Grow—Container-grown birches can be planted anytime except for the hottest summer months. Balled-and-burlapped specimens are best planted while they are dormant, from late fall to winter. Consistent moisture is best, but established specimens will tolerate some drought, though they may drop up to half their leaves.

Care & Problems—Young trees grow very quickly once established. Remove any suckers that form at the base of the trunk. River birches can be messy. Summer leaf and twig drop can mean constant cleanup near driveways, patios, and walkways.

Hardiness—Zones 4a to 9a

Mature Size (H x W)—40 ft. x 25 to 30 ft.

Water Needs—Moderately moist to wet soil

Flowers/Berries—None

Fall Color—Yellow, not particularly showy

SNOWBELL

Styrax japonica

Why It's Special—The very best cultivar on the market, 'Emerald Pagoda', produces pendent, bell-shaped, fragrant white flowers in May, just after the thick, emerald green leaves unfold. Its compact form and shade tolerance give it an edge over many other noteworthy candidates.

How to Plant & Grow—The farther south or toward the coast you go, the more shade snowbell needs to keep from becoming scorched in the summer sun. It prefers deep, rich, moist, acidic soil that is loaded with organic matter. Amend the planting hole thoroughly! Water thoroughly after planting and once or twice per week for the first two months. Keep the soil evenly moist after that.

Care & Problems—Once established, snowbell is nearly care free. Problems with borers have occasionally been reported and the ambrosia beetle is the culprit. Check with your County Extension Service for treatment.

Hardiness—Zones 5b to 8a

Mature Size (H x W)—20 to 30 ft. x 20 to 30 ft.

Water Needs—Evenly moist soil

Flowers/Berries—White flowers in mid-spring

Fall Color—Yellow flushed with red

SOUTHERN MAGNOLIA

Magnolia grandiflora

Why It's Special—Southern magnolia is a champion among fine evergreen trees. In the Carolinas, magnolias are valued for their large, shiny green leaves and 10-inch, creamy white flowers. The sweet fragrance of magnolia blossoms perfumes the air on early-summer nights. The cultivar 'Little Gem', while smaller, can still become a good-sized tree.

How to Plant & Grow—Southern magnolia's fleshy roots make it sensitive to cold or dry conditions. Avoid balled-and-burlapped specimens, as these are difficult to transplant and frequently struggle to get established. Southern magnolia grows naturally in rich, moist soils along river swamps or in damp woods, but will tolerate drier sites if the soil is rich and high in organic matter.

Care & Problems—Abundant leaves that fall at the worst possible time of year—early summer. By letting your magnolias branch low and sweep the ground, you can disguise the problem and the leaves become natural mulch.

Hardiness—Zones 6b to 9b

Mature Size (H x W)—30 to 70 ft. x 20 to 50 ft.

Water Needs—Evenly moist soil

Flowers/Berries—Large white flowers in early summer

Fall Color—Evergreen

SOUTHERN RED OAK

Quercus falcata

Why It's Special—Southern red oak is one of our faster-growing oaks and makes an outstanding street tree, as well as an excellent shade tree for larger landscapes. Its deep, solid root system makes it a sturdy tree with a low risk of being uprooted during storms.

How to Plant & Grow—Plant container-grown or balled-and-burlapped specimens anytime from November to March. They transplant best while they are dormant. Water thoroughly at planting time and then as needed to maintain soil moisture until the tree is established. Soak the soil once or twice each week during hot weather for the first two growing seasons.

Care & Problems—Prune to encourage an open branch structure with strong side branches at perpendicular angles to the trunk. Oak wilt can be a problem. Consult a professional arborist or a County Extension Service agent at the first sign of it.

Hardiness—Zones 6a to 9a

Mature Size (H x W)—50 to 80 ft. x 40 to 60 ft.

Water Needs—Average to slightly dry soil

Flowers/Berries—Small acorns on mature trees

Fall Color—Reddish to rusty bronze

SUGAR MAPLE

Acer saccharum

Why It's Special—For the cooler areas of the Carolinas, no other tree produces the truly stunning fall color like the sugar maple. Its symmetrical form and strong branches make it an excellent choice as a shade tree for properties that can accommodate its size.

How to Plant & Grow—Container-grown trees can be planted anytime the soil can be prepared, while balled-and-burlapped specimens should be planted from late fall to late winter, while they are dormant. This gives the roots a chance to begin to grow before the tree leafs out. Water regularly and deeply during the first growing season.

Care & Problems—The greatest problem with the sugar maple is its shallow root system, which will eventually make its way to the soil surface and render grass—or anything else, for that matter—nearly impossible to grow within the root zone of the tree.

Hardiness—Zones 3a to 8b

Mature Size (H x W)—60 to 70 ft. x 40 to 50 ft.

Water Needs—Evenly moist to slightly dry soil

Flowers/Berries—Insignificant

Fall Color—Truly stunning, orange and gold

TULIP POPLAR

Liriodendron tulipifera

Why It's Special—The tulip poplar is one of the South's most majestic forest trees. It is fast-growing, straight-trunked and well-suited as a large shade tree for Southern landscapes. Even though it grows quickly, it is also strong and long-lived. The tree gets its common name from the pale yellow-green, tulip-like blooms that appear on older specimens.

How to Plant & Grow—Plant field-grown or potted tulip poplar during the dormant season from November to March. Tulip poplar needs a minimum of 6 hours of direct sun each day and appreciates moist, well-drained soil. It is well adapted to a variety of soils and growing conditions but may lose its leaves early in the season in particularly dry conditions. This is not detrimental, and the tree will leaf out normally the following year.

Care & Problems—Water during the first two seasons to keep tulip poplar thriving. Even after it's established, irrigating during times of drought may be beneficial. It is rarely susceptible to pest or disease problems and is a sturdy landscape tree. Thoughtful pruning to encourage a strong, widely branched structure when the tree is young will add to the tree's strength and majestic appearance at maturity.

Hardiness—Zones 5a to 9a

Mature Size—60 to 80 ft. x 40 to 50 ft.

Water Needs—Evenly moist, well drained

Flowers/Berries—Greenish-yellow, tulip-like flowers in mid- to late spring

Fall Color—Can be a good golden yellow in some years

YELLOWWOOD

Cladrastis kentukea

Why It's Special—Yellowwood is valued for its foliage and flowers, but its common name comes from its bright yellow heartwood. This native landscape tree matures gracefully with a rounded, spreading crown, and its deep roots permit landscape beds or turf to flourish beneath it.

How to Plant & Grow—Plant yellowwood during its dormant season, late November to early March, in full sun to light shade. It grows in shadier locations, but may be thin with sparse flowers. It prefers soils that are extremely high in organic matter, and clay soils should be very well amended.

Care & Problems—Prune in summer while the tree is young to encourage a strong leader, though this can only be maintained for a certain time. Sap flows when the tree is pruned, but stops of its own accord. Yellowwood has no serious disease or insect problems.

Hardiness—Zones 4b to 8a

Mature Size (H x W)—30 to 40 ft. x 20 to 30 ft.

Water Needs—Evenly moist to slightly dry soil

Flowers/Berries—White flowers in pendulous clusters in spring

Fall Color—Clear, beautiful yellow

ZELKOVA

Zelkova serrata

Why It's Special—New homeowners desiring fast shade can plant a zelkova. This large, deciduous beauty grows to 70 feet, a perfect size to thwart the hot afternoon sun. First introduced as a replacement for the fast-disappearing American elm, zelkova has found its way from the city street to the suburban back yard.

How to Plant & Grow—Container-grown and balled-and-burlapped specimens are best planted during the dormant season, from December to early March. For maximum growth, plant where the soil is moist and deep in part to full sun. One reason that zelkova has become popular is that it transplants easily.

Care & Problems—Water during the first two growing seasons if summers are dry. Use a soaker hose that can drip slowly for one to two hours. Good drainage is essential and decline of plantings is often attributed to heavy, wet, clay soils that are poorly drained.

Hardiness—Zones 4a to 8b

Mature Size (H x W)—70 ft. x 50 to 60 ft.

Water Needs—Evenly moist soil

Flowers/Berries—None

Fall Color—Occasional gold to bronze, not always showy

MORE ABOUT TREES

PLANTING

Most trees are available in containers or as field-grown balled-and-burlapped plants. Follow these steps to ensure a good start for your new tree:

1. Match the tree to its location. In addition to light levels, be aware of drainage, salt spray, and other factors that can affect the tree's growth.

2. Have your soil tested through your County Extension Service.

3. Dig a wide, shallow hole at least two or three times wider than the diameter of the rootball, but no deeper than the height of the ball. Making the hole as wide as possible allows the roots to grow quickly into the loosened soil, thereby speeding up the plant's establishment in its new home.

4. Slip the plant out of the pot and examine the rootball. Shrubs or trees growing in containers may have roots circling around the outside of the rootball. If you plant it as is, roots will grow from the bottom of the rootball. You should encourage roots to grow along the entire length of the rootball. Use a knife, pruning shears, or the end of a sharp spade to score the rootball in three or four places. Make shallow cuts from the top to the bottom. Tease the sides of the rootball apart. Now this "doctored" plant will produce new roots from these cuts all around the rootball.

5. Remove wire or twine from a balled-and-burlapped plant and cut away as much wrapping material as possible after placing it in the hole. Remove synthetic burlap entirely; it won't break down and will strangle the roots.

6. Plant even with or slightly above the surrounding soil. Place the tree in the hole for fit. Lay your shovel across the hole. The rootball should be level with or slightly above the handle. If, in your zeal, you've gone too deep, shovel some soil back in. Compact it with your feet. You want a firm footing for the rootball so it won't sink below the level of the surrounding grade. That can cause roots to suffocate. In slowly draining soils, set the rootball 1 to 2 inches above the surrounding soil, then cover with mulch.

7. Start backfilling—returning the soil to the planting hole. Tamp the soil lightly as you go, but don't compact it. When half the rootball is covered, add some water to settle any air pockets and remoisten the rootball. Backfill and water again. Do not cover the top of the rootball with soil.

8. Apply 2 to 4 inches of organic mulch, such as compost, leaf litter, shredded wood, or pine straw. Extend it to the outermost reaches of the branches (the drip line). Leave a space of 3 inches or more around the trunk to keep the bark dry.

9. Depending on weather and rainfall, you may need to water daily for the first few weeks. After that, begin cutting back, eventually reaching an "as-needed" basis by testing the soil and rootball for moisture.

WATERING

Not all established trees have to be watered during hot, dry summer months. Drought-tolerant trees can withstand long periods without rain or irrigation. When watering is required, it should be done thoroughly and deeply to encourage roots to grow far into the soil searching for moisture. Drip or soaker hoses are often most effective because they can be allowed to run for several hours at a time so that water reaches to the bottom of the rootball.

Overhead sprinklers also work well, but because of the volume of water they put out, the saturation point at the surface of the soil can be reached quickly and from that point water simply runs off. If you are irrigating with sprinklers, it is helpful to let the sprinkler run for thirty to forty-five minutes and then turn the water off, allowing what you've applied to soak in and saturate the soil as deeply as possible. Then come back the next day and water for another thirty to forty-five minutes. The second day's water will quickly penetrate the top layers of soil that are already moist and will thoroughly saturate the deeper root zone of the tree.

PRUNING

Trees are pruned to improve their health and branching structure. The goal of pruning young trees is to create a strong structure of trunk and limbs to support future growth. The main reason for pruning mature trees (usually by professionals) is to remove weak limbs to focus the tree's resources on the stronger remaining branches. Pruning is easiest during late winter, when trees are still dormant and branches bare, because you can see what you are doing and where you are cutting.

The old adage about measuring twice and cutting once can also apply to your trees. When you're pruning, especially if you are removing larger limbs, determine the limb you think needs to be cut. Then step back several paces from the tree and look closely at that limb. Follow it all the way from where it attaches to the tree's trunk out to its very tip, and see how and where it crosses and interacts with other limbs and branches. Once you've checked it from several angles, then you can proceed. By doing this, you avoid opening up big holes and creating bare spots in the tree that cannot be fixed.

PEST CONTROL

Insects and diseases are two of the most serious threats to your trees' health. Plants that are weakened by unfavorable growing conditions will not be able to tolerate pest attacks. Select better-adapted plants and match them to the site, or concentrate on pest-resistant cultivars. Even if you do so, some pest-resistant trees that are correctly located can still be attacked by pests. It's just nature. A tree ought to be able to support a few insects or diseased leaves if it is kept healthy and vigorous. For serous infestations or infections, consult the professionals at your local garden center or your County Extension Service.

FERTILIZING

Newly planted trees can be fertilized after they become established, which may take months or longer, depending on their size. Once established, fertilizing can stimulate growth and help them fill into their allotted space in the landscape.

Established trees shouldn't be fertilized on a regular basis. Replenishing the mulch over their roots with compost or other "recyclable" organic materials provides them a steady diet of minerals. If your trees are growing in a lawn that is fertilized, do not add additional fertilizer.

Apply fertilizer when it will be readily absorbed by the roots of your trees and when the soil is moist, which can be any time from late spring after new growth emerges to early fall. However, if water is unavailable or when the trees are stressed by drought during the summer months, do not fertilize at all because their roots will be unable to absorb the nutrients.

JANUARY

- If you're planning on pruning your trees this winter, have a purpose in mind as you proceed. This could include removing dead or dying branches, thinning the canopy, removing branches that are rubbing or crossing over one another, or improving the trees' overall shape.

- Do not coat pruning wounds with tar, paints, or other substances. There is no scientific evidence that this practice is actually helpful and some experts believe that covering the wound actually traps moisture and invites trouble.

- If you have newly planted trees that were staked last season, check all straps and stakes to make sure that they are secure, but not cutting into the bark of the tree, and that they are tied at the lowest point on the trunk to allow it to move just slightly. A little bit of movement in the wind encourages the trunk to grow strong and thick.

FEBRUARY

- If you would like to try your hand at fruit trees, now is the time to order, and they will be shipped in just a few weeks at the proper time for planting in your area.

- Large balled-and-burlapped trees can be planted this month anytime the soil is not frozen and a hole can be dug. Planting larger trees while they are still dormant allows them to settle in quickly and easily, barely knowing they have been moved.

- Newly planted trees must be kept moist. It is easy to forget to water during the winter, but it can be a very important task.

This is especially true for evergreens that continue to lose water through their needles, even in winter.

- Begin pruning when the coldest part of winter has passed and before new growth begins. When pruning large limbs, be sure to "undercut" the limb first: make a cut on the underside of the limb you're removing to help prevent it from cracking and stripping the bark down the trunk of the tree.

MARCH

- Planting of new trees can begin in earnest this month.

- If you have evergreens that need to be pruned, March is the perfect time. Do not cut evergreens back past the point where they have active green growth. If you cut back into bare wood, they may not regrow and you'll be left with a bare stub.

- Dormant horticultural oil spray should be applied this month *before* buds begin to break and new leaves begin to grow. This will help to control scale and spider mite problems later in the summer.

APRIL

- It's not too late to plant container-grown or balled-and-burlapped shade and ornamental trees. Pay careful attention to watering during their establishment phase.

- Avoid bumping into tree trunks with your lawnmower or whipping them with a nylon string trimmer. The resulting wounds can be quickly colonized by fungal diseases or infested by borer insects, which can eventually kill the tree.

- Fertilize palms with a slow-release palm fertilizer such as 18-6-12 or 15-5-10 applied according to the label directions. Palms benefit from fertilizers that contain additional micronutrients, especially in sandy Coastal Plain soils, where nutrients leach out quickly. Fertilizers made especially for palms will contain these necessary nutrients.

- Mites begin to get active this season. Keep an eye on evergreens, in particular, and treat with highly refined horticultural oils or soaps—not dormant oil!

MAY

- Update your garden journal with information about spring-flowering trees that performed particularly well this year and others whose show may have been a little lackluster. These notes can help you determine your plants' needs later on.

- If you would like to add palms to your landscape, they transplant best in late spring and summer, when air and soil temperatures have warmed and the palms are in full, active growth.

- If you're not receiving regular rainfall, be prepared to water newly planted trees on a regular basis until rain resumes. Remember to water thoroughly and deeply.

- Aphids are out in force this month, especially on new tender leaves and stems. A medium-strong spray of water will generally dislodge them and alleviate the problem. For severe infestations, insecticidal soaps are a safe and easy way to treat them.

JUNE

- As part of your summer vacation plans, why not find some time to visit private and public gardens in the Carolinas? These gardens can be inspirational and educational, and you can see many new and unusual plants you might like to add to your own landscape.

- Water recently planted trees, which are especially vulnerable to heat and drought. Water thoroughly and deeply to encourage deep rooting. Mulch with a 2- to 3-inch layer of compost to conserve moisture, suppress weeds, and moderate soil temperatures.

- Be on the lookout for aphids, scale insects, spider mites, and dogwood borers. Japanese beetles will be hatching this month as well.

- Keep bagworms at bay by applying the bacterial insecticide Bt (*Bacillus thuringiensis*). It is safe and nontoxic and does a good job of controlling these pernicious and persistent pests.

JULY

- If you are planning a summer vacation, be sure to arrange for someone to water your newly installed trees. Trees are a big investment and losing one (or more) while on vacation would make the return home disappointing.

- Trees should not be fertilized during the heat of the summer. Encouraging soft new growth now means a higher need for water and the possibility of tender new growth scorching in the hot sun.

- Powdery mildew and leaf spot diseases are very active this month. Fungal diseases love the heat and humidity. Proper pruning to increase airflow within the tree can help alleviate these problems.

AUGUST

- If you live along the coast or on barrier islands, you may have a difficult time finding plants that will thrive in the salt breezes and poor sandy soils in your area. Look to native plants that grow naturally in your surroundings. They will be tough and resilient and provide a wonderful "sense of place" in the landscape.

- Continue your summer watering regime. August is often the hottest and driest month of the year, and new trees will need your help to survive this last brutal month of summer.
- Spider mites are very active during hot, dry weather, especially on junipers, arborvitae, hollies, and many other ornamentals. Insecticidal soap is a safe way to help control them.
- Powdery mildew and leaf spot diseases are still running rampant. Try to select resistant cultivars when you are choosing trees for your landscape, and avoid sprinklers that spray high overhead and wet the foliage on trees such as dogwood and crape myrtle.

SEPTEMBER

- This fall, recycle your fallen leaves into mulch or compost. For a fine-textured mulch, shred the leaves with a lawnmower or leaf shredder. Finely cut leaves look more attractive and tend to stay where you put them.
- Avoid doing any major pruning at this time of year. Pruning now can stimulate new growth that will not have time to harden off before cold weather arrives and can then freeze and be killed.
- Fall in the South can be very warm and very dry. Keep an eye to the sky, and if rain isn't falling, it's up to you to keep plants watered and healthy until rain comes again.
- Prepare now to protect your trees from deer and rodents. Protect trees from deer with fencing and repellents. Deter rabbits by installing wire or plastic guards around the trunks of young shade trees with tender, delicious bark.

OCTOBER

- Deciduous trees can light up the autumn sky with an assortment of fiery reds, oranges, and yellows. Look around you as trees begin to color up for fall and decide where you might want to add more colorful trees to your landscape.
- Record notes about the autumn garden in your journal. Pay close attention to trees that have not performed well this year and try to determine the reason why.
- In fall and early winter, don't forget to water newly planted trees to help them become established. A few weeks after planting, start reducing water to every few days or longer, especially with cloudy, rainy, cool weather.
- Remove and destroy bagworm bags on evergreens and other trees. Eggs overwinter in the bags produced by females and will hatch next spring.

NOVEMBER

- When planning to include trees in your landscape, take advantage of their winter beauty. Peeling bark, twisting branches, and architectural forms all give deciduous trees great character.
- Fall is the best time of year to plant or transplant many trees, both deciduous and evergreen. To ensure success, wait until they have gone completely dormant in late November before you begin.
- Fall rains may be adequate for newly planted trees, but keep a close watch on your soil and if it appears to be drying out too much, be prepared to water.
- As leaves fall from deciduous trees, be sure to remove them from the lawn. It doesn't take long for a thick layer of leaves to shade and/or rot out the grass beneath them, leaving you with large bare patches in the lawn.

DECEMBER

- For good establishment, try to transplant at least four weeks before the soil temperature goes below 40 degrees F. Newly planted trees should be watered immediately after planting.
- Try to purchase your Christmas tree several days ahead of when you want to bring it indoors and decorate it. Make a fresh cut at the base—even if they cut it at the tree lot—and stand it up in a 5-gallon bucket in the garage for at least twenty-four hours (forty-eight is better) before bringing it indoors. Really saturating your tree this way will help it last longer indoors.
- It's Christmastime! Be sure to check the water in your Christmas tree stand every day to be sure that it does not dry out.
- When Christmas is over, check to see if Christmas tree recycling occurs in your area.

GOING GREEN

in the Carolinas

CONSERVING WATER IN THE GARDEN

WATER DEEPLY AND LESS OFTEN

Keep plants growing strong—encourage roots to explore deeper into the soil.

In many ways, plants are like some people I know. They don't work any harder than they have to! Consequently, if all the moisture needed is right near the surface, plants won't use extra energy and nutrients to grow roots deeper into the soil where moisture levels are consistently higher.

This is why the key is to water infrequently but deeply. *Reducing* the overall amount of water to plants (and especially lawns) keeps them growing stronger. Deep watering encourages deep roots, and roots that are encouraged to explore farther into the soil to find sustenance have better access to moisture when the area closer to the surface dries out. This upper layer *always* dries out first because soil at or near the surface warms faster and is subject to evaporation and the drying effects of wind.

When a gardener waters every day but for only brief periods, water rarely soaks deeply enough into the soil to encourage roots to grow there. In order for roots that are growing only near the surface to stay healthy and alive, continued frequent watering is *required* to provide them with sufficient moisture. The "pampered" plants never have to develop an extensive root system reaching farther down to find water.

But what happens if you go on vacation and forget to set your irrigation timers, or the batteries fail, or your neighbor forgets to water your lawn or plants? In periods of drought or inconsistent irrigation, plants with deeper roots can still receive adequate moisture in many cases because the roots are where the water is.

Now, deep watering doesn't mean turning on the sprinkler and leaving it on while you go and play a quick nine holes! The surface layer of most soils becomes quickly saturated after watering for only a few minutes, and then all the water applied from that point on runs off and is wasted. Research shows that the most efficient and effective way to get water down deep is to water an area for a short time until the upper surface is saturated—say, ten minutes for most soils (less if it's on a slope)—then stop and let that water soak in for thirty minutes to an hour, and then water again for a few minutes more. This allows the water to be deeply absorbed into the soil while reducing runoff, and ultimately lets you go much longer between watering.

With the exception of container gardens that tend to dry out daily, brief but daily irrigation is an inefficient use of time and water.

IT ALL ADDS UP

By watering deeply but only one-third as often, the average homeowner will reduce his or her landscape water usage by 30 percent, which translates to about 13,000 gallons saved per year for every household.

If everyone does this, it will reduce national water consumption by 820 billion gallons per year!

By watering very early in the morning or at night rather than in the heat of the day, the average homeowner will reduce water usage by 25 percent, and by twice that amount in desert climates. This translates to an average water savings of 11,000 gallons per year, per household.

If everyone in the U.S. does this, we will save 700 billion gallons of water per year.

By keeping a 2-inch layer of mulch on garden beds during the growing season, the average homeowner will reduce water usage by 5 to 10 percent (depending on how much of your landscape is occupied by beds rather than lawn). This translates to 4,400 gallons of water saved per year.

If every household in the U.S. does this, it will save the nation 277 billion gallons of water per year.

WATER AT THE RIGHT TIME OF THE DAY

The time of day that you water can have a significant effect on the water's efficiency.

The hotter it is, the more water is lost to evaporation. Add wind to the equation and even more water is vaporized in the atmosphere before it ever reaches the ground. Depending on your irrigation system and the timing of *when* you water, as much as half the water can be lost to drift and evaporation, especially when using overhead sprinklers.

If you water at night, or very early in the morning, temperatures are cooler and winds are calmer. Late at night or very early in the morning is also the best time to use soaker hoses or drip irrigation. The coolness during darkness along with the calm skies allows soils to soak up the maximum amount of water, without the influence of drying winds or evaporative sunlight.

MULCH, MULCH, MULCH!

Mulch is an important tool for a gardener in more ways than one. As a way to conserve water, it can't be beat.

Mulch is one of the most versatile additions to any garden. It has many uses which are covered throughout this book, but from the standpoint of water conservation, it is a star. A 3- to 5-inch layer of mulch will provide an insulating blanket that greatly reduces surface evaporation, slows runoff, moderates soil temperatures on hot days, and lowers the moisture requirements of the plants. It also dramatically cuts down on weed production, lowering the demand and competition for nutrients and water.

Mulch can be organic, such as leaves, straw, compost, or bark. It can even be gravel or plastic. In all cases, the mulch holds the moisture in place, in the ground, right where it is needed most.

BUILD HEALTHY SOIL BY ADDING ORGANIC MATTER

Whenever you see any information on improving soil, it always stresses the importance of adding organic matter. The natural benefit of rich organic soil will be a reserve of vital nutrients and improved soil quality overall.

Think of soil rich in organic matter as a savings account for your plants. The nutrients are released back to your plants much like a steady income. The more you need, the more you get. The nutrients found in organic matter stay in the soil much longer than water-soluble synthetics, which rapidly leach through the soil.

Now visualize someone who has just been given a lot of money all at once. Rather than putting it in the bank, they spend it all immediately. It feels good temporarily, but when it's gone, it's gone. There are no reserves to draw on over time. That's how I think of water-soluble inorganic fertilizers. They work, but the nutrients that aren't absorbed by the roots quickly pass through the soil, leaving behind potentially damaging salts.

Organic matter is, was, or comes from living things. Some of the most common natural amendments found in nature include decomposed plant residue, dead roots, excreted waste from soil-dwelling organisms, and composted bark, manure, leaves, and sticks. When you think of the lush forest of a woodland setting, all that makes up the soil there is a collection of natural amendments over time. The only fertilizer they receive is what is derived naturally from the soil. And yet how the forest flourishes!

In our home landscapes and gardens, we can create the same effect. In addition to the amendments mentioned above, we might use grass clippings, mushroom compost, peat moss, peanut or coco shells, and so much more. Collectively, it may be just good old compost, but whatever it's made of, it contains billions of living beneficial micro-organisms and includes vital organically-derived nutrients.

There's a second reason that adding organic matter is so important to creating healthy soil. It improves drainage of compacted soils and increases water retention in loose, sandy soils. Amendments incorporated into the soil allow some particulates to bind together while preventing others from creating a mass that is too large. In total, the organic elements along with the native sand, silt, or clay work in harmony to improve the structure, tilth, and texture of any soil while, at the same

Organic matter in the soil helps hold nutrients and water for plant use. In sandy soils, organic matter holds over 10 times more water and nutrients than the sand.

In clay soils, organic matter improves soil structure by binding mineral soil particles together to form aggregates. This creates greater pore space among the aggregated particles, providing optimal conditions for root growth. The increased pore space improves both soil drainage and water-holding capacity, and improves soil aeration.

Organic matter in the soil helps to promote the healthy biological activity of the soil—a complex web of life ranging from microbesto earthworms.

time, building up nutrients and reducing the need for supplemental water and fertilizers.

As you build healthy soil in your home garden and landscape, how much you add will depend on the condition of your soil before you start. The amount will vary, but your goal is to add enough so that compacted soil breaks apart and loose soil binds together.

There's no cookie-cutter recipe for proper soil, but here's a good rule to follow: Your goal for adding organic matter to the soil should be to end up with a texture that binds together when squeezed but breaks apart easily when disturbed. Over time, organic matter will continue to break down and decompose so you will need to periodically add more. But as you do, know that your soil is getting better and healthier all the time, and as you continue to feed the soil, your plants will reward your efforts.

Comparison studies of soil amendments show that plots amended with yard waste compost yield healthier, more productive plants and have more available nutrients in the soil (nitrogen, phosphoric oxide, and potash) than plots treated with synthetic fertilizer.

The slow release of nutrients in compost is less likely to impact groundwater from leaching than quickly-available synthetic fertilizers.

Using compost suppresses some plant diseases, such as fusarium crown and root rot in tomato, brown rot in peaches, fusarium end rot in onions, and numerous fungal diseases of turfgrass.

COMPOST AS A SOIL CONDITIONER AND FERTILIZER

There is no store-bought product better for the garden than compost.

Compost helps add life and fertility to the soil. It improves drainage yet allows soil to retain sufficient moisture. Compost helps create the type of soil structure that is critical for nutrients and water to be absorbed and for roots to spread. It protects plants from certain diseases, moderates pH, feeds earthworms, supports beneficial microorganisms, is known to be a growth stimulant, and even buffers toxins in the soil.

In nature, composting occurs constantly. Plant and animal waste breaks down into soil-like particles over time, with no involvement from us. If you choose to make your own, the simplest compost piles are just that, piles of yard waste and kitchen scraps. There are no fancy systems, containers, bins, or compartments to facilitate the process. Although a simple pile will suffice to make perfectly usable compost, more elaborate systems can be built or purchased to contain the mix and help speed up the decomposition process.

Compost structures come in many shapes and sizes. Your choice will depend on the space and materials you have available. Structures can be made of woven wire, snow fencing, old wooden pallets, concrete blocks or bricks, or a 55-gallon barrel. Successful composting can even be accomplished in a modified garbage can. Structures can also be made with single or multiple compartments. Once you've decided what structure is right for you, position your compost bin near a water source and make sure the bottom has adequate drainage.

There are a few essential elements necessary for compost to occur. They are water, air, heat, carbon (brown stuff, like dead leaves and twigs), and nitrogen (green stuff, like grass clippings or vegetable and salad scraps). To start a compost pile, you don't need anything fancy. A simple accumulation of green waste (10 to 25 percent) and brown waste (75 to 90 percent) will get you going. Although mixing the compost pile is not required for compost to form, you can speed up the decomposition process by turning the pile every week or so. Each time the pile is turned, oxygen is introduced, which will increase the rate of breakdown. Add water periodically to keep the pile at the moisture level of a damp sponge. You will be well on your way to making compost. Depending on the variables, you should be able to have usable compost in about four months to one year.

You can add many items to your compost pile or bin, but whatever you add, make the pieces as small as possible for faster breakdown. Almost anything from the yard or garden can be added, but avoid adding diseased plants. The disease pathogens may not be killed in the composting process, and you can end up introducing diseases to your soil. I also choose not to include weeds in the mix. The seeds can persist for a very long time, and they may survive the composting process only to be spread to other areas of your garden as you add new compost.

When adding household products, the biggest items to avoid are meat, fish, bones, dairy products, and pet wastes. They can attract outdoor pests and can harbor many types of bacteria and disease.

Compost will be ready to use when it's dark brown, earthy-smelling, and crumbly. The result is undoubtedly the best soil food and conditioner available—recycling at its best!

GROW THE RIGHT PLANT IN THE RIGHT PLACE

You've just solved most of the challenges around creating a healthy and thriving garden.

Make it a point to visit private and public gardens. It's no surprise that these gardens are meticulously maintained, lush and thriving. They are free of pests, and there are no plant diseases. They are the types of gardens you and I dream about.

When you ask the person responsible for taking care of the garden: "What's the one thing you are doing to keep these plants looking so good?" You get the same answer time and again.

"PUT THE RIGHT PLANT IN THE RIGHT PLACE"

Plants do have an ideal growing environment. Place them in it, and they will reward you with minimal care.

In the eco-friendly garden, placement is an important consideration. Any plant, no matter how small or big, will flourish when planted where it is happiest. And just in case you don't know by now, a happy plant is a healthy plant. We know through scientific observation, healthy plants are less susceptible to pests and diseases. Even when these forces are present, healthier plants are more resistant and resilient when attacked. The bottom line is this: happy, healthy plants rarely need chemical fixes.

Plants that thrive in full sun will never look their best in even partial shade. Plants that prefer shade will become quickly stressed in full sun conditions. Plants that thrive in dry conditions will look terrible in wet soil and vice versa.

When plants don't look their best, they're under stress. Unknowing gardeners try to fix the problem by throwing extra fertilizer, pesticides, and fungicides at the plant, thinking that will take care of it. That's the worst thing you can do! Plants in the right place won't need to be fixed. They'll look great all on their own.

It sounds so simple and really is, as long as you know what the ideal conditions are for that plant or tree. Unfortunately, we too often buy on impulse, never knowing much about the plant or even where we'll place it once we do get around to planting. Here are some tips to help you put the right plant in the right place:

KNOW THE CONDITIONS OF YOUR YARD OR GARDEN

Do you know what hardiness zone you live in? It's important to know the average minimum and maximum temperatures for your area. Do you have full sun or full shade? In many cases, you'll have some combination. What about soil moisture? Is it constantly damp or as hard as concrete?

To make matters worse, when referring to a site, there is dry shade, moist shade, dry sun, and moist sun. No wonder we sometimes struggle. Unless you get lucky, it's hard to plant the right plant in the right place without knowing all this.

RESEARCH AND READ THE TAG

It's so easy to plunk a plant into any old space just to get it out of the driveway and into the ground. But don't do it. This is where the breakdown usually occurs in the home garden. We make the impulse buy, not knowing where we'll ever plant it. Or we buy a plant, not knowing if it will even grow in the place we have in mind.

Today, there is so much valuable plant information at your fingertips. A simple Internet search with keywords such as, "dry shade, groundcover, Zone 7" will quickly produce several Websites from university extension services, garden forums or discussion rooms, magazine articles, and other authorities. At the very least, all plants should come with a tag that provides preferred growing conditions for sun, shade, and moisture.

The right plant in the right place shouldn't need any supplemental chemicals for pest or disease control, and fertilization can be kept to a minimum. It's an easy rule to follow that really works.

CONTROL PESTS WITH NATURAL CONTROLS FIRST

There are some very effective natural control treatments available. Controls for all pest types in the eco-friendly garden seek to use the least toxic method first.

Organic pest-control methods are generally less environmentally damaging and less toxic to non-targeted insects, mammals, and aquatic life. Unfortunately, in our time-starved world, many people simply want the most potent, one-application product—no matter what the consequences. But since you're reading this book, you understand the costs of such flippancy are great, and you want a more eco-friendly yet effective way.

Pest-control strategies in the eco-friendly garden seek to use the least toxic method first. The good news is, there are some very effective natural control treatments available. With the proper preparation and cultural practices, rarely if ever will you need to go beyond these measures.

The first step in controlling pests, before even applying the most benign treatment, is to create the most hospitable growing environment for your plants. A healthy garden is the single best natural pest-control there is. Healthy plants are less attractive to pests in the first place, and when they are attacked, the plants are better equipped to defend themselves and recover.

Another advantage to the no-spray method of control is that it allows beneficial insects the best opportunity to establish populations in your garden and do the work for you. You may need to exercise a little patience and put up with some cosmetic damage initially, but beneficial insects are incredibly effective.

With any pest-control treatment, the first step should be to identify the offending pest, and target a control method that affects just it. To keep from throwing out the baby with the bathwater, don't apply a non-selective chemical that kills beneficial insects as well. There are a good number of organic options available, and some are more specific to certain pests than others.

If there's a downside to natural pest-control methods, most people would say that although they can be every bit as effective as synthetic controls over time, they are not as fast-acting initially. It seems that's an acceptable tradeoff—a little patience for a healthier environment! Although there are many natural methods for pest-control, here are some of the most common options:

MICROBIAL INSECTICIDES

These insecticides cause pests to get sick, are very specific to the target pest, and do not harm beneficial insects or poison mammals. One of the most popular choices is *Bt (Bacillus thuringiensis)*. Use this whenever necessary to treat a number of worm larvae from hornworms to cabbage loopers and cutworms. The bacteria in *Bt* paralyzes the digestive system of the larvae. They stop eating, and within a couple of days, the pests are dead.

INSECTICIDAL SOAPS

These soaps utilize the salts and fatty acids within them to target many soft-bodied pests including aphids, whiteflies, mealybugs, earwigs, thrips, and the early stages of scale. The soaps penetrate the soft outer shell of these and other pests, causing damage to the cell membranes. The membranes then begin to break down, resulting ultimately in dehydration and starvation.

Insecticidal soaps can be phytotoxic (having a tendency to burn) to certain plants, so be sure to test a small area before applying on a larger scale. The other downside is that soaps are non-selective, so they can be toxic to beneficial insects as well. Use them sparingly, as with any pesticide. Insecticidal

More natural pest-control products are being offered commercially to the home gardener every year. They range from microbial insecticides to insecticidal soaps, Neem oil, and botanical insecticides.

Effective natural controls for plant diseases are also more available, with new products coming on the market every year. For example, potassium bicarbonate marketed as GreenCure is safe for organic production and found to be more effective than a previous natural favorite—baking soda combined with horticultural oil—for treating many plant diseases. Sulfur and lime can also be effective against blackspot, powdery mildew, and rust. Vermicompost teas are being offered in home centers to help control plant disease.

soaps have not been shown to be toxic to humans and other mammals.

You can make your own insecticidal soap by adding a teaspoon of dishwashing soap (not detergent) and a teaspoon of cooking oil to a quart of water in a spray bottle. Insecticidal soaps are available for purchase at nurseries, home improvement centers, or garden centers.

INSECTICIDAL OILS

These oils work by suffocating the pest. The oil coats them with a petroleum-based, horticultural grade liquid, cutting off their oxygen supply. This control method has been around for a long time and is primarily used to kill the eggs and immature stages of insects. These products are very effective because they spread so well and break down quickly. They can and do affect beneficial insects but are less toxic to them than synthetic pesticides.

Oils are used to control aphids, scale insects, spider mites, mealybugs, psylla, and some other insects. These oils can harm your plants and trees by damaging the leaves, so be sure to read the directions that come with the packaging.

Never spray these oils on a hot day, usually not one over 85 degrees, and again, it's best to spray a small area of your plants first. Just spray a test area and wait a few days. If you don't see any damage from the initial spray, commence with a larger application, coating the top and bottom of all leaf surfaces.

DIATOMACEOUS EARTH

This product is the fossilized silica shells of algae. Although microscopic in size, they are covered with sharp projections that cut and penetrate the cuticle of an insect. This piercing causes the pest to leak vital body fluids, resulting in dehydration and death. The unique aspect of diatomaceous earth (DE) is that it is not a poison that causes the damage, but the physical abrasiveness of the dust.

DE is effective against soft-bodied pests including aphids, thrips, whiteflies, caterpillars, root maggots, slugs, and snails. However, DE is non-selective and will potentially kill beneficial insects as well.

Apply DE to the soil for ground-dwelling pests and to the foliage for other pests. DE adheres best to moist foliage, so application is best early in the morning, when leaves are wet from dew, or after a rain. Be sure to use natural-grade, not pool-grade, DE. The latter contains additional chemicals that can be harmful to humans and mammals if inhaled. In either case, it's a good idea to wear a dust mask whenever working with any dusting agent.

NEEM OIL

Neem is a broad-spectrum (non-selective) insecticide, acting as a poison, repellent, and deterrent to feeding. It also sterilizes certain insect species and slows or stops the growth cycle of others. Neem oil is derived from the neem tree, which is native to India. It is applied as a foliar spray or soil drench and is used to kill a wide range of pests, including aphids, thrips, loopers, whiteflies, and mealybugs.

One unique aspect to this biological agent is its systemic properties. Plants take up the Neem extracts through plant foliage and roots, where it is present in the plant tissue. Consequently, Neem is also effective against leaf miners, which are usually not affected by other nonsystemic foliar sprays.

Generally, Neem must be ingested to be toxic and is largely nontoxic to mammals. Although it breaks down quickly, you should spray Neem only when necessary and only on plants known to be affected. In this way, you will minimize the damage to beneficial insects.

BOTANICAL INSECTICIDES

There are a number of botanical insecticides, but we are going to focus on the most popular one, pyrethrin, an active ingredient extracted from the Pyrethrum daisy. Products containing pyrethrin contain compounds that kill on contact. They are considered broad-spectrum (non-selective) and are used to control many chewing and sucking insects. **CAUTION:** Do not confuse natural pyrethrin with the synthetic version called Pyrethroid. It is even more toxic to insects.

Use caution when applying pyrethrin products as they are toxic to fish and moderately toxic to mammals. They are also harmful to some beneficials, including lady beetles.

MULCH TO CONTROL WEEDS

Mulch is a multitasking miracle for the garden. If there were ever a workhorse in the garden, compost and mulch are on top of the list . . . or bed in this case. This leads to the point about using mulch to suppress weeds. When you place a generous layer of mulch on your beds, you are effectively blocking sunlight that otherwise reaches the soil surface and allows seeds to germinate and grow.

Not all weed seeds need light to germinate, but all plants including weeds need it to grow. Weeds that come up each year from seed are referred to as "annual weeds," and mulch is very effective at blocking their germination. Although it's not a sure thing for every weed all the time, mulching should be a standard practice in your garden to reduce the amount of work you'll have to do when it comes to managing weeds later.

Perennial weeds, on the other hand, come back each year from other means. Although seeds are included in the list, rhizomes, stolens, and regrowth from the base of the original plant are the most common sources of these weeds. Since there's not a germination issue in these cases, perennial weeds will often come back with or without mulch.

When mulching, be sure that you apply enough mulch to actually block the sunlight and prevent germination. In general, a 3-inch layer should be sufficient. If you apply less, you certainly open up the possibility for inadvertent bare areas. Too much mulch could pose a different problem: the thick layer that blocks the light and prevents germination may also restrict airflow. Mulch should not be so thick as to suffocate the plant roots underneath.

A 2- to 3-inch layer of mulch can significantly reduce weed growth in an area. The weeds that do manage to germinate in mulched soil are much easier to pull and remove.

Studies show that by mulching an area, the average amount of time required to remove weeds is reduced by two-thirds.

By maintaining a 2- to 3-inch layer of mulch, you can virtually eliminate the need to use herbicides in landscapes and garden beds.

Mulch comes in many varieties. Sometimes the only common denominator of mulch is that it covers the ground. Beyond that, it can be sorted into two categories: organic and inorganic. Organic mulches are natural products such as shredded leaves and wood, bark, straw, pine needles, and coco or peanut shells.

Organic mulches will usually decompose within a season and needs to be replenished consistently in order to maintain effectiveness as a weed suppresser. On the other hand, incorporating composted mulch into the beds at the end of each season is an excellent way to improve the condition of your soil.

Inorganic mulches typically do not break down or they do so slowly. Black plastic is an example of inorganic mulch that will eventually break down and is very effective at weed suppression. Stones, gravel, and even recycled tires can be used. With inorganic mulch, frequent replacement is not necessary. However, it will not improve your soil at the end of the season, either.

There will be times that, in spite of your best efforts, weeds will start growing from your mulch. Usually the weeds you find growing *in* the mulch (as opposed to through it) will come from seeds transported into your mulch from any number of ways, but usually from wind, birds or other animals. It's a common sight, and they are easy to remove by hand pulling since they likely haven't been able to root into the soil yet. Try it. You'll be pleasantly surprised to see how easy it is.

OTHER EASY WAYS TO ELIMINATE WEEDS WITHOUT CHEMICALS

Hand pulling is natural and effective, but so are these options.

Some people actually enjoy pulling weeds. Manual extraction by hand pulling has an element of satisfaction that no other weed control method can offer. If you like instant gratification, it's the only way to go. It's also one of the few ways for selective control. But it's not the only one. (You can breathe a sigh of relief now.)

Although highly satisfying, hand weeding is not always a practical solution to the problem. Time and ambition are usually the two most important assets to taking on a manual project such as this. Furthermore, hand weeding in any size garden is always helped along after a soaking rain. The soil is soft, and roots easily yield to even the gentlest tug.

When you're ready to manage weeds with organic controls but hand pulling is not your style, consider some of these other popular alternatives using eco-friendly methods.

MOWING HIGHER, or letting the grass grow tall, is an excellent non-chemical ways to fight weeds in my lawn. Although there is an upper limit on how tall any variety of grass should be, taller grass has the opportunity to shade out developing and sun-loving weeds before they have a chance to establish. When it is time to mow, remove no more than one-third of the total height of your grass. It's better on the lawn and keeps the grass blades tall enough to still shade most weeds.

BOILING WATER works well at killing most weeds with one application. Some weeds, especially those with taproots such as dandelions, may need multiple applications. Be sure to use extra caution when using boiling water. The risk of burning yourself, children, pets, or others is a real possibility. You might even be wondering about the damage burning water can have to the beneficial microorganisms in the soil—it will kill them as well. However, take comfort in knowing that billions of microbes will fill the void quickly in healthy soil.

ACETIC ACID *(vinegar)* works, but common household vinegar at 5 percent concentration is not effective for mature weeds. Concentrations above 7 percent are needed to manage tougher weeds, and multiple applications may be necessary with taprooted weeds such as thistle. Use caution when using acetic acid as it can burn skin and eyes on contact. Approved sources of acetic acid for herbicide use can be found online or at farm supply stores.

PLANT-BASED INGREDIENTS such as citric oil, clove oil, and garlic are nonselective, post-emergence herbicides also. Use caution, as they will injure or kill all vegetation they come in contact with. Tougher weeds usually require multiple applications for complete control. Ready-to-use products are available through organic gardening supply sources online and in some garden centers.

FLAME WEEDERS are those devices that use the intense heat of a concentrated flame to destroy the cell structure of the plant. Typically powered by a propane canister, these devices are portable and effective. Simply pass the flame over the weed for several seconds. It is not necessary to visibly burn or ignite the weed. A few seconds of intense heat is all that is necessary. The heat will collapse the cell walls and render the plant unable to sustain itself. Because the roots are unaffected, the toughest weeds may require multiple applications. Again, use *extreme* caution when working with this tool.

Taprooted weeds can seem impossible to control no matter what method you are using. Even when the top growth is damaged or destroyed, there is enough energy in the remaining root to regenerate a new plant. If you are hand weeding, be sure to get the *entire* root! The other methods listed above may need repeated applications to destroy the weed.

More than 90 million pounds of herbicides are applied to residential gardens and landscapes every year.

2, 4-D, found in weed-and-feed and other lawn products, is the herbicide most frequently detected in streams and shallow groundwater from urban lawns.

Using combination weed-and-feed products is not the most accurate way to control weeds. Unnecessary herbicides are likely to be broadcast onto lawn areas where there are no weeds and into adjacent areas where non-target plants will be damaged. And certain trees growing in lawn areas can also be damaged when their shallow roots take up herbicides.

By removing weeds mechanically, you will greatly reduce your need to use herbicides.

Although these control options can be directed precisely onto the target weeds, they may not be considered completely selective. Any misdirection or drift can kill any plant they come in contact with. It's up to you to apply these controls only to the targets.

No matter which method of weed control you prefer, prevention is still the best way to make sure you keep the weeds from spreading next year. Although they can still come into your yard through other means, eliminating weeds on your property before they go to seed will save you many hours of work next year and beyond.

STORE CHEMICALS SAFELY

Improperly stored chemicals can have lethal consequences. Perhaps you know of a case firsthand. A child is poisoned because she drank from a container she thought contained juice, soda, or milk. Instead, it was a container being used improperly to hold a pesticide. The results were fatal. What a sad story.

Of course these are extreme cases, but unfortunately they happen all too often. What makes stories like this even harder is that they were easily preventable. In no case should any chemical be stored, even for a moment, in a container other than the one it originally came in.

> A nationwide survey by the EPA revealed that almost one-half of surveyed households with children under the age of 5 had at least one pesticide stored within the child(ren)'s reach.
>
> By storing garden chemicals safely, you protect children and pets from accidental poisoning, you protect the environment from accidental chemical spills, and you protect your chemicals from losing their effectiveness.

There are a number of precautions we can take to ensure accidents with pesticides don't happen under our watch:

- Follow all storage instructions listed on packaging and labels.
- Always store pesticides in their original containers. In addition to the proper identification of the contents, important safety information specific to that product is listed on the container. Such information includes what to do if accidental poisoning takes place, emergency contact numbers, and necessary first aid steps.
- Keep pesticides stored out of the reach of children and pets. When possible, store them in a locked but ventilated cabinet. Even if you don't have children, you never know when a curious person may happen upon these dangerous chemicals. Be safe and take the path of caution.
- Pesticides should never be stored in the same location as food, medical supplies, or animal feed.
- Never transfer pesticides to soft drink bottles or other containers, including milk jugs, juice or water bottles, or coffee cups. It is easy for children and even adults to confuse them for something to drink or eat.
- Use child-resistant packaging correctly. Be sure to close containers tightly and properly after use. Just because a product says "resistant" does not make it childproof. These products should receive the same care and caution as any other when storing.
- Don't stockpile chemicals. Only buy what you'll use that session or season. The less pesticide that remain after it is needed, the lower the accident risk.
- Pesticides should be stored away from places where flooding is possible or where spills or leaks could run into drains, surface water, or watersheds.
- Flammable liquid pesticides should be stored away from the living area and away from any risk of sparks, such as near gas grills, furnaces, and power lawn equipment.
- Never store pesticides in the application equipment. To avoid the problem of having excess product, only mix what is needed for that application. If excess mixture remains after application, apply where appropriate to other parts of your property.
- When in doubt as to the identity of a product or container, do not use. Be sure to dispose of it properly.

MULCH OR COMPOST YOUR LEAVES—DON'T SEND THEM TO THE LANDFILL

Leaves contain more than half the nutrients they took in during the season.

When the mornings are cool and crisp, the leaves are starting to change colors, and college football is in full swing, that's clearly a favorite time of year for many people.

As lovely as hardwood trees appear with their leaves in glorious shades of red, yellow, orange, and rust, my best part of the season is after they have fallen. The now-brown leaves begin to blanket the lawns and beds, and it is compost time!

No, the work of clearing off those leaves isn't much fun. But, what they will mean to the garden and landscape in just a few months will be worth it.

"Beauty is in the eye of the beholder." Where most people see leaf debris, along with hours of raking, bagging, and hauling, they are really garden beds blanketed in rich organic compost. These leaves contain 50 to 80 percent of the nutrients that their trees extracted from the earth this past season. Use them to replenish the soil and nourish all that grows within it.

Earthworms will feast on this debris, burrow deeper into the soil, and then deposit the matter as castings, adding even more valuable nutrients, oxygen, and drainage in the process. Beneficial fungi and bacteria will assist in the decomposition process, consuming this raw leaf material and returning it in a nutrient-rich form that can be utilized by plant and tree roots more efficiently and effectively than anything man has ever created.

Mere months after these shredded leaves are applied around the garden, they'll transform into matter that promotes the life of soil-dwelling organisms, which in turn will fortify plants and trees to be more pest- and disease-resistant.

But let's interrupt this vision to ask a question: Have you ever stopped to consider that no matter what condition soil is in, leaf compost will help make loose soil retain moisture and compacted soil drain better?

Rather than being viewed as trash, these leaves, grass clippings, and other garden trimmings should be going into our own gardens to enrich the soil while reducing the need for supplemental fertilizers and other harmful chemicals.

Yes, we should look forward to gathering up and shredding not only the leaves falling from our trees, but from our neighbor's (and the stranger's down the road) as well. Landscaping crews can bring you the leaves they've collected from their jobs.

What leaves you don't spread into the beds, you can store somewhere else in the yard. Worry about them later. Take some to a neightbor who will appreciate it. It's organic fertilizer, multi-vitamin, and soil conditioner all-in-one, both plentiful and free. It doesn't get any better.

> Leaves comprise about 25 percent of the total amount of yard trimmings that enter the waste stream, about 8 million tons per year.
>
> Up to 4,000 pounds of leaves per acre can be shredded and mulched over a lawn with no negative effects on turf quality, color, thatch accumulation, weed populations, or disease.
>
> Shred your leaves for the compost pile or mulch instead of setting them out for collection, and you can reduce the amount of waste you send to the landfill in the fall by as much as 50 percent.

PLANT TREES, TALL SHRUBS, AND VINES TO REDUCE YOUR HOME'S COOLING NEEDS

The shade cast by plants can play a vital role in energy savings for cooling our homes.

How many of us can remember a time when homes were only heated in the winter and not air-conditioned in the summer? Back then, we weren't used to having the perfect climate inside, and as kids, we really didn't know what we were missing.

That was a long time ago. Today, the majority of us live in a year-round, climate-controlled environment. In fact, 78 percent of single-family homes in America have some form of air conditioning. That's a lot of energy demand, especially as our climate heats up. Going forward, think about how much energy is needed to keep that perfect climate going year-round in your house.

Just as we humans benefit from the cooling effects of shade outside, our home's interior climate benefits as well. It's easy to forget that what's going

Nearly all air conditioning is accomplished with electricity. The average amount of electricity consumed for cooling per home is about 11,000 kilowatt hours per year; nationwide, that accounts for about 9 percent of our total residential energy consumption.

Well-positioned, appropriately chosen trees around your house can reduce indoor temperatures by up to 20 degrees and save between 10 to 40 percent in energy use for cooling each year, compared to a wide open landscape. By growing well-positioned trees around your home, you can reduce your energy use for cooling by 10 to 40 percent.

With the average household using about 11,000 kilowatt hours a year for air conditioning, if just 100,000 households in the U.S. improved their shade plantings and saved a conservative amount of 10 percent of the energy they use for cooling, that would result in a national savings of 110 million kilowatt hours every year.

If every homeowner planted shade trees around his or her house, the energy used for cooling our homes could be slashed by 20 to 40 percent nationwide.

on outside can profoundly affect how our homes operate and feel inside. Planning ahead for plants that keep your home cooler naturally can affect how much energy we consume.

On the west or south side of your house, planting a combination of deciduous trees and very tall shrubs will block those summer rays. The trees will eventually drop their leaves, allowing the warm winter sun into your home. Consider planting large deciduous vines trained on a trellis, arbor, or pergola running in front of or over south- or west-facing windows, doors, and porches. They too will cast welcome shade in the summer and allow sunlight in the winter.

START AN ECO-FRIENDLY GARDEN AT YOUR LOCAL SCHOOL, DAY CARE, OR OTHER FACILITY

Any gardener can attest to the therapeutic benefits of digging in the dirt and of the pleasure derived from nurturing its offspring. Consider developing a healing garden at a hospital, church, retirement home, or local women and children's shelter. These places are often looking for opportunities to involve children or patrons in educational, enriching activities—and usually on a shoestring budget.

It would be especially meaningful to start a garden at your child's school. It sends an important message to children that their parents care so much about the environment, their school, and them, that they're willing to put in the time and effort to build a garden.

Even if you don't have school-age children, being a gardening mentor is a great way to tap into the enthusiasm for nature that nearly all children have. Instilling an appreciation for stewardship at the earliest stages of education teaches lessons that last a lifetime. And it's more than just gardening. Although that's what gets them excited, slip in history about the plants and the origins of the names, have them draw the design and measure the beds, make the plant tags and record the progress, and I'd say you've more than covered all-important reading, writing, and arithmetic requirements for the season. (You can even tap into art, language, math, English, history, and nutrition—gardening as the frame for an entire curriculum!)

Consider talking with classroom teachers about how they can work with you on developing science lessons around the theme of the garden and allow the students to come out and help. It's a great opportunity for hands-on learning.

By letting children take ownership of the garden, from seed to harvest, you instill in them a sense of pride and responsibility and a desire to learn even more. When you include vegetables and herbs and then allow children to experience what truly fresh, homegrown food tastes like, chances are very good they'll be hooked for life. And think of the relationships you'll build as you watch things grow together!

And the biggest reward of all this? When you do it all in an eco-friendly way, you teach children about environmental stewardship, biodiversity, and sustainable ecosystems. Indeed those are big words, but they will come to life in ways that even children can understand when you show them simple but real-life examples. In the eco-friendly way of gardening, you can feel good about knowing they are not exposed to chemicals and pesticides—especially when they sneak a taste of that plump red cherry tomato, fresh from the vine!

Most schools are delighted for parents to help start a garden or tend to an existing one. But don't just stop there. Talk with the principal or the head of the daycare center about green gardening, and watch them really get excited. Consider creating an organic garden that attracts butterflies, includes a compost heap, and of course produces fruits and vegetables for the children to harvest and eat. If you make sure you'll have enough support to keep the project going through the years, you'll likely have no problem getting them on board. A little recruiting on your part should unearth some willing parents who would love to give time back to the school through a gardening project.

Money is usually the biggest obstacle to developing a sustainable gardening program in schools, day cares, and other facilities. But it doesn't have to be. There are many private companies that offer grants to schools and nonprofits for educationally related garden endeavors. Organizations like The National Gardening Association offer opportunities for qualified applicants to apply for financial assistance, and there are many others. Local gardening centers may also be glad to act as sponsors—just make sure that you are in charge of what kinds of products and methods you use!

The garden doesn't have to be outdoors, either. During the cold winter months, encourage teachers to set up indoor gardens in containers, start seeds indoors, or explore hydroponic gardening.

There is no greater joy than to see children delight in the pleasures of gardening. Moreover, it is very reassuring to know that the children are working in safe, eco-friendly conditions. The experience of seeing their faces as they bite into the fruits of their labor for the very first time—it's nearly indescribable. The bonus is knowing that these foods are likely the freshest, most nutritious, and only chemical-free vegetables and fruits they have ever eaten . . . so far.

No matter how busy we are, teaching children about gardening—green gardening—is a priceless opportunity to make memories and teach important lessons that last a lifetime. You'll be cultivating far more than just plants.

START AN ECO-FRIENDLY GARDEN IN YOUR NEIGHBORHOOD

You've probably heard somewhere that "great fences make great neighbors." I guess if you're really into privacy, there's an argument in favor of that statement. But is that really how you want to live? How about a new statement: "Great gardens make great neighbors." And honestly, it doesn't have to be great. But if your neighborhood has a vacant lot, a small park or playground, or any parcel of plantable common ground, it's a green opportunity just waiting to happen.

Stories abound about how neighborhoods across the country transformed from crime-infested war zones to a beehive of all things good when a neighborhood or community garden was installed. There's something both magical and magnetic about a garden. When neighbors come together to create a common garden, it often becomes the catalyst to stimulate social interaction, as well as neighborhood and community development. Strangers become friends, and neighborhoods come together. Quality of life improves, and neighborhoods are beautified. What better way to enhance an unadorned space while creating a place to connect people across intergenerational and multicultural boundaries?

TO CONSIDER AS YOU CREATE YOUR GARDEN

As you create a common garden, an organizing body may decide on the ground rules for the garden. Maybe the space is used as a community vegetable garden and everyone works together in one common plot. Or neighbors may be allotted individual spaces for their own personal gardening where they can plant whatever they want.

But however the garden is laid out, it is good to decide ahead of time the issues that are most important for the individual gardeners and the community as a whole. Your group may want the garden to be entirely eco-friendly. It certainly would be an environmentally responsible way to act locally to protect children and pets, neighbors, the community, and the environment from the hazards associated with nonsustainable gardening practices.

You will also need to address money issues. When it comes to funding the start-up and ongoing costs for smaller projects, individuals may chip into the pot. It is also possible that grants for such plans might be available from the city, state, or federal government or that others will subsidize your project. The city manager's office or state Department of Natural Resources is a good starting point. Corporations that focus on gardening often set aside grant money to promote community gardening efforts. The reference librarian at your local library can help you track down possible grants.

Planting an eco-friendly garden in your neighborhood builds a sense of community like nothing else. Such gardens provide opportunities for exercise, education, therapy, relaxation, and social interaction. In addition, green space is preserved and resources are conserved. Neighborhoods can even come together through their gardens for community outreach programs like Plant a Row for the Hungry. The eco-friendly garden in your community or neighborhood is limited only by your imagination and commitment—but the benefits can reach far beyond its original boundaries.

GET INVOLVED IN TREE PRESERVATION AND PLANTING IN YOUR NEIGHBORHOOD

It's possible to overemphasize the many benefits of trees or even to have too many of them. Beyond their natural beauty, they make a new neighborhood look established, provide blissful shade on hot days, screen cold winds, buffer erosion and runoff, and of course, exchange bad air for good.

So if trees are so good, why are so many cut down to establish new developments, change the landscaping, or simply to . . . well, that part just doesn't make sense. Maybe you've seen what I see: large, mature trees topped like a hat rack for no apparent reason. There is no reason (other than safety or power line obstruction) that necessitates the senseless topping of trees.

Topping trees has been a problem for decades, and it is remarkable how widespread it is. Simply put, topping hideously deforms and can eventually kill a tree. It causes stress when much of the leaf-bearing crown is removed, which can temporarily starve the tree. As a defensive action, the starving tree responds by rapidly sending out multiple shoots from the latent buds below each cut. The new growth that ascends is only anchored in the outermost layers of the parent branch, making the tree weaker and actually more dangerous than before topping it. If you'd like more information about the topic of terrible tree topping (sorry, couldn't resist again), visit www.plantamnesty.org.

By the way, if encroaching branches are truly a problem on our roads, then the wrong tree or shrub was planted there in the first place. Often it is simply a matter of selecting plant material that is more suitable for growing under power lines. Understanding the mature height of a tree or large shrub and putting that knowledge to work is critical to preventing this abusive practice nationally.

As we lose trees that eventually die from topping, clear-cutting, or indiscriminant development, look for the opportunity to plant trees at every turn. An obvious place to start is in neighborhoods, especially new neighborhoods, where the developer has stripped the land of vegetation. If you don't have many trees in your community, organize a neighborhood effort to plant more. A good source for information is a local certified arborist, or contact your Cooperative Extension office to find out what trees are recommended for your area.

If you will be planting trees along a street, it's especially important to choose the right mature-sized tree. Too often, trees are planted in an area that will not support its mature height and width. When planted near obstructions, especially power lines, an inappropriately placed tree is destined for disaster as it grows and encroaches onto those lines.

Other considerations for street plantings should include choosing trees that don't produce a lot of litter, don't have the type of root system that will crack streets and sidewalks, and aren't prone to weak branch structure (which can end up falling on cars). They should also be known for their ability to grow in the often difficult, harsh conditions street trees have to endure.

HELPFUL GARDENING TIPS & HINTS

for the Carolinas

GROWING ROSES

TO HELP YOUR ROSES SURVIVE THE WINTER

- Rose plants should go into the winter in a vigorous state. Plants stressed by drought or lack of fertility, or those defoliated by pests, are more inclined to succumb to cold than robust plants are.
- Roses should be grown in a well-drained location. Roses will not tolerate "wet feet," especially during the winter months.
- Winter winds can dry out the canes of exposed roses, loosen a rose's footing, or bruise canes as they're jostled by the wind. You can plant roses near walls or fences or erect temporary windbreaks of burlap, or the canes may benefit from staking or being tied down. Plant the roses at a distance that is at least four to six times their mature height from the windbreak.
- Mountain gardeners are faced with the freezing and thawing of the soil, called frost-heaving that can lift up plants, causing them to dry out. Carefully push down any plants and maintain a mulch layer to moderate soil temperatures.

Own-rooted roses are varieties grown from cuttings. Old garden roses are typically grown on their own roots, as are some modern roses. Own-rooted roses offer an advantage in the Mountains where winters are very cold. If the top is lost to winter cold, but the rootstock survives, the variety won't be lost. New growth will arise from the roots. When you lose the top of a grafted rose, what's left is a rootstock that is durable but not beautiful.

TOOLS NEEDED FOR PRUNING

Pruning will begin early in the year. Assemble your pruning tools and equipment. If you need any tools, put them on your birthday or Christmas wish list. Pruning tools needed:

- PRUNING SHEARS. The proper tool for most pruning is a sharp set of bypass pruners with curved blades that cut with a scissorlike action and give the cleanest cut. Pruning shears cut canes up to one-fourth inch in diameter. The bypass types are preferred over anvil pruners. These have a single cutting blade that, when cutting, presses the stem against a flat piece of metal (anvil). They should not be used for roses because they crush the stem.
- LONG-HANDLED LOPPING SHEARS (12- to 18-inch-long handles) to cut out thick canes up to ½ inch in diameter. Select bypass types with lightweight metal alloy handles.
- A KEYHOLE SAW about 7 to 8 inches long with a thin pointed tip. It can be used to cut very large canes (one-half-inch diameter or greater) near the crown. Remove large stubs close to the bud union.
- THORN-PROOF GLOVES with gauntlet-type cuffs to protect your hands and forearms when pruning.
- HEDGE SHEARS to prune miniature roses or floribunda hedges.
- SPRAY BOTTLE OF LYSOL. Use it to disinfect tools when cutting into cankers or canes infected with crown gall disease. It's less corrosive than bleach.

SAFE USE OF PESTICIDES

AUTHORS' CAUTION: Remember, it is a violation of state and federal laws to use any pesticide in a manner inconsistent with the label. Products mentioned in this book are used for the sole purpose of education and do not necessarily imply an endorsement. The use of pest controls must remain the choice of each individual gardener. It may not always be necessary to use pesticides to control insects or diseases. Consider the use of alternative means including resistant varieties, the use of botanical and microbial insecticides or soaps, the use of beneficial insects, mechanical means such as screening and handpicking, and improving cultural practices. If you decide to use traditional chemical pest controls, first consult your local county Cooperative Extension Service for correct pest identification and control recommendations. Once you have decided to use a specific product, you must read and follow label directions carefully.

EDUCATION ON THE SAFE USE OF PESTICIDES

A pesticide may be used only on the plants, animals, or sites named in the directions for use. You may not use higher dosages, high concentrations, or more frequent applications. You must follow all directions for use, including directions concerning safety, mixing, diluting, storage, and disposal. You must wear the specified personal protective equipment even though you may be risking only your own safety by not wearing it. The use directions and instructions are not advice, they are requirements.

Federal law does allow you to use pesticides in some ways not specifically mentioned in the labeling. Unless you would be in violation of the laws of your state or tribe, you may:

- apply a pesticide at any dosage, concentration, or frequency less than that listed on the labeling.
- apply a pesticide against any target pest not listed on the labeling if the application is to a plant, animal, or site that is listed.
- use any appropriate equipment or method of application that is not prohibited by the labeling.
- mix a pesticide or pesticides with a fertilizer if the mixture is not prohibited by the labeling. (Understand, however, that certain fertilizers can cause pesticides to precipitate.)
- mix two or more pesticides, if all of the dosages are at or below the recommended rate.

All pesticide labeling contains some instructions for storing the pesticide. These may include both general statements, such as "Keep out of reach of children and pets," and specific directions, such as "Do not store in temperatures below 32 degrees Fahrenheit."

Pesticide labeling also contains some general information about how to dispose of excess pesticide and the pesticide container in ways that are acceptable under federal regulations. State and local laws vary, however, so the labeling usually does not give exact disposal instructions. Storage and disposal statements usually appear in a special section of the labeling titled "Storage and Disposal."

HOW TO PLANT A TREE

After you have selected the right tree for the right site, plant it so the tree will establish quickly and grow into a thing of beauty. The planting hole should be wide and shallow rather than deep and narrow. Here's how to plant a tree:

- Kill the grass within a circle about twice the width of the rootball.
- Spread limestone and superphosphate if called for by a soil test.
- Amend clay or sandy soils by adding organic soil conditioner equal to one-third the amount of existing backfill.
- Dig a planting hole to the depth of the rootball, then put 2 inches of amended soil in the bottom.
- Break up any large clods and remove stones, roots, and debris.
- Inspect the rootball and cut roots that encircle it. If a mat of roots has formed on the bottom of the rootball, prune off the mat.
- Set the tree in the center of the hole, oriented so the best side faces where it will be seen most often.
- Shovel the conditioned soil around the rootball. Firm it down with your shovel handle.
- The backfill should come up to the soil line on the tree and taper down.
- Trickle water around the rootball for an hour or so until it begins to run off.
- Mulch 3 to 4 inches deep over the tilled area.
- Drive two steel fence posts into the soil on opposite sides of the rootball.
- Fasten twine or cotton cord to the posts near the bottom of the tree. Leave a little slack. On

large trees, use wire cushioned with pieces of water hose or, better still, use canvas straps and tree guying kits available at garden shops.
- Water twice weekly for a month, then monthly unless rain does the job for you.

The noteworthy trees in this book are personal favorites and are by no means an exhaustive list of good-quality trees offered by nurseries.

HOW TO PLANT YOUR SHRUBS (EXCEPT FOR AZALEAS, PIERIS, AND RHODENDRONS)

- With the shrub still in its container or wrapping, position it where you plan to plant it. Look at it from several directions. Review the plant label for mature size to make sure the shrub won't crowd your house or block the view from a window when it grows to full size.
- Dig a planting hole to the depth of the rootball and three times its diameter.
- Pile the excavated soil to the side and mix it with one-third organic soil conditioner by volume in sandy or heavy clay soils. Crumble large clods into small pieces. Rototill planting beds.
- Mix in ¼ cup controlled-release fertilizer and ½ cup pelletized limestone. (Prepare beds using limestone and fertilizer as recommended by soil tests.)
- Shovel a cone of crumbled, conditioned soil 4 inches high into the hole.
- If planting a container-grown shrub, slide it out and loosen the roots. Prune off long or girdling roots or, using hand shears or a sharp knife, cut any roots that are circling the rootball. If its balled and burlapped, set the rootball in the hole and loosen the twine around the top.
- On small, container-grown shrubs you can "butterfly" the rootball by using both hands to split open the bottom half of the rootball. This will encourage new roots to form.
- Bang the rootball on the ground a couple of times to dislodge some of the soil around the roots. This will also encourage feeder roots to penetrate the backfill.
- Turn the shrub so that the best side is out, not facing the house.
- Shovel the conditioned soil or unamended good topsoil into the hole in layers. Tamp or firm in each layer using your foot or the shovel handle, but don't overdo it—roots need air.
- The top of the rootball should stand at least 1 to 2 inches above the surrounding soil. Form a low basin with the remaining backfill to catch water.
- Water each shrub with a 5-gallon bucketful. If the water runs off, let the shrub soak for a while then continue watering around the rootball. Water trickled from a hose works best.
- Support tall, slender shrubs by tying them loosely between two stakes using degradable twine or flexible plastic tape. Loose tying allows the shrub to flex but not break in the wind, which strengthens the central stem.
- Spread mulch 3 inches deep to the outermost branches. Spreading three layers of newspaper before you mulch will diminish later problems with weeds and grass sprouting through the mulch. (Wet the newspaper immediately after setting it into place.)

HOW TO PLANT AZALEAS, PIERIS, AND RHODODENDRONS

More ericaceous (acid-loving) shrubs are killed by overwatering than by drought. In the wild, these plants grow in deep, well-drained organic "duff" in high shade. They send roots down into mineral soil to sustain them during dry weather.

Plant these special shrubs with half of the rootball aboveground. Here's how:

- Spade or till the soil in the planting area. Don't walk on it prior to planting.
- Regardless of what you have learned previously, scatter ½ cup pelletized limestone and ½ cup of controlled-release fertilizer over

the area where the shrub will be planted. (Most Carolina soils have been depleted of calcium and magnesium by farming, and the rise in pH won't be significant.)

- Slide the shrub out of the container and loosen the roots. Bang the rootball on the ground a couple of times to shake off some soil particles.
- Pull circling roots loose from the rootball. If a pad of rootlets has formed on the bottom of the rootball, slice it off. Cut off long, stringy roots.
- Borrow 5 gallons of soil from elsewhere in your garden and dump it to the side of the planting site, or buy a bag of topsoil. Crumble the borrowed soil and mix it with an equal volume of organic soil conditioner or leaf compost. Avoid dried cow manure as it is alkaline in reaction.
- Turn the plant so the best side is forward and set it in a shallow hole where it is to grow.
- Pull the conditioned soil around the rootball and taper it down to the original soil level. The plant may seem "high and dry," but it will love the good drainage and aeration.
- Shovel any remaining conditioned soil into a shallow basin to catch water.
- Mulch as directed for other shrubs. Do not use peat moss as a mulch; it repels water. Keep bark mulch away from the crown of plants. It is okay to tuck pinestraw beneath branches to conserve water and keep down weeds.
- Give each plant at least 5 gallons of water trickled from a hose.

PLANTING PERENNIALS

Perennials are almost always sold in larger containers than annuals because they are customarily grown from cuttings or divisions of crowns, tubers, or explants from micropropagation rather than from seeds. Read and save plant labels in a garden journal or record into a database. They will tell you which cultivars demand well-drained soil and those that will thrive in wet, poorly aerated areas. (The latter includes obedient plant, Joe-pye weed, ironweed, turtlehead, cardinal flower, hardy hibiscus, as well as many others.)

Prepare soil as directed. Container-grown perennials can be planted at any time in the Carolinas, but fall through early spring is far and away the best time. In Mountain areas, spring is the best planting time, after the soil has thawed. Cool soil, frequent showers, and decreased transpiration all encourage root development that prepares the plant to bloom the following year. Transplanting perennials from late spring through summer steadily decreases survivability due to increased water needs. You must water every two or three days between rains to keep up with the demands of a developing root system and burgeoning top growth and the loss of soil moisture taken up by roots and transpired through the foliage.

Dig planting holes the recommended distance apart, and have a hose equipped with a water wand or a 5-gallon container of water when you're ready to plant.

Tap the plant out of the container. If only a few roots girdle the rootball or mat at the bottom, set the rootball in the planting hole with as little disturbance to it as possible. More often than not, perennial plants are potbound, with substantial root development girdling the sides of the rootball and matting at the bottom. Using hand shears, snip off the mat and cut major girdling roots. Then, bang the plant on a solid surface to knock off some of the rooting medium and to expose root tips. This seemingly rough treatment prepares the plant to send new developing roots into the surrounding soil.

Set the plant in the planting hole so that the top of the rootball is level with the surface of the surrounding soil or as much as ½ inch above it. Pull the conditioned backfill around the rootball and firm it down lightly. Complete planting the other selections chosen for that spot and soak the area with water without delay.

Toby advocates adding a diluted, water-soluble organic fertilizer to this initial watering. Jim prefers to use only water at planting time and to drench the soil with liquid fertilizer two to three weeks later when the plants have begun to send out new feeder roots. This goes to show you that gardening is more art than science and that personal preference trumps written rules. Both approaches work well.

How to handle home-divided perennials is a different matter. When you dig clumps of perennials during fall or winter, wash the soil off the roots before surgery and cut, saw, or break the clumps into smaller, well-rooted parts. You can set out the divisions at the same time. Or if they are from choice, expensive plants or ones with sentimental value, you can pot the plants in potting soil, grow them for a few weeks, and set them in place with a well-developed root system. The former approach requires more frequent watering to guarantee that your new plants will "take." Both Jim and Toby have small "nurseries" at their homes where they can hold vegetative divisions while they are developing roots. Their holding areas are near water faucets and are protected from foraging by wildlife.

STARTING ANNUALS FROM SEEDS

If you have a sunny south- or west-facing windowsill, you can sprout seeds of annuals successfully and grow them to transplanting size. Even better is a fluorescent light fixture that can be lowered to within 2 inches of the tops of seed pans. Better yet are the metal halide lamps that come even closer to imitating the full spectrum of sunlight and can deliver the footcandles needed by plants when placed further away than fluorescent tubes.

Most flower seeds will sprout (germinate) at soil temperatures of 60 to 65 degrees F. Some species that have a tropical provenance sprout more rapidly at 70 to 80 degrees F. Such warm temperatures can be produced atop a hot water heater or by using a horticultural heating pad with an adjustable thermostat. It is most important that you move the seed pan to a somewhat cooler area just as soon as you see green seedlings emerging. Some gardeners cover seed pans with clear plastic wrap to maintain high humidity; covers must be removed as soon as you see green.

Plastic meat trays about three inches deep make good seed pans. Use an ice pick, auger, or a large nail to punch six to eight drainage holes. Fill pans to within ½ inch of the rim with "seed starting mix" which is formulated from fine Canadian sphagnum peat moss and fine particles of vermiculite or perlite. Use a short length of board to firm down and level the mix. Moisten the starter mix by setting the filled pan in a tray of warm water. Capillarity will pull water up into the mix and saturate it.

Gardeners usually plant the contents of a standard seed packet in a single seed pan. Some prefer to scatter the seeds evenly over the surface; others prefer to plant the seeds in three or four straight lines or "drills." The best topping to cover seeds is "milled sphagnum moss," which is produced by grinding the ropy moss from the surface of peat bogs. It has biological properties which greatly reduce the incidence of damping-off, an infection that kills seedlings at ground level. A very thin topping of seed starter mix will work nearly as well. Certain species require light to sprout, but enough light can penetrate a thin topping to initiate germination.

Gardeners usually start seeds six to eight weeks prior to the spring frost-free date, earlier on species that can tolerate light frosts, and later on fast-sprouting, fast-growing species. The initial bottom-watering should suffice to sprout the seeds, especially if the seed pan is covered with clear plastic wrap. Overwatering seed pans is a fast track to damping off, especially if the germinating area cools to 50 to 60 degrees F at night.

The rate of growth of seedlings depends greatly on the size of the seeds. Large seeds produce robust seedlings with enough stored carbohydrates to nourish them for up to three weeks. If they're given adequate light and the proper range of heat,

you can almost hear them grow. Tiny seeds, on the other hand, produce seedlings almost too small to see. They grow excruciatingly slowly until they can produce enough surface area of foliage to trap a significant amount of light.

When seedlings develop four to six leaves, they can be transplanted to individual 2- to 3-inch pots filled with high quality potting soil formulated for bedding plants. They can be "pricked out" (pried out) of seed pans with a Popsicle stick or a similar tool. Hold seedlings by their leaves, not by their stems, to avoid crushing the tender stem tissue.

Poke a planting hole in the center of the filled pot and lower the seedling into it so that the top of its root system is level with the surface of the soil. Pinch the potting soil to firm it around the root system. Set the potted plant aside for bottom-watering when all the seedlings have been transplanted. Certain species such as lobelia and begonia have such tiny seedlings that they are customarily transplanted in small clumps, grown for a few weeks, then divided into individual plants for transplanting into pots.

Invariably, first-time seed starters are surprised, even overwhelmed, by the geometric increase in space needed at transplanting time. You can go, say, from fifty seedlings in a small pan to fifty individual pots of 2- to 4-inch diameter. All of a sudden, the area lighted by two 48-inch fluorescent tubes must strain to hold the plants from one seed pan. Advanced gardeners often keep a "coldframe" handy, lighted by the sun and perhaps warmed with grounded electric light bulbs, to handle the overflow of plants.

Your reaction to these directions may be to ask, "Why bother?" If you like to try the very newest annuals, you can usually buy seeds a year or two before started plants become widely available. Also, the tall varieties of annuals that are preferred for cutting gardens are rarely available as started plants because they take too long to show color and grow too tall in the process. Neither growers nor retailers like to handle them. Starting from seeds gives gardeners a way to propagate heirloom varieties that are no longer grown by seed companies and to produce plants at a lower unit cost than is possible with purchase of bedding plants. Last but not least, starting from seeds is the mark of a good gardener. It isn't easy to balance light intensity, temperature, and soil moisture to the needs of each species. Prior to World War II, starting from seeds was the only way to grow. If millions of gardeners could master the technique without using fluorescent or halide lamps, surely you can too.

GLOSSARY

ACID SOIL: soil with a pH less than 7.0. The lower the pH, the more acidic or "sour" the soil. Soils are acid when concentrations of bases like calcium and magnesium are low in relation to hydrogen and aluminum. This can occur naturally in forested areas or as a result of leached soils or growing crops. Sulfur is typically added to the soil to make it more acidic.

AERATION: the process of punching holes in the soil to increase the amount of oxygen available to plant roots and correct compaction problems.

ALKALINE SOIL: soil with a pH greater than 7.0. It lacks acidity, often because it has limestone in it.

ALL-PURPOSE FERTILIZER: powdered, liquid, or granular fertilizer with a balanced proportion of the three key nutrients nitrogen (N), phosphorus (P), and potassium (K). It is suitable for maintenance nutrition for most plants.

AMENDMENTS: components added to soil to improve fertility or structure.

ANNUAL: from a botanist's perspective, an annual lasts no longer than one year. To the gardener, an annual is a seasonal plant, growing until winter's cold or summer's heat causes it to decline or die.

BALLED AND BURLAPPED: describes a tree or shrub grown in the field whose soilball was wrapped with protective burlap and twine when the plant was dug up to be sold or transplanted.

BARE ROOT: describes plants that have been packaged without any soil around their roots. (Often young shrubs and trees purchased through the mail arrive with their exposed roots covered with moist peat or sphagnum moss, sawdust, or similar material, and wrapped in plastic.)

BARRIER PLANT: a plant that has intimidating thorns or spines and is sited purposely to block foot traffic or other access to the home or yard.

BENEFICIAL INSECTS: insects or their larvae that prey on pest organisms and their eggs. They may be flying insects, such as ladybugs, parasitic wasps, praying mantids, and soldier bugs, or soil dwellers such as predatory nematodes, spiders, ants, and beetles.

BERM: a narrow raised ring of soil around a tree, used to hold water so it will be directed to the root zone.

BRACT: a modified leaf structure on a plant stem near its flower that resembles a petal. Often it is more colorful and visible than the actual flower, as in dogwood or poinsettia.

BROADLEAVED: plants having leaves of wider breadth in relation to length and thickness, in contrast to grassy plants. Broadleaved, or broadleaf, weeds are typically dicots, whereas grasses are monocots. Dicots and monocots respond differently to chemical controls.

Bt: abbreviation of *Bacillus thuringiensis*, an organism that attacks a certain stage in the life cycle of some pests. Forms of *Bt* can be created to target a particular species. Used as a natural pest control.

BUD UNION: the place where the top of a plant is grafted to the rootstock; usually refers to roses or fruit trees.

CANOPY: the overhead branching area of a tree, usually referring to its extent including foliage.

CHLOROTIC: yellowing of leaves either from pest or nutrient problems.

CLUMPING: a contained growth habit versus a spreading growth habit.

COLD HARDINESS: the ability of a perennial plant to survive the winter cold in a particular area.

COOL-SEASON GRASS: turfgrasses that prefer and thrive in cooler northern conditions. They can remain green during milder winters.

CORING: the act of mechanically removing small plugs of soil from the ground, allowing for better penetration of oxygen and water to alleviate soil compaction, and also providing lodging places for new grass seed. Typically done in preparation for renewing an established lawn or installing a new one. Also called core aeration.

COMPACTION: when soil particles are packed so tightly together that air and water cannot easily penetrate.

COMPLETE FERTILIZER: powdered, liquid, or granular fertilizer with a balanced proportion of the three key nutrients—nitrogen (N), phosphorus (P), and potassium (K). It is suitable for maintenance nutrition for most plants.

COMPOSITE: a flower that is actually composed of many tiny flowers. Typically, they are flat clusters of tiny, tight florets, sometimes surrounded by wider-petaled florets. Composite flowers are highly attractive to bees and beneficial insects.

COMPOST: organic matter that has undergone progressive decomposition by microbial and macrobial activity until it is reduced to a spongy, fluffy texture. Added to soil of any type, it improves the soil's ability to hold air and water and to drain.

CORM: the swollen energy-storing structure, analogous to a bulb, under the soil at the base of the stem of plants, such as crocus and gladiolus.

CROWN: the base of a plant at, or just beneath, the surface of the soil where the roots meet the stems.

CULTIVAR: a CULTIvated VARiety. It is a naturally occurring form of a plant that has been identified as special or superior and is purposely selected for propagation and production.

DEADHEAD: a pruning technique that removes faded flower heads from plants to improve their appearance, abort seed production, and stimulate further flowering.

DECIDUOUS PLANTS: unlike evergreens, these trees and shrubs lose their leaves in the fall.

DESICCATION: drying out of foliage tissues, usually due to drought or wind.

DETHATCHING: the process of raking or removing the mat of partially decomposed remnants of grass lodged at the soil surface, beneath the living grass layer. Can be done manually or mechanically; vertical mowing (or verticutting) is one method.

DICOT: shortening of the word "dicotyledon." Plant with two cotyledons or seed leaves emerging from its seed, such as a bean or an acorn.

DIVISION: the practice of splitting apart perennial plants to create several smaller-rooted segments. The practice is useful for controlling the plant's size and for acquiring more plants; it is also essential to the health and continued flowering of certain ones.

DORMANCY: the period, usually the winter, when perennial plants temporarily cease active growth and rest. Dormant is the verb form, as used in this sentence: Some plants, like spring-blooming bulbs, go dormant in the summer.

DROUGHT TOLERANT: plants able to tolerate dry soil for varying periods of time. However, plants must first be well established before they are drought tolerant.

ESTABLISHED: the point at which a newly planted tree, shrub, or flower begins to produce new growth, either foliage or stems. This is an indication that the roots have recovered from transplant shock and have begun to grow and spread.

EVERGREEN: perennial plants that do not lose their foliage annually with the onset of winter. Needled or broadleaf foliage will persist and continue to function on a plant through one or more winters, aging and dropping unobtrusively in cycles of three or four years or more.

FOLIAR: of or about foliage—usually refers to the practice of spraying foliage, as in fertilizing or treating with insecticide; leaf tissues absorb liquid directly for fast results, and the soil is not affected.

FLORET: a tiny flower, usually one of many forming a cluster, that comprises a single blossom.

FUNGICIDE: a pesticide material for destroying or preventing fungus on plants.

GENUS: a distinct botanical group within a family, typically containing several species. Plural form is "genera," referring to more than one genus.

GERMINATE: to sprout. Germination is a fertile seed's first stage of development.

GRADING: changing the slope of the land, usually to make it more level or a more gradual incline.

GRAFT (UNION): the point on the stem of a woody plant with sturdier roots where a stem from a highly ornamental plant is inserted so that it will join with it. Roses are commonly grafted.

GROWTH RATE: The pace or speed at which plants develop and increase in size. Plants are described as slow, medium, or fast growers. Among shrubs species, hedges are fast growers and dwarf conifers are slow growers. Many ground covers grow slowly.

HANDS: the female flowers on a banana tree; they turn into bananas.

HARDSCAPE: the permanent, structural, nonplant part of a landscape, such as walls, sheds, pools, patios, arbors, and walkways.

HEAT TOLERANCE: the ability of a plant to withstand the summer heat in a particular area.

HERBACEOUS: plants having fleshy or soft stems that die back with frost; the opposite of woody.

HERBICIDE: a pesticide material for killing or preventing weeds.

HYBRID: a plant that is the result of intentional or natural cross-pollination between two or more plants of the same species or genus.

INSECTICIDE: a pesticide material for killing, preventing, or protecting plants against harmful insects.

INTEGRATED PEST MANAGEMENT: a combination of pest management techniques used in order to reduce the need for pesticides. Also referred to by the acronym IPM.

INVASIVE: when a plant has such a vigorous growth habit that it crowds out more desirable plants.

IRRIGATION: manmade systems of pipes, sprinkler heads, and timers installed to provide supplementary water to landscaping.

LEACHING: the removal of nutrients from the soil by excessive amounts of water.

LIFE CYCLE: stages in the life of an organism. With insects it is important to know the cycles of both beneficial and harmful ones, since different stages vary in their locations, vulnerabilities, and eating habits.

LIMING: the practice of incorporating limestone into acid soil to raise the pH level and increase the calcium level to optimize fertilizer benefits.

LOW WATER DEMAND: describes plants that tolerate dry soil for varying periods of time. Typically, they have succulent, hairy, or silvery gray foliage and tuberous roots or taproots.

MICRONUTRIENTS: elements needed in small quantities for plant growth. Sometimes a soil will be deficient in one or more of them and require a particular fertilizer formulation.

MONOCOT: shortening of the word "monocotyledon." Plant with one cotyledon or seed leaf emerging from its seed, such as with corn or grass.

MOWING STRIP: a type of barrier placed between the lawn and landscaped areas that accommodates lawnmower tires, making it easier to mow the lawn edge neatly, and preventing ruts or compaction to the edges of the beds.

MULCH: a layer of material over bare soil to protect it from erosion and compaction by rain, and to discourage weeds. It may be inorganic (gravel, fabric) or organic (wood chips, bark, pine needles, chopped leaves).

MULCHING MOWER: mower that chops grass blades into very fine pieces, eliminating the need to have an attachment that bags the clippings.

NATURALIZE: (*a*) to plant seeds, bulbs, or plants in a random, informal pattern as they would appear in their natural habitat; (*b*) to adapt to and spread throughout adopted habitats (a tendency of some nonnative plants).

NECTAR: the sweet fluid produced by glands on flowers that attract pollinators such as hummingbirds and honeybees for whom it is a source of energy.

NODE: structure on a stem from which leaves, roots, and branches arise.

NON-SELECTIVE: herbicides that have the potential to kill or control any plant to which they are applied.

NUTRIENTS: elements available through soil, air, and water, which the plant utilizes for growth and reproduction.

ORGANIC MATERIAL, ORGANIC MATTER: any material or debris that is derived from plants. It is carbon-based material capable of undergoing decomposition and decay.

OVERSEEDING: distributing new grass seed on an established lawn to thicken the grass coverage or introduce another type of grass to extend green season.

PARTIAL SHADE: situation with filtered or dappled sunlight, or half a day of shade. In the South, part shade often refers to afternoon shade, when the sun is at its brightest and hottest.

PATHOGEN: the causal organism of a plant disease.

PEAT MOSS: organic matter from sphagnum mosses, often used to improve soil texture, especially sandy soils. It is also used in seed-starting mixes and in container plantings.

PERENNIAL: a flowering plant that lives over two or more seasons. Many die back with frost, but their roots live the winter and generate new shoots in the spring.

PH: a measurement of the relative acidity (low pH) or alkalinity (high pH) of soil or water based on a scale of 1 to 14; 7 being neutral. Individual plants require soil to be within a certain range so that nutrients can be available to them.

PINCH: to remove tender stems and/or leaves by pressing them between thumb and forefinger. This pruning technique encourages branching, compactness, and flowering in plants, or it removes aphids clustered at growing tips.

PLUG: piece of sod used in establishing a new lawn. Plugs can also be grown or purchased in small cells or pots within a flat, sometimes referred to as trays.

POLLEN: the yellow, powdery grains in the center of a flower. A plant's male sex cells, they are transferred to the female plant parts by means of wind or animal pollinators to fertilize them and create seeds.

PRE-EMERGENT: an herbicide applied to the soil surface to prevent weed seed from germinating.

POST-EMERGENT: an herbicide applied to already germinated and actively growing weeds to kill or control them.

RACEME: an arrangement of single-stalked flowers along an elongated, unbranched axis.

REEL MOWER: type of mower generally thought of as old fashioned, but with new versions achieving renewed popularity. Blades are arranged horizontally in a cylinder, or reel, that spins, cutting the grass blades against a metal plate.

RENOVATION: renewing an established lawn, partially or completely.

RHIZOME: a swollen energy-storing stem structure, similar to a bulb, that lies horizontally in the soil, with roots emerging from its lower surface and growth shoots from a growing point at or near its tip, as in bearded iris.

ROOTBOUND (OR POTBOUND): the condition of a plant that has been confined in a container too long, its roots having been forced to wrap around themselves and even swell out of the container. Successful transplanting or repotting requires untangling and trimming away of some of the matted roots.

ROOT FLARE: The transition at the base of a tree trunk where the bark tissue begins to differentiate and roots begin to form just before entering the soil. This area should not be covered with soil when planting a tree.

ROTARY MOWER: a mower with its blades arranged under the body of the mower, which cuts by the high speed of the spinning blades.

RUNNER: horizontal stem that grows along the soil surface and forms plantlets at each node. An example is the strawberry.

RUNOFF: when water moves across the landscape without being absorbed, because the slope is steep, the volume of water is greater than the absorption capacity of the soil, the soil is compacted, or the surface is of an impenetrable material. Runoff from areas that have had chemicals applied can cause problems in the areas ultimately receiving the water.

SELECTION: a variation within a species that occurs naturally due to the presence of a multitude of genetic possibilities. Over several generations, plants with the desired characteristic are isolated and propagated. This process has been particularly important in the agronomic industry.

SELECTIVE: herbicides, and other pesticides, that target a particular type of weed or pest.

SELF-SEEDING: the tendency of some plants to sow their seeds freely around the yard. It creates many seedlings the following season that may or may not be welcome.

SEMI-EVERGREEN: tending to be evergreen in a mild climate but deciduous in a rigorous one.

SHADE: An area of filtered light or partial darkness. Not all shade is equal; true shade-loving plants can tolerate morning sun in North Carolina conditions but wither if the shade period is reversed; dappled shade is preferred. The dry, shaded conditions under a maple are extreme compared to those under tall pines. Plants flourish in shade by a stream.

SHADE TOLERANT: a plant's ability to maintain health and continue growth in a shaded location.

SHEARING: the pruning technique whereby plant stems and branches are cut uniformly with long-bladed pruning shears (hedge shears) or powered hedge trimmers. It is used when creating and maintaining hedges and topiary.

SLOW-ACTING FERTILIZER: fertilizer that is water insoluble and therefore releases its nutrients gradually as a function of soil temperature, moisture coating, and related microbial activity. Typically granular, it may be organic or synthetic.

SOD: commercially grown turfgrass sections cut from a field in rectangular panels or rolls, used to establish new lawns.

SOIL CONDITIONER: chemical or organic material which aggregates soil particles for improved structure.

SPECIES: a group of fundamentally identical plants within a genus. Synonymous with the more botanically accurate designation "specific epithet."

SPECIMEN PLANT: An ornamental shrub or tree used alone to create a focal point or accent in the landscape. Often, the plant has some unique features, such as showy bark, fragrant flowers, etc.

SPRIG: part of an underground root or stem that contains nodes, used to establish new plants.

STERILE: producing no viable seeds or spores, and in lawn grasses no flowers, which is an advantage since the flowers are typically taller than the leaf blades and are not attractive. The disadvantage is that such grasses cannot be bought as seed, only as sod.

STOLON: horizontal stem that grows along the soil surface. It can form plantlets at the tips of the stems. An example is the blackberry.

SUCCULENT GROWTH: The sometimes undesirable production of fleshy, water-storing leaves or stems that results from overfertilization.

SUCKER: a new growing shoot. Underground plant roots produce suckers to form new stems and spread by means of these suckering roots to form large plantings, or colonies. Some plants produce root suckers or branch suckers as a result of pruning or wounding.

SUPPLEMENTAL IRRIGATION: The recommended amount of water for gardens from May until September is 1 to 1½ inches per week. When rainfall is short or drought sets in, most plants benefit from watering weekly (less often for trees).

SYNTHETIC: products made to imitate a natural material, as in synthetic fertilizer or pesticide.

TAMP: pressing down on newly installed sod so that the roots have good soil contact. This can also be achieved with "rolling," in which a heavy cylindrical drum is rolled over the sod.

THATCH: layer of undecayed grass found between the soil surface and the living grass blades.

TOPDRESSING: the act of applying granular products such as fertilizer, lime, sand, etc. over the top of lawn grass.

TOPSOIL: the fertile layer of soil where plant roots grow. Sometimes the naturally occurring topsoil is inadequate for certain plants, or has been removed during construction, in which case it might be necessary to purchase topsoil from a local supplier.

TRANSLOCATION: movement of water, minerals, and food within the plant.

TRANSPIRATION: water loss by evaporation from external leaf surfaces.

TRANSPLANTING: moving plants from one location to another.

TUBER: a type of underground storage structure in a plant stem, analogous to a bulb. It generates roots below and stems above ground. A dahlia is a tuberous root. A potato is a tuber.

TURF OR TURFGRASS: grass used to make a lawn.

VARIEGATED: having various colors or color patterns. The term usually refers to plant foliage that is streaked, edged, blotched, or mottled with a contrasting color, often green with yellow, cream, or white.

VARIETY: a group of plants within a species which have stable characteristics separating them from the typical form. Frequently used synonymously with cultivar and selection, even though there are differences in the definitions of the three terms.

VEGETATIVE: non-sexual production of plant material typically achieved by divisions or cuttings and not as a result of flowering, pollination, and seed formation.

VERTICAL MOWING OR VERTICUTTING: mechanical act of cutting into a lawn vertically with sharp blades or tines to lift dead vegetation such as thatch.

VIABILITY: refers to seed that is healthy and able to germinate.

WARM-SEASON GRASS: turfgrasses that thrive and perform in warm southern conditions. They can go dormant during the coldest parts of the winter, then resume growth in the spring.

WATER-LOGGED: soil that holds too much water for most plants to thrive, associated with poor aeration, inadequate drainage, or soil compaction.

WEED: a plant growing where it is not wanted.

WEED-AND-FEED: a product that combines a weed control, usually pre-emergent, and a fertilizer. Timing of an application is critical since a pre-emergent weed control is also capable of preventing grass seed from germinating, and fertilizing before the grass is actively growing might actually promote the growth of existing weeds.

WHITE GRUBS: the larvae of scarab beetles, including Japanese beetles, masked chafers, and May and June beetles. They have plump, cream-colored, C-shaped bodies and distinctive yellow to brown heads. Most have life cycles lasting from several months to three years.

WINGS: (a) the corky tissue that forms edges along the twigs of some woody plants such as winged euonymus; (b) the flat, dried extension of tissue on some seeds, such as maple, that catch the wind and help them disseminate.

BIBLIOGRAPHY

Alabama Gardener's Guide, Jennifer Greer, Cool Springs Press, Franklin, TN, 1997.

The American Horticultural Society Flower Finder, Jacqueline Heriteau, Simon and Schuster, New York, NY, 1992.

Aquatic Plants and Their Cultivation, Helen Nash with Steve Stroupe, Sterling Publishing Co., Inc., New York, NY, 1998.

Bulletproof Flowers for the South, Jim Wilson, Taylor Publishing Co., Dallas, TX, 1999.

The Carolinas Gardener's Guide, Toby Bost and Jim Wilson, Cool Springs Press, Nashville, TN, 2004.

Commonsense Vegetable Gardening for the South, William D. Adams and Thomas LeRoy, Taylor Publishing Co., Dallas, TX, 1995.

Daffodils for American Gardens, Brent and Becky Heath, Elliott & Clark Publishing, Washington, DC, 1995.

Easy Roses for North American Gardens, Tom Christopher, The Reader's Digest Association, Inc., Pleasantville, NY, 1999.

The Encyclopedia of Ornamental Grasses, John Greenlee, Michael Friedman Publishing Group, Inc., New York, NY, 1992.

The Encyclopedia of Roses, Judith C. McKeon, Rodale Press, Inc., Emmaus, PA, 1995.

Garden Bulbs for the South, Scott Ogden, Taylor Publishing Co., Dallas, TX, 1994.

Garden Guide to the Lower South, Trustees' Garden Club (P.O. Box 24215, Savannah, GA), 1991.

Georgia Gardener's Guide, Erica Glasener and Walter Reeves, Cool Springs Press, Franklin, TN, 1996.

The Green Gardener's Guide, Joe Lamp'l, Cool Springs Press, Franklin, TN, 2007.

Growing and Propagating Showy Native Woody Plants, Richard E. Bir, University of North Carolina Press, Chapel Hill, NC, 1992.

Handbook of Water Use and Conservation, Amy Vickers, WaterPlow Press, 2003.

Heat-Zone Gardening, Marc H. Cathey, Time-Life Inc., China, 1998.

Herbs, Norma Jean Lathrop, HP Books, Los Angeles, CA, 1981.

Herbaceous Perennial Plants, 2nd Edition, Allan M. Armitage, Stipes Publishing L.L.C., Champaign, IL, 1997.

House Plants, John Brookes, ed., The Reader's Digest Association, Inc., Pleasantville, NY, 1990.

Identifying Turf Problems, Richard Duble, Florida Turf Digest, Vol. 3, No. 9, 1986.

Improving Landscape Irrigation Efficiency, Amanda Dewees www.awwa.org/waterwiser

Landscape Plants of the Southeast, Gordon R. Halfacre and Anne R. Shawcroft, Sparks Press, Raleigh, NC, 1992.

Landscaping with Natives, Guy Sternberg and Jim Wilson, Chapters Publishing Ltd., Vermont, 1995.

Louisiana Gardener's Guide, Dan Gill and Joe White, Cool Springs Press, Franklin, TN, 1997.

Manual of Woody Landscape Plants, 5th Edition, Michael A. Dirr, Stipes Publishing L.L.C., Champaign, IL, 1998.

Mississippi Gardener's Guide, Norman Winter, Cool Springs Press, Franklin, TN, 2000.

Month by Month Gardening in the Carolinas, Revised Edition, Robert Polomski, Cool Springs Press, Franklin, TN, 2005.

The National Arboretum Book of Outstanding Garden Plants, Jacqueline Heriteau with Dr. H. Marc Cathey, Simon and Schuster, NY, 1990.

North Carolina Gardener's Guide, Toby Bost, Cool Springs Press, Franklin, TN, 1997.

The North Carolina Lawn Guide, Steve Dobbs, Cool Springs Press, Franklin, TN, 2007.

Oklahoma Turfgrass Survey, Glen Martin, OSU, Stillwater, OK, 1987.

Oklahoma Soil Fertility Handbook, Billy Tucker et al., Oklahoma Cooperative Extension Service, Stillwater, OK, 1977.

Ortho's All About Roses, Tommy Cairns, Meredith Books, Des Moines, Iowa, 1999.

The Palm Reader: A Manual for Growing Palms Outdoors in the Southeast, compiled by members of The Southeastern Palm and Exotic Plant Society, 1994.

Passalong Plants, Steve Bender and Felder Rushing, University of North Carolina Press, Chapel Hill, NC, 1993.

Perennials, Pamela Harper and Frederick McGourty, HP Books, Los Angeles, CA. 1985.

Perennials for American Gardens, Ruth Rogers Clausen and Nicolas H. Ekstrom, Random House, NY, 1989.

The Perennial Garden, Jeff and Marilyn Cox, Rodale Press, Emmaus, PA, 1985.

Perennials: How to Select, Grow and Enjoy, Pamela Harper and Frederick McGourty, HP Books, Tucson, AZ, 1985.

Plants That Merit Attention, Vol. 1, Trees, Janet Meakin Poor, ed., Timber Press, Inc., Portland, OR, 1984.

Plants That Merit Attention, Vol. 2, Shrubs, Janet Meakin Poor and Nancy Peterson Brewster, Timber Press, Inc., Portland, OR, 1996.

The Practical Gardener: A Guide to Breaking New Ground, Roger B. Swain, Little, Brown and Co., 1989.

Reader's Digest Success with House Plants, Anthony Huxley, The Reader's Digest Association, Inc., Pleasantville, NY, 1979.

Research Update, Sharp Blades Conserve Fuel, Unknown, Grounds Maintenance 36(8), Overland Park, KS, August 2001.

Rodale's Successful Organic Gardening: Trees, Shrubs, and Vines, Bonnie Lee Appleton and A. F. Scheider, Rodale Press, Emmaus, PA, 1993.

The Rose Book, Maggie Oster, Rodale Press, Emmaus, PA, 1994.

Rose Gardening in the Carolinas: Culture and Care, C. Douglas Baker, Thomas W. Estridge, and Roderick J. Humphreys, The Greater Columbia Rose Society, Columbia, SC, 1997.

Roses for Dummies, Lance Walheim and the editors of the National Gardening Association, IDG Books Worldwide, Inc., Foster City, CA, 1997.

Soil Reaction (pH) for Flowers, Shrubs, and Lawn, J. NeSmith and E.W. McElwee, Circular 352-A, Florida Cooperative Extension Service IFAS, Gainesville, FL, 1974.

South Carolina Gardener's Guide, Jim Wilson, Cool Springs Press, Franklin, TN, 1997.

Southern Gardens, Southern Gardening, William L. Hunt, Duke University Press, Durham, NC, 1992

Southern Living Gardening: Trees and Shrubs, John Alex Floyd, Oxmoor House, Birmingham, AL, 1980.

Southern Living Garden Problem Solver, Steve Bender, ed., Oxmoor House, Inc., Birmingham, AL, 1999.

Southern Seasons: Month-by-Month Gardening in the Piedmont Plateau, Frances Worthington, Shurcliff Press, Greenville, SC, 1993.

Successful Rose Gardening, Meredith Corporation, Des Moines, Iowa. 1993.

Successful Southern Gardening, Sandra F. Ladendorf, University of North Carolina Press, Chapel Hill, NC, 1989.

Sunset Annuals and Perennials, Sunset Publishing Corp., Menlo Park, CA, 1993.

Sunset National Gardening Book, Suzanne E. Eyre, Sunset Books, Inc., Menlo Park, CA, 1997.

Teaming with Microbes: A Gardener's Guide to the Soil Food Web, Jeff Lowenfels and Wayne Lewis, Timber Press, 2006.

The Tennessee Gardener's Guide, Walter Glenn and Lark Foster, Cool Springs Press, Franklin, TN, 1996.

Texas Gardening Guide, Dale Groom, Cool Springs Press, Franklin, TN, 1997.

Treasury of Gardening, C. Colston Burrell et al., Publications International, Ltd., Lincolnwood, IL, 1998.

Trees for Urban and Suburban Landscapes, Edward F. Gilman, Delmar Publishers, Albany, NY, 1997.

Water Gardening, Joseph Tomocik, Pantheon Books, Knopf Publishing Group, NY, 1996.

Water Gardening: Water Lilies and Lotuses, Perry D. Slocum and Peter Robinson with Frances Perry, Timber Press, Inc., Portland, OR, 1996.

Water Gardens, Thomas C. Cooper, Ed., Primedia, Inc., Peoria, IL, 1998.

Well-clad Windowsills: Houseplants for Four Exposures, Tovah Martin, Macmillan, NY, 1994.

The Well-Tended Perennial Garden: Planting and Pruning Techniques, Tracy DiSabato-Aust, Timber Press, Portland, OR, 1998.

The Year in Trees: Superb Woody Plants for Four-season Gardens, Kim E. Tripp and J. C. Raulston, Timber Press, Portland, OR, 1995.

Weeds of Southern Turfgrasses, Tim R. Murphy et al., University of Florida Cooperative Extension Service, Institute of Food and Agricultural Sciences, Gainesville, FL, 2004

Zoysia japonica From Sprigs: Effects of Topdressing and Nitrogen Fertility, John Boyd, and Mike Richardson, University of Arkansas, HortScience 36(2): 377-379, 2001.

MAGAZINES

Carolina Gardener, P.O. Box 4504, Greensboro, NC 27404 (www.carolinagardener.com/)

Horticulture, 98 North Washington Street, Boston, MA 02114 (www.hortmag.com/)

Neil Sperry's Gardens, P.O. Box 864, McKinney, TX 75070-0864 (www.neilsperry.com/cfbeta/)

Assorted publications from:

North Carolina Cooperative Extension Service (www.ces.ncsu.edu/)

Clemson University Cooperative Extension Service (www.clemson.edu/extension/)

American Nurseryman Publishing Co. *American Nurseryman* (semimonthly publication). Chicago, Illinois.

WEBSITES

www.epa.gov/watersense/water/why.htm
www.irrigation.org
www.rainbarrelguide.com
www.beyondpesticides.org/lawn/factsheets/facts&figures.htm
www.organicrosecare.org/articles/worm_castings.php
www.landandwater.com
www.ecocycle.org/tidbits/index.cfm
www.dnr.state.md.us/bay/protect/home.html
www.zerowasteamerica.org/Landfills.htm
www.epa.gov/epaoswer/non-hw/muncpl/facts.htm
www.bae.ncsu.edu/topic/vermicomposting/pubs/composting.pdf
www.wasteage.com/mag/waste_yard_waste_4/:
web.extension.uiuc.edu/homecompost/recycle.html
www.epa.gov/epaoswer/non-hw/green/projects/agriplas.htm
www.agriplasinc.com/index_Page385.htm
www.ces.ncsu.edu/depts/hort/hil/hil-631.html
www.greentagsusa.org
www.epa.gov/heatisland/index.htm
www.mindfully.org.
www.epa.gov/otaq/equip-ld.htm
www.treehugger.com/files/2007/05/ask_treehugger_15.php:
www.countdown2010.net
www.greenfacts.org
www.unep-wcmc.org
www.helpfulgardener.com
www.rodaleinstitute.org
www.nature.org/initiatives/invasivespecies/features/
www.nwf.org/backyard/70000goal.cfm:

INDEX OF COMMON NAMES

BOTANICAL INDEX

MEET TOBY BOST

Born and raised in Piedmont, North Carolina, Toby Bost graduated from North Carolina State University where he holds both Bachelor and Master degrees in Horticulture Science. Toby served Tar Heel gardeners for thirty-one years as an Extension Agent with the N.C. Cooperative Extension Service. For two decades, he recruited and trained more than 400 Master Gardeners in Forsyth and Durham counties, appearing frequently in the media as a gardening educator. He organized professional green industry events to provide training for landscape professionals seeking certification in their respective trade associations.

Toby continues to dedicate his time to helping fellow gardeners conquer stubborn clay soils and grow healthy lawns and ornamentals as the garden writer for *Our State* magazine's online gardening newsletter. He is also co-editor of a newly released book by Blair Publishing, *The Successful Gardener Guide: North Carolina*. Over the years, he has received numerous state and national communication awards from the National Association of County Agricultural Agents for his gardening projects and publications including the Distinguished Service Award, and the Order of the Longleaf Pine Award, presented by the governor's office. He is a member of the American Camellia Society, Paul J. Ceiner Botanical Garden, Forsyth Extension Master Gardener Association, and Old Salem Museum and Gardens Volunteers.

Toby and his wife, Becky, reside in Winston-Salem. They have two adult children who are educators. Toby owns Bost Consulting Group, a landscape gardening service that provides on-site diagnostic and troubleshooting consultations.

MEET ROBERT POLOMSKI

Bob Polomski is widely known and respected for both his down-to-earth gardening expertise and knowledge of the latest technical information. He shares his gardening know-how with gardeners across the Carolinas through numerous print and Internet articles, radio broadcasts, and television appearances.

Polomski's publications range from scientific papers and extension publications to magazine and newspaper articles. For twelve years he wrote the "Questions & Answers" column for *Horticulture* magazine. He has also published articles in *Carolina Gardener*, *Fine Gardening*, *American Rose*, and *American Nurseryman*.

Polomski was a contributing writer for the *Better Homes and Gardens New Garden Book* (Meredith Corp., Des Moines, Iowa) and the *Southern Living Garden Problem Solver* (Oxmoor House, Inc., Birmingham, Alabama). He was technical editor of several books, including the *Miracle-Gro Guides* (Meredith Books, Des Moines, Iowa), the *Yard and Garden Owners Manual* (Meredith Books), *The Complete Perennials Book* (Meredith Books), and *The Carolinas Gardener's Guide* (Cool Springs Press, Nashville, Tennessee).

Attesting to his expertise and communication skills, the author has accumulated many honors, among them national awards from the National Association of County Agricultural Agents (NACAA) for his columns, books, and radio program; Garden Writers Association Silver Award of Achievement for radio on-air talent; a Quill & Trowel Award for his "Listen to Your Lawn: Recycle Your Grass Clippings" public service announcement videotape; and the National Extension Materials Award from the American Society of Horticultural Science. In 2009, Polomski earned a Ph.D. in plant and environmental sciences from Clemson University.

GARDENING NOTES